# Sacraments
## *of* Initiation:
## *A Theology of Rite, Word, and Life*
### SECOND EDITION

Liam G. Walsh, OP

**Hillenbrand**Books

Chicago / Mundelein, Illinois

SACRAMENTS OF INITIATION: A THEOLOGY OF LIFE, WORD, AND RITE,
SECOND EDITION © 2011 Archdiocese of Chicago: Liturgy Training
Publications, 3949 South Racine Avenue, Chicago IL 60609;
1-800-933-1800, fax 1-800-933-7094, e-mail orders@ltp.org. All rights
reserved. See our Web site at www.LTP.org.

**Hillenbrand Books** is an imprint of Liturgy Training Publications (LTP) and
the Liturgical Institute at the University of Saint Mary of the Lake (USML).
The imprint is focused on contemporary and classical theological thought
concerning the liturgy of the Catholic Church. Available at bookstores
everywhere, through LTP by calling 1-800-933-1800, or visiting www.ltp.org.
Further information about the **Hillenbrand Books** publishing program is
available from the University of Saint Mary of the Lake/Mundelein
Seminary, 1000 East Maple Avenue, Mundelein, IL 60060 (847-837-4542),
on the web at www.usml.edu/liturgicalinstitute, or e-mail litinst@usml.edu.

Cover: *The Baptism of St. Augustine*, St. Monica-St. George Church,
Cincinnati, OH. Photo © Denis R. McNamara

Printed in the United States of America.

Library of Congress Control Number: 2011923998

ISBN 978-1-59525-035-3

HSI2

For Sheila, Ann, and Donal,
with Alison and Dick

# Contents

# Preface to Second Edition

The original edition of this book[1] presented a theology of sacraments of the kind that emerged in a Church stirred into new life by the Second Vatican Council. It was part of a series that the Foreword of its general editor, the late Reverend Michael Richards, described in the following terms:

> The Geoffrey Chapman Theology Library sets out to communicate the essentials of each chosen area of study through the personal reflection of an experienced scholar and teacher ... Each volume attempts to survey the documentary materials needed in the investigation of its theme, the special problems and topics of interest that centuries of study have thrown up, and the questions asked in the controversies of the present. As far as possible, Catholic beliefs are expounded and discussed in relation to the established and contemporary teaching of other Christian bodies ...

There seems good reason to believe that the theology of Christian Initiation that was presented in the book is of the kind that has continued to be received in the Catholic Church in the postconciliar years. It is a theology that has been widely practiced and preached in pastoral life, has been given catechetical shape in the *Catechism of the Catholic Church* (1994), and has been appealed to regularly in the recent teachings of popes and bishops. It is, nevertheless, a kind of theology that has also been challenged in those decades. It has been challenged on theoretical grounds: its philosophical and anthropological assumptions have been called into question, and alternative theologies, grounded on contemporary and postmodern philosophies, have been proposed by way of replacement. There have been practical challenges, too. Pastoral and liturgical practices have been introduced that, although claiming to be in the spirit of Vatican II, have gone far beyond anything that could be justified by what the serious theology associated with the council was saying about Christian sacraments and their celebration. On the other side, there have been more recent

---

1. Liam G. Walsh, OP, *The Sacraments of Initiation. Baptism, Confirmation, Eucharist.* Geoffrey Chapman Theology Library 7 (London: Geoffrey Chapman, 1988).

movements of a return to pre-Vatican II forms of celebration that, intentionally or not, raise questions about the theological insights associated with the council and manifest a fear of the consequences that can be drawn from those insights.

An interesting book could be written dealing head-on with these contemporary challenges to mainline Catholic sacramental theology. This is not what is attempted here. It is believed that the theology presented in the first edition of the book can still contribute to contemporary theological discussion and education. It is substantially retained in this edition, with only minor modifications being made here and there to the text, in the interests of greater clarity and of updating documentation, and to take account of comments made by reviewers. Some examples of alternative theologies of sacrament are noted and commented on in Chapter 2. The conclusion suggested there is that the issues they raise are fundamentally philosophical, and that the philosophical proposals they make are not yet sufficiently assured to justify the abandonment of a theology grounded on a more traditional metaphysical view of reality. The issue belongs to a debate that needs to be ongoing, in philosophical and fundamental theology. It is suggested that, in the meantime, these newer sacramental theologies already bring considerable enrichment to an understanding of the anthropological reality of sacraments. It is claimed that this enrichment can be incorporated into the kind of theology being presented in this book, without undermining its traditional metaphysical, and, let it be said, specifically Thomistic structures. It is hoped that something of this sort is actually done in the book, even if it is not explicitly attributed to dialogue with these alternative theologies.

The book gives considerable attention to examining and documenting the ecclesial tradition of sacramental practice and teaching. Texts are given—although a little less extensively here than in the first edition. Biblical and historical studies continue to uncover new riches of that tradition, and some account is taken of recent findings in this new edition. A careful listening to the tradition in all that it has to say about the rites and words of sacramental life is truly indispensable for sacramental theology. It has to be said that, while authors like the four noted in Chapter 2 pay serious attention to the tradition, not all those who have come forward in recent times with new theological ideas and pastoral strategies—whether they take the form of innovation or restoration—have given an equally serious place to the tradition. Neglect of it has led to some quite superficial readings of texts of Vatican II. What seemed to be new and liberating in the teaching of the council was readily exploited, but sometimes with little or no appreciation of how that teaching was grounded on the continuity of the Church's tradition of faith and practice, and could only be rightly understood in the light of it. Irresponsible things were done with the flimsiest of theological justification. In the other direction, there have been movements of restoration that have wanted to revert to preconciliar practices in the name of one particular, for example Tridentine, phase of the tradition. Some of these are inclined to make comparisons between favored forms of a particular age and the liturgical forms that emerged from the council. But they do so in a way that shows very little understanding of how Vatican II resituated all phases of the tradition in a recovery of the great core values of the apostolic tradition, about which so much had been learned in the years that led up to the council. The liturgies that are studied in this book are the liturgies that have been given to the Church under the inspiration of Vatican II. It is believed that the historical chapters presented here will show how they can be seen to be a contemporary expression of fidelity to core values of the apostolic tradition, rather than a privileging of any particular phase, ancient or modern, of its transmission.

The book retains the general structure and arrangement of parts that it had in the first edition. However, the lists for Further Reading that concluded each chapter have now been gathered in an Appendix at the end of the book. The chapters on the *rite* of each sacrament include anthropological considerations that are meant to unveil the human significances of the various rites. These have been put under a distinct heading in this edition, which they did not have in the original. The chapters on the *word* about baptism and confirmation (Chapters 5 and 7) conclude with what is called a "systematic essay"; the systematic essay on the Eucharist is given a separate Chapter 11, which follows two chapters, 9 and 10, devoted to the material on the word. These systematic essays are meant to be speculative in the best sense of the term: they do not dogmatize but rather show how theology might deal with questions that *life* is likely to put to the *word* about the particular *rite* being discussed. Although the questions are believed to arise from real life, they are put here in a form that must necessarily seem general and abstract. They are meant to be contemporary questions, but many of them have been asked before and the answers to them will not necessarily be new. It is for those who read them to discover if they can make these questions their own, and see how they can use them as a framework for dealing with new issues that are arising out of their own experience of contemporary life and practice.

Not all the bibliographical material proposed in the first edition of the book has been retained, and a number of works published since then that have influenced this edition are now included. In spite of that, perceptive readers will recognize that the notes and reading lists still reflect the period in which the book was originally written and the resources on which it drew. This is, of course, something of a limitation. However, it can also express a hope that not everything that was alive and well in the eighties is now out of date. The works that have been retained in the notes and reading lists are believed to have stood the test of time, to be still available, and to be still worth reading. More recent works have carried their researches forward, have sometimes challenged and corrected them, but have not entirely replaced them.

The author continues to feel the gratitude he expressed in the original edition to the late Reverend Michael Richards and the late Reverend Paul O'Leary, OP, as well as to others who helped him in the production of the book. To that must now be added thanks to Mr. Kevin Thornton, Editor of Hillenbrand Books and Publishing Manager of the Liturgical Institute, for his admirable and comforting editorial work on this edition. And to the appreciation expressed in the first edition of the students to whom I taught the course on sacraments at the University of St. Thomas (Angelicum), Rome, for the influence they had on my writing of the book I must now add a similar word of appreciation to the students of the University of Fribourg, Switzerland, where my teaching on sacraments continued from 1988 to 1999, and also to the dedicated group of students whose company and stimulation I enjoyed while teaching a course on the Sacraments of Initiation at the Liturgical Institute in Mundelein during the summer of 2009.

# *Abbreviations*

AAS    *Acta Apostolicae Sedis*

ACW  Ancient Christian Writers

BEM  *Baptism, Eucharist and Ministry* (World Council of Churches, Faith and Order Paper 111)

CCSL  *Corpus Christianorum*, series latina

DACL  *Dictionnaire d'archéologie chrétienne et de liturgie*

DS    H. Denzinger and A. Schönmetzer (eds), *Enchiridion Symbolorum* (32nded.)

DTC  *Dictionnaire de théologie catholique*

ICEL  International Commission on English in the Liturgy

LG    *Lumen Gentium* (Vatican II, Dogmatic Constitution on the Church)

LNPF  Library of Nicene and Post-Nicene Fathers

ND    J. Neuner, SJ, and J. Dupuis, SJ, eds. *The Christian Faith in the Doctrinal Documents of the Catholic Church*. Fifth revised and enlarged ed., London: HarperCollins Religious, 1992; New York: Alba House, 1996.

PG    J.-P. Migne (ed.), *Patrologiae cursus completus, series graeca*

PL    J.-P. Migne (ed.), *Patrologiae cursus completus, series latina*

RCIA  *Rite of Christian Initiation of Adults* (Note: in the interest of pastoral utility and convenience, the definitive ICEL edition somewhat rearranges the contents of the *Praenotanda* of the Latin *editio typica*. Hereafter, references to paragraphs in RCIA give the number from the English definitive edition; followed in some instances by the number from the *editio typica, in* square brackets.)

SC    *Sacrosanctum Concilium* (Vatican II, Constitution on the Sacred Liturgy)

UR    *Unitatis Redintegratio* (Vatican II, Decree on Ecumenism)

WCC  World Council of Churches

# Introduction

## Rite, Word, and Life: Methodological Considerations for a Theology of Sacraments

To become a Christian is to join a community of people who believe that Jesus Christ brought eternal *life* into this world and who celebrate together their sharing in that life while they are waiting for it to be fully realized when Jesus comes again. Believing in life and celebrating the wonder of it is a good description of what it is to be a Christian and a member of the Christian Church. Belief is brought about and expressed in *word*. Christians are known as people of words: they have a story to tell about how God has given eternal life to humans and a doctrine about the meaning of the story. And when they gather to celebrate the life they live and the story they tell, they practice *rites*. They are often known by their rites — as people who go to Mass or to the Lord's Supper (or whatever synonym they use for their ritual meal of bread and wine) and who initiate new members ritually by baptizing and confirming them. But they would like to be known most of all as people of life. The word in which they believe is the word of life. The rites they practice are for the giving and celebrating of life.

The rites of initiation into the Christian community (baptism, confirmation, and Eucharist) are especially concerned with life because they mark the first giving of the fullness of the life in Christ that is proclaimed and made available in the Christian community. They cannot be life-giving in this way unless they are accompanied by the word of life: the story of the giving of eternal life has to be told to the initiates and the essential meaning of it explained. The story and the explanation must deal with the form and meaning of the rites, and with how they serve to insert human life into eternal life. It is the business of the theology of sacraments to work out such an explanation, so that the story can be told in relation to the rites in a way that makes them life-giving.

All theology is a word. It draws from the words of faith—from the story of the giving of eternal life that is told in the scriptures and from the continuous telling and explanation of it in the tradition of the Church. It draws from the words of human wisdom about the reality and meaning of human life. A theology of sacraments, however, has the peculiarity of being a word about the giving of eternal life through a very particular kind of human activity, which is the making of rites. It directs the word of faith toward the human experience inherent in ritual activity, so that when the sacramental rites of the Christian Church are celebrated a word will be available that can make them be truly life-giving.

The interaction of rite, word, and life is a common subject of study by the anthropological sciences. Human life in all its spheres is full of ritual, and of words and stories and myths that go with the rites. The sciences that study human ritual have much to teach the theology of sacraments. They let them see how sacraments can be understood as instances of that irrepressible human instinct to imitate and dramatize things or events or persons that are important for human life, to remember and recreate them symbolically at certain times and in certain places. They give it valuable insights about how rites affect critical moments of human life like birth and death, puberty and marriage, initiations into and affirmations of belonging to a social group—critical moments that are captured and held in a manageable way by rites, so that the life experience and tension in them can be adequately dealt with.

Rites have their own peculiar intelligibility, which can never be fully expressed in words. Although there is a story behind most of them, there is something more in them than any story can tell. They can continue to be performed even when the story that gave rise to them has been forgotten. But rites do seem to call out for a story, and a story may be invented for them when the original one has been lost or is no longer relevant. The story is really an explanation of how the rite has a bearing on human life. The explanation may be a simple narrative but it may also develop into a quite sophisticated philosophical analysis of the rite and its story. The Greeks created myths to explain their rites but they also turned these myths into a kind of theology.

A Christian theology of baptism, confirmation, and Eucharist will want to gather all the words that have been spoken about these rites within the Christian tradition and all the speculation that has been done about them, in order to understand them in the bearing they can have on human life. Classical theology may be more comfortable with words than with the particularity and concreteness of rites. It is itself, indeed, a form of word. But if it is to be a theology of sacraments like baptism, confirmation, and Eucharist it has to be a word not about ideas but about rites, and about their bearing on life.

The anthropological sciences explain how it is within the life of particular communities and their culture that rites develop and have meaning. They, and the words about them, are carried by a tradition, and the community lives by the tradition. People find in their words and their rites a way of dealing with the more critical issues of life that confront them regularly and test their ability to survive and prosper. Birth and death, entry into adulthood, marrying, illness, buying and selling, political decision making, the recurrence of the seasons and the fruitfulness of the earth are the kind of moments in the cycle of life that are solemnized by ritual. Unique events like the conquest of what has become the homeland, decisive battles won, the birth of great leaders are also commemorated ritually, because they have meant the difference between life and death to the community. To the extent that they are human rites, baptism, confirmation, and Eucharist will be touching some such crucial moments in the life of the Christian community, and of the persons who make it up. A theology of these rites will have to identify these moments and explain how the rite with its story allows people to deal with them.

The crucial moments that are dealt with by rites are, even in anthropological terms, sacred moments. Anthropology uses words like mysterious, numinous, fearsome, beyond-the-rational to define this sacredness. In stories that go with rites it is often described in a language that speaks of God, the gods, good and evil spirits and their interventions in human life. Anthropology can be quite neutral about the truth of this language, because it is not concerned with the existence or otherwise of God or the gods, but only with how belief in them affects human behavior. Obviously, theology cannot be neutral about the issue and will claim some competence to judge between the true and the false in the rites and religious stories of humanity. But it can do that without discounting the deep insights into human nature and God's way of dealing with it that are revealed in the anthropological analysis of all human rites, even of those that invoke a god who may be a purely mythical creation, unsubstantiated by any kind of critical verification.

The Christian theology of sacraments has to be about the rites that are celebrated within the Christian community of the Church. The word that it listens to about the rites and how they bear on life has to be the word that is spoken in that Church. There is an anthropological basis for this, even before one considers the imperatives accepted by theology itself in relation to the Word of God and its transmission in the Church. Rites and stories hold communities together and point them toward their future. As a group of people becomes self-conscious and protective about its identity, its stories and rites become official. Not any story will do and not any rite will do to express and give direction to the life the group wants to live and the future it wants for its children. Those who come to hold authority in the community take responsibility for the stories and the rites. The men and women of the word—the storytellers and the thinkers— become themselves authorities about the word, and those who lead the rites come to lay down the law about them. They become the "prophets" and the "priests" that are found in some form in every community. Those who hold general authority over the life of the community (the "kings") also find ways of having a say in what stories and what rites prevail. One can find these authority patterns at work in all kinds of human communities, ranging from primitive societies, with their sages, their priests and priestesses, and their chiefs, to the developed societies of today in which a well-structured establishment controls what is accepted as the national tradition, what ceremonies and holidays appropriately celebrate it, and how traditions and rituals are to be used as factors of political unity and stability.

There is another authority factor that has to be taken into account in studying rites. The written record of rites and of the stories that go with them can itself become sacred. Religious texts are not the only ones that develop this kind of sacredness but they do have it with particular explicitness. When the history of a people is thought to be in the hands of God it is not difficult to see how the telling of that history should also be believed to be cared for by God and somehow inspired by God. The sacred books of religions become a source and a standard for rites and their explanation. They often tell of the origin of rites and of the effect they have on human life, attributing them to God himself. Thus the Christian Scriptures are the normative source for any study of baptism, confirmation, and Eucharist, because it is in them that the story of the origins of the community and of its rites is authoritatively set down.

Once a community like the Christian Church commits itself to a certain account of its origins, to a set of fundamental rites and to an authorized word about them, it faces the problem of keeping rites and words in contact with a life process that is subject to many forces of change. Sacred books are sacrosanct and ritual is uneasy with change. An important part of the function of both is to ensure stability and the homogeneity of a group. However, when stability is conceived in an immobile and purely conservative way, words and rites can lose contact with real life. Both they and the society that they supported can become fossilized. The highly ritualized civilizations of Central and South America, for example, coped no better with the cultural and religious challenges of the Conquistadores than they did with their military assaults, and whole cultures disappeared or went underground. Coping with change is a challenge that faces particularly those who hold authority in the community—whether it be of the prophetic, priestly, or kingly kind. If those who control the rites and their story lack the will or the imagination to see that life is never an exact repetition of the past but a continuity in change, they will cut the rites off from real life and thus destroy their value. It is especially in the word that is spoken with and about the rite that the challenge of change is met. New generations with new life experiences have to be told in a new way how the rite can have a bearing on their lives. Otherwise they will not find in the rite a helpful way of dealing with the crucial moments of their life and a way of making appropriate choices about them. When rites and the words that go with them are not affecting choices about the serious issues of life they gradually lose their status, first for individuals and eventually perhaps for a whole people. They drift toward being fable and folklore, while life begins to look elsewhere for ways of dealing with its crucial moments and expressing its goals. The rites and stories of ancient Egypt, for example, no longer have much effect on the contemporary Egyptian nation, which lives by a different story and by different rites. A new story and new rites may grow up just because the old ones have been found wanting. It may also be imported or imposed from outside. If a new power group wants to change the life of a people it can do this by introducing a new story and new rites, or by distorting, if not suppressing, the old. After the Bolshevik revolution the Russian people received a whole new story about itself and Red Square became the place of assembly for a new set of rituals. The classics of Russian history may still have been read, its art enjoyed and its rituals remembered but officially, at least, this had nothing to do with the real life of the people at that time. Those who thought it did, ran the risk of being considered subversives.

These general anthropological observations about the effect of change on the understanding of rites suggest a further methodological requirement for a theological study of baptism, confirmation, and Eucharist. One must obviously start any study with the scriptures that tell of the origins. But one must then follow the story of how the community of the Church coped with the changes in life experience and perception among its members over the centuries during which it has claimed to have remained faithful to the identity given to it in the apostolic age recorded in scripture. The rites themselves have evolved. More significantly, as the Christian community gathered new people to itself and lived through new ages, the story has grown and the explanations have multiplied. Besides those of the scriptures, the community has a multitude of other words to speak with its rites. This is the liturgical and theological tradition. Some of it was a successful adaptation of rite and word to new life situations. More of it is the checking by Church authorities of adaptations that were feared to be destructive of the original, constitutive tradition that is recorded in scripture. Part of the story is about dangerous periods of decadence when the rites drifted away from life, or when they were being misinterpreted and misused in the interest of goals and values that were not really those of the Christian community. It is only from a study of this entire tradition that one can discover how the rites have come to be what they are today, why they are thought about and spoken about as they are, and how they can still contribute to the continuity of the Christian Church.

The indications about methodology that are suggested by looking at baptism, confirmation, and Eucharist in the anthropological framework of rite, word, and life are important for a theology of these sacraments. Theology has to respect the human reality of things no less than God himself does. It is in the human reality of these rites that God gathers his People together, saves them from sin and brings them to eternal life. They are believed to be divine realities, but they function in the way rites function in any human community. At the same time, anthropological insights into ritual activity are pushed to a new level in theology because the defining interest of theology is in the divine reality that is present in human affairs. Theology will gain much insight into baptism, confirmation, and Eucharist from an anthropological reading of the scriptures and Christian tradition. But its primary task is to draw from these resources the truth about God's presence and action in these rites. It reads the scriptures in faith, accepting them as the Word of God, of the true God, who reveals himself and saves the world in the history and teaching that is recorded in the scriptures. The issue for theology is not just how and why the rites function anthropologically, but how and why they function as actions of God, of the true God, in which he saves his People. The anthropologist can study rites and their story without judging what is true or false in the claims they make about God. The theologian believes that the story is true and he trusts the rites to be works of God. Indeed, he or she speaks in and for a community that stakes its life on the truth and reality of these words and rites.

The theology of sacraments needs to be especially careful about taking to itself anthropological analyses of rites that go beyond the experimental and becomes philosophical speculation about meaning and reality. There are philosophies that make the human experience of existence be the unique gateway to the mystery of being. These anthropological philosophies can be quite rich anthropologically. When taken into theology they can offer many rich insights into sacraments. But theology will be entitled to ask whether they open the human mind to the full reality of the divine, or do not somehow reduce the divine to what is measurable by the human perception of it. There is an ongoing debate in philosophy about how human experience can give access to the reality of the divine. It is a debate that is crucial for all theology, but especially for the theology of sacraments, because it is in sacraments that believers are offered their most characteristically human experience of the divine.

## Outline of this Book

The search for the theological meaning of baptism, confirmation, and Eucharist starts in this book with an examination of some general truths about how Christian faith has experienced and understood the practice of rite and word in the life of God's people. To call this a discussion on "the sacraments in general," as theology might once have done, would be to run the risk of claiming there is some kind of generic notion of "sacrament" in scripture and the tradition that can subsequently be made specific to give one an understanding of each of the seven sacraments. That is not what is being attempted. The assumption is that there are things that can be discovered about the general economy of rite and word that God has patronized throughout the entire history of salvation, and that an understanding of these is an important step toward understanding baptism, confirmation, and Eucharist.

Chapters 1–3 of this book will deal with the general sacramental economy in this perspective. Chapter 1 covers the scriptural material. It examines the relationship between rite, word, and life in biblical religion. This is a critical question in anthropological terms, but even more so in theological analysis. Compared with other religions of humanity, the Old Testament already shows some unique features in its working out of this relationship. In the New Testament the relationship is altogether unique. Jesus, who is way, truth, and life, brings about a total identification of rite, word, and life in his own person. He is *life*, the full embodiment of Eternal Life; he is *word*, Word made flesh; he is *rite*, realizing in the temple of his own body the roles of Priest and Victim. The understanding of Christian rites must be dominated by this truth, because their whole purpose is to continue throughout time and space what God does once for all in Jesus. Rites that are not all that Jesus is have no place in the New Testament.

Chapter 2 examines the tradition of faith about "sacrament," with its derivation from the Greek *musterion* and the Latin *sacramentum*. The Christian community has had to work hard to maintain for itself the unique relationship that Jesus set up between rite, word, and life. In its thinking and in its practice it has continually had to find ways of realizing it anew, to keep pace with its own growth and with changes in the life experience and perceptions of its members.

It has had to deal with all the deviations that any human system of ritual is prone to. It has had to save the rites from superstition as well as incredulity, and from being distorted by a careless or un-Christian word that might put them at the service of a life that was not truly Christian. The struggle, carried on in both theory and practice, is bound up with the fortunes of the word "sacrament." In Latin theology and its derivatives this became the technical Christian word for the rites of the Church. It serves to state the unique relationship that exists in them between rite, word, and life, along with the ground for that, which is Christ's presence in them. The tradition about this word is the key to understanding the theological and liturgical tradition about any of the individual sacraments.

Chapter 3 moves into the domain of systematic theology. In its scriptures and tradition the Christian community remembers its origins and its past. It remembers them, not just for anthropological reasons connected with survival but because it is in them that God has given it his word and given it the rites that are made life-giving by fidelity to that word. Each generation, however, has to do its own reworking of the tradition. It does so on different levels—pastoral practice, catechetics, art and architecture, song and music making, and technical theology. All of these levels are interconnected. Systematic theology has the task of providing an orderly, critical, philosophically grounded setting for all of them. Its own truth is tested by its fidelity to the tradition as well as by its relevance and reasoned response to contemporary questioning. While it is generally done in academic settings, and has to obey accepted scientific criteria, the testing of it has to be done not only in the lecture hall but also in the baptistry and around the altar and, above all, in the lives of those whose participation in the sacraments has been informed by it.

The systematic questions that are put about baptism, confirmation, and Eucharist have in them the more general questions about the whole sacramental system and about how these three sacraments relate to everything else in the sacramental order. The three sacraments form, in fact, the initiation phase of a ritual system that has four other structural sacraments and a multitude of secondary rites called sacramentals. It is by this sacramental system and by the word of faith that accompanies it that the Christian community is constituted as Church, as Body of Christ and as People of God. This is the perspective in which baptism, confirmation, and Eucharist are set in Chapter 3. What is presented there is, in summary form, a general theology of the sacramental economy. It shows the profound ramifications and interconnectedness of the questions that will come up about the individual sacraments. Even though it is put in rather classical terms it is still offered as a theology for today. There can be alternative theologies of sacrament that meet particular ecclesial and cultural situations more immediately. But they, too, need to face eventually the issues that the great theses of classical sacramental theology deal with. A position on these issues is present in every theology of sacraments. It may be a negative position, calling for radical revision of the classical solutions. But in addressing the issues the classical positions will always need to be given their say.

When one begins to look at an individual sacrament in the theological and anthropological perspective being proposed here, one will want to see it as a rite, accompanied by an appropriate word, that gives life. The discussion on each of the three sacraments being dealt with here begins with a chapter on its rite (Chapters 4, 6, and 8). A fairly detailed description of the rite is given as the starting point for theological reflection. The description is taken from the official texts in which the Church prescribes how the rite should be performed. It will read so much more realistically if it is accompanied by some direct experience and observation of actual celebrations of the sacrament. To describe the rite of a sacrament is already to begin to understand it. Although there is an inherent mysteriousness in all rites there is no deliberate cult of obscurity in the Christian sacraments. The rites are made as clear as they can be, and it is believed that the less explanation they require the better. Yet they do gain from some explanation. A first explanatory key is provided in the chapters on rite under the heading "History." Ritual actions are always heavy with tradition, with memories and precedents. These can be brought to the surface by historical information about the origin and development of the rite. A second key is offered under the heading "Anthropological Considerations." Each sacramental rite addresses certain deep human experiences and needs in a way that has parallels in other cultural and religious expressions of the human psyche. The anthropological sciences, especially those dealing with religion, analyze these patterns in ways that give sacramental theology much food for thought. What is offered in the sections of the chapters on rite is no more than a pointer to what is available.

The chapter about the rite of each of the three sacraments is followed by a chapter or chapters on the Word that accompanies the rite (Chapters 5, 7, 9–11). The study of the rite already includes an examination of the words that are spoken at the core of the rite. Although these are somewhat ritualized in the sacrament they are not mere incantations. They give a ritual action, which by itself may be open to any number of interpretations, its specifically Christian meaning. They are accompanied in the celebration of the rite by many other words — by readings, song, and prayers, and preaching. In the rite, words register along the whole range of human perception. As well as enlightening the mind they nourish the poetical instinct, prod memory, and stir the depths of the unconscious. To bring out these values of the ritual words (not just those at the core of the rite — the sacramental "form" — but all the words used throughout the rite) would be to develop a deep theological understanding of the rite in its relationship to human life. One would be doing what could be called a liturgical theology of the sacrament. Such a theology is not presented in detail in this book, although hopefully its presence can be felt.

The chapters on the Word that follow the chapter on the rite of each sacrament do deal with some of the words spoken in the celebration. But they deal mainly with a broader set of words that affect the celebration of the rite and enhance its influence on life. These come from scriptural passages, patristic catecheses, and technical analyses of systematic theology; they are the readings that are proclaimed, the catecheses that are spoken in the church, in the classroom and in the nursery, and they are the words of preaching. Also to be considered are dogmatic pronouncements that were made to settle disagreements among Christians about the meaning and value of the rites. And because dogmatic definitions did not always resolve differences, and Christians went their separate ways with contrasting views on the rite, there are now agreed or convergence statements in which separated Christians try to restore unity to the sacramental belief and practice of the Church. All of these words are about the rite. Their effectiveness comes from how well they give life and light and authenticity to the faith of those who actually practice the sacrament. Although they are always grounded on the words that form part of the rite they go beyond them into explanations and ideas and a vocabulary that suits their particular purpose. This kind of explanatory text is found already in the scriptures, side by side with the descriptive texts that are the source of the actual rites. Paul has theological explanations of baptism that suppose knowledge of what the rite is. John has his discourse on the bread of life that supposes the accounts of the Last Supper but does not repeat them. Later texts express the scriptural teaching about the rites in the pedagogical language of catechetics, or use the technical terms of systematic theology, such as sign and cause, instrument, character, encounter, visibility, *ex opere operato* and so on. The tradition has found these scriptural and other words necessary for the good celebration of the rite. It has taken texts that use them as readings to go with the celebration of the rite, or at least as nourishment for the preaching that is done at it. A theology of a sacrament has to listen to these words and let its own thinking be formed by them.

The chapters on the word concerning baptism and confirmation conclude with an essay in the systematic theology of each sacrament; the third of the three chapters devoted to the word on the Eucharist (Chapter 11) is a systematic essay. A systematic theology of a sacrament should be the point at which the relationship of rite and word to life is most directly examined. A systematic theologian thinks about what is believed, doing so from the standpoint of his or her understanding of reality as it is encountered in human life. In theology, however, thinking about particular matters of belief, such as sacraments, has to be done within a comprehensive, critical vision of how God—the true God—is at work in the world, drawing all the things that he has made back to himself in love. It has to employ principles and presuppositions—such as those about Christ, the Church, the grace of the Holy Spirit—that inevitably come into play in even the most superficial discourse about sacraments. Dealing critically with these great issues can require systematic theology to distance itself provisionally from the particularities in which life is lived. But it only does so in order to be able to bring the light of understanding—the *intellectus fidei*—to bear on these particular situations. Its value is ultimately tested by the way it helps those who have to speak the word about the sacramental rites in particular life situations—pastors, catechists, preachers—to relate the sacraments to life. It is the point that will be made in the Epilogue of this book.

# Chapter 1

# Biblical Orientations

Baptism, confirmation, and Eucharist, as rites of the Christian Church, come out of and receive the first authoritative statement of their meaning in the scriptures of the New Testament. Each of them has roots in the Old Testament, without which its emergence in the New Testament cannot be fully understood. But more importantly, each of them builds on a general experience and understanding of rite that is presented with considerable anthropological and theological richness in the books of the Old Testament. The Bible tells the life story of God's chosen People. It includes descriptions of their rites and accounts of the part they play in life. The Old Testament presents a pattern of interaction between rite, word, and life that has its own historical consistency, but also reaches out to a future transformation. Knowing that pattern and these expectations, one can better appreciate the radical newness, and yet the continuity in contrast of what the books of the New Testament have to say about rite and word in the new life of the People of God, of which they are now the story. The New Testament teaching about individual rites such as baptism and Eucharist can be best understood in this background.

## RITE, WORD, AND LIFE IN THE OLD TESTAMENT

In anthropological terms the Old Testament tells the story of a tribe of nomadic origin that, after a period of settled development and eventual oppression in Egypt of the Pharaohs, found freedom in escape and in a momentous journey across the desert, at the end of which they came to the land between the river Jordan and the Mediterranean, which they conquered and settled as their own. It is the story of their social, economic, religious, and cultural development in that land, of their struggles to survive in difficult times, and to grow in all the areas of human enrichment when circumstances were favorable. Religion, in its beliefs and its rites, plays a central part in this story. It touches every facet of life and is itself filled with the stuff of life.

But the Old Testament is a theological, not just an anthropological, telling of the story of Israel. It is the story of what God was doing for his people and of how they responded to him. It is about the rites in which they found assurance of God's continuing care for them and in which they addressed themselves to him in crucial moments of their lives. It is a covenant story, about the working out of an agreement between God and his People. God is the one who initiated and repeatedly renewed the covenant. He promised blessings to his people—blessings of the most real-life kind: they would have children, many of them, so that they would not only survive but would become a great nation; they would have a land of their own, with food and drink from it; they would conquer their enemies and live in peace; they would know how to dance and sing, and in old age each would sit comfortably under the shade of his or her own vine or fig tree.

God did things for his People. And to make sure they knew it, God told them the true story of what he was doing with them by inspiring their prophets, their storytellers and the writers of their holy books. God gave them a book of the covenant. As well as telling them what God was doing for them, this book also told them what God expected of them. It spelled out in the form of law and exhortation their side of the covenant. It gave them very detailed moral laws about how they should live in the main areas of individual and social choice. It also told them the religious rites they should practice. In the rites they were expected to experience what it was to be God's People and to express their acceptance of that. The rite of circumcision marked the initiation of individuals into the covenant and into membership of God's People. It evoked the original call of Abraham and somehow repeated it for individual Israelites. Other rites recalled what God had done for them at the Exodus. His action of bringing them out of Egypt, through the Red Sea, across the desert and into the land he had given to their fathers had become a prototype of his saving actions and of the response his love generated in his People. The rites of the Passover recalled and somehow repeated the pattern of this saving act of God, and gave Israelites an opportunity to renew their fidelity to the covenant of Sinai. To gather at table with their family and friends, to have the kind of table talk of memory and hope that unleavened bread and bitter herbs and the slaughtered lamb evoked, to eat this food and to drink wine in the cups of blessing—all this was to live the Exodus experience again and to feel it being realized in their own life. It was to make a memorial (*zikkaron* in Hebrew; cf. Chapter 8, "Rites of the Old Covenant" and Chapter 9, "Accounts of Institution") of God's saving act. There was a host of other rites that were to mark the life of an Israelite. Like circumcision and the Passover celebrations, they took their meaning from the story of Israel and from the belief of those who cherished the story that they truly were God's people. The story was told again and again in folk tradition and eventually from books. It began as the story of this particular people but as time went on it gathered into itself the story of all humankind and of the very cosmos. It became a creation story within a salvation story. The rites did not always reflect this wider perspective and there is not a little exasperation in the words of the prophet Malachi when he says, "I have no pleasure in you, says the Lord of hosts, and I will not accept an offering from your hand. For from the rising of the sun to its setting my name is great among the nations, and in every place incense is offered to my name, and a pure offering; for my name is great among the nations, says the Lord of hosts" (Malachi 1:10b–11).

As words and rites established themselves, the authority that emerged in Israel began to take responsibility for them. The men and women of the word always carried authority. They are the *prophets*. The most famous among them were the great preachers and interpreters of the fortunes of the People. Many of the sacred books came to be attributed to them, from Moses, who was thought to have written the five books that stand at the head of the Bible, to Malachi, which was the name given to the last of the prophets to have a book ascribed to him in the Hebrew Bible. Responsibility for the word, especially in its written form, was also vested in people called scribes, who emerged at the time of the exile in Babylon (cf. Ezra the scribe in Nehemiah 8:1; note that in the following verse Ezra is called a priest). *Priests* were responsible for the rites, and a priestly class exercised considerable power in Israel. Once stable political structures developed in Israel, overall responsibility for the life and times of the people was given to the *king*. As life, word, and rite were interdependent so were the offices of prophet, priest, and king. Those who held one would regularly be concerned about the affairs of the others. They would blame each other when things went wrong in the life of the People. For a long time most of the blame was put on the king (cf. the books of Samuel, Kings, and Chronicles). But the hope of better times was also bound up with the coming of an ideal king, a new David. In the course of time this figure of hope gathered to himself, in an ideal balance, the offices of priest and prophet.

The hope of Israel for the coming of a messianic king was nourished by the word spoken through its prophets and sustained by the rites it celebrated under the guidance of its priests. The prophets appeared most often at times of crisis for the people. The crises manifested themselves in real life: crops failed and there was hunger, leaders quarreled and there was internal strife, enemies broke in and destroyed, there was death and deportation, there seemed to be no sign of a happy end to the story. That tested faith in God and his covenant: it was not what he had promised his People. There was a temptation to blame God for the catastrophes. The prophets answer that complaint by proclaiming the absolute fidelity of God to his covenant and putting responsibility for the catastrophes squarely on the shoulders of the people and their kings. They put blame, too, on members of their own class; not all those who claim to be prophets speak the word of God; there are false prophets. And they blame the priests for failures in the way they care for the rites of the covenant. It is not God, then, but the people and their leaders who have been unfaithful. A favorite technique of the prophets is to retell the story of Israel, but in a way that points up its relevance to the contemporary life situation. The message is that the People have forgotten their own story, or not understood it properly, that the Israelites have not been faithful to their own tradition. This new telling of the story ends up by being itself part of the word by which the People live (as in Deuteronomy, Chronicles, and parts of the Wisdom literature) and a recognized projection of it toward the future (as in the strictly prophetic books).

If priests have their faults they can also combine with the prophets, can even themselves exercise a certain prophetic role, in restoring the faith and hope of God's people. With the prophets they see the calamities besetting their people as due to the fact that the rites given by God to his People are being neglected, or have been contaminated with pagan forms of ritual, or are being performed in a purely legalistic way without much relation to the real-life choices of private and public morality. The prophets put into words thoughts that must have also been on the minds of priests, moving them to effect the purification and restoration of the rites. The prophetic word is not a rejection of rites but a call for them to be in accordance with the tradition and to be an honest expression of moral choices. If the Israelites are proclaiming themselves to be God's People in their rites they must behave like God's People in their lives. The prophets often blame the priests and the king for letting the rites deteriorate, but when the king and priests undertake a serious reform they have the support of the prophets. (See, for example, the covenant renewal under King Josiah described in 2 Kings 22–23.)

And yet the prophets do keep alive a certain dissatisfaction with the rites of the Old Testament. They seem to want something less prone to formalism and less liable to become an excuse for avoiding the real choices of life according to the covenant. The book of Jeremiah has a powerful page (Chapter 31) that looks forward to a time when life will be full and abundant again because God will have made a new covenant that will be written on people's hearts. People will act from inner conviction and personal wisdom rather than because somebody else tells them what the law says. There does not seem to be any special place for Temple rites in Jeremiah's city of this new covenant. The whole city, not just a temple area, will be sacred (vv. 38–40). Perhaps Jeremiah is saying that, as the sacred words will have become identified with life through being written on the hearts of people, so will the sacred actions. Isaiah was certainly moving in that direction in his prophecies about the Suffering Servant (42:1–9; 49:1–6; 50:4–11; 52:13–53: 12) whose own life and death would do all that rites of sacrifices were being expected to do in the old covenant, to the point that he himself can be described as the covenant given to the people (42:6; 49:8).

## RITE, WORD, AND LIFE IN THE NEW TESTAMENT

The first Christians believed that in Jesus, God made the definitive covenant promised by the prophets of Israel. They believed themselves to be the People of the New Covenant. No sooner had they come to this certainty, on the day they received the Holy Spirit, than they began to tell their story and to celebrate it in rites. What they told about themselves centered on the event that brought them into existence as a community of believers—the death and resurrection of Jesus and his glorification in power at the right hand of his Father. Their story, written in the books of the New Testament, is the story of him; the rites they began to practice are memorials of him.

The new covenant, like the old, is made with words. There is a story in it and there is a promise; there are explanations and there is a new law. But the story is all about a living person, Jesus, who was born, who died, who rose from the dead, who is with the Father from whom he sends the life-giving Spirit on the whole of creation; the promise is of the second coming of Jesus; the explanations are mostly about the unique way that God is at work in Jesus because of who Jesus is in the deepest level of his person; the law is all about behaving in the way Jesus behaved. Jesus put much of this into words himself: he exercised, although in a special way, the role of a prophet. He commissioned his disciples to go on speaking about him. They are people of the word, a word that they believe to be the word of life. The first letter of John opens with a powerful statement of how the Christian word is identified with the living reality of Jesus. The teaching of the prologue of the gospel of John that Jesus is the Word of God made flesh establishes the most profound continuity between words about Jesus and the reality of God's personal life that is in him, because he is the Word of God in person. The words are realistic because they are of the Word.

The new covenant is also made with actions. These are seen to be in continuity with the rites of the old covenant and are often described in terms of them: there is a new Passover, there is a new circumcision, there is a new anointing. But these are not, in the first place, ritual actions but are the personal life-actions of Jesus. The new covenant is made not only by Jesus but in him; he is the one promised in Isaiah 42:6, "I have given you as a covenant to the people, a light to the nations." His acceptance of his call and his total dedication to the work of his Father is his real circumcision; the choice he made that led to the shedding of his own blood, his acceptance of death, and his being raised to life from the dead was the Passover in which his Father made the new covenant of life; his sitting at the right hand of the

Father in an eschatological triumph that is marked by the outpouring of the Spirit sets up the new community of God's People through whom the world is transformed and the cosmos recreated. It is not through rites that Christ acts but through his own body; his body makes all previous rites obsolete. If people are going to have their lives brought in touch with the work of God, they must now do it by getting in touch with the body of Christ. Indeed, the community of those in whom the work of God is now identifiable is itself called the body of Christ; to be a member of it is to be one of his members. If one is a member of a living body one is oneself alive. If there are to be rites in the community of the new covenant they can only be life-giving by being filled with the life that is in the body of Christ.

The letter to the Hebrews is a proclamation of the coincidence of word, rite, and life in Jesus. It begins by identifying him as the one in whom the word of God reaches its fullness, the one who is uniquely beyond the earlier prophets and the angels, because he is the Son whereas they were only ministers of the word (Hebrews 1–2). The theme of the word brought to its fullness in Jesus is intertwined in Hebrews with the more dominant theme of his priesthood. He is both "apostle and high priest of our confession" (Hebrews 3:1). His priesthood consists first of all in a real-life identification with his brothers and sisters (2:10). He exercises it by offering himself in death and by entering the heavenly sanctuary where he lives to make intercession for us. His priestly action is described in reference to the rites of the old covenant, especially to those practiced in the Temple. In accomplishing these rites in a new way he has made them obsolete. He now lives forever in a heaven that, while it may be described in the imagery of the Temple, is clearly no place for rites.

So overwhelming is Hebrews about the passing of ritual priesthood that one might suppose it leaves no place for rite in the work that God is now doing in the world through Christ and his Spirit. The hard things Paul has to say about the law of the Old Testament and its ritual prescriptions, as well as his polemic against circumcision in Galatians, suggests something similar. Jesus himself, according to the gospels, did not seem to see much future for the Temple and therefore for ritual religion. The age of the Spirit, with its worship in spirit and in truth proclaimed in the writings of John, seems the very antithesis of sacred places and sacred actions and sacred personages. Prophets in the new covenant could make an even stronger case against ritualism than did their predecessors in the old.

Yet rites there were from the beginning, and their introduction is attributed to Jesus himself. Chapter 2 of the Acts of the Apostles relates that when the new covenant was first announced in Jerusalem on the day of Pentecost and the people who accepted the preaching of Peter asked "what shall we do?" they were told, among other things, to "be baptized" (Acts 2: 38). When they were baptized they were gathered together into a community that met regularly for, among other things, "the breaking of bread" (v. 42). The two actions are mentioned regularly enough in the New Testament, and are so related to critical moments of the life of Christians that one is already justified in calling them rites. Other actions like anointing with oil and laying on of hands are already beginning to take on ritual shape. And the making of a marriage can, of course, hardly but be a rite. The New Testament suggests some continuity between these ritual actions and the rites of the Old Testament. Baptism is a new kind of circumcision according to Colossians 2:11–13; Luke's account of the Last Supper presents it as a new Passover meal; marriage, representing the union between Christ and the Church, realizes the dream of oneness between Yahweh and his People that was evoked by marriage in the Old Testament (Ephesians 5:21–33).

## NEW RITES FOR A NEW COVENANT

However, the differences between the rites of the new covenant and those of the old are profound. The originality is in the way the new rites relate to the life that is in Jesus and in his members. This can be perceived by reflecting on:

1. The kind of rites they are.
2. The way the rites are related to the word that is preached about Jesus.
3. The role of the Apostles in regulating the life of the community in which the rites are practiced.
4. How the rites are the abiding of Christ with his own "until he comes again."

## Rites of a New Kind

The rites of the new covenant are drawn from "ordinary" life rather than from the typically religious sphere. Sacrifice of animals, offerings of first fruits, physical marks of initiation, sacred places, incense, reverential gestures are all left aside, and there is no provision for a ritual priesthood to tend any such rites. Instead there is a bathing in water, an eating at table, anointing with oil, hand touches of nearness, comfort, and blessing. The religion of Jesus is of the prophetic sort. It is not forcing things too much to say that, in giving his followers rites drawn more from ordinary life than from the religious patrimony of his people, Jesus was making a prophetic statement about the need to make rites an expression of real life. Such rites could more easily be from the heart, suited to a covenant that was to be written on the heart. They are appropriate to the life that is given within, in the end times when the Spirit is poured out.

There is something still deeper about these rites that relates them uniquely to the life that is in Jesus. They are actions that Jesus performed during his own life, the life that he shared in such obviously human ways with his disciples on earth before he shared it with them in the resurrection. Jesus was baptized in the Jordan, he sat down to eat and drink with his friends, he touched people for healing and comfort, he shared in a wedding feast. When the disciples did these things together after the resurrection, they did them repeatedly and ritually; they were, no doubt, expressing many things that were on their minds about the present and the future. But they could never forget that, in the past, they had done these same actions with Jesus. His "in memory of me" dominated everything and brought the rites into the heart of the life experience they were having in Jesus.

## Rites Accompanied by Words about Jesus

The life that the disciples were receiving from Jesus was being proclaimed in their words. These words of the apostolic preaching provided a setting for the rites. According to the command of Jesus, baptism was to be done within a process of teaching that would call forth faith in Father, Son, and Holy Spirit: "Go therefore and *make disciples* of all nations, baptizing them in the name of the Father and of the Son and of the Holy Spirit, *teaching them to observe* all that I have commanded you . . ." (Matthew 28:19–20). The first baptisms on the day of Pentecost were of "those who *received his word*" (Acts 2:41). The table is a place of conversation and the rite inaugurated at the Last Supper was set in the midst of many words. The breaking of bread that is introduced in Acts 2:42 is accompanied by *"the apostles teaching . . . and the prayers."* All these words and teachings and prayers proclaimed the reality that was present in the rites. They are words of and about Jesus. People who had come to believe in them—and by that very fact had made them their own story, their way of understanding, their law of life—could not but center the rites on Jesus and on their life in him.

## Rites Authorized by the Apostles of Jesus

The rites, like the words, are already becoming recognized in the New Testament, and to that extent subject to the direction of the leaders of the community. The title that Jesus gave to the foundational leaders of the community of his disciples says much about the kind of life he wanted the community to have and about the kind of authority that was to direct it. He called them neither prophets nor priests, nor kings, nor any derivatives of these, but apostles. Although they are men of the word, the apostles are not prophets. There was a category of leaders in the community called prophets, but they are distinguished from the apostles. Nor are the apostles presented as priests. Paul, who is an apostle by a special title, does claim to be "in the priestly service of the Gospel of God, so that the offering of the Gentiles may be acceptable, sanctified by the Holy Spirit" (Romans 15, 16), but there is nothing in this text to link "priestly service" with a priestly performance of rites. Paul did baptize some people, but says he was not sent to baptize (1 Corinthians 1:14–17), and neither he nor any of the other apostles is presented as presiding at the Eucharist. Nor did the apostles give priestly titles to those to whom they gave authority in the communities, but the more neutral, almost secular titles of presbyters and bishops *(episkopoi).* Least of all are the apostles kings. The contrast Jesus made between their authority and that of "the kings of the Gentiles" (Luke 22:24–27) should have made that clear once and for all. If it took two centuries before the Church felt ready to give its leaders priestly titles, it took even longer for it to dare to give them titles or modes of address drawn from the usages of royalty (Lords, Excellencies, Reverend Sirs!).

The title "apostle" presents the leaders of the community of disciples as, above all else, representatives, envoys, messengers of Jesus. Their status and mission is entirely relative to him. Because the fullness of the kingdom has come in Jesus, nothing that is not from him and about him can lay claim to be of God. The apostles are authorized witnesses to Jesus. They lived with him during his days on earth and they recognized him in his resurrection. They authorize the words that are spoken in the community about him. They must also authorize the rites that are done in memory of him. Through this apostolic authorization the community is able to be in touch with the life of Jesus in its words and in its rites. Whatever other authority figures emerge later in the Church, whether they be of the prophetic, priestly, or kingly kind, can only claim to have control over rites and words to the extent that they are faithful to the tradition that comes from the apostles. That is the guarantee that the community is living the life of Jesus.

Through the tradition that comes from the apostles, then, and particularly through the words of the tradition that surround them, the rites of the new covenant remember and embody the reality of Jesus—the reality of his life that he now lives at the right hand of his Father and communicates through the Spirit to those who live in his body, which is the Church. For the believing community the rites of the new covenant have a realism in relation to life that no other rites have ever claimed. They are revelations of the Word made flesh, in whom all prophecy is fulfilled; they are actions of the Eternal High Priest, in whom all worship is centered; they bring about the universal reign of God that is established in Christ and pervades all things through the Spirit. The community that celebrates these rites is alive with his life. Its story is about the working out of his Lordship and its rites are a remembering of his saving action until he comes again.

## Rites of the Presence of Jesus, until He Comes Again

The dream of the prophets about rites that are all of a piece with life has come true in the community of those who believe in Christ—and yet not entirely. On the one hand, there is the euphoric description of the first community in Acts 2:42–47, in which life is gloriously at one

with word and rite. On the other hand, there is soon an outbreak of
"murmuring" in that same community about the distribution of food,
which did not seem to match the table fellowship of the "breaking of
bread" (Acts 6:1). Paul, on the one hand, can serenely dismiss problems
of conscience about eating meat that might have been offered to idols
by appealing to the reality that is encountered in "the cup of blessing
which we bless . . . the bread which we break" (1 Corinthians 10:16).
On the other hand, he has to castigate that same Corinthian community for living in a way that makes nonsense of the rite of "the Lord's
Supper" (1 Corinthians 11:17–34).

Paul's way of dealing with the inconsistency between rite and
life in Corinth shows, however, that the problem is quite different
from what it was under the old covenant. An Old Testament prophet
would have told the Corinthians that, because of the way they were
living, their rite was vain and unacceptable to God. Paul deals with the
question quite differently. He patiently tells them what the tradition
has to say about the rite. It is, he says, the proclaiming, in the bread
and in the cup, of the death of the Lord in the reality of his flesh and
blood. The fault of the Corinthians is that they have not discerned
this reality, which is there whether they discern it or not (and it does
not matter much to the argument whether by "body" in v. 29 Paul
means eucharistic body or ecclesial body, or both). The incongruity
he is pointing out is not between the life of the Corinthians and the
symbolism of the rite they are performing, but between the reality of
their life and the reality of Christ proclaimed in the rite. The value of
the rite comes from the reality of the body and blood of Christ before
it comes from the behavior of the community. If they really knew and
accepted the reality of the body of Christ that is proclaimed and present in the Supper, their lives would soon be changed and they would be
blessed by God accordingly: they would behave differently towards one
another and they would be freed from illness and death (vv. 30–32).
The rite would then have meaning for them because the reality of their
own lives would be in continuity with the reality of Christ.

Paul does not deal any differently with Baptism. In Romans
6:1–14, he explains how Christians have died to sin through being
baptized into Christ Jesus. And yet they still sin! When Paul talks
about the sins of Christians he never suggests that there is anything
wrong with their baptism. The rite does not become empty because of

their sinful lives. He never makes a contrast between baptism of the heart and baptism of the flesh that would be comparable to what he does when discussing circumcision. To question the value of baptism would be to question the reality of Christ. Because it makes one a member of the body of Christ, and because Christ is alive never to die anymore, baptism is always life-giving.

John makes the same point about gospel rites that Paul does, although in a different way. John's gospel does not describe the origins and form of the rite of either baptism or Eucharist. But it alludes to both rites as something its readers would be already practicing, and it has a strong teaching about the reality that believers are to recognize in what they do. The teaching is a call to the disciples to believe that when they celebrate these rites they are to find Jesus, the Word made flesh, the Son sent from the Father, the one from whom the Spirit is poured out, and they are to draw life from him.[1] This understanding of the Christian rites would be a safeguard against ritualism and legalism, such as, for example, might have been carried over into Christianity from some strains of its Jewish inheritance.

The scandal of lives that are not in accord with words and rites should be greater among Christians than among other people because of the uniqueness they claim for the new covenant. Christian theology will always have to wrestle with this problem. Why is it that Christian rites sometimes do not seem to work? Theology will use the analogies of human ritual and the precedents of the Old Testament to try to understand the inconsistency. But in fidelity to the New Testament it will always have to press these explanations to a point that respects the unique relationship of the rites of the new covenant to the word of the gospel and to the life that is in Christ. To a very large extent it was to do this that the word "sacrament" came to be employed in Christian theology as a general name for the principal rites practiced by the community of believers.

---

1. See R. E. Brown, *The Community of the Beloved Disciple (New York: Paulist Press, 1979)*, 88 and *passim*. On the "sacramentalism" of John see Brown, *The Gospel According to John*, Anchor Bible 29, 29a; 2 vols. (Garden City, NY: Doubleday, London: Chapman, 1966, 1971), vol. 1, cxi ff; also *Introduction to the Gospel of John*, ed. P. J. Moloney (New York: Doubleday, 2003), 229ff.

# Chapter 2

# Rites Called Sacraments

"Rite" is a useful generic word that allows one to speak of baptism, confirmation, and Eucharist together and to state some important truths about their place in human and religious experience. Although it is not a biblical word it can denote the biblical realities examined in the preceding chapter. It is, in fact, used in the language of the Church to describe what baptism, confirmation, Eucharist, and other such activities, are in their external shape and form. The books that prescribe how they are to be celebrated can be entitled *Rite of . . .* And yet it is not the word that the tradition of faith has selected to describe what is most profoundly distinctive about these activities. The word that has come to do that is "sacrament." It has come to be the Church's generic word for baptism, confirmation, and Eucharist, as well as for penance and reconciliation, anointing of the sick, matrimony, and Holy Orders. It is a biblical word originally, but in the course of a long history of application to the rites of the Church it has gathered to itself refinements of meaning that it did not have in its biblical origins. There has been an ebb and flow in that history, as new shades of meaning were added to the word or old ones lost. At times the Church has used the word with a technical precision that allowed it to say things that needed to be said about the rites at that particular moment (for example, during the Middle Ages). At other times the word became a bone of contention between churches and they each defined it in their own way to make the point about their differences (for example, during the controversies of the Reformation). Still again it has been used to bring back to the consciousness of faith aspects of the rites that had been somewhat forgotten (as at Vatican II). It is necessary to tell the story of this word and what it said at different times about the rites of the Church before one can sense what it might mean today. The word carries resonances of all the phases of its story and these must affect how we use it to talk about Christian initiation and its rites.

## SACRAMENTUM AND MUSTERION

The English "sacrament" comes from the Latin *sacramentum*. When Christians first began to describe something as *sacramentum* (Tertullian is the earliest Latin writer in whom there is a record of the usage) they were identifying it as related to the sacred; they were also saying that it stood for secret things, that it marked out people as having been initiated into some area of privilege and responsibility, and that it expressed a commitment to some form of service (for different shades of meaning of *sacramentum* in Tertullian see the index to CCSL edition of his works, vol. 2, p. 1604). The oath that soldiers took on entering the service of the emperor was called a *sacramentum*.[1] That particular use of the word evoked many of the qualities that Christians wanted to attribute to their rites, especially to the rites of initiation. Tertullian used the analogy, and it was certainly one of the reasons why he called the rites *sacramenta*. Because the emperor was thought to be divine, a commitment to fight in his service was sacred. One was marked forever by it (quite literally, sometimes, by having some image of the emperor tattooed on one's person). One gained access to all sorts of privileges, as well as to responsibilities, and to the inside information that went with that. To call a Christian rite a *sacramentum* in that sense was to say that it was a commitment to the service of the true God, an entry into the company of other Christians and an initiation into the secret, sacred truth they shared about life and death and eternity. In likening Christian initiation to an oath, *sacramentum* said it was a word, a ritualized word, a binding word about what one wanted to do with one's life.

That was a lot to say about Christian rites. If *sacramentum* could say it that would probably have been enough to justify its place in the Christian vocabulary. But if that was all it said it would hardly have become the distinctive, technical word that it has become in the

---

1. Details in J. C. Navickas, *The Doctrine of St. Cyprian on the Sacraments* (Würzburg, 1924), 7–11.

language of Christian faith. In fact, *sacramentum* acquired another function in Christian language that really made its fortune, and ultimately made it an even more appropriate term for baptism, Eucharist, and the other major Christian rites. It came to be used as a translation of the Greek word *musterion*.

In Greek, *musterion* has a general meaning of "secret," with a sense of the sacredness of all secrets. The Greek Bible used it in that sense. It is the word that the Revised Standard Version (RSV) translates by "secret" in Tobit 12:7: "It is good to guard the secret of a king, but gloriously to reveal the works of God." If kings have their secret plans ("mysteries" in Judith 2:2) and can reveal them to their intimates, the secret of the destiny of all kingdoms is known only to God and can only be revealed by him. *Musterion* is used in the expression of this idea in Daniel 2:18, 27, 47. When Daniel has interpreted the strange dream of Nebuchadnezzar, the king says: "Truly your God is God of Gods and Lord of kings, and a revealer of mysteries, for you have been able to reveal this mystery" (v. 47). The later Wisdom literature of the Old Testament connects Wisdom with the making and the revelation of this secret plan of God for all human history and uses *musterion* for what the RSV translates as "the secret purposes of God" (Wisdom 2:22; *cf.* 6:22).

Saint Paul takes up this language of mystery, and its Old Testament field of thought, to describe the Christian gospel (1 Corinthians 2:6–16; Colossians 1:9–20; 2:2–4; Ephesians 1:9–23; 3:1–6; Romans 16:25–27; the word is also used in Matthew 13:11; Mark 4:11; Luke 8:10; Revelation 1:20; 10:7; 17:5). The mystery, which is God's plan for the reconciliation of all things, is finally realized, and shown to be realized, in the cross of Jesus, in his resurrection and sending of the Spirit. The mystery is put into words and proclaimed in the preaching of the Apostles. Those who believe in their word and enter the Church have the mystery revealed to them.

For all that he has to say about the mystery, the only time Paul comes close to calling a rite of the Christian community a mystery is when he is presenting the Christian meaning of marriage (Ephesians 5:22–33). The marriage of Christians represents and realizes the work of Christ for his Church and the response of the Church to Christ. "This mystery is a profound one," says Paul, "and I am saying that it refers to Christ and the Church" (v. 32). In this text Paul seems to be thinking more of the day-to-day living out of marriage than of the ritual solemnizing of it, so one is not yet at the point of having a Christian rite called a mystery—although rite and life are so close in marriage that the distinction is almost academic. Much of what Paul has to say about baptism and Eucharist, and of the bearing they have on life, is strikingly similar to what he has to say about marriage, but he does not call them mysteries. However, he would surely see the mystery proclaimed in them, since they are an integral part of that gospel which makes the life of the Church be a revelation of the mystery of God.

When Christians came to translate their Greek Scriptures into Latin they sometimes rendered *musterion* by *mysterium*, somewhat as English would later develop the word "mystery" to translate it. But they also translated it by *sacramentum*—and there is no obvious reason why they chose one translation rather than the other. Scholars are not quite sure why they used *sacramentum* as the equivalent of *musterion*. There is no particular precedent for doing so in classical Latin. But it is a fact that they did so, and the fact says a lot about what they thought of *sacramentum* and of anything they called *sacramentum*. When the Greek Fathers came to use the word *musterion* for the rites of the Christian faith, the Latins were ready with *sacramentum* to say everything the Greek word wanted to say about the rites. Their word, in its turn, became enriched with the biblical teaching about the mystery of God and the mystery of Christ, and could consequently bring these fundamental ideas to bear on the understanding of Christian rites.

## CLEMENT AND ORIGEN

In the writings of Clement of Alexandria and Origen one can see some of the important lines of thought that led the Greek patristic tradition to call the rites of the Church *musteria*. The Alexandrians made use of *musterion* and its derivatives to speak of Christian realities. They were interested in the special knowledge of God *(gnosis)* enjoyed by Christians. In broad terms one can say that they thought in Platonic categories, according to which the world of the senses is a world of images and symbols behind which, or above which, lies the true world of divine ideas and ultimate spiritual reality. To get at the reality represented by the images was to enter their mystery, or "mystical" sense. In the Christian world, texts of Scripture, formulations of faith such as the Creeds, and the rites of the Church were special images and symbols that needed this kind of interpretation. In imaging and symbolizing the mystery of God they, too, were somehow mysteries. They allowed one to get in touch with the divine reality when they were suitably, that is mystically, interpreted.[2]

There is little doubt that in the thinking of Clement and Origen the primary bearer of mystery is the word. But they see how the word is ritualized in the celebrations of the Church, especially in baptism: the rite concretizes the biblical types proclaimed in the texts and brings them to bear on the life of Christians. For example, the biblical stories of deliverance by water are made concrete in the water ritual of baptism. Baptism is a mystery because it shows forth the reality of salvation that was already realized, although in a shadowy form, in the events of the Old Testament and was fully realized in the death and resurrection of Christ. The word is at the heart of the mystery that is in baptism. The "bath of water" is likened by Origen, in his Commentary on John VI, to the physical cures worked on peoples' bodies by Jesus. Like them, it is a symbol of the spiritual healing that the word works on those who have faith.[3] It is the word that calls forth faith and in that faith heals. Rite is never separated from word, and both yield up their hidden meaning together by being related to the mystery that is in Christ. It is the task of interpretation and catechesis to reveal this meaning. There is also the task of spelling out the implications of word and rite for life in a moral kind of exegesis.

## The Mystery Religions

Another linguistic usage had to be absorbed before Christians were entirely at home with calling their rites *musteria*. In the early centuries of the Christian era the word was used to describe ritual cults

---

2. B. Neunheuser, OSB, *Baptism and Confirmation*, trans. from German (New York: Herder and Herder, 1964), Ch. 3–4.

3. R. E. Heine, trans., *Origen. Commentary on the Gospel according to John, Book 1–10*, The Fathers of the Church, A New Translation, vol. 80 (Washington, DC: The Catholic University of America Press, 1989), 216.

that were being practiced in the Greco-Roman world side by side
with Christianity. There was nothing very mysterious about the official cult of the emperor: it was civic and civil but not much more. The
religion of the household gods was more intimate, but not very excit-
ing. Out of the eastern parts of the empire, however, had come a variety of cults that claimed to give a deeper encounter with the reality of
nature and the cosmos, and promised an experience of liberation from
the drabness of existence into some kind of fuller life. The devotees of
Demeter went to her shrine at Eleusis in Greece, while the devotees
of Isis and Osiris, and particularly of Mithras, set up their centers
of cult throughout the empire. Each cult had its mysteries. It had a
story, which was usually a myth about how the god or gods made
the world, gave it fertility, and overcame the various death-dealing
forces that trouble it. The story was kept secret and revealed only to
initiates. Initiation was by a series of ritual actions (Mithraism had
seven) during which the initiates were given a progressively fuller
knowledge of the story (which would be at the same time an explanation of the successive ritual stages) until they were finally admitted
into the full secret of the cult. The process of initiation, and the story
that was revealed in it, was supposed to make a profound difference
to the life of people and to admit them to a higher form of existence.
The whole process, including rite and story, had to be kept secret. The
cult was a mystery.

The parallels with Christianity were too close for comfort,
especially when it became known, as it inevitably did, that the story
was sometimes about the death of a god, about the shedding of blood
that brought life, about descents from and ascents to heaven, and that
the rites included sacred meals and various libations and washings.
Already by the year 150, Justin Martyr found it necessary to explain
away the parallels. Having described the Christian Eucharist in his
*First Apology* (n. 66) he adds:

> The evil demons, in imitation of this [what Jesus did at the Last Supper]
> ordered the same thing to be performed in the Mithraic mysteries. For,
> as you know, or may easily learn, bread and a cup of water, together with
> certain incantations, are used in their mystic initiation rites.

Justin does not call the Christian Eucharist a mystery here. Even if
he had seen reasons for doing so, the risks of reducing the Eucharist

to the level of a Mithraic or any other cultic ritual were too great at this stage of the development of Christian language. Tertullian saw the parallels, too, and vigorously rejects any real similarity between the *sacra* of the mystery cults and the *sacramentum* of Christian baptism. His only use of *mysterion* is in reference to pagan rites.

In a development of which historians are still trying to give a coherent account, the reserve about calling the rites of the Christian faith *musteria* was eventually overcome. A beginning had been made by Origen, and by the time of Athanasius the statements are explicit *(Oratio II contra Arianos* 42; *Oratio III contra Arianos* 33: PG 26, 236, and 393). The self-confidence Christians gained during the fourth century and the decline or suppression of the pagan mystery cults made it easier to call the rites of Christian cult *musteria,* and to even allow the word to carry with it some discreet analogies with the pagan cults. Certainly, these cults, with their combination of story and rite, and their offer of a life-changing experience, were better models for showing how Christian rites were rooted in human experience than were the official cults of the State religion. The Greek mystagogical catecheses of the fourth century are quite at home with *musterion* as a word for the Christian rites. The two Latin sets of catecheses that come from Saint Ambrose are called *De Mysteriis* and *De Sacramentis.*

## The Mystagogical Catecheses

The ongoing history of *musterion* and of its application to the rites of the Church by the Greek Fathers from Origen onward would, no doubt, be instructive, as would that of *sacramentum* in Latin, but for the purposes of the present chapter it is sufficient to draw attention to what *musterion* and *sacramentum* had come to stand for around the end of the fourth century when Cyril of Jerusalem, Ambrose of Milan, John Chrysostom, and Theodore of Mopsuestia spoke their great catecheses to those who were experiencing the rites of Christian initiation. Nor is it necessary to work out whatever interdependence there might have been between these four great preachers. It seems reasonable to say that they are four witnesses to a way of thinking and speaking that had become so widespread as to be universal in the fourth century.

While there can be no substitute for actually reading the text of the catecheses,[4] attention can be drawn to some general features of them that bear on the use of *musterion* and *sacramentum*. They are about *rites*, and it is these they call mysteries/sacraments. The rites are the full liturgy of Christian initiation of adults (baptism, confirmation, and Eucharist) solemnly celebrated in the Church at Easter. The word, spoken and read, is an integral part of the rite to be explained. The "explanation" is more an evocation of the deep underlying realities than a logical analysis of meaning. The preparatory rites of the catechumenate are also expounded within the ambit of mystery, but there is a preferential use of "mystery" to refer to the central core of the rite (e.g., Theodore, II, 1). It is the sermons on these central rites of baptism, confirmation, and Eucharist that are properly called "mystagogical" (the *mustagogus* was the one who explained the rites of initiation to candidates in the mystery religions). Mystery and sacrament are not so much definable theological terms which would allow conclusions to be drawn about the rites as mood-words that convey an atmosphere. They express the sacredness, the awesomeness, the hiddenness, and need to keep secret, the symbolic character of the rites that comes from the realities encountered in them. There is not much explicit appeal to the Pauline *musterion*, but the explanation of the rites of baptism and Eucharist is deeply Pauline. There is constant reference to the scriptures—to texts being read in the course of the celebration, but to others as well. Clearly the mystery is in the rite only in the setting of the *word*. The types and figures of the Old Testament give the rites their symbolic resonance; the proclamations of the New Testament about the salvation that is in Christ reveal the grace that is given in the rites. The reality that lies beneath the rites is discovered in the word. The reality is the salvation that comes from God, the climax of the divine mystery accomplished in Christ. The word draws forth faith. It is only in faith that the real meaning of the rites can be accepted (cf. for example Chrysostom, II, 9–11; Theodore, II, 13–16).

The change of *life* brought about by the rites and required by them is also explained in the catecheses. It is a gift given in the rite but it is also a personal decision called for by the rite. There is an element

---

4. Conveniently edited and translated in E. Yarnold, sj, *The Awe-Inspiring Rites of Initiation. The Origins of the R.C.I.A.* 2nd ed. (The Liturgical Press: Collegeville, MN, 1994). References in the text are to this edition.

of contract or covenant in the rite. It is referred to in the explanations of the rite of renouncing Satan. A new contract is being made with Christ, in place of the one that bound people to Satan. The language of mystery/sacrament is used about it (Cyril, I, I–II; Ambrose, I, 5–8; Chrysostom, 11, 17–21; Theodore, II, 1–12). The sense of commitment and oath that *sacramentum* had in the original Latin usage noted in Tertullian is being maintained.

## THE LATIN TRADITION AND SAINT AUGUSTINE

In the catecheses of Ambrose, with the easy interchange of *mysterium* and *sacramentum*, and with the use of both words for diverse things such as texts of Scripture, other doctrinal expressions of the faith, realities of the life of Christ such as the Incarnation and Passion, as well as for the rites of the Church, one is still in a world of thought and language that can be shared comfortably by pastors and theologians from the Greek and other Oriental Churches. Generally speaking, the Churches of the East have remained with that kind of thinking.[5] However, whereas the Greeks had only one word *(musterion)* to deal with, the Latins had two. Almost inevitably one of them, *sacramentum*, came to be favored when it became necessary to talk specifically about the rites, and it became the word that was made to carry the kind of sharpened thinking required by the doctrinal controversies about the rites that bothered the Western Church in the fourth and fifth centuries. *Mysterium* came to be used more particularly for the doctrinal expressions of the realities of salvation, and for the realities themselves in so far as they were thought about in faith (as in "mystery of the Trinity" or "mysteries of Christ"). The distinction came about quite gradually. Indeed the equivalence and interchangeability of the two words was never quite lost in Latin theology. It is periodically reemployed (as in the theology associated with Vatican II), and with great profit for the life of the Church.

The controversies that led to the technical development of *sacramentum* occurred mainly in the Church of North Africa, which, in Tertullian, provided the first evidence of its use. By the end of the fourth century the Church of North Africa had been divided for more

---

5. T. Ware, *The Orthodox Church.* New edition. (London: Penguin Books, 1997), Ch. 14.

than a hundred years by disagreements about the nature of the Church and contrasting views about the ecclesial value of baptisms, ordinations and Eucharists celebrated by sinners.[6]

The origins of the debate can be seen already in Tertullian. He adopted the Montanist position that only the saints *(pneumatici)* formed the true Church and so only they could truly baptize. This touched issues of pastoral decision as well as of teaching. What should be done about people who came to the Church from heretical or schismatic churches in which they had already been baptized, ordained, admitted to the Eucharist? What if they had been admitted to these rites but had never renounced a sinful life? Or what if they had betrayed the faith under persecution? Should they be baptized again, ordained again? And if so why? It was a question of whether the Church could recognize as sacraments rites performed by sinners. Saint Cyprian thought the negative position was more reasonable, and claimed to have the support of 71 of his brother bishops from North Africa. But his reasoning went against the tradition of the Church, which, as his contemporary Pope Saint Stephen reminded him, was the decisive argument in such matters.[7]

One can recognize in Cyprian's reasoning something of the protest of the prophets that rites that were not all of a piece with life made nonsense of the covenant of God. But his logic owes more to the old than to the new covenant. Paul saw the incongruity between the behavior of the Corinthians and their celebration of the Lord's Supper. But because he believed that the Eucharist celebrated a covenant made in the body and blood of Christ, he could not conclude that the rites of the Corinthians were empty. The body of Christ was there, and they were it, if they would but discern the reality. Fortunately Cyprian did not push his logic to the limits that Tertullian did. His ecclesiological instinct, if not his theory, was sound enough to keep him from the puritan hypothesis of the Church as a community of saints. But others

---

6. For the different phases of the dispute see J. N. D. Kelly, *Early Christian Doctrines*, 4th ed. (London: Adam & Charles Black, 1968), 200–211, 409–417; for Cyprian's use of *sacramentum* see J. C. Navickas, *The Doctrine of St. Cyprian on the Sacraments* (Würzburg, 1924).

7. Relevant texts in P. Palmer, sj, *Sacraments and Worship: Liturgy and Doctrinal Development of Baptism, Confirmation, and the Eucharist* (London: Longmans, Green and Co, 1957), 112–113; J. Neuner and J. Dupuis (eds.), *The Christian Faith in the Doctrinal Documents of the Catholic Church*, fifth revised and enlarged ed. (London: Harper Collins Religious, 1992; New York: Alba House, 1996).

who took up the same issue later were not so discreet. Out of a controversy about the ordination of a certain Caecilian as Bishop of Carthage
in 311 came a new, Montanist-type teaching about the Church and
its rites, and a schism that deeply divided the Church in North Africa.
The schismatic groups, who were named Donatists after Donatus,
one of their principal exponents, based their teaching on the view that
the Church was a community of saints that had no place for sinners.
Hence, rites performed by sinners were not really of the Church and
could not be sanctifying. Converted sinners should be baptized into
the church of the saints, i.e., the Donatist church, whether or not they
had already been baptized by and into another church. The scandal of
lives that were not in accordance with Christian rites and words, and
the scandal of rites and words that did not seem to produce effects of
holiness in the lives of people, were thus eliminated, at least theoreti-
cally. The sinners who came from another church had simply never
been baptized or ordained and their Eucharist was not of Christ.

The Donatist theory must have been attractive for people who
were serious about their Christianity, serious about Christian rites, and
serious about the demands of being in the Church. Yet it went against
something that lay deep in the Christian tradition of practice and
teaching. Optatus of Milevis did much to expound orthodox teaching
on the subject.[8] But it was Augustine who brought the full Catholic
tradition to light and, in doing so, gave *sacramentum* technical refinements that have remained with it ever since.

Augustine does not yet reserve the word "sacrament" for the
rites of the Church. Scripture, the Creed, the sign of the cross, the
Lord's Prayer and many other sacred things are still sacraments in his
language. But he does begin to look more carefully at what the word
means when applied to the major rites of the Christian faith. He uses
the anthropological idea of sign *(signum)* to explain what these things
called sacraments are, and shows how that fits them into the normal
psychological and pedagogical procedures of human life (his idea of
sign can be gleaned from, among other places, *Letters* 54 and 55 *Ad
Januarium*, 98 *Ad Bonifatium*, 138 *Ad Marcellinum* [PL 33]; *De Doctrina
Christiana* 3, 13 [PL 34]; *Contra Faustum* tom. 19, nn. 12–14, 17 [PL

---

8. Kelly, *Early Christian Doctrines*, 411–412; texts of Optatus in Palmer, *Sacraments and
Worship*, 115–119.

42]; *De Civitate Dei* 1.10, c. 6, 20 [*PL* 41]). A sign is always a sign of some "thing" (*res* in Latin). The Platonic strain in Augustine's thinking comes into play here. Behind the visible, tangible world of human experience lies the world of invisible reality, the world that is truly real. Our world of the senses is full of signs and images of "the real thing." Christian rites are part of this arrangement. One has to look behind them to discover the thing they signify. This was, of course, something that the tradition had been wanting to say about them by calling them mysteries and sacraments. Augustine has many ways of describing the reality that is signified by the Christian rites, but ultimately they all come to saying that the reality is Christ. If he says that it is the Passion and Resurrection that are signified it is because these are actions (mysteries) of Christ; if he says it is the Church it is because the Church is the whole Christ, head and members; if he says it is grace it is because grace is the life of Christ, the head, given to his members.

That the reality *(res)* signified by a sacrament is Christ is the heart of Augustine's understanding of what it means to call the rites of the Church by that name. It is also the heart of his answer to the Donatists. The rites are what they are, are what the word sacrament says they are, because Christ is in them, because the Church is in them, because grace is in them. This is what is given by ministers of the sacraments and what is received by members of the Church. Augustine explains how ministers and believers give and are given life by being caught up in the sanctifying, Christ-forming, Spirit-filling power of the sacraments. But because of the Donatist controversies he has to think about sacramental celebrations in which this does not happen. Ministers of churches that are in heresy or schism are sinners, cut off themselves from the life of grace. People who receive sacraments in these churches are sinners and do not receive the sanctification of grace. Not alone are they sinners but they sin in celebrating the sacraments unworthily. And there are other sins of which ministers and participants can be guilty besides heresy and schism. Yet, whatever it is, the sin of ministers or participants does not destroy the reality of Christ that is in the rite. Provided it is properly celebrated the rite remains a sign of the reality of salvation. It remains a sacrament.[9]

---

9. Relevant texts of Augustine in Palmer, *Sacraments and Worship*, 119–129.

Obviously, it would be easier to believe that a rite is a real
sacrament if one could explain that even people who are not sanctified
are still somehow affected by it. Augustine works out a theory
on this point that explains the effects of baptism in a way that justifies the practice of not rebaptizing converts from other churches,
which the Catholics were defending against the Donatists. It is a
theory that has had a lasting effect on the theological understanding of
sacrament. He takes up the biblical image of "seal" that the Fathers of
East and West had been using to talk about Christian initiation. Paul
had said that Christians were sealed by the Holy Spirit (2 Corinthians
1:22; Ephesians 1:13–14; 4:30). They were marked, set apart for the
life that was in them through the gift of the Spirit. To be sealed in
this way was to be made like Christ, because the Father had also set
his seal on him (John 6:27). A seal is an identifying mark, a sign of
ownership, a setting-apart or consecration for special purposes. The
original Latin meaning of *sacramentum* conveyed much the same
idea. In describing baptism as a sacrament the Christian tradition
was saying that it marked people out, consecrated them as Christians,
and did so as a kind of visible sign. It was this Christian marking that
Augustine seized on to explain how the baptism of a sinner could have
some real effect. Once the minister made the appropriate sign and
the participant entered freely and intentionally into it, he or she was
"signed, sealed, and delivered" for Christ, whether or not they were
repenting and having their sins forgiven. They had really received a
sacrament of Christ, even if they had not begun to live like Christ.
That sign of belonging to Christ would remain with them. If they did
later repent of their sins and begin to live in Christ it would be the
effect of the sacrament they had already received. They would not need
to be baptized again.[10]

The way of thinking about the effects of a sacrament that
Augustine developed in his controversy with the Donatists about
baptism is also applied by him to ordination and confirmation.[11]
It becomes, with some adjustments for the other sacraments, an
integral part of the sacramental theory that the Western Church

---

10. See J. Galot, sj, *La nature du caractère sacramentel* (Paris-Louvain: Desclée de Brouwer, 1958), I, 3, 36–41.

11. Texts in Palmer, *Sacraments and Worship*, 125–126.

inherited from him. Enlightening and necessary as are the distinctions he made about the effects of a sacrament, they carry a risk. If a sacrament can stand even when its life-giving effects are not being received by the participant, the possibility is opened up of justifying the making of a sacrament for reasons other than its life-giving *effect* on the participant. Or, at least in the case of a sacrament that cannot be repeated, one may be tempted to take a chance: if it does not sanctify the participant now it may do so later. There is in the theory a risk of detaching the sacraments from life and of countenancing a certain formalism in ritual. It is a risk that was not always avoided by those who took over Augustine's teaching in the Middle Ages and subsequently.

There is, however, another essential element in the sacramental theory of Augustine that greatly minimizes the risk of separating rite and life. It is the attention he gives to *word* in relation to the sacramental rite. Augustine lived in a Church that still celebrated many adult baptisms (including his own!) and prepared people for them with an elaborate catechumenate. The word of preaching and instruction enfolded the rite. It is also at the core of the sacramental sign. In a famous passage from his *Treatise on the Gospel of John* (80, 3),[12] he explains how it is the word that gives an element such as water its power to cleanse in baptism. This joining of word and element, in a single sign, makes the sacrament to be a kind of visible word (which, in the context of this passage, relates it for Augustine to the joining of Word and flesh in the incarnation). The spoken word makes a sacrament, not because of its sound or its obvious meaning, but because of the meaning it has for faith, the faith of the Church and of the one receiving the sacrament. The word expressed in the scriptures, the Creed, the preaching and catechesis of the Church is all of a piece with the prayers and formulas that are spoken in the rites. All these words breathe life into the rites and relate the rites to the real life of Christians. They do it, ultimately, because in them is the Word of God in person. He is the reality that gives all these words of faith, and particularly the sacramental words that go along with the element, their life-giving power.

---

12. Text in Palmer, *Sacraments and Worship*, 127.

# THE SCHOLASTICS AND SAINT THOMAS AQUINAS

By the end of the twelfth century a need for pastoral discernment, backed by a growing theological consensus, brought the Latin Church to recognize that seven of its rites had a special status, and that what was believed about that status could be expressed by saying that they, and they only, were sacraments. The theological consensus about seven sacraments was given authoritative expression during the twelfth century in the *Sentences* of Peter Lombard. The doctrine was included in the "Profession of Faith of Michael Palaeologus" read at the Second Council of Lyons in 1274 (DS, 860; ND, 28). Such a development supposed that the word sacrament had a special meaning when applied to these seven rites. Medieval theologians set about synthesizing and refining the Augustinian definitions of the word so that it would express what was peculiar to these rites, and to nothing else in the same way. That produced more precise thinking and language about the rites as sacraments. It also, of course, carried the risk of separating these seven rites from the wider context of symbolic activity and proclamation of the word that was always in the mind of Augustine when he used the word sacrament.

Thomas Aquinas had a determining influence on how the Middle Ages dealt with the Augustinian tradition and handed it on in the Church. While his formal treatment of the sacraments comes in the Third Part of the *Summa*, some of his most interesting thinking about how rites like sacraments could have a place in the work of divine grace is done already in the Second Part, in his consideration of the rites of the Old Testament and how they are related to those of the New. There he examines the institutions that God gave to his People in the Law of the Old Covenant. In his study of the ceremonial precepts of the Old Law (qq. 101–103) he explores the human and religious value that their rites had for the people of Israel, as well as how these prefigured the realities of the New Testament. When he moves on to consider the New Law of the Gospel, he explains how this is no longer a dispensation of words and rites, but is the actual living presence and reality of the grace of the Holy Spirit, given in the coming of Christ (qq. 106–108). The New Law does, nevertheless, have some institutions of word and rite, in the form of teaching and sacraments (q. 106, a.1; q. 107, a.1 ad 3; q. 108, a.2). These have a secondary role, entirely relative to the reality of Christ, which is the only source of grace. All that Thomas will later say about how the grace of Christ is "contained" and objectively present in the sacraments is grounded on this explanation of the radical newness that the actual presence of Christ, source of the grace of the Holy Spirit, gives to the institutions of the New Law.

When he comes to deal formally with the sacraments in the Third Part of the *Summa* (qq. 60–90) Thomas holds fast to Augustine's idea that sacraments are signs. Some of his contemporaries were afraid that sign was too thin an idea to convey the full realism and power that the tradition saw in the sacraments, and were looking to the ideas of cause (of grace) for a more reliable definition. Thomas, however, chooses sign as the defining feature of sacraments (q. 60). His understanding of sign, although basically Augustinian, has more Aristotelianism than Platonism in it. It is a little more intellectualist than mystical: the word that is part of the rite is a word of meaning more than just of shadowy symbolism, and the whole rite offers and calls for instruction. For Thomas the reality signified in the sacrament is sacred and mysterious, but the sign itself should make sense.

Thomas does a careful analysis of how the life of grace comes from sacraments (q. 62). He takes the fact that it does so as a given of the tradition and has already given his basic explanation of why it should be so in his discussion on the New Law. Here he employs the technical categories of causality, particularly of principal and instrumental causality, to explain how God could use something like a sacrament to give divine life to humans. He has introduced the categories of causality early in the *Summa*, explaining God's action in terms of a causality that is at once exemplar and formal, efficient and final (e.g., First Part, q. 5, a. 4). In his causal analysis he does not lose sight of his definition of sacrament as sign. It is in signifying that the rite causes grace (*sacramenta significando causant*, De Veritate, 27, 4 ad 13). God reveals his grace in the sacrament as he gives it. Thus the sacrament gives form and finality to grace as well as giving it existence (q. 62, a. 2). This means they are signs of Christ, because he is the concrete embodiment of grace, giving it existence, form, and finality (Third Part, qq. 7–8). They are signs of the paschal mystery of his death, of the grace that comes from him into our life on earth, and of the glory he promises when he comes again (q. 60, a.3). It is the Passion of Christ that gives the sacraments their meaning as well as their life-giving power (Third Part, q. 60, a. 5). The identification of these causalities, operating in a sign, allows Thomas to explain the personal factors that come into play in the making of a sacrament (q. 64). A sacrament is an act of God (a. 1 and 2), an act of Christ (a. 3 and 4), an act of the Church acting through its ministers (a. 5–10), and none the less for all that (indeed, because of it) it is a grace-act of the participant. For the participant the sacrament is an act of worship which, being itself a fruit of grace, opens the believer to the grace of the sacrament (q. 60, a. 5). This coordination of causalities can be described as Thomas' attempt to put some reasonable order into the many different things that the tradition had been wanting to say about the rites of the Church by calling them mysteries and sacraments and acts of worship. (He connects the *mysteries* of the Incarnate Word with the sacraments of the Church in his Prologue to q. 60 of the Third Part.)

One of the most creative parts of Thomas' theology of sacraments is what he has to say about character (q. 63). Under pressure from the Donatists, Augustine had come to the conclusion that sacraments can have an effect even when they do not give grace, and had used the idea of seal to express his thinking. Thomas is able to develop Augustine's thinking about the seal without the pressure of any polemic and to use it to clarify important ecclesiological and Christological features of the rites called sacraments. Three of the sacraments, baptism, confirmation, and ordination, give a spiritual mark or seal, which he calls character. The Latin *character* transliterates a Greek word that the patristic tradition had already associated with the seal. It means something like "exact reproduction of"—which is what a seal often was. The Fathers noted that in Hebrews 1:3 Christ is said to be the "character of the Father's substance" (RSV: "the very stamp of his nature"). As Christ is the likeness of the Father, so Christians are stamped, sealed with the likeness of Christ by the Holy Spirit: they bear his character.

The character given by sacraments is itself, in the mind of Thomas, a qualification for giving and receiving sacraments. The idea of qualification, or power, has to be seen in the sphere of sign-making activity, since to make a sacrament is to make a sign. It takes qualified people to make effective signs (it takes a policeman to stop traffic with the wave of a hand!). Since the principal cause of the effectiveness of sacraments is God, the power given in the character is instrumental. It enables people to act as God's instruments, either for their own benefit (qualifying them to receive the grace of the sacrament) or for the benefit of others (qualifying them to give grace to others). This giving and receiving of grace is for our justification and the taking away of our sins. But as it occurs in a sacramental rite, it is also, says Thomas, an act of worship *(cultus)*. The signs in which grace is given and received are signs of worship. The character, as a power to make these signs in the Church, is a power to set up and partake of sacramental worship. At this point Thomas is bringing to light something of what the tradition of faith meant by calling the rites of the Church mysteries/sacraments. The rites are, in a term made famous by Odo Casel, "cult-mysteries." The death and resurrection of Christ that they embody is, in a "downward" movement, the source of life for the whole of creation and simultaneously, in an "upward" movement, the worship of God from the whole creation. Because the rites are of Christ they are grace-filled and worship-filled, and they could not be one without the other. In presenting the character as a power to make signs of Christian worship Thomas takes theological reflection beyond any kind of merely *ad hoc* answer to Donatism and makes it carry a profound truth about a full Christian sacrament. This worship side of sacrament is as much a point of identification with Christ for the Christian as is its grace-giving side. Since the only worship now acceptable to God is that of Christ the Priest, Thomas presents the character as a sharing in the priestly power of Christ (Third Part q. 63, a. 3).

    The character thus understood is also a point of identification with the Church as Body of Christ. The Church is the communion of those who live in the grace that Christ, the Head, gives to his Body. At the same time it is the community of those who live institutionally together on earth in the profession of faith and the celebration of sacraments. In presenting the character as a qualification to make those signs of faith that are sacraments Thomas is saying that they make people to be members of the sacramental, institutional Church. Ecclesiology was not a distinctive theological issue for Thomas. But clearly his idea of the character is his way of expressing at one and the same time a deeply ecclesiological view of sacraments and a deeply sacramental view of the Church. He does not lose sight of what Augustine had to assert against the Donatists. The Church continues to be the visible Body of Christ even when some of her members are not living in the grace of Christ. The characters are given, and work, even when the persons who have them are not in grace. They work because they are sacramental sharings in the power of Christ, who is always present in and for his Church. What Augustine defended about particular sacraments against the Donatists is true of the whole character-built Church. This is Thomas' way of accounting for what the tradition meant when it called the whole Church a sacrament.

*Word* continues to be inseparable from *rite* in Thomas' thinking about sacrament. His somewhat intellectualist conception of sign already inclines him to see the sacramental rite as a word, and he regularly refers to the instructive value of sacraments. But he also notes that sacraments themselves demand such instruction (e.g., q. 71, a. 1 on baptism). He has a strong sense of the biblical typology inherent in sacraments and gives explicit attention to it in studying individual sacraments (baptism in q. 70 *passim*; confirmation in q. 72, 2; Eucharist in q. 73, 6). But his most formal attention is given to the sacramental words spoken at the core of the rite. He sees them as a spiritual (i.e., intelligible) factor that gives precision to the significance of the material element or action of the sacrament. It is in this sense, on the level of signification, that he adopts the terminology "matter" and "form" for the element and word that come together to make a sacrament. The element or action has a soft, open, human signification that would work in any number of ways: in this it has something like the openness that Aristotelian philosophy attributed to "prime matter." The words draw out of this openness a precise Christian signification: in this they have something like the existentially determining role that "form" has in relation to "matter." Like Augustine, Thomas insists that the sacramental word is a word of faith. Faith recognizes in it the personal Word of God, and it is this Word who gives power to the sacramental words (Third Part, q. 66, 5 ad 3). The faith in the Word that the Church professes in its sacramental word is the same faith that it professes in its scriptures and its creeds, and that is communicated in its preaching and teaching. In the rite the believer is carried by all these words to the reality of the life of God that is given in the Word made flesh.[13]

    The *life* that Thomas sees coming from the Word in sacraments is the life of grace, virtues, and gifts. Thomas puts his treatment of sacraments at the very end of his theology (only the general resurrection remains to be dealt with after sacraments). Methodologically, this means that he wants to see the sacraments as the ultimate, historical realization of the whole process of God's work of creation and self-giving, and of the moral response in which humans receive that gift. The *Summa* is an exploration of the mystery of God as he is the origin of all things and as he brings all things back to himself in love. Thomas' concern to maintain the sense of this two-fold theological movement, from God and to God, can be seen in his analysis of sacraments as simultaneously sanctification (from God) and worship (to God). It is in this sense, too, that his theology of grace, as sovereignly efficacious gift of God, which is at the same time free moral choice of humans, finds its existential verification in sacraments: they are, at one and the same time, life-giving acts of God for humans and moral decisions of humans to live for God. As such they bring into play the whole earthly striving towards happiness of men and women, as humans and as Christians—all that is involved in the life of grace, virtues, and gifts. But sacraments add something essential to that life (q. 62, a. 2). Life for God has certain critical moments in its continuous development. It is these moments that are specially graced by God by being sacramentalized. By that very fact the whole life of grace, virtues, and gifts—the whole return of the creature to God—is inserted into Christ and into his Body, which is the Church. In the theology of Saint Thomas, when one has fully understood what the sacraments are there is nothing more that needs to be thought about except the return of Christ in glory, something which, of course, they already signify!

---

13. For a critical evaluation of Thomas' teaching on word and sacrament see K. Rahner, SJ, "Introductory Observations on Thomas Aquinas Theology of the Sacraments in General," in *Theological Investigations*. 14. (Baltimore/London, 1980), 152.

## Reformation and the Council of Trent

The tradition of faith carried by the word "sacrament" is alive and well in the theology of Saint Thomas. It is presented in a new analytical way, and with some new technical concepts, as part of a systematic theology. The other great original Scholastic theologians did the same kind of thing. Their views are not always those of Thomas, but one recognizes in them the same basic tradition of faith. However, the very technicality of the Scholastic theology of the sacraments and the new elements in its vocabulary can hide its continuity with the tradition. And it has shorthand phrases that can easily become jargon, pithy principles that can easily become clichés. Movements to renew sacramental theology have been tempted to think that they have to shake off the whole Scholastic analysis of sacrament if they are to recover the tradition.

The Reformers of the sixteenth century certainly believed they had to rescue the faith of the Church about sacraments from Scholasticism. But it is well to know what kind of theology of sacraments the Reformers were hearing from Scholasticism. It was, in fact, a quite decadent version of what had been worked out by Thomas and others in the creative period of medieval theology. In one sense the seeds of decadence were already there at the time of Thomas. They were there in the sacramental practice of the time, which was already becoming ritualistic and losing touch with the language and symbols and feelings of real life.[14] New devotional and even social concerns were having their effect on sacramental practice. By the late Middle Ages liturgical decadence had become even more pronounced. The better Scholastic theory was used by Church authorities to try to correct abuses and to give direction to practice. But at the same time the theory was being pushed along certain eccentric lines in an attempt to make some sense of even dubious practice. It was still accepted that the sacramental rites should have a bearing on life, and that sacramental doctrine and preaching should be a word that would explain the connection with life and promote it. But the life that the rites were being related to was an increasingly strange mixture of traditional Christian

---

14. J. A. Jungmann, sj, *The Mass of the Roman Rite: its origins and development (Missarum Sollemnia)*, New rev. and abridged ed. of *Missarum Sollemnia*, 2 vols., (1949) (New York: Benziger Bros., 1959), 77–100.

values, new devotional forms, and superstition, as well as the sociore-
ligious concerns of a world that was going through major convulsions
like the Black Death, the discovery of the New World, and a cultural
Renaissance. A new word came to be spoken, in order to provide some
explanation of how Christian rites might be connected with this life.
It used jargon and clichés abstracted from Scholasticism, without the
sensitivity of the early Scholastics to the balance of the tradition. For
example, if the practice was to baptize people indiscriminately, and
Jews forcibly, it was justified on the grounds that sacraments were
necessary for salvation and produced their effects *ex opere operato* (a
tag used by some Scholastics to distinguish how sacraments worked
in the giving of grace from the way nonsacramental works of devotion did, which was *ex opere operantis*): a splash of water administered
simultaneously with the appropriate form of words was guaranteed to
get anyone into heaven, and indeed was the only such guarantee that
existed. Baptism on those terms was certainly connected with life. It
was, indeed, believed to give the life of Christ that is proclaimed in
the gospel. But it was also being thought of and used for building up
the life of a particular form of society. It was easier to manage citizens
when they were all baptized into the same Church and subject to its
discipline. The way the necessity of baptism for salvation was understood gave a religious reason for treating those who were not baptized
(particularly Jews) as dangerous dissidents; it added a religious motivation to the ambitions of colonial conquest. The theory about baptism
came to reflect these social concerns, and the sermons of the time have
their stories about the wonderful *ex opere operato* effects of baptism on
converts from Judaism and paganism. The controlling word from the
scriptures and the patristic tradition was not always able to make itself
heard among these stories from contemporary life.

Something similar was happening with the Eucharist. For
example, men were being ordained to the priesthood in numbers that
had little relationship to the traditional ministerial needs and structures of ecclesial communities but a very strong relationship to the
contemporary desire of people to have as many Masses as possible said
for the living and the dead. Elements of the general Scholastic theory
of sacrament and of its theology of the Eucharist were used to justify
this practice. The Eucharist thus understood continued to play a major
part in the life of people and of society. But it was not quite the place

the scriptural and patristic tradition had given the rite. For example, the theory was much less persuasive about the need for actually eating the bread and drinking the cup in the Eucharist than it was about the value of looking at the consecrated host at the elevation.[15] Stories were told about how looking at the host affected one's life, and a theory was ready to explain how that could be so. The economic consequences of this way of practicing and thinking about the Eucharist were considerable: the Mass stipend and the giving and receiving of indulgences played at least as important a role in social life as did the paying and collecting of taxes in a society in which religious faith and the afterlife were taken so seriously.

Nobody is very surprised nowadays that when the Reformers, like the prophets of old, began to speak up against all that they found decadent in the Church they vented a lot of their wrath on everything that the word "sacrament" seemed to stand for in medieval theology. They castigated the way sacraments were practiced and ridiculed the theory that patronized the practice. They wanted to liberate the Church from an understanding of sacrament that they found incompatible with the life of grace that God is giving to his people in the new covenant. They highlighted the teaching that this life is a gift of God, given in his word of promise, realized in Christ who takes away our sins, and experienced in faith by those who accept the word of promise that is fulfilled in Christ. They drew the conclusion that it is the word, accepted in faith, that justifies and gives life: no human works can take away sin and give life. As the Reformers understood it, the Scholastic theory seemed to be purveying sacraments as works that contain and give grace literally "by the work worked" *(ex opere operato)*. This was to claim for them something that only the word of promise, received in faith, can do. It would seem to make them a kind of alternative to the word. The distinction between word and rite, which was an obvious fact of life, was being turned into a distinction between word and sacrament (whereas in the tradition the rite only became sacrament through having the formative power of the word joined to it). Catholics, it could be thought, were for sacraments while Protestants were for the word.

---

15. Jungmann, *The Mass of the Roman Rite*, 90–92.

Protestants, of course, retained some rites, and continued to call them sacraments. Baptism and the Lord's Supper were so clearly required by the scriptures that the Reformers could not but find a place and a meaning for them in Christian life. The word sacrament was so well established among the early Fathers that only the most radical among the Reformers were prepared to abandon it. So the task was to rethink the meaning of the word as a term for those Christian rites that were given in the scriptures. With some appeal to Augustine and other Fathers, sacrament was taken to mean sign. But what the rites were signs of was not something contained within themselves but rather the promise contained in the word of God: they were taken to be pledges added to the word of God, as a kind of visible guarantee that God is faithful to his promise. They could also be thought of as being useful to the believer as a sign of his or her faith in the promise. So the sacraments accompany the grace of justification. But what justifies is the word of promise received in faith, not the sacrament. On this understanding, sacraments of the New Law function no differently from those of the Old. All the difference is in the word that they guarantee, which in the new covenant is a word already fulfilled in Christ.

In putting word right at the centre of sacrament, the Reformers made a powerful bid to make the rites authentic acts of Christian life. The biblical word dominated the rite in the liturgical practice of the Reformers: it was read in the vernacular, it was preached about, it was inculcated as the moral norm of living. Only those rites explicitly required by the scriptures were to be taken as divinely instituted and deserving of the name sacrament. The sacramental words of baptism and Eucharist, because they were biblical words, were also taken as proclamations and were read aloud, in the language of the people. It was only to the extent that the rite served the word of promise and the word of faith that it had value. The rites were redesigned with this in mind and strenuous efforts were made to bring a living, biblical faith to bear on sacraments. The frequency of celebration was to be measured by the needs and possibilities of this faith.[16] All this

---

16. Selected texts of the Reformers in Palmer, *Sacraments and Worship*, 149–166; liturgies of the Reformers and sacramental thinking that underlies them in B. Thompson, *Liturgies of the Western Church* (Cleveland/New York, 1962) and Y. Brilioth, *Eucharistic Faith and Practice, Evangelical and Catholic*, trans. from Swedish (London: SPCK, 1930, 1956).

was certainly in line with a basic imperative of the Christian tradition about the necessary interaction of word, rite, and life, which was something that the Church badly needed to be reminded about in that age of sacramental decadence. But the price paid for the remembering was the forgetting of, or at least a distraction from, a fundamental element of the tradition that had always been associated with the words sacrament and mystery, namely, the guaranteed presence of God, giving life in Christ and the Spirit, in the rites of the Church, and the reality of that presence even when the people making the sacrament were not living in accordance with the rite.

And yet the forgetting was often more a polemical expedient in a debate whose terms had been set by Scholasticism than a real denial. Certain things had to be said, whatever the cost, in order to dislodge the Scholastic theory on the nature of sacrament. But the forgotten elements were remembered in other contexts. Luther took the scriptural words "This is my body . . . this is the cup of my blood" as being literally true, and therefore saw the Eucharist as a mystery/sacrament that contained the living Christ and gave his life to those who received it. Calvin had a strong sense of the presence of Christ in the Eucharist, at least during the celebration of the sacrament. Baptism was still considered by the Reformers to be necessary for salvation and most of them continued to believe that it could save infants who were not yet ready for personal acts of faith. These and other elements of the traditional content of the word sacrament survived the anti-Scholastic polemic and continued to be witnessed to in the sacramental theory and practice of the churches that grew out of the Reformation—even when they did not sit very easily with the idea that sacraments are merely signs of the faith that justifies.

The Council of Trent, in dealing with the challenge of the Reformers, gave the Catholic Church a dogmatic teaching and a way of speaking about its rites that dominated subsequent centuries and will always have to be taken seriously when Christians talk about sacraments. The objective of Trent was to reform the Church, and that included reforming its practice of the sacraments. On sacraments the council believed it had to dissociate itself from many of the reforms initiated by the Protestants and from the thinking that inspired and claimed to justify those reforms. Trent's most-remembered teaching

comes in the form of canons that condemn Protestant errors. Since
what the Protestants denied was most often a Scholastic formulation
of the tradition, the condemnations of Trent are phrased in Scholastic
language and draw special attention to those elements of the tradition
that were being forgotten by Protestants. There is not much attempt
to find common ground with the Protestants—such, for example, as
might have been provided by the Augustinian idea of sign. Rather, the
differences are accentuated. It is assumed that Catholics affirm what
Protestants deny. Catholic doctrine on sacraments comes from Trent,
then, with a heavy concentration on what needed to be reaffirmed
against Protestant denials, and with little attention to what Catholics
and Protestants might have together retained of the tradition. It
comes in Scholastic formulations that are careful enough to avoid the
banalities of late medieval theology (and thus escape the more obvious Protestant objections), and yet firm enough to draw a line between
Catholic and Protestant positions.[17]

    At the heart of what Trent has to say about sacraments is that
they are truly acts of God and of Christ, and that the life that comes
from God through Christ and the Spirit is truly in them and is truly
given by them—which is something that the words mystery and
sacrament had surely meant throughout the Christian tradition. That
is expressed in the canons on sacraments in general by saying that they
are profoundly different from the sacraments of the Old Law (canon 2),
and that they are objectively different from one another (canon 3)
because of the particular gift of divine life they contain. This is the
basic reason for the statement about the sacraments being necessary
for salvation (canon 4), about their containing grace and conferring it
*ex opere operato* on those who do not place an obstacle (canons 6 and
8), about conferring it always (canon 7), about imprinting a character
(canon 9), about requiring an ecclesially competent minister (canons
10 and 11), even if he is a sinner (canon 12), and about the need to
follow approved rites (canon 13). It is the reason why the identification
and numbering of sacraments, and the institution by Christ of each of

---

17. Texts of Trent in Palmer, *Sacraments and Worship*, 166–176; good analysis of them
throughout B. Leeming, sj, *Principles of Sacramental Theology* (London: Longmans, 1956); canons
on sacraments in general in N. P. Tanner, sj, *Decrees of the Ecumenical Councils*, vols. I and II
(London and Washington: Sheed & Ward and Georgetown University Press, 1990), vol. II, 684–
685; ND 1311–1323.

the seven so identified (canon 1), becomes a dogmatic issue (one can only be sure Christ is in them if he has instituted them himself).

## From Trent to Vatican II

The teaching of the Council of Trent about sacraments—about the general meaning of sacrament and about each of the seven sacraments—provided the Catholic Church with an authoritative word about its rites in the centuries that followed the council. It marked the word that was spoken in preaching, in catechetical instruction, in theological discourse. It helped very much to make the rites sources and expressions of that renewed life in Christ that the Church could boast of in the Counter-Reformation period. It was a word that echoed the stresses and passions of the Reformation and continued to irritate and probably mislead Protestants. It was a controlled word that tended to limit readings from the scriptures and the Fathers about the sacraments to what was of apologetical interest. Apart from the rather formal Epistle and Gospel at Mass there was not much reading of the scriptures in association with the celebration of sacraments, nor much biblical preaching. And yet for all its Scholastic dress, one can argue that the Catholic word of Trent preserved the mainstream scriptural and patristic tradition about the rites that the word sacrament stood for, and kept it reasonably close to life. As time went on, the Baroque and the Romantic ages of Catholicism had no great difficulty with the Tridentine word. They molded it, and they molded the celebration of the rites to their own peculiar conception of life, and the Catholic tradition more than held its own. Neo-scholasticism explored the medieval theories of sacramentality once again, sometimes with originality, but generally within the Tridentine framework.[18]

The contemporary Roman Catholic word about sacraments is, however, somewhat different from the Tridentine word. "Sacrament" today says many things about the rites that were said differently, or not said at all, in Trent and Counter-Reformation theology. The pastoral strategy of Vatican II to promote the relationship of rite to life is rather different from that envisaged by the stern, standardizing discipline of Trent and the papal legislation that implemented the

---

18. Leeming, *Principles of Sacramental Theology* is a good representative.

council. To understand historically how this new word has come to be spoken one would need to look at the evolution of human life, at least in the Western World, and of Christian thinking about it, over the last century or so. One would need to have some sense of how the experience of being human, and the way of reflecting on it, has changed under the influence of people like Darwin and Freud and Marx. One would need to bear in mind how different internal currents affected the way the Christian churches interpreted modern life in the light of the gospel word. Initial fears gave rise to many negative words about modernity. In the Catholic Church there was a massive condemnation of Modernism by Pope Pius X, in his Decree *Lamentabili* of 1907, and a relentless campaign to eradicate it from Catholic theology. But that very modernity was gradually harnessed by various pastoral and theological movements that developed in the churches. There was the biblical movement that recovered the original freshness of the inspired word of God in seeing it as a human telling of God's care for his people. There was the patristic movement that restored contact with the classical literature and art of the faith that was created during the centuries when cultured Greek and Latin minds had their earliest encounters with the gospel message. There was the liturgical movement that restored a sense of the richness and diversity of forms of celebration that lay behind the rigid rubrics of current Roman and other liturgies, and gave hope that it would be possible to restore sacraments to more authentic forms and to give them a closer relationship with contemporary life. There was the ecumenical movement that opened up the traditions of the different churches to each other, with a readiness to discover what they shared, and what each could say about the fullness and balance of the tradition of faith and liturgical practice. There was the pastoral and missionary movement that took advantage of each of these other movements to explore how the faith and sacraments of the Church could become life-giving for people of the many different life-experiences and cultures that exist in a world moving into its third millennium.

Each of the movements that marked the Church in the twentieth century had its word to say about sacraments. A theology of sacrament began to emerge that put those words together and analyzed them technically with the help of ideas drawn from the great theological and magisterial tradition, as well as new ideas drawn from current

philosophy and other areas of theology. What "sacrament" had come
to mean in progressive Catholic theology by the time Vatican II
set about renewing the life of the Church could be fairly described
in terms of the work of four major theologians. It could be said to
be the product of the restoration of the patristic sense of "mystery"
that will always be associated with Odo Casel, osb, particularly in his
*Das christliche Kultmysterium;*[19] of the integration of the theology of
sacraments in a theology of the entire liturgy, such as one gets from
Cipriano Vagaggini, osb in *Il senso teologico della liturgia* (1957);[20] of
the powerful demonstration by Karl Rahner, sj, in his *The Church
and the Sacraments* (1963),[21] that underlying the sacramentality of
the seven rites, there is a sacramentality of the Church, which allows
one to call the Church itself a sacrament (the *Ursakrament,* which is
translated "fundamental sacrament"); of the closely reasoned synthe-
sis put together by Edward Schillebeeckx, op in *Christ, the Sacrament
of Encounter with God,*[22] in which the full richness of the tradition
(which Schillebeeckx had studied in detail in an earlier work called
*De Sacramentele Heilseconomie,* 1952) is ordered systematically in terms
dictated predominantly by the theological method of Saint Thomas,
but also by current personalist thinking.

The word that Vatican II comes to say about the rites of the
Church reflects the life-giving movements that had been at work in
Christian experience for half a century or more, and the theology that
had grown out of and at the same time monitored those movements.
It is a word that tries to show how the rites are filled with life: the
mysterious life of Christ and the Spirit, on the one hand; the real life
and concerns of present-day people, lived in the faith of Christ, on the
other. It is a word that states its own continuity with what was said at
Trent, and with the Scholastic theology that gave Trent its ideas and
language. But, in the style of the theology of the day, it gives body

19. Casel, first edition 1932; subsequent editions incorporated in English translation as *The
Mystery of Christian Worship* (London, 1962); paperback edition (New York: Crossroads
Publishing Company, 1999).

20. C. Vagaggini, osb, *Theological Dimensions of the Liturgy,* trans. from Italian (Collegeville,
MN: Liturgical Press, 1959).

21. K. Rahner, sj, *The Church and the Sacraments,* trans. from German (Freiburg/New York/
London: Herder and Herder, 1963).

22. E. Schillebeeckx, op, *Christ the Sacrament of Encounter with God,* trans. from Dutch
(London and New York: Sheed & Ward, 1963).

to the geometric jargon of Scholasticism and Trent with the original apostolic freshness of scriptural statements, the classical roundedness of the Fathers and the images and reminiscences of the premedieval liturgical tradition of East and West. It keeps sacrament as a generic word for the seven rites recognized as such by the Catholic Church, and reaffirms the Tridentine definitions about it. But sacrament is a much richer word in Vatican II than in Trent. As well as being used when describing the rites, it is also used to describe the Church as sign of salvation set up among the nations and instrument by which Christ brings his saving life to the whole universe. This sacramentality attributed to the Church affects, of course, the sacramentality seen in the rites, and their relationship to the Church. The council also restores scriptural and patristic richness to the word "mystery," and transmits that to "sacrament" both by the equivalence it assumes between the two words and by the way it sees the paschal mystery of the death and resurrection of Christ at the heart of all liturgical celebration of Christian sacraments.

## Life, Word, and Rite in the Texts of Vatican II

Vatican II deals most directly with the rites of the Church in its constitution on the Liturgy, *Sacrosanctum Concilium* (SC).[23] At the heart of the liturgy it sees the seven rites called sacraments, and among these it singles out the Eucharist for special attention with a separate chapter (Chapter 2) entitled *De Sacrosancto Eucharistiae Mysterio*. The other six sacraments are dealt with in the following chapter under the title *De Ceteris Sacramentis et de Sacramentalibus* ("The Other Sacraments and the Sacramentals"). While the term sacrament is applied only to the seven rites recognized as such by the Catholic Church, the idea of sacramentality pervades the whole treatment of the liturgy. Right from the beginning the liturgy is put in series with "the mystery of Christ and the real nature of the true Church" (SC, 2), and the nature of the Church that the text goes on to expound would be described by contemporary theology as sacramental. If the sacraments are put

---

23. A. Flannery, OP, ed., *Vatican Council II. The Conciliar and Post-Conciliar Documents*. Revised ed. (Dublin: Dominican Publications and Northport, NY: Costello Publishing Company, 1996), 1–36.

in series inwardly with the Church and with Christ, they are put in series outwardly with that multitude of ritual practices that are called sacramentals, which brings sacramentality into almost any imaginable area of human life. The conception of sacramentality being employed in the constitution is one that puts together life, word, and rite in a careful balance. The pastoral concern to develop in the Church both a liturgy that is filled with life and a Christian life that is nourished by the liturgy is stated in the introductory paragraphs (SC, 1, 2). The theological explanation of how the gift of God is unfolded progressively by word and rite in the Old Testament, in Christ, in the Church ("From the side of Christ came forth the wondrous sacrament of the whole Church") and in the liturgy is given in SC, 5–8; and particularly in SC, 7, which explains how the living Christ is present and active with the Church in its liturgy. The life that Christians are expected to live, responding to and participating in the word and rites celebrated in the Church, is described in SC, 9–13. These theoretical statements are followed by an outline and justification of the practical steps that need to be taken in the Church so that Christians can more effectively put their lives into the liturgy and draw life from it (SC, 14–46). If there was ever a suspicion that the Catholic tradition stood for a ritualism that was formal and somehow removed from the real-life situations of God's people, the word of Vatican II in this first chapter of *Sacrosanctum Concilium* should set it to rest.

The belief that word is inseparable from rite in sacramental liturgy is put in various ways in the first chapter of the constitution. There is an interesting preliminary statement of it in SC, 2 that reflects the council's dominant missionary, but also sacramental, view of what people are in the Church:

> . . . it [the liturgy] marvelously increases their power to preach Christ and thus show forth the Church, a sign lifted up among the nations, to those who are outside, a sign under which the scattered children of God may be gathered together until there is one fold and one shepherd. (SC, 2)

References to the prophetic word, to the ministry of preaching and teaching, to the reading of Scripture go hand in hand with references to the work accomplished in the flesh of Christ and the rites of the Church in SC, 7–13 (SC, 9 is particularly significant on preaching and instruction), while the need to instruct the faithful, and the study required of those who have that responsibility, are highlighted in the statements about liturgical participation in SC, 14–20. The norms for the reform of the liturgy that complete this first chapter, especially those "Based on the Educative and Pastoral Nature of the Liturgy" (SC, 33–36, but especially SC, 35) are full of concern for the word and for its part in making the rites to be life-giving. There is a reference in SC, 33 to what Trent has to say about the need for instruction on and within the Eucharist. But the place that Vatican II gives the word in the making of sacraments is much more profound and pervasive than Trent was able to recognize. Vatican II is able to reach out to that part of the tradition about sacrament that was specially patronized by the Reformers, whereas Trent had to be cool about it because the Protestants seemed to make it the only thing that mattered.

With such a conception of the interaction of word and rite the constitution is able to make this quite sweeping claim about how all human life can be interpenetrated by the sacramental order:

> Thus, for well-disposed members of the faithful the liturgy of the sacraments and sacramentals sanctifies almost every event of their lives with the divine grace which flows from the paschal mystery of the Passion, Death and Resurrection of Christ. From this source all sacraments and sacramentals draw their power. There is scarcely any proper use of material things which cannot thus be directed towards the sanctification of men and the praise of God. (SC, 61)

Among other documents of Vatican II that speak of sacraments the constitution on the Church, *Lumen Gentium* (LG) is particularly important.[24] It develops the sacramental view of the Church noted in *Sacrosanctum Concilium* and explicitly calls the Church the sacrament of salvation (LG, 1, 9, 48). It is "in Christ" that the Church is a sacrament (LG, 1) and it is his life that is manifested and communicated in it. When the constitution comes to explain how Christ's priestly work is continued among God's People, it does so by an analysis of Christian life that weaves together sacraments and virtues (LG, 10 and 11). The life that people draw from the sacraments is lived out in different areas of moral choice by the appropriate virtues. The life of virtue, in turn, gives human realism to the sacraments, and makes the priestly People to be a witnessing and transforming force in the

---

24. Flannery, *Vatican Council II*, 350–426.

world—makes them be that very Church that the constitution calls a sacrament.

The teaching about revelation given in the constitution on divine Revelation, *Dei Verbum* (DV), makes much of the fact that God reveals himself through "deeds and words" (DV, 2 ). This is a truth that underlies the pattern of rite/word/life that is discerned in the sacraments. The doing of the ritual is itself a "deed," an event. The word that is spoken with it, being about the original saving event that is being evoked by the ritual (e.g., the Exodus event by the Passover meal), makes that event present in the making of the ritual. Rite and word together reveal the saving act of God as it occurs here and now in the life of those who are celebrating.

The Constitution of Vatican II that speaks most directly about human life, *Gaudium et Spes* (GS) ("The Church in the Modern World"), has quite a lot to say about the word, but almost nothing about sacraments. There is one striking reference to the Eucharist in a paragraph (GS, 38) dedicated to "Human activity: its fulfillment in the Paschal Mystery." It reads:

> Christ left to his followers a pledge of this hope and food for the journey in the sacrament of faith, in which natural elements, the fruits of man's cultivation, are changed into his glorified Body and Blood, as a supper of brotherly fellowship and a foretaste of the heavenly banquet. (GS, 38)

But a kind of studied reticence seems to be observed in other places where the significance of Christ and the Church in relation to human life is being expounded and one might have expected an explicit reference to the sacraments as well (e.g., GS, 22, 32, 45). Perhaps it is that the theological word on how particular rites of the Church are related to specific experiences of the contemporary world, whose agenda is no longer being set by the Church or even by Christian culture, has yet to be worked out. Certainly, the Vatican Council nowhere offers sacraments as a kind of easy and "pious" solution to the complex issues of contemporary human life, or encourages any exaggerated confidence in sacraments without evangelization and catechesis. Paul VI stated this more positively after the council in *Evangelii Nuntiandi*, 47 (1975) that is a fine statement on the relationship between word, rite, and life (ND 1336).

# Ecumenical Convergence on Sacraments

The theology of sacraments developed in the Western Church shares a common biblical and patristic tradition with the theologies of the churches of the East. But from Augustine onward it developed along lines that were not followed by the theologies of the East. Theologians from those churches continued to think deeply about the liturgical rites of the Church. Among them are numbered great figures such as John Damascene, Simeon of Thessalonika, and Nicholas Cabasilas. They were able to deepen the great insights of the Fathers, without having to face many of the rather technical questions that its Augustinian heritage and its Scholastic methodology required Western theology to address. The Great Schism of 1054 meant the two theological traditions had largely separate developments. But there was a degree of mutual awareness and serious doctrinal divergences remained few. In the ecumenical exchanges of the second half of the twentieth century Catholic theologians have found it easy to embrace Orthodox theologies of the sacraments, and their own contemporary thinking has generally been acceptable to their Orthodox counterparts.

Faced with the way the Roman Catholic Church has been filling out its dogmatic word about sacraments with biblical and patristic material, and letting this enriched word become more operative in the celebration of sacraments, the major churches issued from the Reformation have been losing some of their inhibitions about the sacramentality of rites. Along with increased sacramental practice they are developing a teaching that converges with what Catholics are saying about the rites. There are points of doctrine about individual rites that still divide churches, and there is still disagreement about how many rites should be called sacraments, and in what precise sense. But there is a broad area of agreement about sacraments between Catholics, Protestants, and Orthodox, and it seems to be growing. An important stage in the convergence is represented by the Lima Document of The World Council of Churches on *Baptism, Eucharist and Ministry*, commonly referred to by the acronym BEM.[25] This document, product of several decades of study and consultation by theologians of the different traditions, has already been received positively by many

---

25. *Baptism, Eucharist and Ministry.* Faith and Order Paper no. 111 (Geneva: WCC, 1982).

churches.[26] In its official response, sent by the Secretariat for
Promoting Christian Unity to the Faith and Order Secretariat in
August 1987,[27] the Roman Catholic Church recognizes in BEM much
of its own faith about baptism, Eucharist, and ministry, and much of
what it teaches when it calls these rites sacraments. The word "sacrament," it is true, is used rather sparingly in BEM. Some churches of
the more evangelical Protestant strain are still uncomfortable with it.
The Catholic response accepts the reticence of the document about
sacrament (used of baptism only once, in BEM, 23; of Eucharist in
BEM, 1, 2, 13; of ministry in BEM, 41 and 43) which "because of
its complex history needs a great deal of explanation in inter-church
conversations." However, it does suggest rather firmly that BEM
would have profited from a deeper study of the concept of sacrament
and a more well-defined use of the term. It claims that some of the
ambiguities found in the text might have been avoided, and the way
the rites work and what they do might have been stated more plainly if
the thinking about sacrament had been clearer, especially as regards its
grounding in ecclesiology.

## THEOLOGY OF SACRAMENTS TODAY

The theology that has been described up to now has been done within
the Catholic Church drawing on a philosophical tradition that can
broadly be described as metaphysical. It believes that, even though
God transcends all the categories of being derived from the experience
of created reality, there is a metaphysical way of thinking about reality
that makes it possible to think and speak realistically about God in all
God's transcendence. It claims that one can think and speak meaningfully about how God relates to all reality that is not God, and particularly about how God is present in human action. Medieval theologians,
drawing on what they believed to be the common patristic tradition,
developed sophisticated versions of this philosophy of being, believing
they were providing a reliable grounding for the thinking about God
that they put at the center of their theologies. This thinking is very

---

26. See M. Thurian (ed.), *Churches Respond to* BEM: *Official Responses to the "Baptism, Eucharist
and Ministry" Text*. Vols. I–VI, Faith and Order Papers 129, 132, 135, 137, 143, 144 (Geneva:
WCC, 1986–88).

27. Text in Thurian, *Churches Respond.*

present in their theology of sacraments. It makes those theologies be first and foremost an understanding of God and God's ways. It uses philosophical analyses of causality to understand how God acts in the celebration of actual sacraments to give his gifts to human creatures. On this metaphysical grounding the received Catholic theology of sacraments has also appealed to a philosophically based understanding of the human person, to an anthropology, in order to understand how God's gifts are actually received by humans. In this anthropology what has always been thought to be most significant about humans is that they are made in the image of God. It is this that allows them to receive God's gifts by free God-directed acts of knowledge and love. In line with the recognition that human knowledge and love is exercised necessarily through bodyliness, God's action in human life is seen to occur in and through bodily experience. It occurs uniquely in the body of Christ. What occurs in his personal body is realized throughout human history in his ecclesial body, which is his Church. It is realized in a distinctive way in the bodies of the members of the Church when, at crucial moments of their life experience, they celebrate the God-given rituals in memory of Christ that are called sacraments.

An evocation of the philosophical grounding of the traditional Catholic theology of sacraments is needed here for an understanding of new kinds of sacramental theology that are emerging at the turn of the millennia. These draw largely on philosophical developments that, starting already at the time of the Renaissance and the Reformation, have been challenging the versions of metaphysical thinking that were present in patristic thinking and were worked out in Catholic theology during the Middle Ages. The story of these developments cannot be told here, apart from saying that they gave an increasing centrality to the analysis of the human subject, and to a phenomenology of human existence as the key to unlocking the mystery of being.

For centuries most Catholic theologians resisted these philosophical currents. However, from early in the twentieth century, after the false start of the Modernist period, theologians began to draw on elements of modern and contemporary philosophy. Most of those who first did so retained confidence in the Catholic tradition of metaphysical thinking. They tried to harmonize it with the new philosophical insights they were adopting. In sacramental theology people like Rahner and Schillebeeckx still appealed regularly to Thomas Aquinas.

This way of doing theology continues today. However, towards the end of the twentieth century, some theologians began to accept the full radicalism of the current philosophical critique of metaphysical thinking and began to seek an entirely new philosophical basis for theology. The theology of sacraments provided a particularly promising setting for the search. Sacraments are profoundly human actions within which humans are believed to encounter the mystery of the divine. They are acts of human choice, made at critical moments in the life-history of individuals, expressed in rituals that call into play the symbolic structure of human existence and relationships. It is in their very humanness that they reveal the divine and make it present. They lend themselves to a movement of thought that for philosophical reasons wants to go from the human to the divine.

Four works on the theology of sacraments can be taken to illustrate features of this recent theology of sacraments. The book that one finds most often quoted as representing a theology of sacraments done in the spirit of liberation theology was written in 1968, but took some time to become widely known in the English-speaking world. *The Sacraments Today*, by Juan Luis Segundo, sj and collaborators, looks at the sacramental practice of the Catholic Church in the light of an understanding of the Church that sees it called to a ministry of historical liberation in the world. It wants sacraments to be seen as signs, signs that are given their reality by a Church, or more concretely by ecclesial communities actively engaged in this mission of liberation. It is in signs so constructed that God, present in human history through the death and resurrection of Christ, acts now in the world for its salvation. The signs get their authenticity and effectiveness from the Church community that expresses in them its liberating presence in the world of secular realities. In this sense the making of them has to be constantly adjusted to the historical reality of that world. Segundo contrasts this view of sacrament with what he took to be the prevailing view present in catholic sacramental practice. According to his analysis, established theology was treating the sacraments not as signs, in the sense he understood the term, but as rites. He suggests that this way of understanding and practicing sacraments is derived from non-Christian forms of religiosity that, in the course of time, supplanted the original nonreligious significance given by Jesus to the practices he initiated of baptizing and eating the Lord's Supper. Treating sacraments as rituals entails attributing to them an intrinsic efficacy of the sort claimed for magical practices, because it is thought to be inherent in the rite itself properly performed. This efficacy is for the benefit of the individual recipient who, through the sacraments, builds up a personal "bank balance" of saving grace. Segundo's analysis of sacraments celebrated and understood as rites undoubtedly owed much to his experience of sacramental practice in Latin America. There is much that is anthropologically and pastorally precious in his championing of sign over rituality. However, his dismissal of any attribution of inherent efficacy to sacraments, on the grounds of magical misunderstandings of it that are present in some forms of Christian practice, does scant justice to received theories of sacramental efficacy. It is very much determined, no doubt, by a philosophical position that refuses any meaning to theories that do not come out of actual practice.

*Symbol and Sacrament* by Louis-Marie Chauvet[28] was published in its original French in 1987, and in an English translation in 1995. Chauvet writes out of an evident feel for the liturgical and pastoral richness of the sacraments and for the way in which they engage human existence on a very profound level. It is nothing less than human existence, specifically as it is lived by Christians, that he sets out to understand in the light of a renewed understanding of Christian sacramentality. His book carries the subtitle: *A Sacramental Re-reading of Christian Existence.* He thinks that traditional metaphysically grounded theology of sacraments cannot provide this understanding. He develops this thesis in the first part of the book, which has the title "From the Metaphysical to the Symbolic." To do his critique of metaphysical thinking he takes his stand on the philosophy of Martin Heidegger. With Heidegger he claims that metaphysical thinking gives rise to ontotheology, which is a way of requiring the human perception of being (represented here by the "onto-") to include the postulate of God (hence the "theology" added to the "onto-") and to place God within this idea of being, as the ultimate cause of all being. For Chauvet this inclusion of God in the human grasp of being is a failure to respect the transcendence of God, who is beyond all being as perceived in human existence. It is also a failure to somehow respect

---

28. L-M Chauvet, *Symbol and Sacrament: A Sacramental Re-reading of Christian Existence,* trans. from French (Collegeville, MN: Liturgical Press), 1995.

the existential autonomy of humans. The thesis of standard sacramental theology that seems to Chauvet to most manifest the "onto-theological" fallacy is the affirmation that divine causality is at work in sacraments. He examines some texts of Thomas Aquinas on the subject. His reading of them leads him to claim that Thomas' thinking entails an understanding of God's action in giving grace through the sacraments as a kind of "production." Such theories of causality are, for Chauvet, incapable of providing a way of understanding the ontological reality of the relationship between subjects, as it is achieved in the symbolic world of language and culture and history in which existence is realized. As such they are incapable of providing an understanding of sacraments and sacramentality. The contemporary liberation from metaphysics, on the other hand, makes it possible to see sacraments not as a divine production of something in humans but as a symbolic exchange in which the full reality of the human subject works out its relationship with God. It is this symbolic exchange that Chauvet, with the help of philosophies of the symbolic and philosophies of language, brings quite richly to light in the positive development of his book.

Among the several books Kenan Osborne has written on sacraments is one that works out with particular clarity an alternative to the received Catholic theology of sacraments, such as he finds it, for example, in the Catechism of the Catholic Church.[29] In his *Christian Sacraments in a Post-Modern World* he argues that postmodern thought has established conclusively that the received theology is hermeneutically meaningless in this new millennium. For contemporary people, understanding comes from concentration on the unique, individual subject of human experience, not from general abstract statements about reality or history. He points out repeatedly that sacraments are individual, here and now, unique events in the life of individual human persons. To express this he employs, among other terms, the word *haecceitas*, taken from his thirteenth century Franciscan confrère, Blessed John Duns Scotus. It is a notion that he finds congenial to the postmodern thinking he is espousing. His book is philosophically articulate and includes some enlightening presentations and application of aspects of modern and postmodern philosophy. He takes on

---

29. K. B. Osborne, OFM, *Christian Sacraments in a Postmodern World. A Theology for the Third Millennium* (New York: Paulist Press, 1999); see also his *The Christian Sacraments of Initiation, Baptism, Confirmation, Eucharist* (New York: Paulist Press, 1987).

and radicalizes Chauvet's criticism of "ontotheology." He does not
see any future for the way traditional sacramental theology has been
developed, with the help of elements of modern philosophy, by people
like Rahner and Schillebeeckx. In the sequence of chapters that follow
his opening chapters on the task and method of sacramental theology he does accept some of the patterns that have emerged from the
work of these theologians but the content of the chapters, replete
with the language of hermeneutical theory and postmodern analysis, quite consciously parts company with their thought. His chapter
titles are: 3. Sacramental Structures in the World at Large; 4. Jesus
and Primordiality; 5. The Church as Foundational Sacrament; 6.
Postmodern Sacramentality. All through his book Osborne is mindful
of magisterial teaching on sacraments and his final chapter proposes
the kind of hermeneutic of such solemn Church teaching that is
required by the postmodern mind. Throughout the book Osborne pays
regular attention to the belief that Christian sacrament are works of
God that are at the same time human actions, and he has some good
descriptions of this "dual-dimension action." However, he does not
give much attention to the question of how one can speak meaningfully of God and actions of God in postmodern terms.

All David Power's writings on sacraments draw on a comprehensive knowledge of the Christian liturgical and theological tradition.
In his *Sacrament. The Language of God's Giving*[30] he puts to work the
findings of the most significant currents of contemporary philosophy
and theology to provide an original interpretation of the word sacrament itself, as it comes out of the tradition of Christian faith and
practice and as it needs to be employed in the Church's renewal of
liturgical practice today. He presents the contemporary currents in a
careful and discriminating way, and is as ready to acknowledge in them
some continuity and compatibility with traditional catholic positions
as he is to indicate their sometimes radical questioning of those positions and their alternative proposals. He acknowledges the critique
of onto-theology, and the effect this must have on traditional catholic sacramental theory, but he does not seem to think it is as totally
undermining as others do. In his own theorizing he draws heavily on

---

30. D. N. Power, *Sacrament. The Language of God's Giving* (New York: The Crossroad
Publishing Company, 1999).

contemporary hermeneutical theory, and particularly on the work of Ricoeur. His approach is spelled out most clearly in Chapter 2 of the book, which he himself says is "pivotal to the book" (p.17). The chapter is entitled "Sacrament: Language Event." It begins with a review of sacramental theories, covering authors from Aquinas and Bonaventure to Schillebeeckx and Rahner, and ends with the contemporary critique of that kind of theological thinking. As a way of meeting those criticisms and doing a meaningful theology of sacrament in the present day, it then presents the outline of a philosophy of language, drawn mainly from hermeneutical theory but also from other resources. It goes on to show how this can function for an understanding of sacrament as "God's Word Events through Spirit." Part Two of the book develops the detail of this project, providing a phenomenological and linguistic examination of sacramental celebration in terms of "Community," "Ritual Action," "Verbal Polyphony," and "The Force of the Visual." It has insights into liturgical celebration of the Christian sacraments in the present day that, while they are triggered by postmodern critical and hermeneutical theory, have an anthropological value that can be comfortably drawn on even by those who follow the more conventional sacramental theology that has been criticized earlier in the book.

Part Three of Power's book takes up the deeper philosophical and theological issues of the view of sacraments being put forward in the previous two Parts, and how they relate to a more standard catholic theology. It puts the issue as one of a systematic theology or doctrine. The hard thinking is done and core concepts such as gift, icon, and language event are elaborated in Chapter 9, which is fittingly entitled "The Event of Gift: Systematic Reflection." Here, the issues raised for sacramental theology by contemporary philosophical and theological thinking are dealt with in a way that, while giving full weight to postmodern critiques of traditional metaphysical thinking, is also sensitive to values contained in that tradition and to attempts that are being made to renew it in contemporary terms by people like Lafont, Marion, and Milbank. It contains challenges that have to be taken seriously by those who would want to sustain the metaphysical tradition of sacramental theology.

From the brief presentation of these "third-millennium" authors it appears that for them the crucial issue in the debate about the theology of sacraments is a philosophical one. It has to do with the way in which one can speak meaningfully about reality. In the various solutions that they are proposing there is a strong accent on the anthropological: human experience is the touchstone of all meaningful discourse, even when that discourse is about God. This supposition enables them to provide rich explorations of the anthropological reality of sacraments. But the question remains for the theologian as to whether the invocation of God that occurs in such statements about the anthropological reality of sacraments are by themselves adequate affirmations about the real God of revelation. Human wisdom has in the past elaborated ways of talking about God that have not measured up to the insights of faith about the mystery of God. There are philosophical theologians who, while accepting much of the postmodern critique of what has sometimes passed for metaphysics, especially among theologians, are not yet ready to abandon entirely what can still be called a metaphysical understanding of reality. In the midst of such a debate it would seem wise for theology to want to keep in robust good health an interpretation of the tradition of Christian faith about sacraments that upholds the value of metaphysical thinking about God, about God's causal relationship to created reality, and about the openness of the human person to divine grace. Time will tell if the community of faith will decide to move on from there to widely embrace the kinds of postmodern theologies of sacrament that have been signaled here. In the meantime, the more classical theologies of sacraments can stand their ground. They can begin to absorb, without compromise to their metaphysical grounding, many of the rich veins of anthropological thinking about sacramental life that are being brought to light in the postmodern theologies.

# The Sacraments of Baptism, Confirmation, and Eucharist

When a theologian sets out to talk about baptism, confirmation, and Eucharist as sacraments, in the manner defended at the end of the section on "Ecumenical Convergence on Sacraments," he or she will be carrying the weight and the wisdom of the tradition about the word sacrament that has been sketched in this chapter. The word no longer has the freshness it had when Tertullian first used it about Christian rites. For him *sacramentum* was a familiar word of everyday language, and to use it about a rite of the Church was to use the known to explain the unknown. But by now the word sacrament has gathered such a richness of meaning to itself, but also in some minds caricatural misunderstandings of it, that it needs to be explained itself before it can be useful for understanding the rites of the Church. The explanation requires one to look at the tradition that has affected the meaning of the word and to take a stand on what is most consistent and central in it. For Catholic theology, and probably for ecumenically minded theologians of all the churches, Vatican II may claim to have done a discernment of the tradition that has proved remarkably useful. It has put together the biblical revelation, the patristic tradition, a judicious measure of Scholasticism, the dogmatic teaching of Trent (without its polemical toughness) and ideas developed in contemporary theology by people like Rahner and Schillebecckx, in a way that has provided a platform for understanding the sacramental economy and the place of individual sacraments within it. Certainly, what the Church of Vatican II has done and thought about individual sacraments—the restored rites and the general instructions about them that are presented in the new liturgical books—is hardly intelligible without the kind of general study of the tradition concerning sacrament that has been covered in this chapter.

# Chapter 3

# A Theology of Sacrament

Within the tradition of faith detailed in the preceding chapter, theology continues to do its thinking about sacraments, listening to, being challenged by but also challenging the workings of the contemporary Christian mind. The first level of theological thinking about sacraments is done in pastoral practice. Each sacrament is a unique, unrepeatable life event and must be thought about as such (see Chapter 12, Epilogue). The pastoral thinking about sacramental events will find itself appealing to words and ideas that have grown out of a collective reflection on Christian experience—words like faith, grace, sacrament, but also the great words of theology that are God, Christ, Church. The ideas carried by these words, and the way the relationship between them is understood, can be seen to serve as hermeneutical keys to make sense of the individual experience. They are themselves examined by theology on a level that is described as speculative or systematic. It is called speculative because, although grounded on and drawn from the tradition of faith and pastoral practice, it is the ordered product of human minds attempting to relate what is believed to the words and ideas that are generated from the full range of human experience within which believers live. Human experience gives rise to shared questions and a constant search for meaning. If faith is to be about real life, then it must let itself be confronted by the questions so raised by the human mind, the questions that are dealt with in philosophies. These questions confront it, challenging it to express itself in ways that are coherent with the way the human mind expresses its grasp of reality. If faith does not face up to this challenge it will be left in a state of blind credulousness, and deprived of access to the full reality of human living. This kind of speculative theology is called systematic because at the heart of the human search for meaning is the desire for coherence and consistency. Things become more real and intelligible when they are seen to relate comfortably to one another and make sense together. The theology of sacrament being presented in this chapter—and in the systematic essays that are offered in subsequent chapters about each of the three sacraments of initiation—is such a systematic theology. Because of its speculative nature it must be treated as an unfinished business, always open to further questions and clarifications.

The theology of sacrament must be set within the framework of a general systematic theology. When one talks theologically about sacraments one is bringing into play everything that one knows about God and God's plan for the universe, and about the meaning of human life and history. Sacraments are, in fact, the final events in the historical working out of the relationship between God and humans—the economy of salvation—that is the overall subject of systematic theology. The only thing that remains to happen between God and his People after sacraments is the coming of Christ in glory and the general resurrection. There is a theology of sacraments current in the Church today that has the great merit of situating itself within a deep analysis of the mystery of God and his relationship with the entire creation and its history, which uses a Trinitarian Christology that is at the same time deeply sensitive to the humanness of Jesus, and employs an ecclesiology that sees the community of believers both as gathered together by the grace of Christ and the Spirit and at the same time as mediating that grace to all those who are being saved. It uses the word sacrament on each of these three levels of analysis — theological, Christological, ecclesiological—taking advantage of its analogical elasticity to show how they interpenetrate without being confused: Christ is the Sacrament of God, the Church is the Sacrament of Christ, and the seven sacraments are different actualizations of the basic sacramentality of the Church. Such a systematic understanding of sacramentality uncovers the deep roots of the unity of the sacramental economy and lets one see each individual sacrament in relation to all the others and to the entire economy.

## CHRIST, THE SACRAMENT OF GOD

In very general terms sacramentality refers to any manifestation in a sign of the mystery of God's life—the giving of it by God and the receiving of it by humans. It denotes the simultaneous manifestation and realization of the gift of God, the telling of it that is also the doing of it, the invitation to divine life that has already within it the response. It occurs most perfectly in Christ. He is the Word of God made flesh, who does not just speak for God but is God; he is and does what he says. He is also the perfect human response to God, his Father: he accepts the design of God in obedience and does what he is told to do. He preached the message of salvation from God and gave his life for it on the cross. When God approved him by raising him from the dead he became in his body the full human manifestation of divine life and the perfect possessor of it. He lives to make intercession for us, expressing and making his own our need and desire for salvation. At the same time he is the giver of the gift of God because he is established in power with the Father as the sender of the Spirit. He is, for all these reasons, the primordial Sacrament of God.

As soon as one says that Christ is *the* Sacrament of God one is already bound to say that all other sacramentality is derived from him and draws its power from him. During his life on earth he gathered around him people who would always remember him, and in that remembering carry his salvation throughout time and place. He gave his disciples words and rituals for remembering. When he made his death on the cross to be the expression of his total dedication to the Father he also made the ritual memorials of his death, which would be celebrated by his disciples, to be expressions of his dedication. He adopted them as expressions of his wish to make his death salvific for all those who would remember him in faith. Christ carried this human decision about his death and about every ritual remembering of it into the timelessness of his glorification. This is what allows him to be personally present to every ritual celebration that those who believe in him do in memory of him. In that personal presence his humanness is the instrument of the divine act that gives salvation.

## THE CHURCH, SACRAMENT OF CHRIST

The memory of the risen Christ is kept alive, by word and rite, in the community of believers founded on his apostles. In telling the story of Christ as vouched for by the apostles and in performing the rites given by the apostles in memory of him, the members of the Church make him present throughout time and space, as his personal body made him present to those who saw and heard and touched him during his days on earth and in the event of the resurrection. In Paul's terms, they become his body. The Church itself is very much a matter of "bodies." It is not some kind of impersonal administrative institution but real people of flesh and blood who tell the story and do the rites. They each have their own personal story that they work into the story of salvation; it is the crucial moments of their lives that give point to the rites that are celebrated. In the rites they identify their own story with the story of Christ and their own life-experience with his. Those who look at such a community can hear and see Christ in the lives of its members, and specifically in their words that speak about him and their rites that celebrate him; and they can feel the power of his person. The prophetic, priestly and kingly roles that Christ fulfils in his own person for the salvation of the world are shared by this community. That is why it can be called the Sacrament of Christ.

In this community Christ is both received and given in a visible way, as befits a sacrament. The Church is both the gathered community of the saved and the gathering community of those who bring salvation:

> ... the Church ... in its entirety is at the same time both community of the redeemed and the redeeming institution.[1]

The receiving is the most important and lasting reality of the Church as sacrament, but the giving has a certain logical priority. The community goes out to seek its members. The giving of Christ in the Church is made possible by a series of ministries, both of the prophetic and of the priestly kind, which carry an authority that comes from the kingly power of Christ. All members of the Church are authorized to do the giving in some form or other. Through baptism and confirmation they have a special relationship with Christ that qualifies them to act and be seen to act in his name. Some ministries are reserved to the ordained and the community can only be recognized as the body of Christ when it enjoys the special conformity to Christ that the ordained bring to it. But ultimately it is the receiving of grace that builds up the community in the likeness of Christ. Without the

---

1. E. Schillebeeckx, OP, *Christ, the Sacrament of Encounter with God* (London/New York: Sheed & Ward, 1968), 58; see also Y. M.-J. Congar, OP, *The Mystery of the Church*, 2nd edition (Baltimore: Helicon Press, 1965), 70ff.

receiving, the Church would not be the body of Christ. It would not be his Sacrament. The giving will end when he comes again, but the receiving will last forever. The ministerial Church, with its equipment of sacramental characters and prophetic gifts and pastoral powers, is for the time of waiting; the grace-filled Church, united by and in love, is forever.

Nevertheless, the sacramentality of the Church is consistent with a certain independence of the giving of grace from its receiving. While the objective containing and showing forth of the grace of Christ that is really being lived by people is the full sacramentality of the Church, the ability to go on doing so even when the lives of individual members of the Church, and particularly of those called to be ministers of word and rite, are not fully Christian is an indispensable feature of it. During the time of waiting for the final coming of Christ members of the Church may be unfaithful to his grace. But because Christ has brought them into a special relationship with himself when he called them to be prophets, priests, and kings in his Church, and to some specific ministries in it, they can go on acting in his name even when they are not living in his grace. His fidelity to his choice is stronger than the vacillations of those he has chosen. Theology can use some ideas taken from the traditional theology of the sacramental character, and its distinction from sacramental grace, to express this feature of the Church in sacramental terms. It is not just in the performance of its rites but in its entire prophetic, priestly, and kingly life that the Church is recognized as having a power to make Christ present and visible that can function even when those who are exercising it are not fully living in Christ. In such a theology the objective reliability of individual sacraments and their independence of the holiness of the minister can be seen as a particular instance of something that is part of the very nature of the Church.

## Sacrament and Word

Sacramentality pervades the entire life of the Church. It is not helpful to restrict it to the area of Church rites, although it is realized in a special way in them. Everything about the Church, including its preaching and teaching, is sacramental in the sense already explained. The distinction that came to be made in theology between word and sacrament has sometimes given the impression that these are separate, almost alternative ways of access to grace. Theology has to insist on their complementarity. What needs to be remembered is that the distinction sacrament/word does not correspond exactly to the distinction between rites/words. The distinction between rite and word is descriptive: there are rites in the life of the Church and there are also words. The distinction between sacrament and word, on the other hand, is a theological analysis that invites separate consideration of two aspects of the one reality of the Church, which are present together wherever the Church exists. The sacramentality of the Church is realized through the interaction of words and rites. It is realized in the rites and it is realized in the words as well. The rites of the Church would not be sacraments without the words that are part of them and that surround them as preaching, teaching, and celebration. The words are sacramental because they are directed towards the rites, are made concrete and tangible in them, are confessed and celebrated in them. The rites take on the character of word because they embody the Word and his words, as the actions of his flesh gave concreteness to the Word of life that he was and spoke. They combine with the words to make the whole Church be Word—be that embodied Word that originally took flesh in the concrete historical reality of Christ. Word, then, is not an alternative to sacrament, because it is itself sacramental through its association with the rites of the Church. Sacrament is not a refuge from word because rites are only sacraments by embodying the word. Sacrament and word, then, express two aspects of the life of the Church. The first is affirmed particularly, but not exclusively, by the concreteness of its rituals, the second by the fluency of its words.

## BAPTISM AND EUCHARIST

From Christ, who is the Sacrament of God, through the Church, which is the Sacrament of Christ, are derived the ritual actions and words that are called sacraments in the Church. From a systematic point of view they are sacraments because they are particular realizations of the sacramentality of the Church, and therefore of Christ. Because of that rootedness in Christ and the Church, they are intimately connected with one another. Reasons can be given for the connections. They form part of the theology of each individual sacrament.

Logically and historically the first two sacraments of the Church are baptism and Eucharist. They are the two rites in which, from the very beginning, the Church has expressed itself and drawn people into membership of itself, and thus into Christ. There is no Church without them. The Eucharist is the fullest expression of the sacramentality of the Church. As a festive taking of food it is, from the human point of view, the ultimate ritual celebration of life—of having it and growing in it and anticipating its consummation in the eternal now of God. It has Christ, the source of life, present in it in the fullest possible way: in the community of those gathered in his name by and under those to whom he has entrusted the apostolic ministry; in the word about him that is read from the scriptures, (which are read in it from beginning to end, whereas in other rites only special passages are read) and comprehensively preached; in the bread and wine that are proclaimed to be the body and blood in which he consummates his sacrifice and gives life to the world; and in the Spirit who gathers all who share the one bread and wine into the one body of Christ.

Yet the Church cannot have the sacrament of the Eucharist without the sacrament of baptism. Life has a beginning, and the Eucharist does not ritualize that beginning. To be in the Church one has to leave the world of sin and escape from the power of the devil, and the Eucharist does not ritualize that original deliverance. Being in Christ means passing with him from death to life, and the Eucharist does not ritualize that passage. It is baptism that ritualizes these different aspects of the crucial moment of life's beginning. It gives people their original Christian existence and identity and inaugurates their membership of the Church. It does so, however, not as an end in itself but in view of the Eucharist. Baptism is a once-for-all beginning. The life that it inaugurates is for growing and for ever. Baptism expresses that, not in itself but in its movement toward the Eucharist. The Eucharist is a rite of the continual nourishment and growth and consummation of life: it reenacts day by day the once-for-all sacrifice that is the source of life; it brings together the community in which life is fostered; it tells the complete story of the community in an authoritative word of God, which gives life meaning and direction; it contains the body and blood of Christ, which is the food of life; and it anticipates the banquet of heaven, which is the possession of eternal life. Without its relationship to the Eucharist baptism would not measure up to the full sacramentality of the Church. Thus, the liturgical and doctrinal tradition sees the Eucharist as completing the process of Christian initiation begun in baptism. One is not fully a Christian until one has taken part in it for the first rime. It is only after First Communion that one is ready to live Christian life to the full and to take one's ongoing part in making the Church be the body of Christ.

## Confirmation

In the Catholic and Orthodox traditions the process of Christian initiation has another rite besides baptism and Eucharist that is recognized as a sacrament. This is what is called chrismation in the East and confirmation in the West; confirmation is also found in the Protestant tradition, but it is generally not thought helpful to call it a sacrament. The complexities of the story of confirmation will be dealt with in Chapters 6 and 7. Here it is enough to make some remarks of a systematic sort about confirmation in relation to Christian initiation and the sacramental system, based on well-established practices of the Church and some constants of the theological tradition.

As a sacrament confirmation must ritualize some aspect of the sacramentality of the Church in relation to Christ and his role in sacramentalizing the gifts of God. The scriptural passages read with the rite and the theological tradition about it have linked the rite of confirmation to the Pentecostal outpouring of the Spirit. Baptism already ritualizes Christ's gift of the Spirit in the Church, because there is no beginning of life without the Spirit. But there is an aspect of the gift of the Spirit that is not clearly ritualized in baptism. The Pentecostal outpouring of the Spirit marks the coming of the "last days." God has now done everything he is going to do by way of public salvation event. This means that the proclamation of salvation is now the responsibility of men and women in a way that it never was before. The Church of the New Testament is a missionary community of men and women who know that they, and only they, can save the world before the Lord comes again. They do not expect any new salvation acts of God. But they do not need them because they have received within themselves the Spirit of power and the tongues of fire, with which they can preach the gospel to the ends of the earth. They have an interior strength and giftedness that makes them self-assured about themselves and in their relations with others. To be a member of the Church is to be caught up in this mission and in the unique sense of responsibility it entails; it is to have a sense of maturity about life and behavior that corresponds to the mature age of salvation that was inaugurated at Pentecost and to the maturing inner resources then given to the Church.

There is an explanation here of why the Church would want to confirm everybody. People are not fully Christians until they have experienced ritually this aspect of the gift of God. The Greek churches confirm, as a matter of course, everyone whom they baptize. The Latin churches often separate confirmation from baptism, but they too want eventually to confirm all those they baptize. They do it immediately in danger of death. However, there is an incongruity in the fact that they do admit the baptized to the Eucharist before confirmation. The Eucharist is the sacrament of the full Church, not just the Church of the saints already gathered but the Church that is still in a state of mission, calling out to those who are yet to be saved to come and eat at the table of Lord. To enter fully into this sacramental aspect of the Eucharist one needs to be confirmed as well as baptized.

## CHRISTIAN INITIATION AND THE OTHER SACRAMENTS

Baptism, confirmation, and Eucharist are initiation into Christian life. For all its eschatological fullness that life has to be lived out in time in the midst of the world. The last chapter of the story has, indeed, been written, but in the enigma of the Apocalypse. In the meantime it is still being written in another, more realistic language, in the daily lives of Christians. The rites of initiation reflect this sense of the completeness and yet incompleteness of the Christian story—what some exegetes call the "already" and the "not yet" of biblical eschatology. The Eucharist is both heavenly banquet and food of the pilgrim people. It is at once celebration of praise and thanks for what is already realized and intercession for what has yet to be accomplished in the mission of the Church. What has to be accomplished is directed by the moral imperatives of Christian living that are the consequences of Christian initiation. But there are also rites that mark this earthly phase of

Christian life and enter into its story, four of which are believed by Catholic and Orthodox churches to have a like claim to sacramental status as do the rites of initiation. The initiation into Christian life accomplished in baptism, confirmation, and Eucharist is also initiation into orders, marriage, penance, and anointing of the sick. One cannot understand the sacraments of initiation without at least some general reflection on how they are related to these other four sacraments that sustain Christian life during its time of waiting in the world.

## Orders

When people are initiated sacramentally into Christian life they find themselves in a Church that is ministered to and presided over by persons who continue in different ways the office given by Jesus to the apostles as the foundation of the Church and the guarantee of its unity. Their ministry takes the form of overseeing the words and rites by which the community lives. To accept initiation is to accept their authority over the words and rites that one has made one's own, especially as these are celebrated in the Eucharist. It is to accept them as symbols and guarantors of that unity of word and rite and life, without which the Church would not be the body of Christ and sacrament of his grace. One can do this with security because the giving of this ministry has itself the status of sacrament. The Church commits a distinctive part of its own sacramentality to those whom it ordains as its ministers. By the sacrament of orders it proclaims that its words and rites make it the sacrament of Christ only when they are duly presided over by the ordained. The ordained, for their part, have an essentially sacramental role that has to be consonant with the general sacramentality of the Church. They represent Christ in his action of gathering and pastoring and being head of God's people for the kingdom. That action was priestly, because it was consummated in Christ's giving of himself to his Father and to his brothers and sisters in a sacrificial death. While a sharing in this priesthood of Christ is given to all those who are baptized into him, there is an aspect of it that has to be specially sacramentalized so that his presence can be recognized and made active in the community of believers. Christ gives priestly holiness to those who are being saved in him. As the one who gives, he is the head of the Body. Through ordination he gives some members of the community the power to sacramentalize his headship, designating them to gather in his name the members of his Body, so that they can be the recipients of his priesthood.

The special service of the ordained to the priesthood of Christ belongs, first and foremost to bishops, and under their leadership to presbyters. Because they can sacramentalize the sacrifice of Christ in presiding at the Eucharist they have a ministry to priesthood in the Church, which allows them to be called priests in a special way. Deacons are also ordained to serve in the sacramentalizing of the priesthood of Christ in the Church. Because they minister by way of service to bishops and presbyters, rather than as being themselves heads of a community of believers, and because they do not preside at the Eucharist, they are not called priests. The ministerial priesthood has to respect all that makes the Church a sacrament of Christ, and all that Christian initiation conveys. Those ordained to the priesthood cannot just be persons who tend the sacred rites. They also have a particular responsibility for the prophetic word spoken in the Church, without which the Church would not be the sacrament of Christ. Although ordination gives real power in the Church, its exercise must be seen as a sacramental service, that allows the baptized, who are already prophets and priests by their baptism, to be the Body of Christ. Ordination gives leadership and authority within the mission of the Church, but its sacramentality requires it to operate in a way that respects the gifts and missionary responsibilities of the confirmed, by which they represent the presence of the eschatological Spirit within the Church. Although ordination gives a consecration to make the eucharistic offering in the person of Christ, it must be seen to acknowledge the right of the initiated to eat at the table of the Lord and to be seen to be his Body.

## The Sacrament of Matrimony

While recognizing that a decision not to marry (1 Corinthians 7:25–40; Matthew 19:11–12; 22:30) was an appropriate expression of the eschatological urgency inherent in Christian initiation, Christians, following the gospels and Paul, also recognized in marriage the values of the life into which they had been initiated, particularly the pilgrim and missionary side of it. The stable bonds of marriage, and the opening of human love in it to the future, in the persons of children and childrens' children, is what makes the world continue and creates its time and its history. Marriage is a commitment of human love to the *saeculum*, to the world. Christians recognize that, as a pilgrim people with a mission of giving life to the world in its time of waiting, their marriages give visibility and effectiveness to the special quality of human love that they have learned in Christ. One of the favorite images for that love in the Christian story has always been the love of husband and wife. The image becomes a reality in the marriages of Christians. The way that married Christians express human love in dealing with sexuality, with nurture and responsibility for children, with community-building, with social structures and politics, with their entire worldly involvement makes the Kingdom of God come. To say that Christian marriage is the sacrament of human love in time is to say that it remakes and retells the story of the world in terms of Christ's love for his People and makes that love a force in shaping human history, until he comes again.

The sacraments of initiation prepare people for the sacrament of marriage and so get some of their own meaning from it. Baptism has consequences for the living-out of human love in the area of sexuality. It enables those who marry to give themselves in human love to their partner with a completeness that matches the baptismal way Christ gave himself to his Church (Ephesians 5:25–30). This is the kind of marriage the baptized are called to—not just because Canon Law requires it but because in Christ they have entered a new life and begun a new story about human love that calls out to be expressed in a Christian rite. Their contribution to the story of the world as husband and wife, as parents establishing a family tree in and through their children, as citizens caught up by their marriage in the social and economic realities of their own place and time is made visibly Christian by the sacrament of marriage. Their lives can become an unfolding of the gospel and a making of the kingdom in all the richness that human love gives to life in the world of time.

Confirmation initiates Christians into a witnessing and missionary status that is lived out in sacramental marriage, and its own meaning is brought to light in its relationship with marriage. Marriages can build up nuclear families, a tribe, a social class, a nation, and can cement loyalties within these groups. By that very fact they can also become a factor of inward-looking particularism and self-centeredness in any one of these groups and can contribute to hostilities between them and other such groups. Its grounding in confirmation will not allow Christian marriage to be of this sort. The men and women who received the Spirit at Pentecost became people for whom human love sealed in marriage could never again lock them into any kind of tribal or linguistic particularism, because they were now committed to living and preaching a gospel story that breaks down all such barriers and hostilities. Those confirmed in this Pentecostal Spirit have the same responsibilities. When they marry they can never let their marriages be caught up in the self-centered, predatory interests of any particular group to which they might become related. They will rather stand for a human love that reaches across such barriers, that keeps open house and hospitality from which no one is excluded simply because he or she is not of the family. They will want to work for relationships that build a social order in which class is not discriminatory. Nothing less is consonant with a marriage whose sacramentality is grounded on confirmation.

The Eucharist provides initiation into Christian marriage in a still more intimate way. It unites the body of a Christian to the body of Christ. It is that same body that becomes one with the body of a marriage partner. It is because the bodies of Christians are seen to be made one with Christ in the Eucharist that their becoming one with one another in the sexual bond of marriage becomes Christ-bearing and Christ-revealing, and can be a sacrament of the human love of Christ for his brothers and sisters who form His Church.

## The Sacrament of Penance and Reconciliation

The life to which people are initiated by baptism, confirmation and Eucharist is meant to grow toward that fullness of life that is already celebrated in the Eucharist. During the time of waiting for the coming of the Lord, however, it can stop growing, and thereby be threatened with extinction. Or it can be deliberately renounced, as it has been deliberately chosen. The Eucharist ceases in these cases to be an expression of life and a nourishment of life. The person is once again a sinner and cut off from the life that courses through the eucharistic community that is the Church. And yet not entirely. There are sins that are not "unto death" (cf. 1 John 5:17). They leave members of the Church diminished in spiritual energy but still alive. But even a dead member is still attached to the body. The sacramental character of baptism guarantees that. The eucharistic community reaches out to its members who have put their life in the body at risk by sinning no less than to those who have not yet begun to live with it. When its call to reconversion and its offer of pardon are accepted by those who have sinned, it has a rite for reconciliation and readmission to sacramental life, and it recognizes this rite to be one of its constitutive sacraments. The essential requirements of the sacrament are changeless (repentance, confession of sin within the Church, works of penance, absolution by a minister of the Church), but the form they have taken and the way they have been put together has varied strikingly over the centuries (variations in the number of times the sacrament could be availed of, in the kind of detail required in the confession of sin, in the type and severity of works of penance, in the form of absolution). Christian initiation has been affected by the different ways the sacrament of penance and reconciliation has been celebrated in the Church. When the penitential discipline was very severe people sometimes thought it might be a good idea to postpone their initiation until late in life, so that they might be less likely to sin after their baptism and thus avoid the rigorous demands of sacramental penance. When the discipline of penance has been relatively easy, people may have seen it as a convenient way of remedying sinful ways not completely renounced in baptism and so have paid insufficient attention to the radical conversion that baptism requires. But whatever view of penance prevails it is clear that Christian initiation has to take account of the possibility of subsequent sin, and of the sacrament by which sinners can be reconciled again to the Church and restored to Christian life and growth in the Eucharist.

## The Anointing of the Sick

Christian initiation carries with it the guarantee and the anticipation of bodily resurrection. Baptism begins it and the Eucharist is the daily promise of it. Illness and death might seem to be a blight on the hope embodied in the eucharistic community. Paul has an enigmatic remark in 1 Corinthians 11:30 ("That is why many of you are ill and infirm, and a considerable number are dying . . .") that seems to suggest that a Christian community that celebrated the Eucharist properly would be free of illness and death. He is more sober in his expectations later in the epistle when he talks about the resurrection (Chapter 15). There he recognizes that some Christians will have died before the Lord's coming and will be raised from the dead at the last trumpet (v. 52). All others will be changed "For that which is corruptible must clothe itself with incorruptibility . . ." (v. 53). Baptism is not far from the mind of Paul in this discussion (cf. v. 29) and his thinking about the body of Christ is at the heart of his argument. It is in this perspective of the resurrection, proclaimed in word and sacrament, that one can best understand how the Christian community cares for its members who are sick and in danger of death. It has a ritual of anointing and prayer done by the heads of the community that calls the sick back to health and back to the eucharistic assembly in which they are nourished for life and resurrection. In the Catholic tradition this ritual healing is recognized as a sacrament. If bodily health is restored the rite acts as a sign and anticipation of the resurrection, as the healing miracles of Jesus were signs and anticipations of the kingdom. If the person anointed does not recover and dies, the sacrament is seen as entry into that final healing that is the resurrection; it is believed to be effective in removing the final vestiges of sin that would block the full fruits of resurrection that give entry to the banquet of heaven. In this case anointing is joined with a final participation in Eucharistic communion.

Christian initiation, then, includes being given access to a sacramental way of dealing with illness and death during the time of waiting for the coming of the Lord. By this sacrament the Church is able to ensure that its eucharistic assembly is not distressed unduly by the wear and tear of age and the disruptive effects of illness. It has a guarantee that it will be graced by healthy people, whether health takes the form of physical well-being, or of peaceful, sin-free coping with illness, old age and death, or of the ultimate life-ensuring passage to resurrection.

## TECHNICAL QUESTIONS ABOUT SACRAMENTS

The life of the Christian community is affected by many rites besides the seven called sacraments. Some of these are called sacramentals. They can have much in common with sacraments and form an integrated ritual pattern with them. Civil rituals, too, like those that express patriotic sentiments and civic duty, can be integrated in the sacramental life of Christians. But the theological claims made for the seven sacraments and for the way they incorporate the sacramentality of the Church and of Christ are quite distinctive and separate them from all other rites. There are some standard technical questions that have been devised by sacramental theology to identify sacraments and define what distinguishes them from all other rites. The origin and drift of these questions have been seen in the preceding chapter. It is useful to outline here how they are put and answered in general terms within the theological tradition being presented here, and to take a position on them, which will then serve for dealing with the individual sacraments of baptism, confirmation, and Eucharist.

### Signs

The first question that needs to be asked about sacraments is what *kind of thing* they are. Everything else that one has to say about them will be affected by the answer given. The words mystery and sacrament tell one already that in sacraments one is not dealing with banal realities but with things that are a lot more than they seem to be. What one sees and does is putting one in touch with deeper reality. One of the first words that was used in Christian theology to express this characteristic of sacraments was "sign." Augustine used it. Thomas made it the key to his theology of sacraments. In Augustine and Thomas, understanding of the term was heavily influenced by the philosophical anthropology of Plato, and had Aristotelian features added to it by Thomas. Its meaning was worked out in the analysis of human perception. A distinction had to be made in the sign between what was perceived on the level of sense knowledge and the reality that was reached in the perception: the one could be called the *signum* and the other the *res*; there was the sign that was signifying and the reality that was signified.

There were risks in saying that sacraments are signs. The world is full of signs that do nothing beyond giving information about something totally other, and that can be forgotten as soon as their message is learned. But sacraments are not just that. For Christian faith they do something, and they hold within themselves the power to do it: they give the grace of salvation. If one says they are only signs one risks being thought to mean that all they do is give a hint that something is being done somewhere else and by something else. At the Reformation, Protestant theologians were happy to say sacraments were signs somewhat in this sense: they served as signs of saving faith in what is done only in and by the cross of Christ. This made Catholic theologians think they were denying all that the tradition of faith had said about the divine reality that was not just indicated by, but was really present within sacraments—all that made them be mysteries. They became coy about saying sacraments are signs, and the Council of Trent rarely if ever uses the terms. Counter-Reformation Catholic theology became much more intent on affirming and explaining how sacraments were *causes* rather than signs of grace. Students of Thomas kept the idea alive and it became important again in some currents of neo-scholasticism, although often being given an excessively cognitive sense. Twentieth century theology developed the notion of sign greatly, taking advantage of important analyses of the role of symbolism in human life that are to be found in many currents of recent philosophy.

Speculation on how human life thrives on the symbolic can greatly enrich the theology of sacraments. It is being done by the contemporary theologians mentioned in chapter 2. Their analyses of the symbolic, of language, of imagination, of community give new and valuable insights into anthropological values of sacraments. It is true that, as has been pointed out, serious questions can be raised about the philosophical and theological weight that these insights are being expected to carry in the theology of sacraments, such as whether by themselves they can give a satisfactory account of their divine reality, and of other matters traditionally dealt with by metaphysical thinking. But this gives no excuse for not thinking in terms of the symbolic about all that is said and done and used and made into art in sacramental celebrations. Otherwise sacraments will be thought about simply as objects to be manipulated and regulated, and not for what they truly are, which is the revealing, sanctifying presence of God being given shape and color and sound in the most engaging forms of human activity.

All presence of God in human activity is a mirror held up to Christ. The signs and symbols that are sacraments put humans, body and spirit, in contact with Christ. They are multidirectional signs. They look to past, present, and future. To say sacraments are signs helps one to understand how they can put memory in touch with Christ as he came in the past, can put hope in touch with Christ as he will come in the future, and can put faith and love in touch with him as he is here and now. It also helps one to understand how sacraments gather humans into the double movement of grace that is in Christ, "upward" to his Father in worship, "downward" to his sisters and brothers in sanctification. What is "signed" in sacraments is, at one and the same time, the human giving of worship to God and the human receiving of sanctification from God.

## Divine Institution

The fundamental question for distinguishing a sacrament from any other human rite is a question about its origin. If it is to be all that it is claimed to be it must somehow come from God. It must express a verifiable divine initiative rather than be a merely human invention. But exactly what about a sacrament must have come from God? The meaning of the question, and therefore the answer to it, supposes an analysis of the makeup of a sacrament. Anthropologically, a sacrament is a rite made up of actions and words; actions and words involve people, who do and say things and have things done and said to them; and their actions and words may involve the use of objects. This complex of actions, words, objects, and people makes up a sign or symbol. A sacrament is a sign, and it is precisely as a sign that it is believed to give God an opportunity to enter human life with his grace in a way that is congenial to humans and allows them to respond appropriately. It is about a sign that one wants assurances of divine origin, not about the material elements of the rite, which can come from a variety of human sources. It is what is signified by the way they are put together that one would want to trace to God, because that is what indicates that God is acting and what God is doing.

The way this question is dealt with is further affected by another piece of analysis that is needed in sacramental theology. One can identify a central core of symbolism in each sacrament that stays constant under a variety of ritual forms. It is found in some central words and actions/objects of the rite. These were called the "matter" and "form" of the sacrament from the Middle Ages until quite recently. Even if the terminology has been dropped, the idea that gave rise to it (but which it did not always subsequently convey) remains in the thinking of the Church. It is thought necessary to define for every sacrament what are the words and actions without which one cannot have its essential symbolism, and therefore the sacrament itself; and with which, in extreme situations, one can have it even if all the rest of the rite cannot be performed. All sorts of practical judgments about the celebration of sacraments depend on the definition of how this core symbolism is assured, and the law and teaching of the Church state it as clearly as the needs of the time demand.

It is theologically tempting to make the question about the divine origin of a sacrament be a question about these essential words and actions that the Church identifies. There have been periods in the history of theology when the question was so understood, and valiant efforts were made to prove that each of the seven sacraments was divinely instituted in this sense. However, theology nowadays sees the question of divine origin as bearing on the *signification* of the rite before it bears on the ritual words and elements. It is the meaning of the rite that is the unchanging substance of the sacrament. And this is what is divinely given and unchangeable. It may in some cases be so bound up with particular elements that it is inexpressible without them, but in itself it is a meaning more than a matter. The Church may have considerable discretion about the ritual elements but it has absolutely none about the meaning to be signified by the rite. Apart from sidestepping many of the difficulties that exegesis and historical investigation have raised against attempts to establish a divine origin for central words and elements of all seven sacraments, this way of putting the question of the divine origin of sacraments seems to be more in keeping with the Church's belief that sacraments are signs. What is looked for, then, to establish the divine origin of a sacrament is evidence of the divine intention to be present in grace at a particular moment of human life in a significant rite, rather than evidence of the choice of the rite itself. The rite, however, is not indifferent to the divine choice. All the sacramental rites come out of the story and images and historical experiences in which the intentions of God have been revealed. The Church has never felt free to go outside that tradition in any choices it has had to make about rites. Some of the rites are attributed to the personal choice of Jesus by the scriptures (baptism and Eucharist); the others can be all traced to the Church of the apostles, although a precise determination of some of them has been made by the later Church (confirmation, orders). But what is of more importance for the divine origin of a sacrament is to be able to find something in the life, if not in the commands, of Christ that establishes a divine intention to communicate a gift of salvation in a particular human life situation, a gift to be ritualized in memory of him. Christ is seen to institute a sacrament as much by what he was and did, and by the imagery and historical tradition in which his life was expressed, as by commands he gave to perform certain rites.

## Participants and Ministers

Questions about divine origin or institution consider sacraments on the properly theological level—the level on which they are identified as acts of God in Christ on behalf of human salvation. Their divine origin distinguishes them from all other human rites. There is another series of questions that explores the ecclesiological level of sacraments. A sacrament has to be recognizably an act of the Church, calling into play its status as sacrament of Christ. The Church itself already affirms this about seven rites when it lists them as its sacraments, defines their meaning, provides for their celebration in its official liturgical books, and gives them priority in its pastoral care. They are also singled out by the stipulations that the Church makes about the people who participate in them and about those who minister in them. It takes people to make a sacramental sign, people who receive and people who give. The theological questions that are asked about them reveal something of how the Church is expressing itself in sacraments.

Because the Church is the community of believers it requires that the participants (those for whose benefit the sacrament is being celebrated, those who receive it) have faith. The Church will only celebrate one of its sacraments with and for those who share its faith.

Because the Church is the community of those who save and are being saved, the participant is also expected to have some intention of making the rite a step on the way to his or her salvation. Even if the theological analysis of this intention shows that a minimal degree of explicitness is adequate to meet the needs of the Church, it also shows that it can never be dispensed with entirely. To receive a sacrament is to join in an ecclesial act; it is to contribute to the making of the Church. The Church will only recognize itself in those who join it by choice, and therefore by some kind of intention. Along with faith and intention the Church requires that the recipient of a sacrament should respect the interconnectedness of the sacraments, and particularly the priority of the sacraments of initiation. One has, for example, to be at least baptized before receiving the Eucharist, and to be confirmed before being ordained. The Church is constructed by this interlocking pattern of sacraments and without respecting it one cannot properly take advantage of the Church. Finally, the Church requires of the one who receives a sacrament an openness to the gift of grace, at least to the extent of not putting any moral obstacle in its way. The Church is the community of people who make holy and are being made holy. It wants no sacramental commerce with those who refuse holiness. Sometimes it happens that the Church is deceived into celebrating a sacrament with those who refuse holiness, or even with those who do not believe or have no intention of seeing the rite as a sacrament of salvation. Sometimes these deceptions will destroy all sacramentality and what is done will be only an empty rite. At other times there may still be a real sacrament because the Church finds in some others among its members a response to the gift of God that takes the place of the contribution to the sacrament refused by the one for whom it was originally celebrated. But this does not diminish in any way the insistence of the Church that those who participate in sacraments must have faith, intention, and openness to grace. It cannot do otherwise if it believes that these people have an essential part to play in making sacraments be an expression of the Church's own sacramentality.

In sacraments the Church is both giver and receiver. The giving is examined in the theological questions that are asked about the minister. He gives as representative of Christ, acting in and through his Church. He acts by human choice and therefore must have some intention of doing what the Church does. He is obviously expected to believe in what he is doing and to act out of the kind of love that makes the Church want to give the grace of God to its members. If he does not believe, or if though believing he does not care much for those to whom he ministers sacraments, the Church community will nevertheless let its own faith and love take hold of the rite and make it be a sacrament. Anything else would not be consonant with the missionary responsibility of the Church to save all humankind, and would be rather unfair to the participant whose faith in God entails a faith in the Church. But there is one ministerial requirement that the Church does not believe it can supply for, because it is rooted in the sacramental system that makes the Church be itself. The interconnectedness of the sacraments can sometimes require a competence in the minister that is given by a prior sacrament. This arises when the signification of the sacramental words and actions depends on the significance of the person who says and does them, and when he gets that signification from another sacrament. Ordination gives a special ability to represent Christ in relation to the baptized, to represent his giving in relation to his being received. The Church will not be able to express itself in the rite without such a sacramentally qualified minister. A Eucharist celebrated by a community that is not presided over by an ordained priest cannot sacramentalize the Church in the way the Eucharist is designed to, nor can a rite of reconciliation or an anointing of the sick. Without an appropriately ordained minister they are not sacraments. The phase of initiation represented by the rite of confirmation likewise requires that its minister be an ordained head of an ecclesial community. Orders can only be given on behalf of the Church by those who already have them. These, and all the other ministerial requirements, are an obedience by the Church to its own sacramentality and to the way it is realized in the different rites that it calls sacraments.

The qualification to be a participant and a minister in sacraments is associated theologically with the sacramental characters. The characters of baptism, confirmation, and orders are variously required for action and reception in sacraments. Following authors like Schillebeeckx,[2] theology handles questions about the character, and its

---

2. E.Schillebeeckx, OP, *Christ the Sacrament of Encounter with God*, trans. from Dutch (London and New York: Sheed & Ward, 1963).

relationship to grace, in a way that also probes the ecclesiological level of sacraments. Grace and character have traditionally been presented as two distinct, separable effects of sacraments. This has sometimes been done in a way that gave the impression that they are two end products of sacraments, with the character being a kind of second-best gift of God that one can hold on to even when one does not accept grace. Theology can draw attention to the tradition that the character is not just an *effect* of a sacrament but is itself a contributing factor to the making of sacraments. In the language derived from Augustine it is a *res et sacramentum*. The character is seen as giving one a capacity to function as a member of Christ and of his Church in the process of one's own sanctification and that of others. The accent is less on how it marks the soul than on how it gives an ecclesiological and Christological qualification to human action, which allows a person to make ritual signs that are, and are recognized to be, acts of the Church and of Christ, and therefore grace-bearing. Characters are required of participants and ministers in sacraments because the Church of Christ is required in them.

## Sacramental Effectiveness

There is a further set of theological questions that probe the distinctive reality of sacrament even more profoundly than do questions about institution and ministerial requirements. They are questions about how sacraments realize their effects, and about the kind of divine and human activity that is at work when they do. It is here that theology explores the ultimate meaning of divine institution and the reason why ministerial and participation requirements of sacraments are sharply distinguished from those of sacramentals in the law of the Church. The law stipulates that certain things are necessary for the validity of a sacrament. However, it must be always remembered that it is not its validity that makes a sacrament work. Thomas almost never talks about the validity of sacraments, but very often about their truth *(veritas)*. A sacrament works because it is a truly significant action of God taking place within a truly significant human action.

No rereading of the tradition about how God gives grace in and through sacraments can avoid the question of how God acts in and on his creatures. If one excludes or is agnostic about such divine action one will hardly get beyond an anthropological understanding of sacraments. Assuming a realistic metaphysics of divine action on creatures (such as one finds, for example, throughout the First Part of the *Summa* of Saint Thomas, especially in Ia, q. 6, q. 8, q. 15, q. 20, q. 43, q. 44, q. 105), one will want to give due attention to the peculiar way in which God acts on free, responsible creatures. Using the analysis of the different kinds of causality that Thomas inherited from Aristotle, it can be stated as a general law of the divine ordering of things that when God acts (as "efficient cause") on creatures who are responsible for their own destiny, he makes them aware of the form of action he is moving them to (as its "formal/exemplar cause") and makes them desire the goal of the action (as "final cause"): this allows the person being moved to make the action that God is causing in them and its finality be their own.[3] It was unfortunate that many theologians claiming to draw from the thought of Aquinas concentrated exclusively on God's efficient causality in their explanations of how sacraments give grace. A theology of sacraments that isolated that causality from the formal and final causality of God did lay itself, and the Thomas it claimed to be interpreting, open to the charge of "productionism" that Chauvet makes against it.[4]

When God's action and its goal are movements of saving grace, there is not just the realization of grace but also its manifestation. The human action that it gives rise to takes on a form and a finality that are also from God. In sacraments the form is manifested in the sacramental sign of grace that the recipient makes the expression of his or her own life choices, and the finality is felt in the thrust of worship that is expressed in the liturgy of each sacrament. The same pattern of divine causality is found in Christ, who is both the manifestation and the realization of salvation, for the glory of God. In sacraments the mystery of Christ is brought to bear on people in the Church. God gives life in Christ to his people in sacraments. His life-giving action takes the form of words that reveal him to them as pattern and goal of the life they are receiving, and of rites that make that revelation suitably concrete and tangible for creatures who live in the body. These

---

3. On the interdependence of efficient, formal and final cause see Saint Thomas, First Part, q. 5, a. 4.

4. L.-M. Chauvet, *Symbol and Sacrament: A Sacramental Re-reading of Christian Existence*, trans. from French (Collegeville, MN: The Liturgical Press, 1997), Ch. I.

words and rites simultaneously give concrete form and finality to the activity of those who come to life in response to God's grace. In this pattern of causality, words and rites act as signs, not as things. They express the reciprocal action of God and of his People, and in expressing it make it occur. But they are signs of salvific human action only because they are first signs of God who is causing that action.

The technical term "instrument" has served throughout much of the Christian tradition to state the subordinate status, and yet the dignity and indispensability, of human action in relation to the divine (which is the principal cause) in sacraments. Something like it will always be needed to keep the anthropological in line with the theological in the analysis of sacraments. The Thomistic tradition has paid special attention to the physical realism of this instrumentality of human action in the making of sacraments. It would argue that an explanation of sacramental action in terms of moral causality (the view that a sacrament causes grace because it has an intrinsic value or worth that establishes a claim in God's grace) does not by itself do justice to the mysterious power and presence of God that the tradition has generally recognized to be at work in sacraments. Modern studies about the "mystery" inherent in acts of Christian worship seem to confirm the theological preference for a physical rather than a merely moral instrumentality. However, these same studies, and the general development of sacramental theology, make it clear that to reduce the instrumental causality of sacraments to the merely physical is to fail to do justice to another aspect of the tradition about sacramentality. Sacraments are not simply a point of contact between God and his People, in which something invisible happens. They are moments of communication, through the medium of signs. All the intentional elements—the way the sacrament notifies the intentions of God to cause grace here and now to designated recipients, as well as the kind of grace he intends to give and the particular response he expects to it—are included in the instrumentality of the sacrament. A theory of sacramental causality along these lines rejoins, from what it would claim to be a deeper metaphysical perspective, contemporary personalist theologies of sacraments, and fits well into the categories of invitation/response and the phenomenology of sign that they use to analyze the interaction of the divine and human in terms of personal relations. Because it offers a metaphysical ground for the application of personalist categories to God, it probably sits more comfortably than merely personalist theologies with the dogmatic tradition about the ontological reality of sacraments, which the Council of Trent defined in terms of "containing grace" and causing it *ex opere operato*. It locates the ultimate basis for the objective reality of sacraments, and of their reliability in the face of human fallibility, in the guaranteed action of God. When humans carry out their proper ministerial and participatory tasks in making a sacramental sign in and for the Church, Christ is truly present as both gift of God and perfect human response, and the work of God is unfailingly being done, even if in some cases it is destined to be obstructed by some obstacles to grace placed by individual recipients.

The theological analysis of the unique causality of grace that occurs in sacraments sets them apart from all other rites and activities of the Church. It shows how profoundly they are linked with God's saving action through Christ and the Church. It is also the basis for the statements that are made about sacraments being necessary for salvation. However, theology has to be careful to explain that this necessity is not absolute: sacramental experience is, indeed, necessary for human salvation but God can and does act to save outside the Christian sacraments; some sacraments are necessary for all believers, others only in particular circumstances; the grace of sacraments can be given in certain cases without the actual sacrament. What emerges from these considerations is that sacraments are for the benefit of humans and their salvation. When they serve that purpose God wants them to be used. When they do not, he gives people another way. And yet the sacramental way has a kind of normative value in the history of salvation and the other ways of salvation that God uses will always show traces of it.

The theological discussions that have been outlined in this chapter are part of the Christian story within which the rites of the Church are celebrated day-by-day. It is the part of the story that deals with the general place and meaning of rites in Christian life. When theology explores these general questions, when it relates each one of the sacraments to the others within the sacramental system, when it relates them to the sacramentality of the Church, and that in turn to the sacramentality of Christ, and when it situates that whole pattern of sacramentality within a general theology, it is building up a critical and systematic account of the place of rites in the story of God's People. This is the story that has to be told if the rites are to remain really in touch with life. There are other ways of telling it besides the way of systematic theology, and in an actual celebration of a sacrament other ways are usually more appropriate. But the systematic does provide a critical basis for the biblical and liturgical telling, and for the preaching and catechesis, and the praying and the singing that are needed if the sacramental rites of the Christian people are to be fully life-giving and life-expressing.

# Chapter 4

# Baptism: The Rite

## DESCRIPTION

It is well to begin the study of baptism with a summary description of the rite. It is in the rite that the sacramental event that theology sets out to understand is experienced. It is best to have primarily in mind the rite for adults.[1] It is in this that the Church expresses all that it means by baptism, without qualification. Other forms of the rite, such as that for children, are no less baptisms. But because they are adapting the sacrament to particular circumstances, they are best understood by comparing their special features with the unqualified rite, which is that for adults.

The essential core of the rite of baptism is a bathing in water, with an invoking of the names of Father, Son, and Holy Spirit. This is the universal belief and practice of Christians (apart from a few rare groups who have a "baptism of the Spirit" without the use of a water rite). They do the bathing in different ways. Almost all agree that the most appropriate way of doing it is to immerse the person being baptized wholly or in part in water. The churches of the Eastern tradition, both Orthodox and Catholic, do this as a matter of course (although allowing exceptions in emergency situations). Some of the evangelical churches of the Latin and Western traditions will only baptize in this way. But most churches of the West settle in practice for a pouring of water on the head of the one being baptized. There is also a practice, which has always been problematical, of sprinkling water over those to be baptized. The immersion or pouring is usually done three times, corresponding to the three names that are invoked.

---

1. RCIA, 48–224; *The Rites of the Catholic Church, Initiation*, 40–102.

A person is baptized in a particular Christian community—
normally a parish—that takes responsibility for the sacrament
and registers it. The rite is celebrated by that community, gathered under the presidency of its ordained ministers, one of whom
(bishop, priest, or deacon) does the actual baptizing. One or more
members of the church sponsor the person to be baptized and take
special responsibility for him or her. The rite is celebrated in a part
of the church building set aside for baptism, which in its location
and design expresses that baptism is the way of entry into the community, and in its decoration evokes the meaning of the sacrament.
The time for celebrating baptism is set by the general rhythm of
the Church's liturgical life. The Vigil of Easter, when the death and
resurrection of Christ is being celebrated with special solemnity, is
considered the most appropriate time. The feast of Pentecost is also
favored. Within the weekly rhythm, Sunday, the day of the Lord's
resurrection, is the preferred day.

The sacramental rite of baptism is celebrated at the end of a
period of pastoral and catechetical preparation called the catechumenate. During it candidates are tested and affirmed in the conversion of
life that gives them the desire for baptism, are schooled in the hearing
of the word of God, and are introduced to prayer in the Church. The
life-changing experience of the catechumenate is itself provided by the
interplay of word and rite. These touch the body in a series of blessings, signings, and anointings; they address the mind in words and
teachings; and they monitor and approve the progressive commitment
being made. Viewed in the theological framework of rite/word/life,
the catechumenate marks the gradual introduction of a person to the
full Christian story (it includes, for example, the ritualized giving of
the sacred books and the learning of the words of the Creed and of the
Our Father) and the gradual transition to the way of life of the community that lives by that story.

In the sacramental celebration itself, the core ritual is preceded
by preliminary words and rites that provide a reprise of the catechumenate. They welcome the candidate, let them hear the Word of God,
express the transition they are making from one way of life (dominated
by sin and the devil) to another (in Christ and his Church), and profess
their faith in Christ. With this kind of preparation the central rite of baptism—the bathing in water—becomes a real acceptance of the climax

of the Christian story—the death and resurrection of Jesus—and a real entry into new life through the ritual reenactment of it.

The central rite of the sacrament is followed by ceremonies that express the new life that the baptized enjoy in Christ and the Church. They are anointed with perfumed oil called chrism. When a continuous rite of initiation is being celebrated this anointing is the sacrament of Confirmation. When, however, the baptized person is not to be confirmed at that time there is still an anointing with chrism, but with a prayer that refers it to the consecration of the baptized as prophet, priest, and king in the body of Christ, rather than to the special gift of the Holy Spirit that Confirmation gives (RCIA, 222 [224]). After anointing the initiated are dressed in white and given a candle that has been lighted from the Easter candle. The Church then proceeds to the celebration of the Eucharist and the newly baptized/confirmed take full part in it, receiving holy communion for the first time. In the weeks following their baptism new Christians are meant to receive special attention from the Church, especially in liturgical assemblies. They are meant to be told in the fullest possible terms the meaning of their first experiences of Christian rites and the effects this should be having in their lives. It is ultimately in life that rite and word have their mettle tested.

## HISTORY

Because ritual needs to be stable it is important to be able to state that baptism today is substantially the same as it has been from the beginning. However, there have been some developments in the rite, and the way it is done today can he better understood with the help of some remembering. One can go right back to the Jewish roots of Christianity.[2] Ritual bathings were practiced in Judaism. They usually had to do with the procedures of cultic purification. In the period of Christian origins it seems that ritual washings were also used in the initiation of pagans into Judaism. And they were also used in those movements and sects, like that associated with Qumran, that

---

2. J. Delorme in A. George, SM, *Baptism in the New Testament: A Symposium*, trans. from French (1956) (London: Chapman, 1964), 25ff; R. T. Beckwith, "The Jewish Background to Christian Worship" in C. Jones, G. Wainwright, E. Yarnold, SJ, and P. Bradshaw, eds. *The Study of Liturgy* (London: SPCK and Oxford: Oxford University Press, revised edition, 1992).

dedicated themselves to righteousness and expected the coming of the kingdom. Baptism was so prominently associated with the preaching of righteousness and the coming of the kingdom in the message of John that he was called John the Baptizer. He drew people out into the desert and baptized those who accepted his call to conversion in the river Jordan, presumably by some form of immersion. This is how Jesus was baptized. It must have set something of a pattern for the way the apostles subsequently baptized in the name of Jesus. The New Testament, however, does not give any information about their rite of baptism beyond the essential statement that it was to be done in water and "in the name of the Father and of the Son and of the Holy Spirit" (Matthew 28:19). When Acts speaks of baptism or baptizing "in the name of Jesus" (2:38; 8:16; 10:48; 19:5; 22:16) it does not seem to be giving an alternative liturgical formula (although confession of faith in the name of Jesus would, in New Testament terms, imply a confession of faith in Father, Son, and Holy Spirit), but rather describing Christian baptism by way of what sets it apart from the baptism of John or any other type of baptism.[3]

There are two important texts about the rite of baptism from the second century. The *Didaché*, generally dated about 100 AD, already allows a triple pouring of water on the head in place of immersion in running water. It recommends that baptism be preceded by some days of fasting, by the baptizer as well as the baptized, and by others who can do so.[4] Saint Justin gives a more detailed description of the process of baptism, with special attention to how the community takes an active part in it.[5] There is a phase of preparation during which the community prays and fasts with those who "are persuaded and believe that those things which we teach and describe are true, and undertake to live accordingly." The candidates are then "led by us to a place

---

3. B. Neunheuser, OSB, *Baptism and Confirmation*, trans. from German (New York: Herder and Herder, 1964), Chapters 1, 4; on a possible primitive baptismal formula in Acts 8:37 see O. Cullmann, *Baptism in the New Testament*, trans. from German (London: SCM Press, 1950 and 1973), 71ff.

4. *Didaché* 7: text in P. Palmer, *Sacraments and Worship: Liturgy and Doctrinal Development of Baptism, Confirmation, and Eucharist* (London: Longmans, Green and Co., 1957), 1–2 and E. C. Whitaker and M. E. Johnson, *Documents of the Baptismal Liturgy*, revised and expanded 3rd ed. (Collegeville, MN: The Liturgical Press, 2003), 1.

5. *First: Apology*, 61: text in Palmer, *Sacraments and Worship*, 3–4 and Whitaker, *Documents of the Baptismal Liturgy*, 1–2.

where there is water" and are "washed in the water in the Name of the Father and Lord God of all things, and of our Savior Jesus Christ, and of the Holy Spirit".... Afterward they join the community, "those who are called brethren" in common prayer "for ourselves, for him that has been enlightened, and for all men everywhere. . . ." They then take part in the Eucharist.

Justin's account of Christian baptism, being addressed to pagans, is marked by a certain discretion. The next important document on the rite of baptism is an internal document of the Christian Church and has no such reticences or circumlocutions. *The Treatise on the Apostolic Tradition*, attributed to Saint Hippolytus of Rome, who would have been writing about AD 215, gives a very full description of Christian initiation in XVI–XXIII.[6] It includes almost all the elements of our present-day Roman rite of baptism. There is a catechumenate, which may go on for two or three years, during which there are regular assemblies for teaching, examination of conduct, prayer, blessings, and exorcisms; the candidates are assisted by sponsors. During the period immediately preceding the baptism there are daily assemblies for prayer and exorcism. On Friday and Saturday, presumably preceding the feast of Easter, there is fasting and on Saturday night there is a vigil during which there is reading from Scripture and instruction. At dawn the water and oils are blessed, the candidates, including children, undress; they are invited to renounce Satan and are anointed with an Oil of Exorcism, they go down into the water and are immersed three times, responding "I believe" each time to the Trinitarian profession of faith pronounced in the form of a question by the one who baptizes. Afterward they are anointed with an Oil of Thanksgiving, dress, and join the assembled Church. There the Bishop lays hands on them, prays over them for the gift of the Holy Spirit, anoints them with consecrated oil, seals them on the forehead and gives them the kiss of peace. They then join for the first time in the Prayer of the Faithful and go on to take part in the Eucharist.

Whether or not the rite described in *The Apostolic Tradition* had much historical influence, it certainly has most of the elements

---

6. Text in Palmer, *Sacraments*, 8–12; and in Whitaker, Johnson, *Documents of the Baptismal Liturgy*, 4–8 , where the text is "attributed to Hippolytus of Rome" but it is pointed out that some recent scholarly opinion questions this attribution; for convenience and without prejudice to that discussion we will continue to attribute the text to Hippolytus.

that form the classical shape of the rite of baptism. Some of these elements are not yet found in the early records of other liturgical traditions, or are found in a different order. There are differences about the anointings, especially those done immediately after the bathing in water. The Syrian tradition has the Trinitarian words said in the form of a statement or prayer rather than in the form of questions as in Hippolytus.[7] This eventually became common practice. Some rites, like the Roman, retain the questions immediately before the bathing, which is then done "in the name of Father, Son, and Holy Spirit."

The development of the Roman rite of baptism from those early centuries to the present day can be followed in the liturgical books.[8] One may note some of the factors that help to explain how the rite reached its present state. The liturgical season of Lent, set up as a time of conversion, fasting, prayer, and instruction in preparation for Easter, and therefore also for baptism, took to itself many of the tasks of the catechumenate. This enriched the liturgy of baptism, even if it did carry the risk of formalizing it. It was particularly useful for those who had been baptized as infants, helping them to work out the full sacramentality of their baptism; it also prepared Christians to exercise their responsibilities for the newly baptized, particularly if these were their own children. However, as the centuries went by, the practice of celebrating baptism outside the preferred seasons of Easter and Pentecost became more common. Away from Lent the catechumenate was less easy to manage. When Europe became almost entirely Christian the great majority of those to be baptized were infants. A rite was developed for baptizing them which was a rather ill-disguised adaptation of the rite for adults. It provided the dominant experience of baptism in the established churches. Of necessity it gave more prominence to the passive ritual elements that suited an infant than to the elements of the rite that called forth personal prayer and decision. The participation of the community in infant baptism became quite limited from the Middle Ages onward. In the course of time a rather passive ritualism came to be accepted as normal, even in the baptism of adults. Adults were, indeed, prepared for baptism by instruction and

7. Whitaker, *Documents of the Baptismal Liturgy*, 24–26.
8. Texts in Whitaker, *Documents of the Baptismal Liturgy*.

prayer, but these exercises were not often ritualized in liturgies— although this was provided for in the Latin liturgical books. That situation lasted in the Catholic Church until the reforms associated with Vatican II.

The reforms called for by the council (SC, 64–70) were meant to restore values of the tradition that had become obscured. The post-conciliar rites are a call to recover the truth and realism of the ritual that one senses in the early tradition. This is particularly evident in the full rite for adults that has already been described. The rite for children is realistically designed to meet their situation. It draws the community and the parents of the child into the rite in a way that expresses their acceptance of responsibility for the Christian nurture of the child, without which the Baptism cannot normally be celebrated.

## ANTHROPOLOGICAL CONSIDERATIONS

### A Rite of Initiation

One can get a feel for the rite of baptism not only from its own history but also from the way it matches general patterns of human behavior that are revealed by anthropological studies, especially in the domain of religion. Baptism can be classed as an initiation rite. One does not need to be a professional anthropologist to have a sense of what initiation is and how it is ritualized. Life is full of beginnings and of passages from one stage of life to another. There are the passages of age, from childhood to teenage, to young adulthood, to middle age, to old age. The way one dresses, the company one keeps, the language one uses change as one passes from one of these ages to another; and there are significant moments when one feels the change and gives it expression in some decisive, socially recognized gesture. These are the rites of passage, of initiation to a new stage of life. There is another experience of initiation when people join something. They commit themselves to an ideal (like scouting), or to a social task (in a political party), or to an enthusiasm (a fan club). Something changes in their life and they develop new relationships. The rites of joining may be little more than giving one's name and paying a subscription, accepting a card or badge, making some promises, but in their own way these are rites of passage that mark a new beginning.

Christian baptism is such a rite of passage or initiation. One is joining something, starting to keep new company, thinking and feeling differently about certain things. Even if the rite is simple the issues are serious. They are matters of life and death. Anthropology and other social and psychological sciences can help one to understand something of what is going on. They can explain how deep psychic and social life forces are at work and issues of life and death are being worked out in rites of passage that may on the surface be banal and even slightly ridiculous to outsiders. Initiation rites in primitive cultures are a fruitful area of study and comparison here, because they show the human life process in unspoiled and unself-conscious simplicity.[9] An analysis of them can help one to understand how the rites of Christian baptism can be touching the human spirit on the deep level where it wrestles with issues of life and death.

The Jewish initiation rite of circumcision is of particular interest for understanding baptism.[10] While circumcision was, and still is in a variety of cultures, a rite of tribal initiation, it was believed to be among Israelites a divinely given sign of their being God's People, bound to him by covenant. It was the way of entry into the covenant community and the mark of belonging to it. The physical intimacy of it ensured that it had a deep impact on the sense of identity, life, and destiny of a whole race of people. The Christian tradition has found many features of it that typify baptism as the initiation rite of the new covenant (Colossians 2:11–12).[11]

And yet baptism is as different from circumcision as the new covenant is from the old. Christianity has, in fact, distanced itself from the kind of rites that are an inevitable part of being born and growing up within a particular racial or cultural tradition. Baptism is not a rite of tribal or cultural initiation. It is a rite of freely chosen entry into a community in which the only basis of belonging is the choice of God, and in which there is no longer Jew or Greek, slave or free, male

---

9. cf. M. Eliade, *Rites and Symbols of Initiation* (first published as *Birth and Rebirth*) (New York/London: Harper and Row, 1958).

10. See R. de Vaux, OP, *Ancient Israel: Its Life and Institutions*, trans. from French (London: Darton, Longman & Todd, 1961), 46–48; O. Cullmann, *Baptism in the New Testament*, trans. from German (London: SCM Press, 1950 and 1973), 56–70.

11. For the Fathers see J. Danielou, SJ, *The Bible and the Liturgy*, trans. from French (Notre Dame: University of Notre Dame Press, 1965), 63–67 and Saint Thomas, *Summa*, First Part, q. 70.

or female. From this point of view, rites of free choice and personal conversion offer a better anthropological model for baptism than do rites of growing up and growing old within a particular culture. The study of the mystery religions of the Greco-Roman world is helpful here (see Chapter 2, "The Mystery Religions"). On a more secular and contemporary plane, one could examine the rites by which people enter various political movements, especially of the radical sort—even if they are no more than the growing of a "Che Guevara" beard! In these, as in the initiation rites of the mystery religions, there is a preoccupation with salvation or liberation, with escape from all that leads to slavery and death, with patterns of change that have once proved themselves and may be repeated again, with joining and helping to create a new people who will enjoy life and freedom in a new world to come.

## A Water Rite with Words

Anthropologically, rites call out for words. The words that surround and accompany them can be stories, incantations, songs; they can be invocations addressed to persons, to those who are at the origin of the rite or those to whom the rite is here and now addressed. The words gather the rite into all that language means to humans, and make it itself be a kind of language. Learning about how language functions in human life can be a precious key for entering into the human richness of sacraments. The writings of sacramental theologians like Chauvet and Power can be read with great profit on this level.

Even a simple reflection on how the stories told around the rite of baptism contribute to its celebration can introduce one to this type of study. Baptism is a ritual of initiation into a salvation process that is thought to have been going on for a long time. The story of it is told in the Bible. It is a story about the God who made the world and brings it to its consummation, about the God who has been doing wonderful works of salvation since time began. There are patterns in those salvation events that throw light on what is now being experienced in a baptism. There are things that have been done in, with, and through water. Retelling the stories about these events, and recalling what has been thought about them in the past, brings to light and gives form to what God is now doing in the water rite of baptism.

The telling is more than just a bringing to mind of past events. There are themes and images in the stories that can provoke deep responses in the human psyche. The psychological sciences probe the impact, conscious and unconscious, of stories, images, and dreams about water. There are well-established patterns linking water to the human way of dealing with great issues such as life and death, birth and rebirth, creation and renewal, salvation and destruction.[12] Among the biblical stories about water are those that tell how it was from a watery chaos that the world was originally formed, how the waters of the Flood brought drowning and death to sinners but carried Noah and his family to new life, how water bogged down the Egyptians and gave freedom to the Israelites at the crossing of the Red Sea, how water was given in the desert and how the waters of the Jordan stood back to let God's People enter the promised land, how the mystique of water was used by the prophets of Israel, how Jesus was baptized in the waters of the Jordan, how he used bathing and the water image in his preaching. It can be shown how the biblical stories about water heard in the celebration of baptism can call into play a healthy working out of images and emotions, even below the level of consciousness, that can give the experience of salvation a deep hold on the human psyche. It is true that, for the believer, the Bible is not just a set of stories invented to provide ways of dealing with various peculiarities of the human condition, as are many religious myths. There are real events, and there is a real God, underlying the biblical stories about how God made and saved the world through water. But the stories are real stories and function the way stories do.

The Biblical words that speak of baptism have been transmitted in the Church in a tradition that generated its own words, and some of these have become a standard part of the making of the rite of baptism. The creeds are an early distillation of the biblical story, putting it in an articulated series of affirmations that can be proclaimed by those being baptized. Prayers have been composed, drawing on biblical precedents and images. The prayers of blessing that are said over the water before it is used in baptism *(RCIA,* 215) are a beautiful example of biblical evocation in a prayer of the Church. Songs have been written to accompany the rite. The classical architecture, furnishing, and

---

12. E.g., M. Eliade, *Patterns in Comparative Religion* (London: Sheed & Ward, 1958), 188ff.

décor of baptisteries have become words set in stone and color. As well as the words that have found their way into the actual making of the ritual there are others that surround the rite without forming part of it. There are the words of catechesis spoken before and after the rite, some of which, such as the Mystagogical Catecheses of the Fourth Century Fathers of the Church have classical authority. And there are words coming out of theological controversy and constructive theological reflection. These, along with the general corpus of biblical words about the sacrament, will be the subject of the next chapter. What needs to be appreciated here are the words that are spoken within the rite itself.

## Calling by Name

The words that are spoken with the central rite of baptism personalize the action. In the words "John/Mary, I baptize you in the name of the Father and of the Son and of the Holy Spirit" the one being baptized is named; the one who is baptizing says "I" (in the Roman rite; in the Eastern rites the passive voice, "be baptized," is used); and the God for whom the baptizer acts and from whom the one being baptized believes salvation is coming is personally named as Father, Son, and Holy Spirit.

Words commonly have a personalizing function in religious ritual.[13] They say what one person is doing to and for another in the rite. They can, of course, become mere incantations, and then the rite becomes a thing rather than a personal action. But when they are speech, and not just sound, they put the "I" and the "Thou" into ritual. When there is speech there is a person speaking and a person being spoken to. The baptizer is an "I." However, he or she is a minister, acting in the name of someone else. The minister baptizes in the name of God, Father, Son, and Holy Spirit. The personal name of God can be spoken because God has revealed himself, through all the events and words of the history of salvation, to be Father, Son, and Holy Spirit. The saving events that are being remembered in the water rite belong to this self-revelation of God. The baptism of Jesus, at which the

---

13. L. Bouyer, *Rite and Man*, trans. from French (Notre Dame: Notre Dame Press, 1963), Ch. IV.

Father identified him as his Son, and the Holy Spirit came upon him, is a climactic moment in that personal revelation of God. Christian baptism is such a moment when it is done in the name of Father, Son, and Holy Spirit. The Trinitarian personal name of God distils the whole history of salvation, and underpins its summarizing in the creeds of the Church. In making his name known to people God gave them a certain power over him—not a magical power but a power that comes from a freely given familiarity. It is this power that a baptizer calls on when he or she acts in the name of Father, Son, and Holy Spirit. The baptizing is recognized as being the saving action of Father, Son, and Holy Spirit, of the One God who is the personal heart of the whole history of salvation.

The person being baptized becomes the "Thou" in face of the "I" that speaks and acts. The ritual is his or her personal response to the Trinitarian God who is present and active in it. Even if the words of baptism no longer take the form of a profession of faith, as they did in the rite given in *The Apostolic Tradition*, they are still an act of faith in the whole history of salvation, and in the credal formulations of it, because they are an acceptance of the personal God who reveals himself in these saving actions to be Father, Son, Spirit.

That the sacramental words are words of faith marks a critical difference between Christian baptism and all rites that rely on myth. A myth is a good story, which can have its beneficent effect whether what it tells happened or not. Writing a letter to Santa Claus or visiting him has had a profound effect on countless children, even though they eventually discovered that there was no such person in reality. The nature rites of all ages have been founded on cosmic myths; the rites "worked" even though the stories were fantasies. Christianity, however, says that God really exists, and believes that God really is Father, Son, and Holy Spirit. What the Son did for our salvation really happened and will happen when he comes again. The Spirit is a real person, who is transforming us and our world. To believe is to affirm the reality of things. The Bible, from Genesis through the gospels and right up to Revelation, is a story. There are mythical elements in its telling, and it is all the better for that. But it is a true story and a dream come true. The words that accompany the water rite of baptism mean just that. They mean that what is being done is not merely an imaginative working out of some human urge or need for a salvation experience, but that it is an objective gift of a God who is really there, and who is revealing himself in this gift as Father, Son, and Holy Spirit. It is in these words of faith that the sacramentality of baptism is ultimately affirmed.

# Chapter 5

# Baptism: The Word

From the previous chapter it is clear that many words, and different kinds of words, are spoken in celebrating the rite of baptism. We will find this to be true also of confirmation, and Eucharist, as indeed it would be true of almost any rite. Words that accompany rites can be a straight narrative of things that happened in the past; they can be an idealizing of events in poetry and song; they can be a moralizing application of lessons learned from past events to human behavior; they can take the form of prayer; they can be instruction about the meaning and practice of the rite; they can be a polemical comparison of the true understanding of the rite with false versions of it; they can be a reflective, even critical review of things that have been said about the rite in the past in the light of various philosophical-type questions that may arise about it. One can find many of these kinds of words used about the covenant of salvation and its rites in the Old Testament. The historical books speak words about it in one way, the Psalms in another; the legal codes moralize about it and the prophets can be polemical about distortions of it; the Wisdom literature is reflective and philosophical. One can find the same variety of literary forms in the words written in the New Testament.

The Scriptural words about baptism, in the variety of forms they take, are the first and most fundamental words that have to be examined in a theology of the sacrament. The way those words have been transmitted and spoken about in the tradition of faith has then to be studied. Again, there is variety in the forms taken by the words. As well as the early accounts of how baptism was actually celebrated, there are the creeds that have strong connections with the sacrament. There are commentaries on scriptural texts dealing with baptism. There are baptismal catecheses, some of which give a moral teaching about the preparation and dispositions needed for the sacrament and the obligations that follow from it, others of which expound the mystical meaning of the sacrament to those who have already received it. There are prayers and hymns and poetry (and also music and painting) in the tradition about baptism. With time there emerges a polemical literature about baptism, which defends its true relationship to the work of salvation against distortions. And a reflective literature appears that reasons in a systematic way about the questions that thinking people have wanted to ask about how this rite could be all that Christians claim it to be.

Baptism uses these different kinds of words in accordance with its own needs. It incorporates some of them directly into the rite. The Trinitarian words that are spoken at the core of the rite are the quintessential statement of the Christian story, because they are a naming of the God who is its constant subject. The creed that is used fills out this "biography" of God. The prayers used in the rite are part of the poetry of belief, expressing human response to what is happening in the rite. The scriptural passages that are read are the first, normative statements of why Christians baptize and of how they understand the rite. These texts, however, are already less central to the rite itself than are the sacramental words and the prayers. They find their place in the scene-setting for the rite, during the catechumenate, during the Liturgy of the Word that precedes the water ritual, and in the explanatory instructions that follow the sacrament. Still farther away from the center are the words that have been deposited in the tradition by the moralizing, polemical, and systematic reflection that has accompanied the celebration of baptism in the postscriptural era. There is no casuistical moral theologizing within the rite of baptism; the technical word "original sin" is used only once in the Roman rite, and then in a very secondary prayer; the word "character" never appears; there is hardly an echo of the polemics of the Reformation.

Yet the words of the tradition that remain unspoken in the rite itself have a profound influence on baptism. They are an essential part of the story that Christian believers bring to bear on their celebration of the rite. If they are not remembered, or are remembered badly, the rite will deteriorate into formalism, magic, or nonsense. It is the task of

Christian theology to keep them always present and influential, even when the rite itself does not directly use them. And to the extent that new words become necessary to keep the story truthful and effective it is the task of theology to coin these words. The rite is for life, and life keeps on throwing up new questions about what that means. The answer is there in the words that have been spoken about baptism from its beginning. But old words can only speak through interpreters. Theology tries to do that constant critical interpretation of the rite of baptism in the light of the words that belong to it, and to do that for the sake of life. The magisterial authorities of the Church monitor the interpretation for continuity and genuineness. Preachers, especially in the actual celebration of the rite, and catechists in preparing people for the rite, play an indispensable part in this theological relating of rite and word to life. It is with these words of catechists, preachers, theologians, and *magisterium* that this chapter is concerned. It is from them that it will try to develop a systematic theology of baptism.

## THE NEW TESTAMENT

Along with descriptive texts that say what baptism is, and prescriptive texts that command that it be done, there are in the New Testament explanatory texts about baptism that say what it means in the design of God for the salvation of his people.[1] This meaning already begins to show through in the descriptive texts, especially when they are read against their Old Testament background. In Acts 2:37–42 baptism is presented as the way in which those who "receive the word" about Jesus (that by his death and resurrection he has been established by God his Father as Lord and Christ: vv. 14–36) and who repent, are granted forgiveness of their sins and receive the gift of the Holy Spirit; by baptism they are gathered into the community of those who "devote themselves to the apostles' teaching and fellowship, to the breaking of bread and the prayers." The core ideas that are developed in the teaching about baptism are already in that text. Some of them are found again in the description of the baptism of the eunuch

---

1. The texts are catalogued in A. George, SM and others, *Baptism in the New Testament: A Symposium*, trans. from French (1956) (London: Chapman, 1964), 13–22.

from Ethiopia by Philip in Acts 8:26–40. They are present, although in a more condensed way, in the command of Jesus to the apostles in Matthew 28:16–20. The command, made in virtue of the power that has been given to him, is to go and teach all nations, gathering together as disciples those who believe in their preaching, baptizing them in the name of Father, Son, and Holy Spirit, teaching them to live in the way Jesus commands; all this to be done in the assurance that Jesus himself remains with them until the work of salvation is complete.

The accounts of the baptism of Jesus in the Synoptic gospels include, in their own way, a theology of Christian baptism. They present baptism as a beginning by placing it at the beginning of the ministry of Jesus. They relate it to divine sonship by making the baptism of Jesus be the occasion when he is proclaimed by the Father to be his beloved Son. They relate it to the outpouring of the eschatological Spirit (baptism is "in water and the Holy Spirit") by telling how the Spirit came upon Jesus, confirming the voice of the Father and identifying him as the Son of God. These texts give baptism its Christological and Trinitarian ground. They also give it a soteriological basis by relating it to the death and resurrection of Christ. When John would have refused to baptize Jesus he was persuaded to change his mind by the words " . . . for thus it is fitting for us to fulfill all righteousness" (Matthew 3:15). The righteousness of God, foreshadowed and realized progressively in the purification of God's people throughout the Old Testament, is about to be fulfilled. It had been foretold that it would be brought about through the righteousness of a Suffering Servant of the Lord (Isaiah 42, 49, 50, 52), in whose suffering the sins of God's people would be taken away. The promise of that righteousness is about to be fulfilled in Jesus. He, though not a sinner, is embarking on a proclamation of the coming of God's kingdom that will draw down suffering and death on him. In being baptized, he gives ritual expression to his readiness to accept the way of righteousness that brings sinful humanity back to the full righteousness of God. His baptism is an anticipation of his death on the cross. He does, in fact, speak later of his death as a baptism (Luke 12:49–50), and invites the sons of Zebedee to "be baptized with the baptism with which I am baptized . . ." (Mark 10:38).

Saint Paul makes frequent reference to baptism and has a well-developed theology of it.[2] He places the rite within the working out of the gift of faith, by which those who are called to justification take hold of the grace of Christ. Although baptism is done by the Church and its ministers, it is above all an action of Christ taking hold of those who are being saved, and a way in which sinners take to themselves the salvation that Christ brings. It is this Christ-centeredness that gives baptism its power to draw people together into one, regardless of who baptized them (1 Corinthians 1:12–17), or whether they are Jew or Greek, slave or free, male or female (1 Corinthians 12:13; Galatians 3:27–29). It is in the Church that this gathering of people in Christ takes place: or rather, the Church *is* this gathering of people in Christ. Paul tells those who are gathered together in the Church that they are the body of Christ (1 Corinthians 12:27; Romans 12:5). The community is the body of Christ in the sociological sense of the term, because it is an organized group of people who, having different gifts and tasks, hold together and co-operate in the name of and for the sake of Christ. But for Paul the Church is body of Christ in a much deeper sense. The Semitic realism of his thinking makes him envisage contact between persons as something that occurs in a concrete, bodily fashion. To contact Christ is somehow to contact him bodily. The realism of the contact is experienced when the Church gathers to break a bread that is "a participation in the body of Christ," as a result of which "we who are many are one body" (1 Corinthians 10:16–17). Paul's language about baptism has to be given the same kind of realistic interpretation. His words "as many of you as were baptized into Christ have put on Christ" (Galatians 3:27) describe a relationship with Christ that is a flesh-and-blood sharing with him that makes people sons of God, as he is Son. To believe in Christ and to be baptized into him is to be joined to his body; to draw life from him is to be a member of his body (see 1 Corinthians 6:12–20). Because the baptized are members of Christ they are members of one another (Romans

2. Chapters by J. Duplacy, J. Giblet, and B. Tremel, OP, in George, *Baptism in the New Testament*,; O. Cullmann, *Baptism in the New Testament,* trans. from German (London: SCM Press, 1950 and 1973); R. Schnackenburg, *Baptism in the Thought of St. Paul,* trans. from German (London: Basil Blackwell, New York: Herder and Herder Oxford, 1964).

12:3–8). Together in him they build up the body of Christ, which is the Church.

In Romans 6 Paul explains the manner in which baptism effects the identification with Christ that grafts people into his body and makes them form the Church as his body. He explains how baptism is a life-giving contact because it takes away sin and death and gives new life through resurrection. The underlying principle is that Christ took away sin by his dying and rising: he died to sin once and for all, and he rose to new life in God (vv. 9–10). The application to baptism is by way of the symbolism of the rite: going down into the water provides an experience of dying, and coming up, revived and refreshed, provides an experience of resurrection. The death and resurrection is with and in the death and resurrection of Christ, in which victory over sin is believed to be achieved. Hence, those who are baptized into Christ Jesus die to sin and rise to newness of life. Their sins are taken away: they are free of them; they no longer live in them but in God. All this is the grace of God, justifying those who believe, making them slaves of righteousness where they had once been slaves of sin, and assuring them that "the return you get is sanctification and its end, eternal life" (v. 22).

To be baptized into Christ in the sense expounded in Romans 6 is to belong to Christ and to somehow share his status and his destiny. It is on this basis that Paul links baptism with the theme of "sonship" in Galatians and explains how it makes the baptized be children of the Father along with Christ: "For as many of you as were baptized into Christ have put on Christ .... And if you are Christ's, then you are Abraham's offspring, heirs according to his promise ... when we were children we were slaves to the elemental spirits of the universe. But when the time had fully come, God sent forth his Son, born of woman, born under the law, to redeem those who were under the law, so that we might receive adoption as sons. And because you are sons, God has sent the Spirit of his Son into our hearts, crying, 'Abba! Father!' So through God you are no longer a slave but a son, and if a son then an heir" (Galatians 3:27–4:7). By introducing the "Spirit of his Son" into his line of thought, Paul is opening the way for the prominent place given to the Spirit in the New Testament understanding of baptism. This is the Spirit that came on Jesus at his baptism, identifying him as the Son of God come into the world in the fullness of time. Elsewhere Paul uses the symbolic language of anointing and sealing to affirm this gift of the Spirit (2 Corinthians 1:21–22; Ephesians 1:13–14, 4:30). One cannot claim that he is alluding to baptism, but his language will fit easily with the developing theology of the rite. The Spirit given in baptism is an anointing that makes people holy to God, with the holiness that belongs primordially to Christ; it is a seal that marks them forever as belonging to God in a way that will identify and save them in the conflicts of the end times (cf. Revelation 7:2-4, 9:4). Paul also expounds the idea of sonship in connection with the work of the Spirit in Chapter 8 of Romans. He does not mention baptism there, but it is arguable that the movement of his thought is still being influenced by what he had said about baptism in Chapter 6.

The theology of baptism in the Johannine writings is done more by way of allusion than by direct reference to the rite (see Chapter 1, "Rite, Word, and Life in the New Testament"). Symbols and images drawn from the Exodus story and the preaching of the prophets about the latter days are used to deepen the understanding that Christian communities should have of their by now familiar rite of water baptism. They come in the statements of John the Baptist about Jesus (John 1:19–36), in the discussion with the Samaritan woman (4:7–15), in the discourse at the feast of Tabernacles (7:37–39), in the account of the healing of the man born blind (John 9), in describing the washing of the feet (13:1–11), and in the Passion narrative, especially in 19:31–37. These texts convey the paschal meaning of the rite of baptism (Jesus the lamb . . . blood and water . . .) and its connection with the eschatological outpouring of the Spirit. In the discourse with Nicodemus (John 3) there is a direct reference to baptism. It is presented as a rebirth "of water and the Spirit" (using, among other things, the womb symbolism of water), without which one cannot enter the kingdom of God (v. 5). The source of this baptismal rebirth is indicated by references to the Spirit (v. 8), to the cross (v. 14), to the saving will of God (the Father who sends his Son, vv. 16–18), and its acceptance is by faith (vv. 15, 18) and living according to the light (vv. 19–21).

Although it does not have explicit references to baptism, the First Letter of Peter does refer to some important baptismal themes. It has, indeed, been suggested that the first part of it is a kind of baptismal catechesis. In Chapter 1 there are references to being "born anew" (1 Peter 1:3; 1:23; cf. 2:2), through the resurrection of Jesus Christ from the dead (1:3), through "the living and abiding word of God" (1 Peter: 23). The themes of the "spiritual house" and the "holy priesthood" introduced in Chapter 2 subsequently became closely associated with the theology of baptism.

## THE THEOLOGICAL TRADITION: THE FATHERS

Baptism is so central in Christian life that there are very few Christian writers of consequence who have not contributed something to the theological tradition about it. There have also been doctrinal deviations and heresies about it, and these have given rise to definitions and directives from the *magisterium* of the Church. The tradition has been documented and analyzed by historians of doctrine (see Appendix 2: Further Reading). An important strand of it is associated with the development of the theological concept of sacrament, already outlined in Chapter 2 of this book, much of which occurred by way of reflection on baptism. Some other technical issues that have arisen will come up in the systematic theology of baptism to be presented below. Here it is enough to introduce some major theological works from different periods of the patristic tradition, and the principal magisterial texts that deal explicitly with baptism. These are texts that serious students of the theology of baptism will want to look at in their entirety and not just in occasional quotations.

The oldest theological monograph about baptism is the *De Baptismo* of Tertullian, written in North Africa about 200, while Tertullian was still a Catholic.[3] His subject in these twenty brief chapters is the rite of baptism, which he describes in some detail. To explain it he employs most of the themes and images that are provided in the New Testament; and he adds some ideas of his own associated with the word "sacrament" (cf. Chapter 2, "*sacramentum* and *mysterion*"). He sets out to explain, against some heretics who were already beginning to question it, how such ordinary things that are used in the Christian rite could produce such divine effects that were claimed

---

3. Latin text in CCSL I, 275–295; English translation in A. Souter, *Tertullian's Treatises Concerning Prayer, Concerning Baptism* (London: SPCK, 1919).

for it: in other words, he opens up the fundamental problem of sacramentality. In his explanations he uses some analogies from pagan cults, but at the same time strenuously denies that baptism is on their level. He deals with practical issues that were arising in the Church of his day—the necessity of baptism for salvation, the baptism of infants (he thinks it better to delay their baptism until they can choose Christ for themselves), the forgiveness of sins committed after baptism, the relationship between martyrdom and baptism, the baptism of heretics (which he considers valueless) and the relationship of baptism to the Eucharist. In short, he does what a theologian of baptism will always have to do: he thinks critically and coherently about the rite practiced in the Church in the light of what the Word of God has to say about it, in a way that relates it to contemporary human experience (pagan religions, military service . . .), that answers the misunderstandings and objections of heretics and nonbelievers and that gives direction on various pastoral issues that were arising in the Church.

The Mystagogical Catecheses already introduced in Chapter 2 contain classical theological teaching on baptism.[4] The subject of the Catecheses is the rite, as it has been experienced by the newly baptized. They deal with the fundamental theological issue of the sacramentality of the rite, and with its effects. They do so in a language and set of ideas that are predominantly biblical. Because of the catechetical setting in which they were given they do not give much attention to the kind of theological question that might be divisive in the Church or to philosophical explanations of how baptism works. And yet there is firm reasoning and logic in them. They give the Church a thoughtful account of its own rites of initiation that is a product of cultured classical minds, retelling the primitive scriptural story in an appropriate way to people formed in that Hellenistic culture.

Even though the Greek Fathers of the fourth century did not produce systematic treatises on baptism, they thought deeply about it. One can get the flavor of their thinking from reading a sermon on

---

4. Significant sections of the texts can be read in P. Palmer, sj, *Sacraments and Worship: Liturgy and Doctrinal Development of Baptism, Confirmation, and the Eucharist,* (London: Longmans, Green and Co., 1957) and E. Yarnold, sj, *The Awe-Inspiring Rites of Initiation: The Origins of the R.C.I.A.* 2nd ed. (The Liturgical Press: Collegeville MN, 1994).

baptism by Saint Gregory of Nazianzus (Sermon 40, PG 36, 361–396)[5]
Two ideas about baptism that were specially important for the Greek
Fathers can be found well expressed in this sermon: baptism is an
"illumination" (*photismos* in Greek); baptism is a "seal" *(sphragis)*. The
idea of illumination or light coming from Christ goes back to the
scriptures, especially to Saint John. Saint Justin uses it about baptism
in his *First Apology*, 61: "This washing is called enlightenment, because
those that are experiencing these things have their minds enlightened."
The idea is also important in the general sacramental theology of
Clement and Origen. In them and in the Greek Fathers generally it
is connected theologically with the word and the instruction that goes
with baptism, and with the insight that baptismal faith gives into the
mystery of God and its ways. It means more than intellectual knowledge: the light that illumines is also a fire that burns with the intensity
of love and the penetration of mystical insight. The idea of seal is used
by the Greek Fathers especially in connection with the work of the
Holy Spirit in baptism. It says that baptism definitively transforms,
marks, anoints, and consecrates as God's possession the one who gives
himself to Christ. Whereas in the Latin tradition the idea of seal
becomes concentrated in the concept of baptismal character, it remains
a much more comprehensive idea in the Greek Fathers, which can
draw to itself almost everything that needs to be said about baptism.

Saint Augustine develops much of his theology of sacrament
in connection with baptism, as indicated in Chapter 2, "The Latin
Tradition and St. Augustine." His *De Baptismo contra Donatistas* is a
classical statement of the theology of baptism as sacrament (PL 43,
107–244). It sets an important part of the agenda for subsequent
theology of baptism in the Latin Church. The technical development
he gives to the texts that associate baptism with the giving of a seal
contribute to the development of the theology of the baptismal character and of its status as a sign (the Latin Bible translated *sphragis* and
its cognates by using the verb *signare*). Another major contribution of
Augustine to the theology of baptism comes out of his dogmatic controversies with the Pelagians. One of the flaws that Augustine identified in their theology of grace showed in their claim that infants did

---

5. Translated in C. G. Browne and J. E. Swallow, eds. and trans. *Select Orations of Saint
Gregory Nazianzen,* LNPF ser. 2, vol. 7 (Buffalo and New York, 1900, reprinted Grand Rapids,
1952).

not need to be baptized. Augustine pointed to the Church's practice of baptizing infants and argued from it that infants need the grace that comes in baptism because they are sinners, involved in that original sin that affects all those born of Adam. In baptism they are joined to the New Adam and receive from him the grace that takes away the original sin and establishes them in holiness. Since Augustine could not imagine a baptism that would be without faith, he appeals to the faith of parents or sponsors to explain how the baptism of an infant is a true baptism. Without this baptism infants remain in original sin. If they die they cannot see the face of God. Augustine was not able to find a way out of the awful theoretical consequences of this position, which would be that unbaptized infants who die are condemned to hell. Putting them on the fringe *(limbus)* of hell was the best he could do (Sermon 244: PL 38, 1337). Later theologians would wrestle with this Augustinian problem about the fate of unbaptized infants and some would propose less drastic solutions than he did. But what they rarely called into question was the link that Augustine established between baptism and original sin. The doctrine of original sin has its biblical roots in the Pauline teaching about how the sin of Adam brought death into the world, and in the Genesis story of the Fall. It drew strength and got its theological language from the tradition of baptizing infants and from Augustine's reasoning about that (see his *De peccatorum meritis et remissione et de baptismo parvulorum ad Marcellinum* PL 44, 109–2001, esp. Lib. I). Belief in original sin eventually became an indispensable dogmatic constituent of the theology of baptism in the Western Church.

## SAINT THOMAS AQUINAS

From Scholastic theology one can profitably read the questions that Saint Thomas devotes to baptism in the *Summa* (Third Part, qq. 66–71; Blackfriars edition, vol. 57). By the time Thomas was writing baptism had become clearly separated, both ritually and theologically, from confirmation. Thomas studies it according to the technical framework for the analysis of sacrament that was becoming standard in his day: the rite itself in terms of sign, institution, essential matter and form, ceremonial, alternatives (baptism of desire and of blood); the minister; the persons who should be baptized and what is required of them; the many-sided effects of baptism; circumcision as its principal Old Testament type; the role of catechesis and exorcism in it. Thomas' theology of baptism is still a theology of the whole rite of the sacrament. It is a theology that is still patently biblical, even while it employs the technical categories of sacramentality. It also reflects the pastoral, liturgical, and even sociological (e.g., the discussion about baptizing children of Jewish parents) situation of the Church of his day. If he does set apart the essential matter and form for special analysis he does not consider his theological reflection complete until he situates this core sign within the full rite of the Church (q. 66, a.10). In his justification of the rite and his explanation of why it includes catechesis and exorcism (q. 71) he shows a traditional appreciation of the role of the word in baptism. This appears also in what he has to say about the relationship between baptism and faith—although his belief in their intrinsic connection is somewhat obscured by his insistence on the sacramental principle that a baptism can be a true sacrament even if the recipient or the minister does not have explicit faith. The faith of the Church is always present and active in a baptism (cf. q. 68, a. 9). Properly celebrated, it is a sacrament because the faith of the Church is present and active in it.

## THE REFORMATION AND TRENT

The relationship between baptism and faith became a major point of controversy at the Reformation. Later generations of Scholastics had paid relatively little attention to the place of faith in baptism and, in a general way, to the subjective side of the sacraments. It is significant that although the Decree for the Armenians issued by the Council of Florence in 1439[6] presents the faith of the Church about baptism in a definitely Scholastic schema, it omits anything that would correspond to Saint Thomas' question 68 about the persons who should receive— called the "recipients" in later theology—the sacrament. The views of the Reformers on baptism were in keeping with their view on justification and sacraments. Justification of the sinner is by faith alone;

---

6. N. P. Tanner, sj, *Decrees of the Ecumenical Councils*, vols. I and II (London and Washington: Sheed & Ward and Georgetown University Press, 1990), 540–550; J. Neuner, sj, and J. Dupuis, sj, eds., *The Christian Faith in the Doctrinal Documents of the Catholic Church*, Fifth revised and enlarged ed. (London: HarperCollins Religious, 1992; New York: Alba House, 1996), 1412.

sacraments are of value to the extent that they are signs of subjectively experienced saving faith. The sacraments of the new covenant are not really different in this from the rites and ceremonies of the old law. Of themselves they are merely works. Some Reformers (the Anabaptists) carried this principle to the point of defying the age-old tradition of baptizing infants and of never repeating a baptism for them or anyone else: they baptized only adults; and they rebaptized those who might have been baptized as infants when they came to experience justifying faith and conversion later in life. The majority of Protestants, however, respected the traditional belief that infants could and should be baptized. Nevertheless, in their theology they saw baptism as a sign of the personal faith that justified rather than as an act of God who justifies in and through the sacramental sign of faith. The canons of the Council of Trent condemning what were thought to be Protestant errors on baptism[7] have to be read in this light. It is to be noted that these canons were promulgated by Trent after its decrees on Original Sin and Justification. There is already a teaching about baptism in the Decree on Original Sin[8] and there are texts that situate baptism within the process of justification in the Decree on Justification.[9] The Reformers had no doubt that baptism had to do with the removal of original sin. But their explanations of how baptism dealt with sin were in line with their general theory of justification. To Catholics they seemed to be saying that the taking away of sin was a kind of covering-over or nonimputation rather than an effective removal. In dealing with these issues Trent gave dogmatic status to a realistic doctrine of original sin, and to a realistic role for baptism in taking it away.

## Trent to Vatican II

Catholic Counter-Reformation theology of baptism was solidly Tridentine. It used mainly Scholastic categories to expound and defend the faith of the Church. It was interested in doctrine more than in rites. When it did deal with the rite it was mainly to examine what was necessary for canonical validity, rather than to reflect on how the

---

7. Tanner, *Decrees,* vol. I, 685–686; ND 1420–1433.

8. Tanner, *Decrees,* vol. I, 665–667; ND 507–513.

9. Tanner, *Decrees,* vol. I, 671–681; ND 1928–1934.

rite could be a humanly satisfying, word-enlightened experience of
the work of salvation. But toward the end of the nineteenth century
the theology of baptism began to be affected by studies on the history
and psychology of religion, and on the history of Christian liturgy and
its interpretation in doctrine. Baptism, because of its anthropological
richness, lent itself particularly well to the general liberal interpretation of religious phenomena that was being developed around the turn
of the century. Established Catholic theology reacted strongly against
what it saw as the reductionist tendencies of this new kind of theology. The condemnation of Modernism by Pope Pius X included, in the
Decree *Lamentabili* of 1907, a reference to errors about Baptism (ND
1437–1444). But mainline theology eventually found ways of reconciling the dogmatic tradition about baptism with the new sciences. It
did for baptism what it was doing generally for sacramental theology
(chapter 2, "From Trent to Vatican II"). This is the kind of theology of
baptism that one finds in the constitution on the Church (LG, 7, 10,
11, 14) and the Decree on Ecumenism (UR, 22) of the Second Vatican
Council, and it is well respected by the canonical prescription about
baptism in the 1983 Code of Canon Law (can. 849–878). It appears
in the Introductions to the revised liturgical rites and in the Catechism
of the Catholic Church.

## ECUMENICAL CONVERGENCE

The theology of baptism promoted by the Second Vatican Council
is shared in its main lines by theologians of Orthodox, Anglican, and
most Protestant churches. However, Baptist theologians, maintaining a strong Reformation understanding of justification, continue to
affirm the need for personal faith in Baptism, and their churches will
only baptize those who can and actually do confess faith in Jesus as
Savior. Their position is often shared by Christians of Evangelical
and Pentecostal communities. That position was also put forward
with high theological seriousness in the early twentieth century by
Karl Barth. In a lecture published in English as *The Teaching of the
Church regarding Baptism*[10] he argued that, because justification was

---

10. K. Barth, *The Teaching of the Church Regarding Baptism,* trans. from German (of 1943)
(London: SCM Press, 1948).

by faith in God's word of promise, baptism only made sense as an expression of personal faith and conversion. He did not, then, see a place for infant baptism in the Church. Barth built his case on an exegesis of the New Testament texts about justification and baptism. He claimed that the reasons why infant baptism had been introduced and maintained in the Church, even by the major leaders of the Reformation, were extraneous to scriptural teaching and often of a political nature. Not all admirers of Barth followed his views on baptism. His exegetical arguments were countered by Cullmann and Jeremias. Catholic theologians also contributed to the debate on exegetical grounds.[11]

Major ecumenical work on baptism has been done by the Faith and Order Commission of the World Council of Churches, expressed particularly in its document commonly known as BEM.[12] The particular question of the practical recognition by churches of one another's baptisms was subsequently addressed by the Joint Working Group between the Roman Catholic Church and the World Council of Churches (JWG) and its findings are printed as an appendix to its Eighth Report (1999–2005). The largely positive responses of so many churches to BEM (see Chapter 2, "Ecumenical Convergence on Sacraments") show how far Christians have come together in their theological understanding of baptism. The responses do show up some problem areas that still remain for discussion between the churches. In the official Catholic response to BEM there is a request for greater clarity in the notion of sacrament being used to describe baptism and for more attention to the ecclesiological significance of baptism. There is a call for explicit attention to the doctrine of original sin in defining the range and kind of sinfulness that is overcome by baptism, for a clearer exposition of the necessity of baptism for human salvation, for a treatment of the "seal of the Spirit" that might explain why baptism is not repeated, and for more clarity in stating the relationship between baptism and confirmation. These are doctrinal concerns expressed in rather distinctive Catholic terms. Ecumenically minded Catholic theologians will have to continue working to see how it is possible to gain acceptance for ways of expressing their Church's faith about baptism

---

11. See J. Duplacy in George, *Baptism in the New Testament*, 118–158.

12. *Baptism, Eucharist and Ministry*. Faith and Order Paper no. 111 (Geneva: WCC, 1982).

that might be less reliant on its own theological language and more open to formulations around which all the churches could unite.

# A Systematic Essay

To do a systematic theology of baptism is to try to see with some clarity how God is at work in the rite, gracing a crucial moment of human life, in a way that brings people toward their fulfilment in God. To do this one has inevitably to use a whole structured set of ideas, worked out in other areas of systematic theology, about God and the world, about God's grace and human response to it, about the sending and mediatorial work of Christ, about the Holy Spirit and the Church, about the general pattern of sacramentality that marks the gracing of human life and its return to God in the Church, through Christ and the Spirit. For a Christian theology of baptism one has to use ideas that are the fruit of reflection on the Christian tradition of faith. For systematic theology these ideas have to be made intellectually coherent. And they have to be made to reflect real human experience if they are to provide a word that will help Christians to relate whatever is being thought about theologically—in this case the rite of baptism— to their real life.

## Summary Statement about Baptism

One can begin with a summary statement of what a systematic theology might say about baptism. This is presented neither as a thesis about, nor a definition of baptism, but as a convenient organized putting together of the important things that have to be said about baptism. They will be taken in order in the commentary that follows. A few other issues that are not made explicit in this summary will be dealt with after the commentary, under the heading of "Additional Questions." The commentary will be using material from the tradition of faith about baptism that has already been presented in this chapter ("New Testament" through "Ecumenical Convergence"). The ideas will not be documented again. The value of a systematic essay should lie in the clarity it brings to an already known tradition of faith. It should be an *intellectus fidei* that reviews an *auditus fidei*. The proposed summary reads:

Baptism is a work of God, in which God realizes his intention of giving salvation and the forgiveness of sin to all humankind, by incorporating into Christ, through regeneration in the grace of the Holy Spirit and adoption to divine sonship, those who believe in the gospel and are converted from sin; this work is realized in and through the Church, which is the community of those who proclaim Christ's death and resurrection and reenact it in a water rite that, as a sacrament, signifies and effects regeneration, incorporation, and adoption by Father, Son, and Holy Spirit.

## A Work of God

If systematic theology is presenting things from God's point of view, the first thing it must say about baptism is that God is acting in it. This is to say what the tradition has been wanting to say about baptism from the beginning by calling it a mystery and later a sacrament. It is to call into play for the understanding of baptism the whole theological analysis of God's being and action, which carries the mind beyond myth to metaphysics. It is to affirm the ontological ground and reality of baptism. It is also to require that the celebration of baptism be in some way a mystical, contemplative experience, an experience of God, without being for that any less a human experience.

## Salvation to All

Systematic theology analyzes the history of salvation from God's point of view. A fundamental principle of the analysis is that God wishes all to be saved. In this present phase of the history of salvation baptism embodies that divine intention. It is offered to all—Jew and Greek, slave and free, man and woman. It is a simple rite using an element that is universally available and having a symbolism that is universally appealing. It is carried throughout the world by believers with a missionary urgency that sometimes borders on the reckless, and is administered with a generosity that is always prepared to give the benefit of the doubt. For it is believed to be the gift of a God who wishes all to be saved by it. If it is claimed to be necessary for salvation this is thought to be a blessing, not a constraint. God's saving action will never be restricted to its actual use. There are other theological principles, to be considered in a moment, that require a certain moderating of the passion to baptize everyone. But they will not deaden the missionary urgency to baptize because they do not negate the principle that baptism embodies the universal salvific will of God.

## The Forgiveness of Sin

The history of salvation that is analyzed in systematic theology is the revelation of a loving, merciful God. The full depth of this loving mercy is seen in a salvation that is not just the divinization of creatures but is also the justification of sinners. In theology, "sin" is more than ethical failure and deviation from moral norms. It is also, and primarily, a paradoxical reflection of the mercy of God. It can be called *felix culpa*, "happy fault," in the Easter Proclamation. Sin is only perceived for what it is in the light of the mercy of God: it is recognized to be a human refusal to respond to the love of God, a love that in accepting God for what God is, accepts humans for the frailty and fallibility that is theirs as creatures. Correspondingly, the mercy of God is the assurance that, as far as God is concerned, sin is there to be forgiven. The universal salvation that gives divine meaning to baptism entails the forgiveness of sin. Indeed, the salvation given by baptism is sometimes described in the scriptures simply as the forgiveness of sin (e.g., Acts 2:38). This is also how the Church's faith in baptism came to be formulated in the Creed of Nicaea-Constantinople: "We acknowledge one Baptism for the forgiveness of sins."

When the scriptures and the creeds say baptism is "for the forgiveness of sins" they are referring to the full range of sins that adult humans commit, and that they repent of when they are baptized. Baptism is for the remission of personal sins. But there is in the theological tradition another facet of sin that has had a profound influence on the theological understanding of baptism. It is expressed in the doctrine of original sin. One has to be careful about the way this doctrine is used in the theology of baptism. While belief in universal human sinfulness, stemming from Adam and Eve, is taught clearly in scripture, the distinctive doctrine of original sin, as it emerged notably in Augustine, is very much bound up with reflection on the baptism of infants in the context of the controversy with Pelagianism. To make the forgiveness of original sin in this sense be the distinctive purpose of baptism is to make infant rather than adult baptism the model for understanding the sacrament. This carries the risk of obscuring the personal response that God requires of sinners when he forgives them in baptism. It could make the personal sins of an adult seem some kind of secondary condition that has to be remedied incidentally in the sacrament. It could encourage the tendency, which always has to be resisted by Catholic sacramental theology, to think of baptism as having some kind of automatic, quasi-magical effectiveness in relation to original sin. Such a view does justice neither to baptism nor to original sin. Infants are given the grace of God in baptism: it is a grace for "the forgiveness of sins" because they have inherited sinfulness from Adam and can only be sanctified by having that link with Adam broken. The inheritance of Adam takes a different existential form in adults. They make a decision about it in their personal moral life. They either choose God, and by that very fact are freed from all their sin; or they refuse God, and to that extent "convert" original sin into personal sins. It is this personalized sin of theirs that is forgiven in baptism. That is why the sacrament is designed to call forth personal faith and conversion. One can go on from there to provide a theological explanation of how this principle is verified in infant baptism. It is much more difficult to give personal faith and conversion their due place in the theology of baptism if one starts with infants and their original sin.

On this issue of baptism and sin it is important to keep firmly in mind the connection between sin and death that is central in Paul's reflection on what came to be called original sin. While later theology found the key to the universality of sin in our being born from Adam, Paul finds it rather in the death we inherit from Adam. Death is the manifestation of our sinfulness in all its forms. And everyone dies. Salvation and the forgiveness of sin will somehow have to make sense of universal death and in doing so overcome it. This is the perspective that will allow one to understand baptism as a rite of death and life, in which sin is overcome. It will also allow one to understand why all humans are called to baptism.

With deliverance from sin and death comes liberation from all the forces that promote death and evil throughout the universe. These powers of death are variously imagined and conceived in the Christian tradition. The liturgy of baptism uses the biblical images of the Devil and of the worldly institutions that seem to represent his dark power and pressure on humans to refuse the reign of God and the saving Spirit of Christ. Baptism is an act of faith in the victory of Christ over these powers of darkness. The baptized renounce them and are made aware that, in the power of the sacrament, they are delivered from them.

## Incorporating into Christ

The most distinctive component of Christian systematic theology is the analysis of how God's will to save humankind is realized in the sending of his Son to be human in solidarity with all other humans, to live with them, to die for them, to rise from the dead as the firstborn of a new creation, to send the Spirit into the world for completing the work of salvation, and to come again at the end to restore all things to his Father. Christ is recognized as the only Savior. He was that in anticipation for those who lived before his coming. He is so for all those who are now alive and for those yet to be born. The issue of salvation is now somehow or other a choice for or against Christ. This is the Christological presupposition of baptism. To be baptized is to choose Christ as the only Savior.

To choose Christ is to choose a very specific way of salvation. In choosing one who saved by dying and rising from the dead, one is accepting that life comes out of death. One is accepting that the overcoming of sin is done by the overcoming of death. Jesus is one of us who went through death without sin, crowning with his death a life of loving obedience to God his Father that had never been marred by any sin. His passage to resurrection is the definitive human victory over death and over sin. This is the soteriological ground of baptism. Christ invited those who would be saved from their sins to die with him in order to rise again. He described his own death as a baptism and was actually baptized in a ritual anticipation of the death he would die "to fulfill all righteousness" (Matthew 3:15). It is because of this, confirmed by an explicit command attributed to himself in the gospels, that to choose Christ as Savior is, in practice, to choose baptism. The choice for Christ is indeed, made by faith. But faith is a decision to identify with this concrete historical person, whose gospel says that he is available for this kind of contact in the rite of baptism. The words are categorical. One cannot have Christ without baptism. The qualifications made in "The Forgiveness of Sin" have to be made again here. As God has ways of saving those who do not explicitly choose him,

so God has ways of saving those who do not explicitly choose Christ.
God has ways of saving those who are not actually baptized. However,
the necessity of baptism as the way of contacting Christ remains a
central affirmation of Christian faith, and a central motivation of
Christian missionary effort.

The contact with Christ that is made in baptism is called
incorporation. The word is derived from the Latin word for body
*(corpus)*. Human contacts occur in and through the body. Life on all
its levels is transmitted through bodily contact. Systematic theology
has an analysis of how Christ in his body is the instrument of God's
saving action, and of how the life of grace is communicated to us by
bodily contact with Christ. Baptism is the first moment of contact,
and it is a contact that holds. The other sacraments, and particularly
the Eucharist, develop the contact. Because it is the first and basic
contact with the body of Christ, baptism is said to incorporate us into
him. This theology is, of course, derived from Paul's teaching about
the body of Christ. His ideas will have to be discussed more fully in
a moment when the ecclesiological principles engaged in baptism are
being looked at. For the present it is enough to note the bodily realism
that is inherent in Paul's Christology and soteriology, and in his understanding of how humans lay hold of salvation in Christ. In statements
like "Do you not know that your bodies are members of Christ . . . ?"
(1 Corinthians 6:15) he is inviting theology to give a strongly realistic
interpretation to that first life-giving contact with Christ that occurs
in baptism and that is called incorporation.

## Regeneration in the Grace of the Holy Spirit

Systematic theology can analyze the reality of the Holy Spirit on different levels. On the Trinitarian level it studies the person of the Spirit
and the mission of the Spirit in relation to the Father and the Son.
The concrete realization of the mission of the Spirit is studied in the
theology of creation and of grace. It is on this level that the biblical
story of the Spirit, starting at creation and culminating in Pentecost,
and the theological reflection of the New Testament authors on this
gift, can be analyzed. The Spirit is the ultimate gift of God's love,
who creates and recreates the universe, peopling it with children of
God by giving a new life of grace to those who were dead in sin. The

Spirit, sent by Christ from the Father, is the immediate divine agent
of the justification of sinners, and the grace of the Holy Spirit, (called
habitual or sanctifying) is the created transformation that makes saints
of sinners.

The action of the Spirit in baptism, and the corresponding
effect of it in the person being baptized, is well described by the word
regeneration. It is one of the classical words in the tradition about baptism. Taken literally, it simply means rebirth but imaginatively it draws
its color from the rite that it describes, which is a passage through
the waters of death and burial to a new birth from the womb of those
same waters. It suits the creating and life-giving role attributed to the
Spirit in Scripture and the Creed. It is the pneumatological counter-
part of incorporation: it says that baptism makes one be alive in the
Body of Christ by giving one rebirth in the Spirit.

Christian baptism is in water and the Holy Spirit. The Spirit
is active in Baptism and is given in it. Scriptural and patristic statements about the gift of the Spirit in baptism are frequent and clear.
What has led to some uncertainty in the tradition is the attempt of
theology, begun perhaps already in the New Testament, to relate the
different phases of the work of salvation to different phases of the rites
of Christian initiation. Acts 8:14–17 seems to associate the gift of the
Spirit with a laying on of hands by the apostles that could be separated
from the water rite of baptism in the name of Jesus. In some of the
patristic theologies of initiation the gift of the Spirit is associated with
an anointing and "sealing" that follows the baptismal bathing. As long
as Christian initiation was a single, continuous rite, all of which could
be called baptism, there was little danger that this line of thought
would separate the gift of the Spirit from the water rite of baptism.
However, when the rite called confirmation came to be recognized as
a sacrament distinct from baptism, having a certain independence of
it, some theologies thought they could define its distinct theological
meaning by reserving the gift of the Holy Spirit to it, leaving baptism
to be defined Christologically: baptism would be entry into the death
and resurrection of Christ, confirmation would be the acceptance
of the Pentecostal gift of the Spirit. This question will be dealt with
later, when the ritual and theological tradition about confirmation has
been examined. For the present it is enough to say that it is theologically inconceivable that baptism could be incorporation into Christ,

the forgiveness of sins, and the laying hold of God's salvation without being also the grace of the Holy Spirit.

## Adoption to Divine Sonship

Those who are regenerated in the Spirit and incorporated in the Son of necessity become children of the Father: they become "sons in the Son." Here one might like to replace "son" in the translation with "child." However, one needs to note that in Paul "son" carries connotations of inheritance rights that "child" does not. Whatever translation is used it means that women and men share equally in the inheritance rights of Christ, in whom there is neither male nor female. The theme of adoptive sonship is constant in the tradition about baptism. Along with regeneration and incorporation it reflects the Trinitarian pattern of the sacrament. It is the distinctive action of the Father in baptism and expresses the distinctive relationship that the baptized have to him.

## Believers are Converted

The mystery of grace is that the Holy Spirit actually causes the very human response in which grace is received, and that the response remains fully human and fully free. Systematic theology does the best it can to understand this mystery of how the works of grace are simultaneously gift and free moral choice. It is such a theology of grace that one needs in order to understand how the gift of God in baptism requires human acts of moral choice. This is a theology of justification. It is affected by the controversies of the Reformation and, for Catholics, is guided by the dogmatic decrees of the Council of Trent. All Christians agree that baptism requires faith and conversion on the part of the one being baptized. The catechumenate that prepares for baptism is a school of faith and conversion. The water rite with its words is a decisive act of faith and conversion. A ritual washing even with the appropriate words that is not being met somehow by faith and conversion is not Christian baptism. Faith here means an assent to and choice of Christ as Savior, not just for the generality of humans but specifically in one's own personal regard. It is an assent to his person as witnessed to and catechized by the word of teaching that is spoken in the apostolic Church. It is an assent to Christ through

assent to credal statements of the Church and such dogmatic teachings as have been found necessary for their elucidation and defense.
Conversion is a turning away from sin in a turning toward God: it is
a life-changing decision to put an end to sin in one's life and to make
a beginning of life in the new creation inaugurated by Christ and the
Spirit. In this sense faith and conversion belong to the most radical level of moral choice. They have to if they are to correspond to
the radicalness of baptism. Baptism is about a decision for or against
the God who saves the world in Christ. It brings one to the crucial
moment of choice between life and death. To call it a crucial moment
is to evoke the cross ("crucial" comes from *crux*, the Latin word for
cross) where the issue of life and death was played out to its ultimate,
prototypical conclusion. To accept baptism is to choose life over death.
It is to pass from death to life. Only a choice as radical as that made in
faith and conversion could give human reality to that passage.

Catholic no less than Protestant theology sees faith and conversion as gifts of God. But there are theological differences between
the Catholic and Protestant view of how the human effort that goes
into them is evaluated morally and anthropologically. The Catholic
tradition sees no threat to the gift of God in crediting human choices
with moral and meritorious value. It sees grace as a transformation
of the ontological roots of human behavior more than as a subjective stirring of the spirit. It has an approach to baptism that is cool
and pedagogical by comparison with the appeal to strong subjective
faith-experiences of sinfulness and of being forgiven that seems more
typically Protestant. The Catholic tradition can claim, too, that its
ontological view of grace can offer a better explanation of how the
requirement of faith and conversion are met in the baptism of infants
(see below, "The Baptism of Children"). The Protestant theology of
grace is more likely to find the practice problematical.

## In and Through the Church

A systematic theology will include an ecclesiology, in which it will
explain how the grace of Christ and the Spirit is mediated through
the community of believers, and how it builds those who are being
saved into the body of Christ and the temple of the Spirit, until Christ
comes again to restore all things to the Father. The Church "is at the

same time both community of the redeemed and redeeming institution" (Chapter 3, "The Church, Sacrament of Christ"). This two-sided
reality of the Church is, in one sense, the fruit of reflection on the
whole sacramental economy. Once it has been established, however, it
becomes an important key for understanding baptism, and particularly
why it is said to have the twofold effect of grace and character.

The Church is a "redeeming institution," or instrument of
salvation, in that it is a community equipped to preach the gospel
and celebrate rites in which people take the gospel into their lives
and make it their own personal story. In its preaching and its rites the
Church makes Christ present to people in a tangible way and gives
the Spirit in an experiential way. It is in the community of the Church
that Christ is contacted in the body and people are incorporated into
him. Here one must take up again Paul's idea of the Church as body
of Christ. The Church is the body of Christ in the sense that any
organized group of people can be called a body. But Paul transforms
the banal, metaphorical use of the term with the physical realism
that he sees in the contact there is between Christ and those who are
joined to him by grace. To say that the Church is the body of Christ
is to say that it is a socially organized group of people who, in the
diversity of their gifts and services, do bodily things like speaking and
caring and ritualizing, by which they bring those who are to be saved
(including themselves) into bodily contact with Christ. Baptism is
the first full contact that is offered. In it the Church joins people to
the body of Christ, incorporating them into him. In that very process it incorporates them into itself. Being made members of Christ,
they simultaneously are made members of the Church. They begin to
act as Church people, joining in the task of building up the community as body of Christ. Their action brings the gift of the Holy Spirit,
from which flow new life, spiritual gifts, and lively participation in the
communion and mission of the Church, to themselves and to others.
To be baptized is to make oneself part of the Church as community of
the redeemed. It is to be ready to take full part in the Eucharist as the
banquet of those who are saved in Christ. It is to contribute one's gifts
to making the Church the instrument of salvation for others as well as
for oneself.

Here one has the ecclesiological correlative of the two levels of
effectiveness that are claimed for baptism: it is said to give a character

and to give grace. It is grace that makes the Church be the community of saints. But the Church itself cooperates in the receiving and giving of that grace. The cooperation takes bodily form: it is done by acts of speaking, caring, and ritualizing, in each of which there is giving and receiving. As ecclesial actions these are Christ-actions. They are recognized to be his actions because they are done by people who are baptized. Baptism qualifies and equips them to represent him. It is this ability that is technically called the baptismal character. In Scholastic language the character is said to be the *res et sacramentum* of baptism. It is a *res* (reality) in that it is signified and given by the rite of baptism (which is the *sacramenturn tantum*). It is simultaneously a *sacramentum* (sign) because it marks a person out as someone who can make the symbolic actions of the Church be actions of Christ, and therefore grace giving (grace being the ultimate *res tantum* of every sacrament). If it is by the grace of baptism that Christians are built into the body of Christ, which is the Church, it is by the baptismal character that they themselves participate in the making of the sacrament that gives this grace.

The baptismal character is said to be a sharing in the priesthood of Christ. The Church is able to mediate salvation only because it contains within itself the priestly mediation of Christ. This priestly quality of its mediation is realized in its celebration of sacraments. It sets up a system of ritual worship that is grace giving because it is the visible realization of the priestly worship of Christ: it is so because the members of the Church share in different ways in the priesthood of Christ. This sharing has been identified since Saint Thomas with the sacramental characters. When the baptismal character is said to be a sharing in Christ's priesthood it is being defined as a qualification to perform ritual acts of worship in the Church that Christ will make to be individual instances of his priestly work of salvation.

Because there is giving and receiving of grace in the Church, the priesthood of Christ is shared in different ways by those who minister and by those who receive. The way of the recipient has a real priority. Christ can only be expected to make his priestly action available when someone calls out for it and is open to it. It is only in the face of a recipient that a minister acts in the Church. A person who is being baptized makes a gesture of appeal and openness to grace undergoing the rite. The minister of the rite makes a gesture of giving.

Their interaction makes it possible for Christ to realize his priestly action in the sacrament. If a person being baptized can make this priestly contribution to his own baptism it must be because baptism itself gives a sharing in Christ's priesthood that then becomes operative in the sacrament. That is precisely what the character (as *res et sacramentum*) is claimed to be. It is an effect of baptism that allows a person to participate in his or her own sanctification. It is a sharing in Christ's priesthood that makes the sacrament be an act of Christ on the recipient's own behalf. Because it is for receiving, the baptismal character has been described as a passive power. This does not mean the role of the participant in baptism is merely passive. He or she has to do something—all participation in sacraments is active. But what is done symbolizes receiving rather than giving. It is the minister who represents the giving side of the sacrament and shows forth that side of the Church. This is true even when the one who ministers is not an ordained person, as in a baptism done by a layperson or even by a nonbeliever. They represent the Church as the giver of salvation. It is even more obvious when the minister is ordained. The character of Order is said to be active. But the active characters build on the passive ones and depend on them. Without baptismal sharing in Christ's priesthood the sacraments would not be what they are supposed to be and the Church would not be what it is believed to be.

There is another truth about the Church that is reflected in the distinction made between grace and character in baptism. There are sinners as well as saints in the Church. There are baptized people who fall back into sin. There may even be people who were baptized but never accepted the grace of the Holy Spirit. There is the possibility of rejecting the Spirit even in the very act of baptism. Something can go wrong with the faith and conversion that is the personal moral reality of baptism. The very communion of grace that binds people together in the body of Christ can be refused. If all faith and conversion were refused there would simply be no baptism, because there would be a deliberate refusal to give the rite any Christian or ecclesial significance. There would be no intention of being baptized. But it is possible for a person to refuse conversion and the normal consequences of faith, and yet maintain some kind of assent to and vague yearning for the salvation that is offered in baptism. To do that would be to go along with what the Church thinks it is doing in baptism (to "have the intention of doing what the Church does"). In that case the Church truly baptizes. The baptized person takes hold of something of Christ, even if not accepting full incorporation into him. He or she becomes a member of the Church. The possibility is kept open that at some future date the baptized person might be able to take advantage of being in the Church to accept the gift of the Spirit by full faith and conversion. The Latin tradition spoke in this sense of a "revival" *(revivificentia)* of sacraments.[13] There is a theological explanation of this possibility in the baptismal character. It is seen as a real belonging to Christ. The one who has it can never be totally rejected by the Church (there may, of course, be various disciplinary degrees of exclusion) but must be ministered to for his or her salvation. Such people may also themselves minister to the salvation of others. When they are eventually brought to faith and conversion their decision will be referred back to their original baptism. They will never need to be baptized again. The character thus understood is a power that abides, because one never ceases to be baptized and one can always claim to act in virtue of one's baptismal status. It marks one on a very deep level of one's personality (in a body/soul anthropology it is said to be a quality or mark of the soul), because it is concerned with that most profound of personal choices, which is to believe or not to believe in the salvation offered by Christ.

The ecumenical force of baptism can also be articulated by the distinction between grace and character. When the communion of love is broken in the Church and the ministries of grace of one ecclesial community are refused by or to another, people find themselves being baptized into different churches. And yet there is one baptism of Christ that incorporates into His Church. When ecumenical efforts begin to be made to restore unity the motive force is surely grace, the grace that overcomes the sins of separation. It is a grace that, like the "revived" grace of baptism in those who received the sacrament without repentance, comes from their baptism. The oneness of baptism remains a constant bond, unspoiled by the sins that brought about the original divisions, or by those that hardened them in time and that

---

13. See E. Schillebeeckx, *Christ, the Sacrament of Encounter with God* (London/New York: Sheed & Ward, 1963), 181ff.

weigh today on those who have inherited them. It is a designation
and a call in every Christian to restore the unity of Christ's Church.
It is more basic than grace because it is an ontological urge that keeps
prompting Christians even when they are yet far from that full baptismal grace that will unite the churches in love. Ecumenical Christians
see in one another's baptism a permanent reality—and Catholics can
call it the character—that is a shared belonging to Christ and to his
one Church, and an openness to grace and to the ecclesial ministries
of grace once they can be identified and agreed upon. Just as the fact
of being baptized remains a lifeline for sinners within the Church and
can eventually bring them to the ministries of grace, so it is a bond for
separated Christians that points them ontologically towards a common search for full communion in grace and for shared access to the
ministries of grace. It is a powerful bond, because it entitles Christians
to call on the unfailing priesthood of Christ that is drawing all things
into grace and communion.

If baptism builds up the Church in both the giving and the
receiving of grace, it is important for the understanding of the sacrament to remember that the Church is the instrument of salvation
(giver of grace) only in order that it may become the communion of
saints (receiver of grace). The instrumentality of the Church, and all
that the sacramental characters stand for, will end with the coming
of the Lord at the Parousia and only the communion of grace will
remain. The baptismal character is functional and is at the service of
baptismal holiness. Incorporation into Christ in the Church is meant
to be a growth towards the full maturity of being in Christ, through a
progressive transformation by the Holy Spirit. It is meant to be part
of a collective growth of the body of Christ in which faith and conversion grow into love and communion. This is the full ecclesial effect of
baptism. It is where baptism reaches into the Eucharist.

## Proclaims Death and Resurrection Rite

Since it is by his death and resurrection that Christ is the universal
Savior, it is as dying and rising that the Church must present him
to those who are to be saved. It does so by telling the story of those
events and proclaiming their meaning for human life in its preaching.

Within that preaching it celebrates baptism as a rite in which humans act out a dying and rising that they believe to be the dying and rising of Christ: they go down to be buried with him in the waters of death and come forth cleansed, refreshed, reborn to resurrection. Baptism is the first point of contact and identification with the body of Christ. It is incorporation into Christ by identifying with what he did—living and dying and rising—in his own body.

## Sacrament That Signifies and Effects

At this point a general theology of sacraments (see Chapter 3) can make its contribution to the understanding of baptism. The water rite and words are a sign, in the sense that term has in sacramental theology. They provide people with a congenial human experience through which God's action is mediated to them and their own response is simultaneously expressed. The experience is congenial for all the reasons that sacramental theology gives for the use of signs in human sanctification. In practice, a considerable pedagogy may be needed to make it so, using the kind of images and ideas dealt with earlier in this chapter and in Chapter 4.

The rite and words of baptism, when properly performed, cause what they signify. The technical analysis of sacramental causality (see Chapter 3, "Sacramental Effectiveness") can help to put order and a certain philosophical toughness into one's understanding of the process that has been described in the preceding commentary. The action of God, of Christ in his humanness, of the Church in its community and ministers, and of the participant can, in a Scholastic-type theology, be coordinated in terms of principal and secondary as well as instrumental causality—provided that is done in a way that respects the proper causality of signs. A theology working with phenomenological tools of analysis will do the same thing in the categories of personal encounter. There can also be technical explanations of how an obstacle can be put in the way of the grace of baptism so that no grace effect is produced even though there is a real sacrament.

The effect of baptism is described as "regeneration, incorporation, and adoption." The fact that it takes three ideas to describe it is a reflection of the Trinitarian God who works in it. God has revealed himself in the events of the history of human salvation to be Father,

Son, and Spirit. Each divine Person has been revealed in a distinctive personal role and relationship. Baptism brings that total work of salvation to bear on the individual being saved by invoking the divine Persons by their biblical names and calling forth a Trinitarian profession of faith; it signifies and causes the distinctive effect of each divine person and relates the person being baptized to each of them in a distinctive way.

## ADDITIONAL THEOLOGICAL QUESTIONS

There are other questions that a sacramental theology may want to ask in its own particular terms about baptism. Among them are: what are the precise elements and words that make up the essential sign (the "matter and form"); how was the sacrament instituted; who is its minister; what are its effects? These questions can be answered readily enough on the basis of the ideas and information about baptism already presented. The essential sign is made up of a bathing in water and the Trinitarian words. The institution (see Chapter 3, "Divine Institution") is attributed explicitly to Christ in the New Testament. The normal minister of it is bishop, priest, or deacon, but "in imminent danger of death and especially at the moment of death, when no priest or deacon is available, any member of the faithful, indeed anyone with the right intention, may and sometimes must administer baptism" (*General Introduction to the Rite of Christian Initiation*, 16); what is required of the minister is the intention of doing what the Church does, which is normally verified by the correct and respectful carrying-out of the rite of the Church. The effects of baptism are the grace of incorporation into Christ, regeneration in the Holy Spirit and adoption by the Father, as well as the baptismal character.

In the history of theology one can find elaborate discussion about each of these points. Some of it came out of meticulous philosophical enquiry. Much of it, however, originated in a rather ritualistic and legalistic approach to sacraments, and in the need to solve corresponding problems of pastoral casuistry. The recovery of a more traditional sense of sacrament has made many of the details of those debates rather irrelevant. One admires the calm and simple statements about baptism and its requirements in the *General Introduction to the*

*Rite of Christian Initiation* of 1972. They provide a sensible perspective for dealing with most of the practical questions and intellectual curiosities that are likely to arise about baptism.

There are, however, some theological questions about the necessity of baptism for salvation that can still benefit from a somewhat extended discussion. There is little difficulty about the application of the principles concerning the necessity of sacraments for salvation (Chapter 3, "Participants and Ministers") to baptism in the case of those who know about it and can actually be baptized. They are quite simply refusing salvation if they culpably refuse baptism. It is pointed out in this context that the necessity in question is not just something that arises from a command *(necessitas precepti)* but that it arises from the very nature of things *(necessitas medii)*. There is an ontological, not just a legal connection between baptism and salvation. A consequence of this is that those who do not know about baptism, or who cannot be baptized, are not simply dispensed from it. A distinction is made between the reality of baptism *(res)* and the rite *(sacramentum)*. One of these can be had without the other. Those who through no fault of their own cannot receive the rite of baptism must receive the reality of it, whether they know it or not, if they are to be saved. How they do it has been thought about theologically in the Church in connection with three questions: (1) the salvation of those who, although not baptized in water, make a personal choice for salvation in what are called baptism of blood and baptism of desire; (2) the baptism of children; (3) the fate of children who die without baptism.

## Baptism of Blood and of Desire

The scriptural texts that require baptism for salvation (Matthew 28:19; Mark 16:16; John 3:5) seem categorical. No alternatives are offered to those who want to be saved after the resurrection. The assumption seems to be that there could be no neutrality about the God of the Lord Jesus Christ. If one did not accept him one was rejecting him, either by clinging to the God of the Law or by worshipping the gods of Greece and Rome. Though the principle enunciated in 1 Timothy 2:3–4 ("God our Savior, who desires all men to be saved and to come to the knowledge of the truth") is maintained, the earliest known Christian admissions that people are actually saved without the rite of baptism come from the third and fourth centuries (Hippolytus, *Apostolic Tradition*, XIX, 2; Irenaeus, *Adversus Haereses*, III, 16, 4; Cyprian, *Letter 73, ad Jubaianum*; Ambrose, *De Obitu Valentiniani*, 51: *PL* 16, 1374–1375). They are about catechumens who die before they can be baptized, especially when they die as martyrs. They are, therefore, about people who already believe in Jesus Christ as Savior and accept his Church. If they are martyred for his name they do realistically what baptism is designed to do ritually. Their death, indeed, expresses their faith in a better and more decisive way than ritual baptism: they actually die with Christ, with a view to sharing in his resurrection; they become members of the heavenly Church even though they have never been full members of the earthly Church. In these early texts and in the subsequent tradition martyrdom is called a baptism of blood. That terminology says something about martyrdom and it says something about baptism. About baptism, it says that the reality of the sacrament is brought about essentially by faith in Christ and sharing in his death: any significant human action that manifests these choices unequivocally is entitled to be called a baptism. About martyrdom, the term baptism of blood says that shedding one's blood gives salvation only to the extent that it is an act of faith in and imitation of the death of Christ: only when dying stands for what the rite of baptism stands for does it guarantee salvation and resurrection. The martyr can do without ritual baptism because he or she achieves the reality that the rite is designed to express, and eventually to cause, in another, more immediate way. Saint Thomas (Third Part, q. 66, a. 12) and Catholic theology generally considers baptism of blood to be an even better way of salvation than ritual baptism. In this it is also saying that what should be aimed at in ritual baptism is the kind of faith and identification with Christ unto death that the martyrs show.

Reflection on martyrdom let theology see that what goes on in the mind and heart of a person can have a baptismal effect whether it is expressed in the rite of baptism or in some other significant way. That modified the seeming intransigence of the biblical texts about the necessity of baptism, and made it easier to recognize that anybody who lived and died well could be said to be baptized and therefore saved. The earliest texts on this envisage only the case of catechumens who died before there was time to baptize them. They had faith and conversion and the intention to be baptized. This intention found expression in their acceptance of the catechumenate. But it also found expression in their death which, presumably, they experienced in faith as a dying in Christ. Such a readiness to die in Christ was inherent in their intention to be baptized. The term that eventually emerged to describe this way of salvation is "baptism of desire." Like the term "baptism of blood" it says that the reality of salvation is gained essentially by faith and conversion that are somehow related to dying in Christ. Actual death takes the place of ritual dying also in this case. But natural death does not have the inherent challenge to the Christian that death by martyrdom does. To refuse ritual baptism on the grounds that one would eventually be baptized in one's own death would be to refuse the very guarantee given in the gospel that one's death would be Christian. Catholic theology has accompanied its teaching about baptism of desire with a warning that anyone who, knowing what the gospel says about the necessity of baptism for salvation, does not take reasonable steps to be baptized in water cannot claim to be saved through baptism of desire. (The magisterial statements on the necessity of baptism, at least of desire, for salvation are in ND 510, 1405, 1408, 1419, 1424, 1437/42, 1928.)

The concept of baptism of desire can be sustained easily enough when it is postulated for catechumens who die before being baptized. Baptism of desire, in this case, includes an actual desire of baptism. It is more difficult to see why it should be postulated for explaining the salvation of the far greater number of people who know nothing whatever about baptism and have no explicit faith in Christ. A case might be made for doing a theological turnabout on the question: one might first work out a general theology of salvation without any reference to baptism, and then introduce baptism as a particular, privileged way of salvation for those who are called to the Christian faith; there would then be no need to postulate a baptism of desire for those who know nothing about Christ or baptism. In favor of this view, one might even appeal to the fact that Vatican II does not use the term "baptism of desire" when explaining in LG 16 how nonbelievers are saved and belong to the People of God. However, while such a theology might seem to have some advantages, it would have lost one of the compelling ways for understanding the centrality of Christ in God's plan of salvation, the place of the Church in it, and the claims of Christian eschatology. The necessity of some

form of baptism for salvation is an expression of these great truths of
Christian faith.

To dispense with the postulate of baptism of desire would
deprive Christian theology of a valuable image for expressing the belief
that the salvation to be found in any religion or ethical system ultimately rejoins the salvation that is given in Christ and in his Church.
All salvation requires a successful coping with the mystery of life and
death. Christian faith affirms that anyone who lives well, in accordance
with conscience, is being saved. The notion of conscience supposes
some form of belief in an ultimate good to which one gives oneself in
a decisive act of choice, and for which one is ready to renounce anything in one's life that is incompatible. To do this is to choose life. But
one can only choose life when one has made some sense of the enigma
of death. The choice of good and the renunciation of evil must be
strong enough to hold in the face of death, because death puts a question mark before every hope of life. To choose to live well is somehow
to take the sting out of death. It is to be ready to die well. This profound truth about the human condition is given theological color by
the claim that baptism of desire is required by all for salvation. What
baptism stands for in any of its forms is an act of faith that life has
conquered death, that there is a way of experiencing death that gives
life. To talk about baptism of desire for all who are saved is to say that,
however they express it, all must make a choice for life that overcomes
death, that they must leave aside all that is not life-giving, that they
must identify with people and institutions that care for life and oppose
all who are hostile to it. That is to say something profoundly helpful
about human life. It is to provide an insight into what it is in the great
religions of humankind and in all forms of religious experience as well
as in secular humanism that makes them salvific. It is, at the same
time, to say that all human salvation replicates the victory of life over
death that God gave humanity once for all in Christ.

The theology of baptism of desire, then, remains a way of
expressing the Christian faith that all salvation comes through Christ
and the Church. Anyone who chooses the victory of life over death
implicitly accepts all that gives life, whether he or she can identify it
or not. Because it believes the ultimate victory of life over death occurs
in Christ, Christian theology finds implicit in every choice of life
over death the choice of Christ and the Church, and calls it baptism

of desire. Implicit in it, too, is the acceptance of the eschatology that sees the ultimate choice facing the whole of creation as a choice for or against Christ; and that he is believed to be the one who will eventually judge all human choices; and that—although it will come as a surprise to many—he will judge them in reference to himself (Matthew 25:34–46). Because it believes it has a mission to bring about this final consummation of things in Christ the Church will never let a teaching about baptism of desire become an excuse for not proclaiming the gospel way of salvation to all, calling them to join Christ and his Church already in time through the water rite of baptism.

## The Baptism of Children

There is nothing in the early records of the Christian tradition to suggest that there was a time when the Church did not baptize children. While some statements of the scriptures about the place of faith in baptism can raise theoretical difficulties about the practice[14] there is no factual evidence that it was not done. There is no reason to believe, for example, that when whole households are said to have been baptized (Acts 10:44–48; 16:15; 16:33; 1 Corinthians 1:16) the children, even of tender years, were excluded. It is known that, at the time the scriptures were being written, children of Jewish proselytes were baptized into the Jewish faith along with their parents. There is no evidence that Christians did otherwise.[15] Although there are some indications in the second century that children were baptized, the positive evidence does not appear until about AD 200. Tertullian in Africa, Hippolytus in Rome and Origen in Egypt (references in Duplacy, p. 129) say it is the common practice of the Church and has been from the beginning. Tertullian did not think it was a very good idea and would have preferred that children were not baptized until they could know Christ, but his view on this is reckoned to have been eccentric. When a significant number of potential Christians began, especially in the fourth century, to postpone baptism it was often for less worthy motives. The reaction of pastoral leaders of the Church to these delays

---

14. cf. K. Barth, *Baptism*.

15. Cullmann, *Baptism in the New Testament*, 25, 51–53; J. Jeremias, *The Origins of Infant Baptism*, trans. from German (Naperville, IL: A.R. Allenson, 1963), Ch. 1; Duplacy in George, *Baptism in the New Testament*, 127–133.

restates and gives reasons for the tradition of baptizing people as soon
as possible, and even in infancy. Pelagian thinking challenged some of
these reasons, especially those that saw infants as being subject to sin
and therefore in real need of baptism. But their denials were concerned
more with the meaning of infant baptism than with the fact of it.

Saint Augustine, in taking up the challenge of Pelagianism,
did some influential thinking about how baptism worked in children
and on why they needed it. The part of his teaching that became
notorious is the connection he made between the baptism of children
and original sin: children are born in original sin, and the only way
they can be freed from it is by baptism in water. It followed from this,
Augustine had to reluctantly admit, that if they died without baptism
they could not be saved. The acceptance of the teaching of Augustine
on this point in the Western Church confirmed and intensified the
sense of urgency about baptizing infants, especially if they were in
danger of death. This becomes the dominant concern in magisterial pronouncement up to the Reformation (ND 1405, 1407, 1419).
Of course, there is more than this to the teaching of Augustine, and
of the tradition generally, about the baptism of children. There are
explanations of how baptism incorporates children into Christ and
into the Church, and of how the faith of parents and other members
of the Church enfolds them and gives significance to their baptism
(Saint Thomas, Third Part, q. 68, 9; q. 69, 6). Protestants had difficulty about this doctrine because of the way they understood justification by faith. But only some of them refused to continue the practice
of baptizing children or practiced rebaptism of those who had been
baptized as infants. The justification of infant baptism by the Council
of Trent comes in canon 4 of its Decree on Original Sin,[16] and is
entirely in terms of original sin. One has to wait for the post-Vatican
II *Rite of Baptism for Children* (1969, 1973) and an Instruction on
Infant Baptism, *Pastoralis Actio* (1980) from the Congregation for the
Doctrine of Faith (ND 1443–1446) for a fuller magisterial teaching
on the subject. Both these documents give careful attention to the
assumption that has always been in the tradition—even if it has not
always been reflected in practice—that infant baptism only makes
sense to the Church when the parents of the child want it and are

---

16. Tanner, *Decrees*, vol. II, 666; ND 511.

ready, with the help of the Church, to ensure that the child will be formed in accordance with the life that has been given to it in baptism. It is forbidden to baptize a child without these assurances. The prohibition does not hold when the child is in danger of death. It has, indeed, been the practice for many centuries to baptize all infants in danger of death, unless their parents positively oppose it. It is believed that the sacrament makes them children of God, frees them from original sin and makes their death be a passage to resurrection.

A theological understanding of the full Christian tradition about infant baptism is best gained by looking first at the gift of God that is in it and then, in the light of that, at the human need that it meets. As a general rule one only gets a good theological understanding of human need when one has first thought about what God has done for human fulfilment. God offers salvation to all through Christ and the Church gathered in the Holy Spirit. He gives that salvation to everyone who does not actually refuse it. His gift (grace) produces within them the appropriate response that accepts it. They are brought to life and freedom and human fulfilment by the gift of God. What God does for them is not something they can afford to be indifferent to: to refuse it is to refuse their own human fulfilment from the God who made them be what they are. Baptism embodies not only the offer and action of grace from God, but also the human response to it. It embodies it as given and received in the Church. For this reason it has within it not just the ministry of the Church that gives grace but also the Church's response of faith and love that receives grace. The response of the individual to the grace of baptism is always cultivated and carried within this response of the community. The cultivating and carrying that the community does takes the form of a comprehensive human solidarity with the person to be baptized, which enables him or her to comfortably take hold of the grace of God being given in the sacrament.

Christians show this solidarity in different ways with different people. Already in helping their fellow Christians to live out their baptismal gift they are ready to support one another in all their human needs. Then, they show solidarity with those who are not yet Christians by enfolding the desire they have to save them within a readiness to care for whatever human need they discover in them. They do not do the caring just to attract them to baptism, but the

caring surely facilitates their response to the grace of baptism should
God give them that call. The Christian community cares in a special
way for its catechumens, helping them on all levels of human care
to respond to the gift of God that is being given them. It is in that
same movement of caring for the full flowering of the gifts of God
in human life that the Christian community addresses the children
born to its members. It makes its own everything that parents want,
or should want, for their child, everything that will help the child
to grow up in good health and in the ability to make good personal
decisions about life and love. The community may have to help to
feed the child if the family is poor; it may want to provide suitable
schooling if that is not otherwise available. It is within this pattern
of solidarity and caring that the gift of baptism is offered. It is gift
before it is remedy. If it is remedial it is in function of the flourish-
ing of the gift—as the vaccinations given to an infant are not ends in
themselves but preventive measures to allow the body to develop in
its own strengths.

Central among the choices for which parents want to prepare
their children is the one to be made about God and his offer of salvation. It is this, and not the choice about what church they will belong
to or what religion they will practice, that is at stake in the baptism of
children. If parents do believe that it is in Christ and his Church that
God offers the fullness of life to humans they will want their child to
have the opportunity of belonging to the Church, as they will want
it to have all other opportunities of growing towards life-fulfilling
choices. They will want this belonging to be as complete as possible, to
the point of being a real belonging to Christ. Such a being in Christ,
in the Church, is the most secure, objective guarantee that the nurture the child receives from its earliest days will bring it to a personal
choice for God when it becomes capable of such a choice. For believing parents to deprive their children of such a rooted nurturing in
grace would be like—even if on a different plane—letting them face
their first sexual encounter without giving them any prior experience
of the tenderness of human love, or any instruction about sexuality, or
without showing any care for their proper physical development. It
would never occur to parents that in giving their child this kind of care
they are somehow depriving the child of freedom to choose. When
they understand baptism as the kind of gift of God it is they will never

be persuaded that they are forcing their child into something that inhibits their freedom.

There is nothing in this explanation of the baptism of children that requires a distorting or truncating of the sacrament itself. Baptism as already defined for adults can also work for children. It is an act of God being met by an appropriate human response of faith. The faith as always is a gift of God. It is being professed by parents, sponsors, and other Church members in the rite of baptism. They ask, in faith, for the baptismal grace that leads to faith for one for whom they are responsible and who is dependent on them for his or her very being. A child is vulnerable to every act of care or carelessness that enfolds it, beginning from the womb of its mother. The fact that it reaches adult life is the result of what others do for it; and the direction that its life takes is affected by everything that happens to it. The Christian community provides a mothering, beginning it with the womb-experience of baptism, that makes it possible for the child to receive the gift of grace in the way it receives all other gifts. There are charming analyses in psychological literature of how all the care that a baby is given—cuddling, bathing, talking to—and the reactions that these call forth, affect its growth into personhood.[17] The grace of God is in all these forms of care, especially when they begin to take explicitly Christian forms such as praying with the child and telling it the Christian story. This is how the grace of baptism is able to produce its effects until it is eventually appropriated personally, in faith by the child who becomes an adult. The baptism that has been a physically experienced symbolic event with psychological, social, and educational consequences, gives a grace that is an ontological reality having moral consequences. This is sanctifying grace, given in a habitual state and subsequently activated as the child awakens to moral responsibility and the demands of the life of virtue.

The grace of God given in baptism is a redeeming and remedial gift. It justifies in taking away sin. It is a passage from belonging to the old Adam to being under the headship of Christ, the new Adam. It takes away original sin. In adults this sin has become the object of personal decision, which has either removed it (baptism of desire) or affirmed it by personal sins (see "The Forgiveness of Sin").

---

17. Noted in Schillebeeckx, *Christ, the Sacrament*, 133–137.

By the mere fact of being born, a child shares the ungraced state of the race, which is what is meant by being under the headship of Adam. It has made no moral choice about its situation and therefore the most that original sin can be for it is the absence of justifying grace. This grace is given to it when it is baptized into Christ, the new Adam. It is given for growth towards its own acceptance in faith. By that very fact it is given for the taking away of everything that would prevent or distort growth. The negative influences that an adult has to struggle against in order to persevere and grow in grace also affect a child. Although these negativities are rooted in its own being, they are brought to the surface by the people and institutions that surround it. The Church community that brings it to growth will be working to overcome these influences wherever they are found, and to protect children from them. The overcoming of sin in the child by the action of the community belongs to the grace of baptism. It is an integral part of the taking away of original sin. It is theologically feasible that this taking away of sin should begin without a conscious personal act of conversion, because the sin in question is an inherited, not a freely chosen state in the child. The conscious rejection of sin will come when the child becomes an adult, and will be the fruit of the grace into which the child has grown. If that rejection is not made in due course the person once baptized will become a sinner again. His or her sin will be affected by, but not attributable to, the sinful state of the human race because it will now be the result of a personal choice. In the Catholic tradition it is dealt with in the Church by the sacrament of reconciliation, not by any repetition of baptism.

If it is considered to be more profitable theologically to think about the baptism of children as growth in grace before thinking of it as the removal of original sin, one will take the requirements that the Church sets for such baptism very seriously. One will simply not baptize until one has reliable guarantees of the intentions and ability of parents to form the child toward a full adult life of grace, and until one can count on the kind of support from an ecclesial community, without which this cannot be realized. However, a certain theological and pastoral unease can be generated by such a theology and practice, and some parents can find it oppressive. Against the apparent strictness of such a discipline, appeal is made to another theological principle and its consequences: baptism is necessary for salvation; for

adults it may take the form of baptism of desire or of blood if they
cannot be baptized in water, but for children there is no alternative to
baptism of water; if they die without it they die in original sin. From
the fourth century onward this way of reasoning has loomed large
in much Christian thinking about the baptism of infants. One must
baptize them, and quickly, because one must not put their salvation at
risk. Every possible measure, including baptizing unborn or aborted
fetuses, is to be taken to ensure baptism in danger of death. Children
of parents who are not Christian are also to be baptized in danger of
death, even surreptitiously when it is thought the parents might object.
The theological and even magisterial weight behind this view has to
be given due respect. However, its application depends on how one
understands the risk of losing salvation that unbaptized children are
exposed to. The greater the risk the more strenuously one will work to
eliminate it. If, on the other hand, there are alternative ways of salvation for unbaptized infants one will be under less pressure to baptize at
all costs.

## Children who Die without Baptism

Augustine could see no way of salvation for children who die without baptism. He first thought they might have enjoyed some sort of
middle way between beatitude and damnation (*De Libero Arbitrio*,
III, 66: PL 32, 1302) but under pressure from his polemic against
Pelagianism he eventually concluded that salvation was all or nothing: infants who did not receive it through baptism went to hell; their
punishment was as mild as could be, but they were deprived of the
vision of God. Other Latin Fathers and the Greeks who dealt with the
issue were less absolute. Still it is Augustine's anti-Pelagian position
that has always haunted Western theology. Because many of his prem-
ises, and especially his concern to maintain the dogmatic truth of the
necessity of baptism for salvation, were shared, it was hard to refuse
his conclusions about unbaptized infants. Much of the effort was to
soften it rather than to challenge it. Of course, theologians often made
the point that God has ways of saving people that we know nothing
about, and that he works miracles. Now and again some daring ones
tried to work out a theory of how it might be done. The question was
not very much discussed during the Middle Ages. When it was, use

was made of a standard theoretical distinction between the punishment for personal sins, which was hell, and the punishment of original
sin, which was exclusion from the vision of God, without any further
afflictions. It could be said, by way of modification of the Augustinian
position, that infants dying without baptism would at least not suffer
the pains of hell, although they would be deprived of the vision of God
because they had never been reborn in grace. There was some attention given to the place where those being punished for original sin
would be consigned. It was thought about by analogy with that *limbus
Patrum* where the just of the Old Testament waited, on the fringe (the
Latin *limbus* means "fringe") of hell, for the coming of Christ, and from
where he freed them when he "descended into hell" after his death.
The Fathers could be freed because they had had faith in Christ who
was to come. There was no such hope for those in the *limbus puerorum*,
where unbaptized infants were consigned. However, Limbo played a
very insignificant part in the theology of the major Scholastics. Saint
Thomas, for example, does not allude to it in his theology of baptism
in the *Summa*. The theological questions the hypothesis might have
raised—its scriptural warrant, its coherence with theories of nature and
grace, its implications for a theory of the general resurrection—were
not dealt with to any extent.

In the sixteenth century Cardinal Cajetan questioned the
Augustinian assumptions of Scholasticism about the salvation of
unbaptized infants. He reasoned that at least the children of Christian
parents could be saved without actual baptism because of the desire
of their parents to have them baptized. It seems that some complaints
were made about his theory at the Council of Trent, but it was not
censured. The *magisterium* has had, in fact, very little to say about the
lot of unbaptized infants over the centuries. The Council of Florence
(1439–1445) commands that the baptism of infants should not be
delayed because "the only remedy available to them" if they die is
baptism.[18] It also affirms that "the souls of those who depart this life
in actual mortal sin, or in original sin alone, go down straightaway to
hell to be punished, but with unequal pains."[19] This reflects the teaching about the nonsalvation of unbaptized infants—they are those

---

18. Tanner, *Decrees*, vol. I, 576; (ND 1419).
19. Tanner, *Decrees*, vol. I, 528; ND 2309.

who die "in original sin alone"—that was common at the time. It is recognized that they do not suffer the same pain as those who die in personal sin. But it is noteworthy that Florence omits the words "in different places" *(locis disparibus)* that were to be found in an earlier papal text (cf. DS 926), which it is citing here. It is saying nothing about Limbo. It will be a few hundred years later, in 1794, that the illegal Synod of Pistoia will be censured by Pope Pius VI for making light of the teaching about the place "which the faithful commonly call Limbo of the Children" (DS 2626). The existence of Limbo was not being taught, but the right of theologians to speculate about it was being defended. Nothing more explicit or binding can be found in the formal teaching of the *magisterium*. An attempt to have the First Vatican Council define that unbaptized infants did not enjoy the beatific vision came to nothing. When Pope Pius XII stated in an address to Catholic midwives in 1951, "In the present economy there is no other means than Baptism of communicating this [supernatural] life to the infant who has not yet got the use of reason. So that of all men it is true that 'unless a man be born again of water and the Holy Spirit he cannot enter the kingdom of Heaven.' Those who die in original sin go to Limbo," he was taking advantage of a familiar piece of Catholic theology to make a strong case for baptizing infants in danger of death, rather than teaching authoritatively about Limbo. Limbo was a familiar, if frightening, part of the Catholic cosmography, which could be counted on to move the midwives to action. One of the preparatory schemas for the Second Vatican Council revived the proposal that had been disregarded at Vatican I, and once again it was disregarded. By then theologians were beginning to seriously review the appeal to Limbo in the theology of baptism and various explanations of how unbaptized infants could be explained were being put forward. Eventually the question was referred by the Holy See to its International Theological Commission. The study of the Commission, published in 2007 under the title *The Hope of Salvation for Infants who Die without Being Baptized,* has brought considerable clarity to the status of the theology associated with Limbo, showing how it is no more than a particular current of theological opinion, not official Church teaching. More importantly, it has pointed the direction that theology can take in working out explanations of the salvation of unbaptized infants in a way that will not call into question dogmatic teaching about the necessity of baptism for salvation. One of its introductory paragraphs states:

> The conclusion of this study is that there are theological and liturgical reasons to hope that infants who die without baptism may be saved and brought into eternal happiness, even if there is not an explicit teaching on this question found in Revelation. However, none of the considerations proposed in this text to motivate a new approach to the question may be used to negate the necessity of baptism, nor to delay the conferral of the sacrament. Rather, there are reasons to hope that God will save these infants precisely because it was not possible to do for them what would have been most desirable—to baptize them in the faith of the Church and incorporate them visibly into the Body of Christ.

The search for an understanding of how unbaptized infants can be saved has a properly theological motivation. True, it is even more deeply motivated by feelings of mercy, and by the desire to comfort families that have lost a baby before he or she could be baptized, and by a wish to truly honor the mercy of God—and theology is not indifferent to these reasons of the heart. But in a strictly theological sense the search is motivated by the need to reconcile two indisputable theological principles. One of these is that baptism is necessary for salvation. The other is that God wishes all to be saved. The second principle is at least as high in the hierarchy of truths as the first. No teaching about the necessity of baptism that contradicts it can be acceptable. Of course, it can be argued that, even if God wishes all to be saved, he does not in fact save all, and therefore to say that unbaptized infants are not saved does not deny the principle. In reply it must be said that the reason some people are not saved is that they refuse the grace God gives them; or, as it is sometimes put in the theology of justification, God does not refuse his grace to anyone who does what he or she can do to accept salvation. Infants do not refuse the grace of God in any way; there seems no reason, then, why God's universal saving will should not be fulfilled in them. In truth, it is hard to believe that a God who so loved the world as to give his only begotten Son for the salvation of all, and who is believed to take more delight in the saving of one lost soul than in the ninety-nine who are already safe, would set a baptismal requirement so rigid that it would exclude from salvation an infant who, through no fault of its own, does not fulfill it literally. Theology has managed to understand how God saves adults who do not fulfill literally the command to be baptized. It has been able to distinguish between the reality of baptism *(res)* and the rite *(sacramenturn)*. If the reality can be given to adults without the rite, one cannot *a priori* exclude the possibility that the same thing can be done for infants. One cannot exclude it simply because one has not discovered how it could be done. One owes it to the God who wishes all to be saved to go on trying to find an explanation. The study of the International Theological Commission looks at various solutions that have been proposed and, on the basis of its own very thorough examination of scripture and the tradition of faith, indicates some lines along which more comprehensive solutions might be found. While it does not itself propose a particular solution it encourages theologians to put forward their proposals.

One quite compelling solution can be suggested here. It has the advantage of bypassing the Augustinian formulation of the problem and working directly from the scriptures. In a book called *From Limbo to Heaven. An Essay on the Economy of Redemption*, published posthumously in 1961, Rev. V. Wilkin, SJ, did a scriptural, mainly Pauline, restatement of the doctrine of redemption that opened the way to a theological theory to explain the salvation of infants who died without being baptized ("the blamelessly unbaptized"). What is proposed here is a summary, with some adaptation, of his ideas. Everyone born into this world is a child of Adam and comes under his headship. All are afflicted by his sin. This original sin is a sin of the race. People have it because, and as soon as, they are born into solidarity with the situation of the race. It is manifested in the death to which all are condemned. Christ overcame sin in overcoming death. In rising from death he made it possible for all who belong to the human race to overcome death and to rise with him. He became the new head of the human race, the new Adam, the new Lord of all creation and giver of the Spirit. He is bringing all things under his Lordship in the course of time, and will complete the transformation at the final resurrection, when he will deliver all to the Father. When that happens the human race will owe nothing any more to the headship of Adam because it will have come entirely under the headship of Christ. Infants who are not yet baptized are children of Adam. They represent the fallen, unredeemed state of the race. They represent it simply because they are human. They have contributed nothing personal to human sin-fulness. Like all humans they are threatened with death and eternal exclusion from the kingdom of God unless they are somehow rescued from the headship of Adam and brought under the headship of Christ. Baptism is what makes this happen. But if they die without being actually baptized in water there is still another way of being baptized that can unite them to Christ. Since Christ conquered death for the human race, human death has a different significance from what it had under the headship of Adam. All who die now rise again and, by that very fact, some under the headship of Christ. Those who have died in personal sins will have put an obstacle to the full taking possession of them by Christ, to his full Lordship over them. But unbaptized infants will have put no such obstacle. Christ can see their death as an unimpeded sharing in his own death and their risen bodies as belonging entirely to himself. In the resurrection, for an infant just to be human is to belong fully to Christ, as at its first birth to be human was to belong to Adam. The infant represents the state of the race at its best as it once represented it at its worst. So, infants are saved by the very fact of their resurrection, without exercising any choice, as they were afflicted by original sin by the very fact of being born (about which they also exercised no choice). Rev. Wilkin calls this a baptism of the resurrection.

The use of the term baptism of the resurrection maintains the principle of no salvation without baptism, as baptism of desire and baptism of blood do in the case of adults. Like these other terms it indicates that the reality *(res)* of baptism is given without the rite *(signum)*. Rev. Wilkin was prepared to admit that unbaptized infants would have to wait until the general resurrection for their saving transformation in Christ, and would allow that their place of waiting could be some kind of Limbo. But at the resurrection Limbo becomes for them "the baptistry of heaven."

A theory along these lines certainly does justice to the principle that God wishes all to be saved. It follows Paul's teaching and imagery about how the divine will to save is actually worked out in the history of salvation. Within that vision it finds a significant event—resurrection—that has an obvious bearing on the issue of life and death for which baptism is designed. It is a physical event (a new creation) that matches at the end of time the event at the beginning of time (creation) that is blighted by original sin. It respects the universality of original sin and the universal need to have it taken away by a reality of grace that comes in a form that can be called baptism. Such a theory is not an invitation to become careless about baptizing infants, as if it would make no difference anymore whether they were baptized in water or not. It is not just caution but theological rigueur that demands that no risks ever be taken with human salvation. Besides, there are many more reasons for baptizing children than the minimal one of taking away original sin. The prescriptions of the Church about baptizing infants in the first weeks of their life, and immediately if they are in danger of death (Code of Canon Law, can. 867) are not undermined by a theological proposal that they may, as a last resort, be saved by a baptism of the resurrection. However, a lot of the anxiety that the prescriptions may generate in parents and ministers of the Church, and the subsequent scruples and agony these may suffer if they have not succeeded in obeying these prescriptions, can be taken away by a credible explanation, grounded on God's own word, of how it is that God's will to save all is realized in unbaptized infants. It can also bring more serenity into people's obedience to the prescriptions of the Church (can. 868) that baptism may only be given to infants whose parents request it, outside danger of death, when a Catholic upbringing can be guaranteed for them. Finally, such a theory accords well with, and can reinforce, a good general theology of baptism. It sees baptism not as some sort of mechanical, magical rite but as a sacrament of God's love that respects the human condition, taking ritual form when this is what brings the best out of people but taking other forms when that is what is best for them. The word that makes the rite of baptism to be life-giving rightly includes a word about when and how life is given without the rite.

# Chapter 6

# Confirmation: The Rite

## DESCRIPTION

The primary form of the rite of confirmation in the Latin Catholic Church is that given within the continuous rite of initiation for adults (RCIA, 225–229; *Rites*, Initiation, 227–231, pp. 102–104). A form is also provided for the celebration of confirmation apart from baptism. It is designed to take place within the Eucharist (*Rites*, Confirmation, 20–31, pp. 306–311), or it may stand alone, as a separate sacramental celebration (*Rites*, Confirmation, nn. 34–49, pp. 314–322). There is no special rite of confirmation for children. The rite given for confirmation in danger of death (*Rites*, Confirmation, nn. 52–55, p. 324) is for use with children as well as adults. It states: "It is of the greatest importance that the initiation of every baptized Christian be completed by the sacraments of confirmation and the Eucharist . . . In the case of a child who has not yet reached the age of reason, confirmation is given in accord with the same principles and norms as for baptism" (*Rites*, Confirmation 52).

The rite of confirmation, whether as part of a continuous initiation or as a separate celebration, is meant to take place in a full assembly of the Christian community into which the person is being initiated. Ordinarily it is presided over by the bishop, who acts as minister of the rite. When, in the absence of the bishop, a presbyter is presiding at the ceremony of initiation of an adult he may confirm as well as baptize in one continuous rite. Those to be confirmed are accompanied by sponsors who present them and take responsibility for them before the community, as they or others will have already done for them at baptism. The rite begins with instruction and prayer that evoke the baptism that has preceded this moment and the gift of the Holy Spirit that is to be given. This phase is quite brief when confirmation is part of a continuous initiation; it takes the more extended form of a liturgy of the word with a renewal of baptismal vows and profession of baptismal faith by the whole community when the confirmation is being done as a separate rite. Then, the presiding minister, and presbyters who may be authorized to assist him, stretch their hands over the candidates, while the minister prays the Father of Our Lord Jesus Christ to send the Holy Spirit and his messianic gifts on those who have been given new life already by water and the Holy Spirit (*Rites*, Initiation, n. 227, p. 103). Each candidate then comes forward, accompanied by a sponsor, who places a hand on his or her right shoulder, and is anointed with a perfumed oil called chrism, which will have been blessed by the local bishop during the liturgy of the previous Holy Week. The minister does the anointing by dipping his thumb in the chrism, and (usually while placing the palm of his hand on the head of the candidate, although this detail is no longer prescribed) tracing a sign of the cross with his thumb on the forehead; while doing this he addresses the person by name and says: "N., be sealed with the Gift of the Holy Spirit" (*Rites*, Initiation, n. 231, p. 104). The confirmed person answers "Amen" and receives a greeting of peace from the minister. In the continuous rite of initiation, or when it is celebrated apart from baptism but with Eucharist, confirmation is followed by the Prayer of the Faithful and the Liturgy of the Eucharist. Otherwise the rite concludes with the General Intercessions and the Lord's Prayer.

## History

The history of any rite can help one to enter into its present meaning. However, in the case of the rite of confirmation, history is not an easy teacher. There is no mention of a rite called confirmation in the records of Christian origins. When history does identify something from which such a rite is believed to have developed, it still leaves many gaps and puzzles in documenting an evolution to the point where confirmation is recognized as a sacramental rite distinct from baptism. The task is not made easier by the uncertainty that exists about the theological definition of confirmation. Theological positions inevitably interact with the reading of historical sources: what one finds is affected by what one is looking for. Allowing for these

limitations, and without pretending to give a complete history of the
rite or to be altogether innocent of a particular theological point of
view, one can still look at some well-established historical material
and suggest how it throws light on the contemporary rite of confirmation. The material about the rite will also be useful background for the
study of the theological word about the sacrament that will be undertaken in Chapter 7.

There are two ritual actions, and a set of significant words
to go with each, in the present rite of confirmation. The actions are a
laying on of hands and an anointing with perfumed oil, called chrism.
They come out of the biblical tradition. From the earliest times the
hands were used to call down a blessing on specially chosen people
(Genesis 48:13–16), and to designate individuals for some status or
role in the work of God (Numbers 8:10; 27:15–23; Deuteronomy
34:9). Jesus laid hands on children as a gesture of blessing (Mark
10:16) and on the sick for healing (Luke 13:13). As well as doing it for
healing (Mark 16:18), the apostles laid hands on whole communities
so that they would receive the gift of the Holy Spirit (Acts 8:17; 19:6).
The gesture was also used for setting people apart for ministry in the
Church (Acts 6:6; 13:3; 2 Timothy 1:6). It is listed in Hebrews 6:2 as
one of those topics that should be dealt with in the basic instruction
of Christians. Anointing with oil, especially with perfumed oil, was
one of the rituals of joy and festive celebration in the Old Testament
(Amos 6:6; Proverbs 27:9); it was offered to guests as a mark of honor
(Psalm 23:5); to forgo or be deprived of it was a sign of trouble and
mourning (Deuteronomy 28:40; Daniel 10:3); to enjoy it would be
part of the celebration of messianic times (Isaiah 61:3; Psalm 45:7).
Anointing was used to initiate kings into their reign (1 Samuel 10:1;
16:13; 1 Kings 1:39), and in the consecration of priests (Exodus 29:7;
Leviticus 8:12; Numbers 3:3). There are texts that speak of the anointing of prophets (1 Kings 19:16–19; Isaiah 61:1) but it seems that this
is a metaphorical way of describing their call rather than reference to
an actual rite.

Jesus was anointed by the woman who was a sinner, after she
had bathed his feet with her tears (Luke 7:38 and 46), when his host
had refused him these honors; and he is anointed by Mary the sister
of Lazarus in spite of the indignation of Judas and the disciples (John
12:1–8; see Matthew 26:6–13). In both these cases the gesture is given

a messianic interpretation by the evangelists. The language of anointing is used in connection with the baptism of Jesus to describe how he was filled with the Holy Spirit (Acts 10:38) and also in a passage of Hebrews about his divine sonship (1:9). It is in a similar metaphorical sense that it is used in 2 Corinthians 1:21–22 and in 1 John 2:20 and 27 to describe how Christians share through Christ in the messianic gift of the Spirit and of truth. This text from 2 Corinthians brings together three words that are subsequently important in the language of confirmation. The Greek word translated "commissioned" in the Revised Standard Version (RSV) is literally "anointed"; the word translated "he has put his seal" is in the same participle form as "anointed," which suggests that the act of anointing is the act of sealing; and the word that is translated "establishes us" could be translated "confirmed" (the Latin Vulgate has *confirmat*). For all this, it cannot be said that the language that Paul uses here evokes an actual Christian rite of anointing and sealing. The only ritual use of anointing attested by the New Testament is in the healing of the sick and the casting out of demons (Mark 6:13). One might, of course, hazard a guess that if the bathing of baptism was in any way realistic it would have been completed, like a normal bath, with some kind of anointing and perfuming, and that this would have been readily given a Christian significance.

Such evidence as there is for the rites of Christian initiation in the second century has no mention of laying on of hands or anointing. But from around 200 CE onward there is frequent mention of both rites. Tertullian seems to be following the sequence of rites in Christian initiation when he says: "The flesh is washed that the soul may be made spotless: the flesh is anointed that the soul may be consecrated: the flesh is signed [with the cross] that the soul too may be protected: the flesh is overshadowed by the imposition of the hand that the soul also may be illumined by the Spirit: the flesh feeds on the Body and Blood of Christ so that the soul as well may be replete with God" (*De Resurrections Carnis*, c. 8).[1]

There are several mentions of both rites in the letters of Saint Cyprian, and indications that in danger of death and in reception into the Church of those baptized in heresy they could be separated

---

1. This and other texts of Tertullian in E. C. Whitaker and M. E. Johnson eds. *Documents of the Baptismal Liturgy* revised and expanded 3rd ed. (Collegeville, MN: The Liturgical Press, 2003), 7–10.

from the other rites of Christian initiation.[2] Meanwhile, from the full description of the rites of initiation given in *The Apostolic Tradition*,[3] one learns that there was an anointing before the rite of baptizing and two anointings after it, and a laying on of hands in the act of baptizing as well as another afterward. The prebaptismal anointing is a rite of exorcism, and the oil used is called the oil of exorcism. The anointing immediately after the baptizing, with what is called the oil of thanksgiving, is accompanied by words that relate it to Christ. The second anointing, with consecrated oil, is done by the bishop. He lays his hand on the head as he anoints and seals the forehead, using a Trinitarian form of words to describe what he is doing. This second postbaptismal anointing is preceded by a laying on of hands by the bishop during which he prays that the Holy Spirit will come upon those who have been baptized.

The liturgical evidence from the fourth century shows rites of anointing and laying on of hands to be a regular part of Christian initiation in both East and West, in a pattern that broadly corresponds to that of *The Apostolic Tradition*. More prominence seems to be given in the East to the anointing than to the laying on of hands in connection with the gift of the Holy Spirit. There is, however, one important liturgical tradition that differs from all others that are known about. The church of Antioch, and the many churches of the East that followed its discipline, had a signing with the cross and an anointing with perfumed oil, not just of the head but of the whole body, before the act of baptizing; and it had the laying on of hands in the baptism itself. It is with this laying on of hands that the gift of the Holy Spirit is associated.[4] Only in a few late accounts of this liturgy does an anointing or signing appear after baptism. This form of the rite of initiation lasted in the Antiochean tradition into the fifth century but then gradually gave way to the more general pattern. However, one cannot ignore the significance of the fact that, in this earliest documented phase of the tradition, there was such an important divergence, which did not cause any problems of discipline or communion in the Church, about the

---

2. Texts in Whitaker, *Documents of the Baptismal Liturgy*, 10–12.

3. G. Dix, The Apostolic Tradition of St. Hippolytus of Rome, 2nd ed., intro H. Chadwick (London, 1968), Ch 4.

4. A. Milner, OP, *The Theology of Confirmation* (Cork: Mercier Press, 1971), 2–15; texts in Whitaker, *Documents of the Baptismal Liturgy*, 12–20.

place and meaning of anointing and laying on of hands in Christian initiation. It has to be taken along with the fact that even within the more generally accepted tradition there were different kinds of anointing, with different kinds of oil, and different ways of laying on hands and signing with the cross; the words used with the rite also differ, as do the theological explanations of it (see Chapter 7). The truth is that the reality to be ritualized in Christian initiation is more fundamental to the faith of the Church than the particular ritual form in which it is expressed. There is, indeed, an inalienable core to that ritual, which is baptism in water; there are other rites that come out of the biblical and apostolic tradition, but without the binding force of baptism; they have a natural affinity with the rite of bathing and somehow suppose it; they have been used from earliest times to express aspects of initiation that it was thought good to ritualize more strikingly than the simple rite of baptizing did; what they express particularly is the messianic gift of the Holy Spirit, which is an essential component of any Christian initiation; in exceptional circumstances these rites can be separated from the rite of baptizing, but they are normally celebrated and thought about as part of a single process of initiation.

It was in the Western Church, in the Roman liturgy, that a separate rite of laying on of hands and anointing for the giving of the Holy Spirit was developed and came to be called confirmation. These actions had been associated from the beginning, in all liturgical traditions, with the ministry of the bishop. It was he who normally presided at the ceremonies of initiation. Even though presbyters and deacons did many of the baptismal rites, the laying on of hands and anointing for the giving of the Spirit was to be done by the bishop. And it was he who was to preside at the Eucharist that completed initiation. It was obviously fitting that he, as head of the Church into which people were being initiated, should be the one to complete the process.

When the bishop was absent the rite of initiation would be presided over by a presbyter. In the Eastern churches, and in the churches of Africa and Spain, all the rites, including laying on of hands and anointing, were done by the presbyter in that case. The unity of initiation was a paramount value. The reference to the bishop was always present, in the sense that the initiation was an act of the Church of which he was the head. It was required also that the chrism used would be blessed by him. The Roman Church, however, reserved the laying on of hands and anointing to the bishop. When initiation came to be celebrated without his presence, these rites were postponed. An anointing with oil, similar to that prescribed by *The Apostolic Tradition* to be done by a presbyter immediately after the newly baptized had come out of the water, was done and all were admitted to the Eucharist. But they had to wait until they could be brought to the bishop, or he could come to them, for the laying on of hands and the anointing and signing with chrism for the gift of the Holy Spirit. This happened more and more frequently as the number of those to be initiated increased, the majority of them now being children of Christian parents, and as parishes were set up, many of them at some distance from the bishop's cathedral church. Outside Rome the practice first appears in the south of France during the fifth century and there are some decisions of local councils about whether the bishop both anoints and lays on hands or simply lays on hands in such a case.[5] It is here for the first time that the bishop is said to "confirm" what has been done in baptism, and the rite he performs is called confirmation. Other parts of Western Europe took longer to accept the need for a further episcopal rite of initiation if people had already been anointed by a presbyter after their baptism, but eventually, by the tenth century, it had become standard practice in the Latin Church.[6] The rite, which eventually came to be written out in a separate book for the convenience of the bishop, consists of a laying of hands over all the candidates together, with a prayer that is a development of the basic text given by *The Apostolic Tradition*; this is followed by an anointing with chrism on the forehead and a signing with the cross, accompanied by a form of words that by the tenth century had come to be: "N., I sign you with the sign of the cross and I confirm you with the chrism of salvation in the name of the Father, and of the Son, and of the Holy Ghost." The Roman rite of confirmation remained quite stable from then until the reforms of the Second Vatican Council. The gesture of anointing became more stylized: the palm of the hand was laid on the head and the thumb dipped in chrism was used to trace the sign of the cross on the forehead. It was a way of combining the laying on of hands and the anointing. Another odd development occurred: the kiss

---

5. Milner, *The Theology of Confirmation*, 42–44.

6. Milner, *The Theology of Confirmation*, 42–65.

of peace that the bishop would give turned into a slap on the cheek! It is surmised that the kiss first became a caress on the cheek, which was easier to do when most of those confirmed were children, and that subsequently, under the influence of a somewhat militaristic theology of confirmation that will be examined in Chapter 7, the caress turned into a slap that symbolically tested the fortitude of the newly confirmed in face of the hostilities of the world.

The Roman discipline of delaying confirmation until it could be administered by the bishop came to interact with another peculiarity of the Roman rites of initiation. In the early centuries children were given the full rite of initiation, culminating in Eucharistic communion, in all the churches. This is still the practice in the East. It lasted in the Roman Church until the thirteenth century. When the bishop was present infants received all the stages of initiation at once. When he was not they had to wait for the imposition of hands like everybody else, but they did receive the Eucharist. It was not always easy for parents to get young children to the bishop. They may also have lost some of the sense of urgency about the sacrament since it came to be thought that confirmation was not necessary for the salvation of their child in the way that baptism was. In the early Middle Ages there are exhortations and ecclesiastical canons against the abuse of delaying the confirmation of those who have been baptized as infants. It is variously required that it be done within a year of baptism, or at the age of three, or at the age of seven. But then in the late thirteenth century a line of theological reasoning begins to appear that actually favors delaying confirmation: it is argued that children would not understand the sacrament before they reached the age of seven and hence they should not receive it before then. This line of thinking eventually prevailed in the Latin Church. The Catechism of the Council of Trent takes this rather cautious position: "Here it is to be observed that, after baptism, the sacrament of confirmation may indeed be administered to all; but that until children have attained the age of reason its administration is inexpedient. If not, therefore, to be postponed to the age of twelve, it is most proper to defer this sacrament at least to that of seven years." In parts of the post-Tridentine Church confirmation was given at an even later age than seven. The practice of giving First Communion to children when they were being initiated, even without confirmation, had died out in the Latin

Church by the thirteenth century. The pattern of initiation for children had thus come to comprise three distinct and separate sacramental rites—baptism, confirmation and Eucharist. The order between confirmation and Eucharist varied. But it was only after the introduction by Pope Pius X of first communion for children once they had reached the use of reason that it became standard practice for children to be admitted to the Eucharist before they were confirmed.

Significant features of the present-day Roman rite of confirmation (described earlier) stand out more clearly against the historical background that has been traced here. In keeping with the general aims of Vatican II there is an attempt to recover the full richness of the tradition about Christian initiation in a viable, contemporary form. The rite recovers the sense that confirmation belongs within a fuller process. It looks back to baptism and forward to the Eucharist. This is obvious in the rites, whether for adults (RCIA, 208 [34]), or for children of catechetical age (RCIA, 281 [306], but especially 281 [344]). The possibility of maintaining this unity even when a bishop is not presiding is opened up by allowing a priest to confirm in the continuous rite. However, the unified process of initiation is not restored for infants. In danger of death they are, indeed, confirmed after baptism, but do not receive the Eucharist. A continuous rite is provided for children of catechetical age, so that their confirmation precedes their First Communion. For children who have been baptized in infancy the Introduction to the Rite of Confirmation says:

> With regard to children, in the Latin Church the administration of confirmation is generally postponed until about the seventh year. For pastoral reasons, however, especially to strengthen the faithful in complete obedience to Christ the Lord and in loyal testimony to him, episcopal conferences may choose an age which seems more appropriate, so that the sacrament is given at a more mature age after appropriate formation. In this case the necessary precautions should be taken so that children will be confirmed at the proper time, even before the use of reason, where there is danger of death or other serious difficulty. They should not be deprived of the benefit of this sacrament (*Rites*, Confirmation, 11).

In the Code of Canon Law (1983) the "age of discretion" is made normative for confirmation. This makes it possible, if it does not actually demand, that all children can be confirmed before they receive their First Communion. Nevertheless, the Code does not seem to impose this order of initiation. It allows episcopal conferences to determine another age for confirmation, which would presumably be later than the age of discretion and the reception of first communion. At the same time it also allows confirmation at an earlier age, not only when the child is in danger of death, but when "in the judgment of the minister a grave cause urges otherwise" (can. 891). The legislation in no way inhibits the efforts that have been made in recent decades by a small number of dioceses to restore the traditional order of the sacraments of initiation by confirming children as soon as they reach the age of discretion and making the sacrament be a key part of their preparation for first eucharistic communion.

The decision made by Pope Paul VI in the wake of the Second Vatican Council to highlight the anointing with oil and to recognize it as the essential core of the rite can be appreciated better when one remembers how the tradition has associated the giving of the Holy Spirit in initiation with anointing as well as with the laying on of hands, and with various combinations of these. The Catholic Church has now recognized that there is no single decisive tradition about the "matter of the sacrament," that could claim the authority of Christ or the apostles. It has felt free to make a decision about what is best for the Church today. In assuming responsibility for fixing the essence of a sacramental rite, instead of claiming that it has been fixed from the beginning by the apostles, the Church has done something that has an important bearing on how theology ought to understand the divine institution of sacraments (see Chapter 3, "Divine Institution"). But the history of confirmation shows that the decision is in no way arbitrary. It is an attempt to get the best out of the tradition, bearing in mind the criteria of sacramental theology and of the theologically informed pastoral strategy promoted by Vatican II. It also has the ecumenical value of adopting a form of the rite that is close to what is practiced in the Orthodox churches. They have always centered the giving of the Holy Spirit on the rite of anointing with chrism, and actually call the rite corresponding to the Latin confirmation by the name "chrismation." The ecumenical factor is also to be noted in the decision to prefer the ancient form of words that has been maintained in the Eastern churches over the later Latin form, for expressing the meaning of the act of anointing. There are other good theological reasons for this preference, which will be examined in the next chapter. Merely from the ritual point of view it has the value of being a richer and more direct form that highlights, mysteriously but without ambiguity, the reality that confirmation sacramentalizes: the sealing of Christians with the eschatological gift of the Holy Spirit.

## ANTHROPOLOGICAL CONSIDERATIONS

One can enter into the meaning of the rite of a Christian sacrament by developing a feeling for the symbols it employs and an awareness of the roots these have in human experience. There are difficulties about doing this with confirmation. The symbols are ambivalent even in Christian terms. Oil is used in baptism, in ordinations, in anointing of the sick as well as in confirmation. Hands are laid on in baptism, ordinations, and reconciliation. And the Holy Spirit is invoked and prayed for in every sacrament. The moment of human life to which the rite of confirmation corresponds cannot be easily stated in reference to the stages of human growth, because there is no consistent tradition about the age at which people are confirmed. Nor does theology give decisive guidelines, because there is no particularly established theology of confirmation. There is agreement that confirmation ritualizes the giving of the Holy Spirit, but it is not quite so clear what particular aspect of the gift is being singled out, and how this differs from what is ritualized in baptism and other sacraments. There is also the difficulty of finding credible equivalents to the Christian gift of the Holy Spirit in other religions or in secular social forms, and therefore of identifying parallel rites that might throw light on confirmation. One has, therefore, to be tentative in proposing an anthropological reading of the symbols of confirmation and admit that one's suggestions are affected by one's particular theology of the sacrament.

### Rites of Going Public

The first Christians to receive the Pentecostal gift of the Holy Spirit became public people. They went out into the streets of Jerusalem, and subsequently into the streets of the whole known world and spoke publicly about Jesus. It might be reasonable, then, to look for an anthropological grounding for confirmation in the human experience of going public. As one grows up, one has to come to a point of taking a stand in relation not just to the people who form one's own family, with whom there are certain ready grooves and patterns of interaction, but also to outsiders who are independent and unpredictable in their attitudes and reactions. One has to accept being part of a society in which relationships are established not only by the intimacy of blood ties but also by the free and open exchange of ideas and choices. At such moments one takes oneself seriously and wants to be taken seriously by people from whom one has no claim to attention other than what one is by personal statement and behavior. These moments are generally associated with entry into adult age. But they do not have to be so. Children can be caught up in the public stance of their parents. Children of some ethnic communities, for example, have often had to suffer from the same discriminations that an intolerant society visited on their parents, and the children of politically important families have little choice about what society expects of them. On the other hand, the need to go public may come later than entry into adulthood. A person who develops intellectual or political convictions late in life often has to go through a process of taking a public stand about them.

Nevertheless, the rites of entry into adulthood can serve as a convenient paradigm for how people go public. There are rites connected with going public as a sexual being—accepting oneself and having oneself accepted as a man or a woman. These are the rites of puberty, like debutante balls, or the more earthy forms of sexual initiation that may be practiced in primitive societies; they are also the many informal rites that teenagers develop among themselves in Western society. There are rites connected with going public in the matter of eating and drinking, such as taking one's first drink in a pub. There are rites for assuming public responsibility, like getting a driver's license or voting for the first time. And there are rites connected with one's career, like graduation or completing apprenticeship in a particular profession or trade. Rites like these provide a paradigm for confirmation, not because they are generally rites of adulthood but because they are rites of going public. To use them theologically in a way that dwells too much on the age at which they occur in human life would be to become locked into a position on the best age for confirmation—making it a sacrament of transition to adult age—that cannot claim any more support from the tradition than that which favors confirmation in infancy.

In any case, what one is trying to understand in confirmation is a rite of anointing with perfumed oil. Perfumed oil has nothing distinctively to do with becoming an adult, but it can have a lot to do with going public. To be comfortable in one's body, to be well groomed and smell pleasantly does wonders for one's self-confidence and one's ability to face the world. Advertisers of lotions and deodorants play shamelessly on people's fears of not being appropriately "sanitized," and promote the belief that the right-smelling cream or spray will make them an instant success in public. It is not without significance for the understanding of confirmation that lotions and perfumes are often connected with bathing. They are more effective when the skin or hair has been washed clean. Indeed, bathing is somehow incomplete without these additional rites. There is also something significant in the fact that babies are oiled and powdered. It is not just for the comfort of the babies but also of their parents who want to show them off in public and to teach them gradually how to relate confidently to strangers. It is this rather earthy sense of the uses of oil and perfume that underlies the biblical symbolism already noted in the history of confirmation. Anointing with oil had to do with public appearances: it prepared people for feasting with their friends, and was given as a mark of public honor to distinguished guests; it was used to designate people for public office (kings and priests) and it became a metaphor for the call to prophecy; it was employed in the New Testament as a symbol of the power of Christians to speak and act convincingly in the name of Christ, to be the "good odor" of Christ.

There are other strains of symbolism in oil that reinforce its suitability for a rite of going public. It is used by athletes and people given to strenuous physical effort. So it becomes a metaphor for strength and of the ability to deal with competition and conflict. This is a line of symbolism found congenial by a theology of confirmation that sees it primarily as the sacrament of Christian strength in the battle against the enemies of Christian life. The limits of such a theology will be discussed in Chapter 7. For the moment it is enough to note that, while it exploits a real symbolism of anointing with oil, it does not explain why the liturgy has always insisted that the oil used after baptism should be perfumed (chrism), and by that fact different from the oil used during the catechumenate and in anointing of the sick. To make strength the dominant symbolism of oil in confirmation could give the impression that to become a Christian is to take a belligerent or defensive stance towards the world, and to deprive the sacrament of something of that joyful, outgoing attitude of sharing and celebrating the good news of salvation that is communicated by the festive symbolism of perfumed oil.

Oil gains further symbolism from the fact that it can be poured out: one can see and feel it flow, and yet it does not run off like water but stays on skin or hair; it penetrates the body, becomes part of it, keeps it moist and supple and, when it is perfumed, keeps it fragrant. Flowing, moistening oil that keeps hair from drying up and becoming ratty and disheveled is taken as a symbol of conviviality and friendship in Psalm 133: "How good and how pleasant it is, when brothers live in unity! It is like the precious oil upon the head, running down upon the beard, running down upon Aaron's beard, upon the collar of his robes."

## The Sealing of Gifts

The words that accompany the anointing with perfumed oil in the rite of confirmation are "N., be sealed with the Gift of the Holy Spirit." The words invite one to think of confirmation in terms of how people are marked definitively and distinctively by their gifts. Following up the anthropological model of "going public" that has been proposed for understanding confirmation, one can reflect that a public person is required to have some kind of distinctive personality; otherwise he or she is exposed as a nonentity. Genuine distinctiveness, as opposed to the projection of an artificially created image, is provided by a person's real gifts, and specifically by the gifts of their adult age. The gifts of infants and children are very real and charming, but many of them disappear with growth in age. Others, however, such as lineage, continue into adulthood. Still others are already embedded in the personality of the child and are developed by education. The gifts that eventually mark a personality are the ones that last and are confirmed in adult life. That is how a person is remembered; that is what one likes to see already unfolding in childhood. Gifts also set up relationships between people. They can bond together and form community with people who are

marked by similar or complementary gifts. And they can look with
some sense of identification and veneration on someone who had the
gifts they themselves enjoy in some kind of eminent or heroic degree.

To define a person, gifts of adult age need to have a certain
permanence—to be signed, sealed, and delivered. Any ritual of sealing
signifies that some process has now been completed. It marks something as belonging definitively to someone and authorizes it to carry
weight on behalf of that person. As used in confirmation, the image
of being sealed evokes the completion of gifting that comes with
Pentecost. The Holy Spirit is the ultimate gift of God, of which God
does not repent and after which God has nothing else to give. It corresponds to the ultimate messianic event that occurs in Christ. The gift
of the Spirit puts the identifying stamp of Christ on the person being
initiated, as it was the Spirit who identified Christ as the Son of God
at his baptism. Christ will be recognizable henceforth in the Christian
through the presence in him or her of the Spirit. The Gift that is
the Spirit may be given visibility in Christians by special charismatic
manifestations, but it is fundamentally manifested and documented by
their being signed in the rite of confirmation, which is an integral part
of the making of a Christian. The Spirit that is given deploys itself in
many particular gifts, orchestrated differently in each Christian, and
it is this diversity that makes each a distinctive individual, bonded
nevertheless with others in the one Spirit common to all. Because this
gift and these gifts are given in a definitive way, the person is sealed
with, marked by them forever. When someone does not develop well
in adult life we do not say that their gifts failed but that they failed to
live up to their gifts. The Spirit given in confirmation may be grieved
and the gifts left unused, but the Spirit once given is there forever.
Once sealed with this gift one is forever signed, sealed, and delivered
for Christ and the Spirit.

## Co-Missioned

One can get a feel for the symbolism of the laying on of hands that is
part of the rite of confirmation from a consideration of the way gifts
are connected with authority in human communities. The personal
gifts that people have already give them a certain authority: they are
able to get things done in the area of their giftedness; others look to

them and depend on them. Communities have their ways of recognizing this and of taking the gifts of their members into their own authority structures. Doing so is one of the tasks of those who are responsible for the exercise of authority in a community. Authority is said to be "handed on" to people who are judged to have gifts that can serve the community. The authority of their gift is recognized officially. They are commissioned to act henceforth on behalf of the community. A hand gesture is often used to express this "handing on"—whether it be a handshake, or a salute or, as in many religious traditions, a laying on of hands. Christian initiation entails the gifting of members of the community and the making official of the authority that goes with those gifts. Those being initiated are recognized as belonging to a community of adults, with that special adulthood that comes into being with the definitive giving of God's Spirit at Pentecost. The head of the community, the bishop or a priest acting in his place, imposes hands on them. The adulthood that comes to them with the gifts of the Spirit is confirmed, and they are commissioned to use those gifts in the interest of the community. And because the community is uniquely charged with the mission of bringing God's salvation to the whole world, the commissioning that is symbolized in the laying on of hands in confirmation is a "co-missioning," that is to say, a being incorporated into the mission of the Church.

# Chapter 7

# Confirmation: The Word

The fact that the rite of confirmation has shadowy beginnings and an uncertain early history raises a difficulty about setting down the words that have bound it to life in the Christian Church throughout its history. One cannot say with certainty that any given text from the scriptures or the writers of the first few centuries is about confirmation because one cannot identify any rite with certainty as being that of confirmation. However, there are two constants of the tradition that can be used as guidelines in the search for texts. The first is that, from early times, Christian initiation included ritual elements in addition to the water rite of baptism and first partaking of the Eucharist, and that anointing with perfumed oil and laying on of hands were prominent among these. The second constant is that these rites are related to the gift of the Holy Spirit that occurs in initiation. The word of the Church that can be taken to refer to confirmation, then, is the word about the gift of the Holy Spirit, and about the way that gift is expressed ritually in Christian initiation. The issues one will be looking for a word on are: what is the role of the Holy Spirit in the making of a Christian; what is the justification for postulating that a rite beyond the water rite of baptism is needed to convey this gift of the Spirit; how does this further rite relate to the rite of baptism in the giving of one and the same Spirit; what is the essential core of this other rite; what are the circumstances in which it is celebrated, who is its minister and in what conditions can it be separated from the other rites that make up full Christian initiation? The choice made throughout the chapter of texts that answer these questions owes a great deal to the work of Milner;[1] some translations used are his.

---

1. A. Milner, OP, *The Theology of Confirmation* (Cork: Mercier Press, 1971).

# The New Testament

Milner makes fine theological use of the exegetical material on the Holy Spirit that is to be found in vol. VI of Kittel, *Theological Dictionary of the New Testament*, particularly in that of E. Schweizer on *pneuma*.[2] The various currents of thought about the Holy Spirit are analysed there. It appears that in broad terms they can be reduced to two.[3] One of these is found predominantly in Luke (Acts and gospel) with support from Matthew and Mark. The other is in Paul and John. The first draws mainly on Jewish tradition for its ideas and images; the second seems to have absorbed some Hellenistic influences. Although chronologically the writings of Paul come before those of Luke it is convenient to take the texts from Luke first. They seem to represent a more primitive and simpler tradition. One can understand the Pauline and Johannine teaching better in relation to them rather than the other way around.

## Saint Luke

The theology of the Holy Spirit in the writings of Luke owes much to Old Testament teaching about the "spirit of God." The spirit, whether it is personified or not, is God's power in action, doing wonders in the history of his People for their salvation as well as selecting and inspiring the prophets and other leaders they need for the working out of their destiny. In the Old Testament the spirit is transient and unpredictable in its manifestations. But the prophets do tell that it will be poured out in a definitive, abiding fullness at the end of time, as a force for the making of the messianic age. Luke sees this Spirit of God given and active in Jesus: in his birth (1:35); in his baptism (3:22); in the conflict with the Devil that marks the inauguration of his ministry (4:1); and in identifying his preaching as messianic (4:18). Jesus is full of the Spirit. The messianic age has begun in him. Jesus, in turn, promises his disciples that the Spirit would be with them to teach them what to say when they were brought before synagogues and rulers and authorities because of the gospel they preached (Luke 12:11–12). After the

---

2. E. Schweizer and others, "Pneuma," in *Theological Dictionary of the New Testament*, vol. IV, ed. G. Friedrich Kittel (Grand Rapids: Wm. B. Eerdmans, 1964), 332–452.

3. See Milner, op, *The Theology of Confirmation*, 81–86.

resurrection, before he was carried up to heaven, he told the disciples (Luke 24:47–49) that "repentance and forgiveness of sins should be preached in his name to all nations, beginning from Jerusalem," and that they were to be "witnesses of these things." In view of this he would "send the promise of my Father upon you; but stay in the city until you are clothed with power from on high." Luke repeats this promise of Jesus in the opening chapter of Acts, in a form that is more explicit about the connection between the power they were to be given and the gift of the Holy Spirit: "you shall receive power when the Holy Spirit has come upon you; and you shall be my witnesses in Jerusalem and in all Judea and Samaria and to the end of the earth" (Acts 1:8). The Spirit is given to them on the day of Pentecost (Acts 2:1–4). It is a dramatic coming of the power of God, in audible and visible manifestations: a sound like a mighty wind is heard and felt, and tongues as of fire are seen and felt. They are "all filled with the Holy Spirit." As Peter will soon explain (vv. 16–21) this fullness that is visibly manifested is the eschatological, messianic outpouring of the Spirit promised by the prophets. It has an immediate and spectacular effect. The disciples who had been gathered in the privacy of the upper room go out and begin to speak to everyone they meet in a language that their hearers understand: "how is it that we hear, each of us in his own native language? . . . we hear them telling in our own tongues the mighty works of God" (vv. 8–11). The preaching of the gospel to the end of the earth has begun. The disciples, filled with the Holy Spirit, are seen to be the ones who will carry it out. It may take time for this final work of salvation to be completed—there is a place for patience in the eschatology of Luke—but, however long it takes, it is the final work, and those who announce it have the last word to say.

The Spirit continues to be with the first disciples and to manifest its presence in striking ways. It moves them to a new way of praying the psalms (4:25) and when their prayer ends, the place where they are gathered is shaken (4:31); they speak in tongues (10:46 and 19:6); they prophesy (11:28); they are filled with joy (13:52); they stand heroically firm and are articulate in the face of persecution (7:55). Clearly they are people who have been transformed utterly and from within. Luke, however, is more interested in the external manifestations of the change than with analyzing its inner reality. The ecstatic, spectacular expressions of what they have become are functional. They give the disciples a public impact and a boldness to speak the word about Jesus at each stage of that outward journey from Jerusalem to the ends of the earth. It is from the Spirit that their inspiration and courage come to take the initiatives required for the preaching of the gospel (8:29; 10:19; 11:12; 13:4; 15:28; 16:6; 20:22).

On the day of Pentecost Peter promised that those who accepted his word, repented, and were baptized would themselves receive the gift of the Holy Spirit (2:38). Three thousand people "were added" that day (2:41). Luke says they were baptized, but says nothing about them receiving the Holy Spirit. However, the gift of the Spirit is prominent in other accounts that he gives of conversion and initiation. In Acts 8 he describes how a large group of people in Samaria were converted to Christ by the preaching of Philip and were baptized. When the apostles in Jerusalem heard about it they "sent to them Peter and John, who came down and prayed for them that they might receive the Holy Spirit; for it had not yet fallen on any of them, but they had only been baptized in the name of the Lord Jesus. Then they laid their hands on them and they received the Holy Spirit" (vv. 14–17). What they had not received with their baptism and did receive with the laying on of hands was some kind of visible manifestation of the Spirit. It must have been something quite impressive—like the speaking in tongues that accompanied the coming of the Spirit at Pentecost—because Simon, a man who had earned the reputation of being "that power of God which is called Great" (v. 10) because of the magic he performed, wanted to buy the power of giving the Spirit from Peter, so that "any one on whom I lay my hands may receive the Holy Spirit" (v. 19). Peter's indignation was not because Simon had associated the gift of the Holy Spirit with a laying on of hands but that he had "neither part nor lot in this matter, for your heart is not right before God" (v. 21). Simon had, indeed, been baptized with the other Samaritans, but he had not really repented. He did not belong in his heart to the community. Belonging is, in fact, a significant factor in the giving of the Spirit, according to Luke's account. The reason Peter and John were sent from Jerusalem was, it seems, to join this new community of Samaria in fellowship with the principal church, the church of the apostles in Jerusalem. The Spirit is given within this Church. It is the need for communion with the mother-church rather than any inadequacy in the power of the "deacon" Philip that requires the presence of the apostles. Nor is there any suggestion that they alone had the power to give the Holy Spirit by the laying on of hands. The phrase "they had only been baptized in the name of the Lord Jesus" (v. 16) does not imply any shortcoming in such a baptism; but it does give the impression that baptism itself did not necessarily give the gift of the spirit *in a recognizable form.*

Luke's description of the conversion of Paul and his initiation into the community of believers by Ananias (Acts 9:10–19) also gives a central place to the Holy Spirit. Ananias came to the house where Saul was:

> And laying his hands on him he said: "Brother Saul, the Lord Jesus who appeared to you on the road by which you came has sent me that you may regain your sight and be filled with the Holy Spirit." And immediately something like scales fell from his eyes and he regained his sight. Then he rose and was baptized, and took food and was strengthened. For several days he was with the disciples at Damascus. And in the synagogues immediately he proclaimed Jesus, saying "He is the Son of God." And all who heard him were amazed . . . But Saul increased all the more in strength, and confounded the Jews . . . proving that Jesus was the Christ.

This is an account of Saul's acceptance into the community of believers at Damascus. It is the working out of what Ananias had been sent to do by the Lord Jesus, so that Paul would regain his sight and "be filled with the Holy Spirit." The laying on of hands is not directly referred to the giving of the Spirit here, but rather to the healing of Paul's blindness. The blindness and its healing are, however, closely woven into the process of Paul's conversion and initiation in Luke's account. (Later, a symbolical opening of the senses will find a place in Christian initiation, and illumination will be one of its more important images.) Paul is baptized. He then takes food. The reference to food could be a banal statement of fact: Paul needed strengthening because he had not eaten or drunk for three days (v. 9). But it could also be saying something about his initiation: taking food with people expresses fellowship with them, especially when it is done for the first time by one who had previously been an enemy; Luke had earlier coupled "partaking of food with glad and generous hearts" with "the breaking of bread" in his capsule description of the first Christian community in Acts 2:46–47. What manifests Paul's being filled with the Holy Spirit—which, according to the words of Ananias, should be the climax of the process—is not, however, any rite or gesture but his dramatic public appearance among his fellow Jews as one who now believes and proves that Jesus is the Messiah. Like the charismatic manifestations on the day of Pentecost it provokes amazement among the Jews. Paul increases in "strength" (the Greek word is the one Luke used in his accounts of Jesus' promise of the Spirit). He stands firm in the face of opposition. His behavior surely confirmed his standing in the community. It was the disciples who arranged his escape over the wall of the city when he was threatened with death. Luke follows up his account of the acceptance of Paul by the community at Damascus by telling how he came to be accepted by the Church in Jerusalem. The pattern is similar to that of the conversion of the Samaritans. Paul has some difficulty in being accepted by the disciples at Jerusalem, who found it hard to believe that he was a disciple (v. 26) until he is vouched for by Barnabas as one who had "preached boldly in the name of Jesus" in Damascus (v. 27). Once he is accepted he again preaches boldly in the name of the Lord, disputing this time with the Hellenists (v. 29). When his life is in danger it is once again his newly found brethren who rescue him. Paul is recognized as one of them, as being filled with the Spirit, by his bold and public preaching of the name of Jesus. And this happens at the very beginning of his life as a disciple, quite some time before he, along with Barnabas, is set apart by the Holy Spirit and the laying on of hands for his missionary journeys.

Luke's account of the conversion and initiation of Cornelius with his family and friends (Acts 10) is the story of how the gospel was first preached to people who were not Jews. It is in obedience to the Spirit that Peter goes to Cornelius (v. 19). As he tells him and his assembled relatives and friends about Jesus "the Holy Spirit fell on all who heard the word" (v. 44). The evidence offered for this out-pouring of the Spirit is that those who had come with Peter "heard them speaking in tongues and extolling God" (v. 46). Peter reasons from this phenomenon to the legitimacy of baptizing them, and he commands this to be done "in the name of Jesus Christ" (v. 48). At their request Peter remains with the new converts for some days. The Spirit is here given without any action, ritual or otherwise, on the part of Peter, other than the preaching about Jesus. Its coming is visibly manifested by charismatic activity. The manifestation precedes the rite of baptizing. Later, when Peter is telling the Jerusalem community about the incident, he links the gift of the Holy Spirit with baptism: he recalls (11:16) a word of the Lord, "John baptized with water, but you shall be baptized with the Holy Spirit." Taken literally, "baptism with the Holy Spirit" could here be a metaphor for the messianic outpouring of the Spirit, contrasted with the ritual baptism with water. Peter, however, saw the gift of the Spirit as an irresistible invitation to baptize Cornelius ritually. It is more likely then that "baptism with the Holy Spirit" is being taken here as referring to the distinctively Christian way of manifesting repentance, which includes baptism and a visible giving of the Spirit. It is for this that the Jerusalem community "glorified God, saying: 'Then to the Gentiles also God has granted repentance unto life'" (v. 18). Luke does not see the gift of the Spirit given to Cornelius and his friends manifested in any missionary preaching. But the fact that they, who were not Jews, would be using the gift of tongues for "extolling God" (10:46) was already a remarkable testimony and had a decisive influence on the missionary expansion of the Church.

There is another story of conversion and initiation in Acts 19, where Luke tells how Paul brought the gift of the Holy Spirit to some people in Ephesus who, although they believed in Jesus, had received only the baptism of John and knew nothing about the Holy Spirit. They had learned about Jesus but without any normal communion with the Church. It was a situation that even the great Apollos had been in, until he had been taken in hand by Priscilla and Aquila (Acts 18:24–28). Paul explains to the group at Ephesus that John baptized "with the baptism of repentance" in view of the one who was to come after him (v. 4). To explain what he is going to do for them he does not use a contrast between baptism of water and baptism in the Spirit. What he does, in fact, is to baptize them again, "in the name of the Lord Jesus." This must mean baptizing them in a fuller confession of faith than they had made when first baptized. Essential to this full confession of faith would be that Jesus is the Messiah who sends the Spirit that is poured out in the latter days. On that basis Paul would not just baptize them but would also lay his hands on them for the receiving of the Spirit. They are initiated into the eschatological community of the Church, in which Paul is now recognized to be an apostle: the Holy Spirit comes upon them and they speak in tongues and prophesy (v. 6). They can then be counted as members of the Church: "There were about twelve of them in all" (v. 7).

In the interests of finding scriptural roots for a tradition about confirmation it seems fair to summarize the thought of Luke along the following lines. The Holy Spirit is that eschatological presence of the saving power of God that Jesus, the Messiah, brought about on earth. It is known to be given when it is manifested in visible, tangible forms that are characteristic of the end times. It is given in a primordial way to the community of men and women gathered under the leadership of the apostles of Jesus in Jerusalem. It is further given to those who, hearing the word about Jesus, believe in him, repent and have their faith and repentance ritualized by baptism. It does not coincide with baptism, and may precede as well as follow it. In whatever form it is manifested it provides an entitlement to be admitted to the fellowship of the Church of the apostles. In this sense, *manifest* reception of the Spirit is a required part of Christian initiation. The manifestation may come as a surprise to the leadership of the Church (the conversion of Cornelius), in which case it is accepted by them and they provide the other elements of initiation. Or it may come at their initiative (Samaria), as a result of prayer and a ritual gesture with which they complete an initiation already begun. The form in which the manifestation of the presence of the eschatological, messianic Spirit is given varies: it may be charismatic behavior, especially that connected with preaching; it may be, as in the case of Paul, the preaching itself, which is a convincing sign no less than an effect of the coming of the Spirit; it may be the prayerfulness and joy and security evidenced in the community ("the comfort of the Holy Spirit" as Luke calls it in Acts 9:31, using the same word that will give the Spirit a personal name—Comforter/Paraclete—in John's account of the farewell discourse of Jesus).

If Luke seems to always require some such *visible manifestation* that the gift of the eschatological, messianic Spirit is being received by those who are being admitted to the community, one can claim to have a scriptural basis for a hypothesis that it is this *visibility* of the giving of the Holy Spirit, characteristic of the messianic age, that is being ritualized in the part of initiation that eventually came to be called confirmation. The effect being sought would be the effect that Luke attributes to all such manifestations of the Spirit: to make those who believe strong enough to take their faith into public places and play their part in the coming-of-age of salvation, which is the proclamation of Jesus as the only Savior, with the conflicts that this inevitably provokes.

## Saint Paul

It appears that Paul has an understanding of "spirit" that reflects particularly the thought of the Wisdom literature. He sees the gift of the Spirit less as a transient, spectacular act of the power of God working through humans, than as an abiding divine reality that is given for a permanent possession to those who believe in Christ, dying and rising with him in baptism and thenceforward living in him. By the Spirit people are drawn out of the domain of the flesh, are reborn in Christ and become new spiritual creatures, holy and belonging to the heavenly world, children of God. Men and women enjoy this spiritual quality, this access to the wisdom and power of God solely because they have received the gift of God's Holy Spirit; left to themselves, in the flesh, they have nothing to glory in (Romans 8:1–17; 1 Corinthians 2). The Spirit is given in the Church, which is the body of Christ, within which it is the bond of unity (1 Corinthians 12:4–11; Ephesians 4:3–7). Paul, no less than Luke, sees the Spirit as inspiring and giving strength to the Church's preaching of the gospel (Romans 15:18–19; 2 Timothy 1:6–9). But even more so, he sees it as the source of a marvelous variety of spiritual gifts, charismatic in every sense of the word, that build up the Church brought into being by the gospel (1 Corinthians 12; 1 Thessalonians 5:19–21; Galatians 3:2–5; Romans 12:6). It is also the source of prayer, in its interior depth (Romans 8:26–27) and in its external expression in "psalms and hymns and spiritual songs" (Ephesians 5:19). However, while recognizing as Luke does the significance of all these gifts and the value of the ecstatic behavior in which they are sometimes expressed, Paul is more impressed by what he calls "the higher gifts" (1 Corinthians 12:31). Charity holds the highest place (1 Corinthians 13; Romans 5:5); the deep insight that faith gives into the mystery of God is another major gift of the Spirit (1 Corinthians 2); the fruit of the Spirit that Paul celebrates "is love, joy, peace, patience, kindness, goodness, faithfulness, gentleness, self-control" (Galatians 5:22–23). These gifts are not without relevance to the eschatological status and task of the Church in Paul. But Paul, even more than Luke, is careful about eschatological expectations. He is writing to communities that are already having to outgrow any illusions there may have been that the coming of the eschatological age meant that the return of the Lord was imminent, to the point of making the world of time irrelevant. For Paul the inner, long-term gifts are more important for the Church and its mission in the midst of the world than the more spectacular but short-lived enthusiasm of the ecstatic charisms. He sees the Spirit that abides within Christians as the first fruit of the new creation, the permanent guarantee that the work of God will be completed in a resurrection that has already been realized in Christ (Romans 8:18–26). This beginning of the new, eschatological creation shows in the abiding gifts of love and peace, and in the inner strength of faith and prayer, more than in transient gifts like tongues and prophecy.

The significance of Paul's teaching about the Holy Spirit for an eventual theological understanding of confirmation must lie in the way it establishes the inner, abiding strength that the Spirit gives to those who must live and proclaim their faith publicly and build up the Church in the eschatological age. The difficulty that Paul's theology of the Spirit raises for a theology of confirmation is that the giving of the Spirit is so closely related to baptism that there does not seem to be much room left for postulating another rite for the giving of the Spirit. It is true that Paul does not give any descriptions of Christian initiation. The nearest he comes to it is in Romans 6:1–11, and one might make something of the fact that there he speaks about baptism without any mention of the Holy Spirit. But in 1 Corinthians he does say: "you were washed, you were sanctified, you were justified in the name of the Lord Jesus Christ and in the Spirit of our God." (6:11) and "For by one Spirit we were all baptized into one body—Jews or Greeks, slaves or free—and all were made to drink of one Spirit" (12:13). The "higher gifts" of the Spirit that he so emphasizes are gifts and effects that he commonly associates with baptism. Nor does he refer to any rite that could become confirmation. When the laying on of hands is mentioned in the Pauline corpus it is for the giving of ministry. He does speak of Christians being anointed and sealed and given the Spirit as a guarantee (2 Corinthians 1:21–22; Ephesians 1:13–14) but it would seem that this language is metaphorical rather than a reference to anything actually done in the rite of Christian initiation.

## Saint John

The teaching about the Spirit in the Johannine writings is closer to the tradition of Paul than it is to Luke. It presents the Spirit as an abiding reality more than as a force manifested in action. In the gospel and epistles of John there is no mention of charismatic, ecstatic behavior resulting from the presence of the Spirit. The book of Revelation, on the other hand, is entirely an account of prophecy "in the Spirit" (1:10; 4:2; 17:3; 21:10) that reveals and guides, in apocalyptic images, the destiny of the Christian community in the conflicts of the eschatological age. In being with the Church ("the Spirit and the Bride say" 22:17) in these enlightening visions and messages, the Spirit is the kind of Counselor (Paraclete, Comforter) that Jesus promised he would be. However, the abiding of the Spirit with the community that is presented in the gospel and epistles goes deeper and is more pervasive than what is manifested by the gift of prophecy. The Spirit is first in Jesus (John 1:32–34). Given the way John's christology sees the unity of Jesus with the Father as a oneness of being, the Spirit must be conceived as belonging to the very reality of this oneness, rather than simply as a divine power that takes possession of the man Jesus and makes him Son of God. After he has been glorified Jesus can give the Spirit to those who believe in him (John 7:37–39). What the Spirit is and does for the disciples is explained in the discourse and prayer of Jesus at the Last Supper (John 14–17). The Spirit is from the Father on the level that Jesus is from the Father and relates to him as Son. He is another Counselor, on the level that Jesus is himself Counselor. As Jesus does, so does the Spirit make the disciples of Jesus live in the real world of God, instead of in the world of appearance and unreality associated with the flesh and the world. The Spirit reveals the ultimate truth about the world, convincing it of sin and of righteousness and of judgment. The Spirit admits the disciples to the truth of things, especially as this is contained in the words of Jesus. So Jesus can pray the Father to keep them safe and united in the midst of the world and its hostilities, sanctifying them in the truth, so that through their word others may come to believe that Jesus himself is the one sent by the Father. It is the Spirit who will be with them in this mission: "But when the Counselor comes, whom I shall send to you from the Father, even the Spirit of truth, who proceeds from the Father, he will bear witness to me; and you also are witnesses, because you have been with me from the beginning" (John 15:26–27). Jesus gives them this Spirit on the day of his resurrection (John 20:21–23). There is no "waiting in the city" for a Pentecostal experience. The Spirit will give standing to what they do in the community, specifically to their forgiving of sins.

It is in baptism that John sees the Spirit being given to those who believe in Jesus (John 3). John does not describe the rite of baptism, as he does not describe the rite of the Eucharist in his account of the Last Supper. He is noted for dealing with the rites of the Church symbolically and theologically rather than ritually. He takes water as a symbol of the Spirit. People drink of the Spirit (John 7:37–39). What he sees in baptism is rebirth in water and the Spirit (John 3:5–6) into the real world of God, beyond the flesh and the sinfulness that belongs to it. The reality that John wants people to see symbolized in their baptism is the reality that the Spirit gives witness to (cf. also 1 John 5:6–9). Breath, or the wind is also a symbol of the Spirit: when John describes Jesus giving the Spirit by breathing upon the disciples (John 20:22) he is drawing attention to a symbolic image rather than to a ritual action. The symbolical language of anointing is used in 1 John 2:20. It is used to contrast those who "went out from us, but they were not of us" (v. 19) with those who "have been anointed by the Holy One." The issue is not unlike that raised by Peter in his rebuke to Simon the magician. It has to do with belonging or not belonging to the community of true believers. The true believers are "anointed by the Holy One." Although the anointing is not attributed to the Spirit, the consequence of it, "you all know . . . the truth," is a characteristic work of the Spirit in John. A later verse points in the same direction: "the anointing which you received from him abides in you, and you have no need that anyone should teach you; as his anointing teaches you about everything, and is true, and is no lie, just as it has taught you, abide in him" (v. 27). The text goes on to develop the idea of abiding in terms of being children of God, avoiding sin, and living in the truth about Jesus and in love, before eventually relating it explicitly to the Holy Spirit: "By this we know that we abide in him and he in us, because he has given us of his own Spirit" (4:13). By this assurance of our abiding in God that comes from the Holy Spirit "is love perfected with us, that we may have confidence for the day of judgment, because as he is so are we in this world . . . perfect love casts out fear" (vv. 17–18). From a different standpoint (that of inner experience) the text reaches a conclusion that has affinities with the teaching of Luke: the Spirit is strength for the Christian in the eschatological era.

Johannine literature speaks symbolically rather than descriptively of Christian rites: if the Eucharist is not described in the account of the Last Supper, the imagery of it does permeate the theology of the Eucharist that is expounded in John 6. One might wonder if the symbolical language about the Holy Spirit in terms of anointing does not likewise depend on a real rite that was practiced in the Church as part of Christian initiation. But as there is no corroborative evidence for such a rite in the New Testament, such as there is for the rites of baptism and Eucharist, one cannot claim with any confidence that the fine theology of the Holy Spirit in John is a reflection on an actual part of the rite of initiation that would eventually be recognized as confirmation.

## From Scripture to its Tradition

The distinction that has been made within the New Testament between a theology of the Holy Spirit found in Luke and another that comes from Paul and is further developed in John can have consequences for a reading of the subsequent tradition, and for a theology of confirmation. There are uncertainties and apparent divergences in the tradition about how and in what particular rite the Spirit is given in Christian initiation. There is a view that it is given in the act of baptizing. There is also a view that links it with an anointing or laying on of hands that follows baptism and eventually identifies these rites as being a sacrament, distinct from baptism, for the giving of the Holy Spirit. It is tempting to propose that the theology of the Spirit that is being transmitted in the first of these traditions is derived from Paul/John, whereas the second represents Luke. One might suggest that, in the early centuries, the more developed, Hellenistic theologies of Paul and John, centered on baptism, supplanted the more primitive Jewish theology that had survived in Luke, but that there was a subsequent revival of Luke's ideas, especially in relation to the rites

of laying on of hands and anointing that had become part of the rite
of Christian initiation. These hypotheses are certainly of some help
for a reading of the tradition. But they can also be misleading. While
Luke does not give great attention to the inner sanctifying presence
of the Holy Spirit in Christians he in no way excludes it. His repeated
reference to prayer as the setting in which the Spirit is given, and the
reasoning he attributes to Peter about why Simon the magician could
not give the Holy Spirit, show that he believes the Spirit belongs to
holy people who live in the faith and love of Christ. To say that he
does not make the Spirit be the direct principle of holiness does not
mean that he thinks the gift of the Spirit is irrelevant to it. There
is no trace in Luke of an Old Testament idea that the spirit of God
could take hold of people against their wills, or that it could use evil
people for God's purposes (oddly enough, it is John who says that
Caiaphas prophesied without knowing it because he was high priest,
John 11:49–51). Paul and John do highlight the inner sanctifying
presence of the Spirit. But they also see the presence of the Spirit
as affecting the mission of the Church to preach the gospel. Their
emphasis on the interiority and abiding reality of the gift of the Spirit
gives a new depth to that self-confidence and sense of being chosen
and gifted to bring about the saving work of God in the world of
the last days that Luke attributes to the Holy Spirit. They put the
Spirit-given strength of Christians on a firmer basis by locating it
in their faith and love, in their knowing and doing the truth in love,
rather than merely in their charismatic gifts. They deepen rather than
discount the mission-centered theology of the Holy Spirit that Luke
champions.

From such a starting point the theological issue to be traced
in the tradition is not so much whether or how a particular New
Testament theology of the Holy Spirit gave rise to a rite and theology
of confirmation, as one of how the full richness of all the theologies
took sacramental shape in a complex rite made up of baptism and
confirmation and Eucharist. The Spirit is given in Christian initiation,
with all the effects that Luke and Paul and John assign to it. The theological question about confirmation is about there being a particular
aspect of this gift, that is consistently revealed in the New Testament,
and is subsequently recognized in the Church as being symbolized and
realized in a part of the rite of initiation other than the baptizing in

water, even if it takes some centuries for this other rite to find a settled and independent form.

## THE FATHERS

In the Apostolic Fathers and Apologists the Spirit is commonly "the prophetic Spirit." It is not particularly connected with initiation, except to the extent that the Holy Spirit is named in the formula of baptism (which Justin explains in *First Apology*, 64 by saying ". . . in the name of the Holy Spirit, who through the prophets foretold all things concerning Jesus"). Irenaeus, however, has a rich theology of the Holy Spirit that has a distinct bearing on initiation. In a text from *Adversus Haereses*, III, 17 (used in Office of Readings for Pentecost Sunday) he weaves together different themes, images, and theologies of the Holy Spirit. He associates the Spirit with baptism. The Spirit descended on Christ like a dove and was given by him to his disciples as a "power to confer rebirth into the life of God" by preaching and baptizing. The Spirit is the gift poured out at the end of time, manifested in prophecy, and at the same time providing a principle of new life. There is no discontinuity between the action of the Spirit in bringing back distant tribes into unity and the action that moistens us and makes us fruitful of life. The Spirit "makes us fit for God's purposes. Just as dry flour cannot coalesce into a lump of dough, still less a loaf, without moisture, so too we, being many, could not become one in Christ Jesus without the water which comes from heaven." He then illustrates his understanding of the gift of the Spirit by a curious interpretation of the parable of the good Samaritan. The man fallen among thieves represents fallen humanity: "For the Lord entrusts to the Holy Spirit this man who had fallen among thieves. Taking pity on him he has bound up his wounds, and given two imperial coins, stamped with the image of the Spirit and the inscription of the Father and the Son. We are to accept them, and make the coin entrusted to us bear fruit and multiply for the Lord." There is no particular justification in the gospel text for saying, as Irenaeus does, that the Lord "commits him to the Holy Spirit," unless it is in the reference to the pouring of oil (and wine) in the description of how the Samaritan took care of the injured man (Luke 10:34). Is the remark of Irenaeus an allusion to a ritual anointing with oil for the giving of the Holy Spirit in the rite of initiation?

He has a reference in *Adversus Haereses*, I, 14 to the use of such a rite in initiation by a Christian Gnostic sect. It is also worth noting that he goes beyond the scriptural text in arguing from the fact that the two "imperial coins" have an image and inscription on them to the claim that the Spirit stamps the image of Father and Son on the Christian. This stamping of an image by the Holy Spirit would make more sense if Irenaeus were referring, even obliquely, to some rite of marking or sealing in Christian initiation.[4]

Tertullian sees the Spirit of God in the waters of baptism but says it is actually given to the Christian at the laying on of hands that follows the water rite and the anointing with chrism: "At this point that most Holy Spirit willingly comes down from the Father upon bodies cleansed and blessed" (*De Baptismo*, c. 8; cf. c. 4). However, when he is explaining the difference between Christian baptism and the baptism of John he says clearly that even the remission of sins is given by the Holy Spirit (c. 10). He recommends that those who are baptized should pray for the charisms of the Holy Spirit (c. 20) but does not give charismatic gifts any special attention. His views on the Spirit and on the charisms surely changed when he joined the Montanists. They gave a central place to prophecy and other ecstatic forms of behavior, which they attributed to the Spirit. Against them, and all other sects and schismatic groups, various writers of the third century contended that the Holy Spirit was received and given only within the unity of the Catholic Church. The accent came to be put on the unifying work of the Spirit within the existing Church more than on the strength for missionary expansion that the Spirit also gave to the Church. Cyprian was a major proponent of the unity of the Church against heretical and schismatic groups. He argued that these groups did not have the Spirit because they were cut off from the unity of the Church. Because they did not have the Spirit they could not give it. Cyprian used this principle in making his case for rebaptizing heretics. He argued that because heretics did not have the Holy Spirit the baptism they gave was no baptism. His assumption is that there is no baptism without the gift of the Holy Spirit. And yet it is with the laying on of hands that follows the rite of baptizing that Cyprian

---

4. Other texts of Irenaeus and analysis in Milner, *The Theology of Confirmation*, 19–22, and J. D. C. Fisher, *Confirmation Then and Now* (London: S.P.C.K., 1978; Chicago/Mundelein: Hillenbrand Books, 2005).

normally associates the giving of the Spirit. He argues his case about baptism on that basis. He notes that the opponents of rebaptism in the Church do, in fact, lay hands on converted heretics for the giving of the Spirit. Later theology might have called this the Sacrament of Reconciliation, but Cyprian takes it to be the first ritual giving of the Spirit. He sees in this practice of his opponents an admission that heretics did not have the Spirit. He accuses them of inconsistency in allowing that baptism given by heretics has value and should not be repeated, whereas their laying on of hands was being given no value and had to be repeated. He develops this argument cogently in his Letter 74 *Ad Pompeium*.[5]

The argument of Cyprian in favor of rebaptism can be answered with the help of distinctions worked out in later theology between a valid and a fruitful baptism. These will also throw light on the ambiguity in his thought about whether the Spirit is given in the baptizing or in the laying on of hands. Cyprian was probably so conscious of the unity of Christian initiation and so insistent that one could only be initiated in the one true Church that the assigning of the gift of the Spirit to one or other of the rites would not mean the exclusion of it from the other. The laying on of hands is an episcopal and manifestly ecclesial ritual action. It makes the gift of the Spirit decisively visible because it manifests admission to the one and only Church. But it is meaningless without baptism. Cyprian also mentions an anointing with chrism in Christian initiation (*Letter* 70) and says that those who join the Church from heresy are "perfected with" the Lord's seal as well as having hands laid on them (*Letter* 73).

Cyprian's arguments in favor of rebaptizing heretics did not convince the Western church. The tradition affirmed by Pope Stephen against Cyprian was eventually sanctioned by the Council of Arles (314 CE), which ruled that those who had been baptized and confessed the Catholic Creed in an heretical or schismatic sect were to be admitted to the Church by having the bishop lay hands on them "for the receiving of the Holy Spirit" (DS 123). The theological reflection about Christian initiation provoked by the question of the admission

---

5. R. J. Deferrari, ed. and trans. *St. Cyprian, Treatises*. The Fathers of the Church. A New Translation, vol. 36 (Washington, DC: The Catholic University of America Press, 1958), 288–290; R. B. Donna, csj, *St. Cyprian, Letters (1-81)*. The Fathers of the Church. A New Translation, vol. 51 (Washington, DC: The Catholic University of America Press, 1964).

of heretics into the Church gave prominence to the role of the Holy Spirit in building up the internal unity of the Church. Unity was becoming a critical issue in that third century, as the pressures that could give rise to heresy and schism multiplied within the growing complexity of the communion of faith. The Church was also sufficiently public for it to become sensitive to the effect that its internal divisions could have on what the world thought of it. It would make more sense to see the Spirit that was received at initiation as the Spirit that gathered people together in the Church before seeing it as the Spirit that sent them out in missionary expansion. The unity of the Church was, no doubt, seen in relation to its mission to the world. But a phrase like Cyprian's famous "outside the Church no salvation" suggests a conception of unity that would make mission be a drawing of people into the Church, within which they would receive the Spirit, rather than an outward expansion of a Spirit-filled Church. In such a perspective the Spirit given in initiation is more for the security of salvation than for the adventure of mission.

The theology of the Holy Spirit and of the place of the Spirit in the life of Christians in the Church is marvelously developed in the writing of the Greek Fathers during the fourth century. One touches only the fringes of it in the mystagogical catecheses of Cyril of Jerusalem, John Chrysostom, and Theodore of Mopsuestia.[6] What they have to say, however, links the pneumatology of the East to the rites of Christian initiation and will have an important influence on the theology of confirmation. Cyril gives his teaching especially when commenting in Sermon 3 (Yarnold, pp. 81–85) on the anointing with chrism that comes after baptizing in the rite of initiation. Although he associates the gift of the Spirit with the anointing rather than with the baptizing, the natural continuity between bathing and anointing allows him to join the Christ-effect and the Spirit-effect closely. The baptizing is putting on Christ; the anointing also makes the baptized be "christs" (anointed ones). At the same time, by referring the anointing to what happened at Christ's baptism he can say that "the anointing is the Holy Spirit." The Spirit is the messianic Spirit promised by Isaiah, with which the Father anointed Jesus when he "chose him to be

---

6. Texts are quoted here from E. Yarnold, SJ *The Awe-Inspiring Rites of Initiation. The Origins of the R.C.I.A.* 2nd ed. (The Liturgical Press: Collegeville, MN, 1994).

Savior of the whole world." It is the messianic "oil of gladness" foretold by David, given to Christ "the author of spiritual joy," and by him to those who have been anointed. Cyril draws a daring parallel between the bread of the Eucharist and the chrism which "after the invocation is no longer ordinary ointment but Christ's grace, which through the presence of the Holy Spirit instills his divinity into us." The grace of Christ, the presence of the Holy Spirit, divinization—these are different aspects of what is given in the anointing. After explaining to the neophytes why they were anointed in different parts of the body he reminds them that Christ, after receiving the Spirit, went forth to do battle with the enemy, "so you also, after your holy baptism and sacramental anointing, put on the armor of the Holy Spirit, confront the power of the enemy, and reduce it saying: 'I can do all things in Christ who Strengthens me.'" It is the theme of strength and of battle against the enemy that will become classical in the theology of confirmation. Cyril continues to explain it in messianic terms, playing on the equivalence of Christ, Messiah, Anointed One: by the anointing the neophytes are entitled to be called Christians; they are the ones in whom the typological anointings of Aaron and Solomon are fulfilled ("not in figure but in truth, for you were truly anointed by the Holy Spirit"); they are taught all things, in the Johannine sense; and the salvation promised to all nations is being worked out in them: "so the blessed Isaiah prophesied long ago: 'The Lord shall make provision for all nations on this mountain' (by mountain he means the Church . . . ). They will drink of wine and gladness, and be anointed with chrism. To convince you utterly, hear what he says about the sacramental nature of this chrism: 'Give all these things to the nations, for the Lord's counsel is to all nations.'"

Explanations of how the Holy Spirit is given in Christian initiation coming from the tradition of Antioch are affected by the peculiarities of the Antiochean rite of initiation: the anointing with chrism precedes the act of baptizing, the laying on of hands is done at the moment of baptism and there is no anointing afterward, at least until the late fourth century and then it is not associated with the gift of the Spirit (see Chapter 6, "History"). John Chrysostom comments on the anointing with chrism in a way that will become familiar in later theologies of confirmation. The anointing makes one be "a soldier . . . signed on for a spiritual contest." The anointing has just been preceded by renunciation of the Devil. The anointed persons, "renouncing him, . . . have changed their allegiance and publicly enlisted with Christ . . . the bishop anoints you on your forehead and marks you with the seal, to make the devil turn away his eyes . . . you will confront him in battle and this is why the bishop anoints you as athletes of Christ before leading you into the spiritual arena" (*Homily* 2, 22, in Yarnold, pp. 160–161). However, it is significant that John does not attribute any of these agonistic consequences of anointing and sealing to the Holy Spirit. It is only at the moment of baptizing that the Spirit is given: "Then by the words of the bishop and by his hand the presence of the Holy Spirit flies down upon you" (ibid., 25, p. 161). According to John's account the baptism is followed immediately by the welcome of the community, with a kiss, and the Eucharist, which he does associate with the Spirit: "For as soon as they come up from the font, they are led to the awesome table which is laden with all good things. They taste the body and blood of the Lord and become the dwelling place of the Spirit" (ibid., 27, p. 163). But further on, near the end of his homily, he mentions something that comes between baptism and access to the table. It is a prayer for others, in the Church and in the world. The *Apostolic Tradition* also prescribes prayer with the assembled community at this point of the rite of initiation— corresponding to what would come to be called The Prayer of the Faithful, or The General Intercessions. For Chrysostom, it is a prayer that looks forward to the Eucharist, but that also looks backward to the gift that has been given in baptism. He does not relate it particularly to the Holy Spirit. But his exhortation does recall the battle with the devil that he had associated with anointing and appeals to the self-confidence proper to those who have been made friends and children of God; he also highlights the unity of the Church and the salvation of the world, both of which are characteristic works of the Spirit. He says:

> As you step out of the sacred waters and express your resurrection by the act of coming up from them, ask for alliance with him so that you may show great vigilance in guarding what has been given to you, and so be immune from the tricks of the Enemy. Pray for the peace of the Churches. Intercede for those who are still wandering . . . You were once diffident; God has given you great assurance. You were once slaves . . . he has raised you up and adopted you as sons . . . When he sees you showing such

concern for those who are your own members and anxious about the salvation of others, because of this he will count you worthy to receive great
assurance. (ibid., 29–30, pp. 163–164)

Theodore of Mopsuestia is inclined to speak in general terms
about the action of the Holy Spirit in initiation rather than to locate
the giving of the Spirit in any particular rite. The Spirit is in the water
by reason of the blessing of the bishop (*Homily* 3, 9, in Yarnold,
pp. 185–187); it is the principle of new birth in the womb of the water
(*ibid.* and already in 3, 3, Yarnold, p. 181–182); it is the principle and
guarantee of resurrection and immortality that will have its full effect
at the resurrection (ibid., 3, 7–10, Yarnold, pp. 184–187). Theodore
stands apart from previous writers in the Antiochean liturgical tradition in commenting on a sealing that is done after baptizing and in
relating it explicitly to the Holy Spirit (Homily 3, 27, in Yarnold,
p. 198–200 and footnote 65). He seems to see this rite as a kind of
résumé of the gift of the Spirit given throughout initiation rather than
as the rite in which the Spirit is actually given. It recalls the messianic
Spirit that came on Jesus and stayed with him as an anointing. It is
this abiding, definitive quality of the gift of the messianic Spirit rather
than the gift itself that he reads into this postbaptismal sealing and
anointing of Christians: "You too, then, must he sealed on the forehead. While the bishop is putting the seal on you, he says: 'N. is sealed
in the name of the Father, etc.' This sign shows you that, when the
Father, the Son and the Holy Spirit were named, the Holy Spirit came
upon you. You were anointed by him and received him by God's grace.
He is yours and remains within you . . ." (*Homily* 3, 27, in Yarnold,
pp. 198–199).

Saint Ambrose attributes the work of baptism to the Holy
Spirit who descends and consecrates the water; the Spirit comes
because Jesus first went down into the water at his baptism and the
Spirit came upon him (*Sermon* 1, 15–19, in Yarnold, pp. 105–109). In
his second sermon, reflecting on the presence of the Spirit in baptism
(*Sermon* 2, 14–15, in Yarnold, p. 114–115), he interprets the dove that
came on Jesus at his baptism as a sign given "to call the incredulous
to faith." This leads him to a general reflection about signs that is an
important component of his sacramental theology: "In the beginning there had to be a sign; in the ages which followed there has to be

fulfillment." He goes on to illustrate this distinction with a comment
on the outpouring of the Spirit at Pentecost:

> There was a loud roaring as though a fierce wind was blowing, and parted
> tongues were seen, as of fire. What does this signify, except the descent
> of the Holy Spirit? He wished to show himself corporally to unbelievers;
> corporally by a sign, but spiritually by the sacrament. This was an evident
> proof of his coming; but now in our case the privilege of faith is offered. In
> the beginning there were signs for the sake of unbelievers; but for us who
> live in the time of the Church's full growth the truth is to be grasped, not
> by signs but by faith.

He appears to be saying that what the spectacular manifestations of the Spirit at Pentecost once did for unbelievers the sacrament now does for believers. Both are manifestations that establish
the coming of the Spirit: one does it by way of proof, the other by
way of faith. The sacrament to which he refers is still, at this point of
his commentary, the water rite of baptism. When he comes later to
explain the postbaptismal sealing (Sermon 3, 8–10, in Yarnold, pp.
124–125) he says that "after the ceremonies of the font, it still remains
to bring the whole to perfect fulfilment. This happens when the Holy
Spirit is infused at the priest's invocation." The invocation for the
giving of the Spirit is the part of the sacrament that "brings the whole
to perfect fulfillment." The Spirit that is received is the Spirit of the
seven messianic gifts read about in Isaiah. For Ambrose, "These are
the seven virtues you receive when you are sealed. For . . . the Holy
Spirit is multiform and has a whole variety of virtues." Ambrose was
probably playing on the fact that the Latin word for "virtue" is the
same as the word used in Acts 1:18 for what the apostles are said to
receive when the Spirit comes upon them (translated "power" in RSV).
It is to this variety of gifts that he returns when, at the end of his
catechesis, he wants to show how the sanctifying action in Christian
initiation is common to the three Persons of the Trinity, and yet that
special aspects of it are peculiar to individual Persons (Sermon 6, 5–10,
in Yarnold, p. 147–149). Neither there nor elsewhere does he relate
these gifts of the Spirit to any kind of public or missionary activity in
the Church. Still less does he see anything charismatic about them.
His earlier remark about Pentecost seems to suggest that the era of
miraculous "signs" is now past and has given way to the era of faith in

which the Church has reached full growth. He seems to be presenting the sacraments, and the faith that perceives the truth and reality within them, as an alternative to the charisms in manifesting the presence of the Spirit, and indeed as something more appropriate to what he calls "the time of the Church's full growth." It is an idea that is not without interest for a theology of sacraments and particularly for the theology of confirmation.

Saint Augustine must have imbibed some of his theology of Christian initiation from Ambrose when he was baptized by him. He uses the distinction between sign and sacrament when discussing the anointing with chrism that follows baptism. But he differs from Ambrose in using it to distinguish between the external rite of anointing with oil, which is what he calls the sign, and the internal anointing with the gift of the Spirit, which is the sacrament (cf. In Psalm 44, 19: PL 36, 505). Augustine is also influenced by the experiences and problems of the church of Africa. He identifies the gift of the Spirit given in Christian initiation with charity. There can be a true, unrepeatable baptism, in which breaches in the bond of charity impede the giving of the Spirit. In such cases the Spirit can be given subsequently to those who repent by the laying on of hands. It is not altogether clear whether this is the rite that will come to be recognized as the Sacrament of Reconciliation, in which sins are forgiven through the power of the Holy Spirit, or the completion of Christian initiation in which the Spirit is given for the first time. However, in the normal process of initiation within the Catholic Church it is in the anointing with chrism that Augustine sees the Spirit being given. He recognizes that since the forgiveness of sin cannot be given in baptism without the action of the Spirit, there is already a gift of the Spirit before the anointing. What is given by the anointing is the special gift foretold by the prophets and promised by Christ (*Sermon* 71, 19: PL 38, 454–455). It is the sevenfold messianic Spirit promised in Isaiah. (*Sermon* 249, 3: PL 38, 1162). But these, like all gifts of the Spirit, are for growth in charity. Augustine does not see anything charismatic about them. Charity, of course, is a very powerful concept in Augustine, both for the building-up of the Church and for its role in the salvation of the world. The gift of the Spirit given by anointing with oil in Christian initiation is certainly not a private preserve.

## WESTERN THEOLOGIANS

As a separate rite of laying on of hands for the giving of the Spirit, that could be done only by the bishop, developed in the Latin West during the fifth century (see Chapter 6, "History"), it became necessary to preach about it and to explain it theologically. Of the many sermons that must have been preached on the subject one came to have a special influence on the whole of Western theology, and even on the magisterial statements that accompany it. It is thought to have been preached by a certain Faustus, once Abbot of Lérins and then Bishop of Riez in the south of France, on a feast of Pentecost sometime during the second half of the fifth century.[7] The text of it survived. Much later, in the ninth century, segments of it, carrying the name and authority of various early Popes, were incorporated in the False Decretals—a canonical collection put together to justify various liturgical and disciplinary reforms of the Frankish church—which became an important authority in theological discussion during the Scholastic period. In the original sermon Faustus explains what this rite of the laying on of hands does. Beginning with the quotation "I will pour out my Spirit upon all flesh" he says that the laying on of hands now does what Pentecost did for the first assembly of the faithful. He then has to explain what this gift could add to the gift already received in baptism. He does so by using an analogy that was already well established in explanations of Christian initiation. It is the military image of the Christian as soldier of Christ. It had often been used to explain the anointings and signings that occur in initiation. Faustus stretches it because what he has to explain is a rite of the laying on of hands by the bishop, rather than an anointing:[8]

> Military proceedings require that when a commander receives a man into the number of his soldiers, he should not only put his mark upon him, but also equip him with arms suitable for fighting with. So for a baptized man the blessing [of Confirmation] is a giving of arms. You have given a soldier; give him also the implements of warfare. What good is it for a parent to bestow great wealth on a small child unless he also provides him with a guardian? The Paraclete is precisely such a protector,

---

7. Milner, *The Theology of Confirmation*, 44; for original text, see L. A. van Buchem, *L'Homélie Pseudo-Eusébienne de Pentecôte* (Nijmegen, 1967).

8. Trans. from Milner, *The Theology of Confirmation*, 44–47.

counselor and guardian of those who are reborn in Christ. Therefore the divine word says: "Unless the Lord guard the city, in vain do the watchmen keep vigil."

He softens the military image with the somewhat problematical one of child and guardian. But when he goes on to pin down more precisely the continuity and complementarity of baptism and confirmation, it is the image of battle that prevails:

So the Holy Spirit, who descended upon the baptismal waters bearing salvation, gave at the font all that is needed for innocence: at confirmation he gives an increase for grace, for in this world those who survive through the different stages of life, must walk among dangers and invisible enemies. In baptism we are born again to life, after baptism we are confirmed for battle. In baptism we are washed, after baptism we are strengthened.

Confirmation is a strengthening. This is an idea that will be canonized by the use of the *False Decretals* make of the text of Faustus, and will find its way into most Western theology, as well as into documents of the *magisterium*. The idea of strength could be related to that "power from on high" that Luke says the Holy Spirit would give the disciples (Luke 24:49 and Acts 1:8). But that is not quite what Faustus has in mind. Rather than use the Latin word *virtus* found in that text of Luke he uses the verb *roboremur*, "we are strengthened" (from it will come the expression *ad robur*, which medieval theology, from Peter Lombard on, will make the classical qualification for the distinctive way the Spirit is given in confirmation). The strength that Faustus sees given by confirmation is not so much for preaching the gospel to the ends of the earth as for living the Christian life in the midst of conflicts and battles of this world. The monastic background of Faustus would certainly make this theme dear to him. Using it to understand confirmation leads him to say, against most of the tradition, that those who die immediately after baptism do not need confirmation: "Thus for those who die at once the benefits of rebirth are sufficient, but for those who survive the aids of confirmation are necessary." The remainder of the homily expands Faustus' view that the gift of the Holy Spirit is given in confirmation, as it was given to the apostles at Pentecost, for personal spiritual growth and strength.

Other strands of the tradition, however, remain alive in Western theology. Three centuries after Faustus, when Charlemagne was having the Roman rite of episcopal confirmation imposed in his domains, one finds a solution being given to the question about baptism and confirmation that differs from what Faustus proposed. Charlemagne's ecclesiastical mentor Alcuin (d. 804) has a pithy statement of the effect of confirmation in one of his letters: whereas in baptism the Christian is endowed with grace for eternal life, in confirmation "he receives the Spirit of sevenfold grace so that he may be strengthened by the Holy Spirit to preach to others."[9] The thought is more fully developed by his pupil Rabanus Maurus (d. 856). Like all the Carolingian reformers he is emphasizing that it is the episcopal laying on of hands that brings the gift of the Spirit for the completing and perfecting of initiation. The anointing with chrism, and the giving of the Spirit that it undoubtedly brings, belongs rather with the grace of baptism. On the episcopal rite of confirmation he says:

> Finally the Holy Ghost, the Paraclete, is conferred upon him by the chief priest through the laying on of the hand, that he may be fortified by the Holy Spirit to preach to others the gift which he himself gained in baptism when he was endowed by grace with eternal life. For the baptized is signed by the priest on the top of the head, by the bishop on his forehead. The first anointing signifies the descent of the Holy Spirit upon him to consecrate a dwelling for God; by the second it is declared that the sevenfold grace of the same Holy Spirit has come upon the man with all the fullness of sanctity for the knowledge of the truth . . . to bear the name of Christ fearlessly before the kings and rulers of this world and preach it with a free voice.[10]

In the prominence given to messianic, eschatological words and images ("fortified by the Holy Spirit," "sevenfold grace," "fullness of sanctity," "knowledge of the truth," "seal," "strengthened," "bearing the name of Christ fearlessly before kings." . . .), and in centering the special gift of the Holy Spirit that comes with confirmation on preaching the gospel to others, Rabanus and Alcuin are recovering the Lucan emphasis in teaching about the Spirit. There is little trace of the

---

9. *Letter* 134: quoted in Milner, *The Theology of Confirmation*, 58.

10. *De Clericorum Institutione* (PL 107, 293–420A) 1, 30: quoted in Milner, *The Theology of Confirmation*, 60.

outgoing, missionary interpretation of the gift of the Spirit in Faustus: the battle he is concerned with is the personal battle against sin rather than the battle against those who oppose the preaching of the gospel in the world. As a background to the views of Alcuin and Rabanus it is worth noting that the Carolingian churches were quite missionary-minded. They sent preachers among the pagan barbarians and had the experience of forming and initiating adult converts. Rabanus was a noted evangelizer when he became Archbishop of Mainz and his *De Clericorum Institutione*, from which the earlier quotation is taken, was written for the training of monks and clerics who would be active in the evangelization of Germany.

## SAINT THOMAS AQUINAS

Medieval scholastic theology of confirmation can be represented by Saint Thomas. He deals with confirmation in a single question in the *Summa* (Third Part, q. 72). He is influenced by some passages from Faustus that by his time had become authoritative, canonical, and even magisterial statements carrying the name of Pope Melchiades. However, he manages to put his finger on some key themes of the tradition that go beyond what came to him through the texts from Faustus. In q. 72, a. 6 sed con., he quotes as authoritative the words of Rabanus Maurus: "Last of all the Paraclete is given to the baptized person by the bishop through the laying on of hands in order that he be strengthened by the Holy Spirit to proclaim the faith (*ut roboretur per Spiritum Sanctum ad praedicandum*)." It is a text that seems to have had considerable influence on Thomas' theology of the sacrament. He presents confirmation as the sacrament of the fullness of the grace of the Holy Spirit (a. 1 ad 1). This fullness is the reality that was given at Pentecost: there it was given visibly but not in a sacramental rite (a. 2 ad 1; a. 4 ad 1). It is now given in the Church by the rite of anointing with chrism (a. 2). It is in this anointing rather than in the laying on of hands that Thomas sees the sacrament. He evokes many of the traditional themes in his explanation of why chrism is a suitable "matter" for a sacrament that gives the fullness of the Spirit. He relates its symbolism to the requirements of human life that are met by different sacraments. Baptism, he says, corresponds to birth, and is the beginning of life. The life begun in baptism has then to grow and increase *(augmentum)* to a certain point of fullness before it is perfectly human. It is this entry into being fully human, into *aetas perfecta*, that provides Thomas with his analogy for what confirmation does in the life of grace. Significantly, he says that the distinctive thing about perfect age is that then one "begins to live in communication with others, whereas previously one lived as it were solely for oneself (a. 2)." In using the analogy of "perfect age" for confirmation Thomas is not saying anything about the age at which people can or ought to be confirmed. He is quite sure that confirmation can and should be given to all, including infants (a. 8). His argument is that God's intention is to bring everyone who is born to the perfection of their human nature, and that because human perfection is a matter of the spirit rather than of the body, infants are capable of receiving it—as elderly people are capable of receiving the birth of baptism. Confirmation, then, has to do with a divinely intended quality of Christian grace— its being objectively perfect—rather than with a subjective stage of development in grace of the person being confirmed. The grace that Christians are initiated into is grace come-of-age at Pentecost. The perfection of grace is characteristic of the new covenant. This is the reason Thomas gives for saying there was nothing corresponding to confirmation in the Old Law: "Confirmation is the sacrament of the fullness of grace and therefore there could not be anything corresponding to it in the Old Law because 'the law made nothing perfect'" (a. 1 ad 2). Thomas also uses the word *robur* (strength), which had been canonized in the text from Faustus, to characterize this perfect age. It is a spiritual strength coming from the Trinity within, and from the mark or sign of Christ that distinguishes those who do battle under the leadership of Christ (a. 4). Among the components of the strength given by confirmation is the sacramental character. Thomas had been somewhat uncertain about the distinction between the character of confirmation and that of baptism in Third Part, q. 63, a. 6. What he has to say in q. 72, a. 5 is more decisive, although it still leaves some questions unanswered. In confirmation the Holy Spirit gives the power (here Thomas uses the Latin *potestas*, which comes from the Arisotelian categories in which he analyses the character, rather than the biblical word *virtus*) to perform sacred actions, not just for one's own salvation (which is what is given in baptism) but for battle against the enemies of faith; the model of this power is what

the apostles received at Pentecost (a. 5). There is a personal battle
that all the baptized have to fight against invisible enemies; but the
confirmed have to take a stand against the external enemies of the
faith in confessing the name of Christ (a. 5 ad 1). All the baptized
are called to profess faith personally by living the sacramental life of
the Church; when they are also confirmed they are given power to
profess the faith publicly in words, and by a kind of commission *quasi
ex officio* (a. 5 ad 2). Thomas had likened confirmation to ordination
in Third Part, q. 65, a. 3 ad 2, in that they both confer special offices.
In q. 72 he notes the difference between them. He bases the distinction on the different effects that the Holy Spirit had at Pentecost
on the apostles and on the other disciples: it made the apostles be
"teachers of the faith," whereas it made the others be able to do those
things that are needed for "the building-up of the faithful" (a. 2 ad 1;
a. 8 ad 1). He is not very specific, in fact, about what the confirmed
are equipped or commissioned to do. That makes theological sense if
one is seeing confirmation as a normal part of all Christian initiation,
expressing the fullness of grace and perfect age that all Christians
ought to have because they belong to an age in which the Spirit has
been given. Thomas does not follow up a thought he had in q. 63, a.
6 about confirmation being somehow a power to receive other sacraments. Nor does he try to go beyond what he said about sacramental
characters being sharings in Christ's priesthood in q. 63, a. 3, by, for
example, raising the possibility of a sharing in Christ's prophetic
office through confirmation. However, he does consistently describe
the effects of confirmation in terms of confessing the faith, in words,
publicly, in the face of opposition, for the building-up of the faithful.
This is in keeping with his original intuition about "perfect age" being
characterized by communication with other people.

## FROM FLORENCE (1439) TO VATICAN II

The first extended doctrinal statement about confirmation from
the Catholic *magisterium* is in the Decree for the Armenians of
the Council of Florence, which was promulgated in 1439.[11] It is a

---

11. N. P. Tanner, SJ, ed., *Decrees of the Ecumenical Councils,* vol. I (London and Washington:
Sheed & Ward and Georgetown University Press, 1990), 544–545; DS 1317; ND 1416–1418.

résumé of the Latin tradition, expressed in the Scholastic framework of numbered sacraments, matter and form, minister and effects. The matter is chrism; the form is "I sign you with the sign of the cross and I confirm you with the chrism of salvation in the name of the Father and of the Son and of the Holy Spirit." The ordinary minister is the bishop: the reason given is that "we read that only the apostles, whose place the bishops hold, imparted the Holy Spirit by the laying on of hands . . . (Acts 8:14–17) . . . Confirmation given by the Church takes the place of that imposition of hands." After admitting that in the past "through a dispensation of the Apostolic See" regular priests have been known to confirm, with chrism prepared by the bishop, the text states:

> The effect of this sacrament is that in it the Holy Spirit is given for strength *(ad robur)*, as He was given to the apostles on the day of Pentecost, in order that the Christian may courageously confess the name of Christ. And therefore the one to be confirmed is anointed on the forehead which is the seat of shame, so that he may not be ashamed to confess the name of Christ, and chiefly his cross, which, according to the apostle, is a stumbling block for the Jews and foolishness for the Gentiles (cf. 1 Corinthians 1:23). This is why he is signed with the sign of the cross.

Many of the Reformers retained a rite corresponding to confirmation, consisting of a laying on of hands with a prayer for the giving of the Spirit; but, in keeping with their general theology of justification, they usually refused to recognize it as a sacrament in the sense defined by the Council of Florence. It was seen as a public profession of faith, to be made by those who had been baptized in infancy; it was preceded by a period of more intensive study of catechism, and was itself the immediate preparation for First Communion. The Council of Trent condemned this view of confirmation in three canons,[12] but did not itself give any positive teaching about the sacrament. The Anglican Church kept the rite of confirmation or "Laying on of Hands upon Those that are Baptized and Come to Years of Discretion" in its Prayer Book, but without an anointing with oil. Its theologians also kept a lively interest in the meaning of the rite and its relationship with baptism, especially as regards the giving of the Holy Spirit. Over the past century much scholarly work has been done

---

12. Tanner, *Decrees of the Ecumenical Councils*, vol. I, 686; ND 1434–1436.

by Anglicans on the question,[13] and the works of Lampe, Dix, and Fisher have offered rich, though contrasting theologies of the sacrament. Roman Catholics also joined in the debate, especially when it became clear that biblical and historical evidence to which standard Catholic theologies appealed was not always as straightforward as had been claimed. But more importantly, the theology of confirmation became caught up in the general renewal of sacramental theology and in the sensitivities that developed in pastoral liturgy over the past half century. The teaching of Vatican II about confirmation reflects these developments—both the progress that has been made and the uncertainties that remain.

Baptism and confirmation are kept closely together in the teaching of Vatican II. The Constitution on the Church attributes the priesthood of all God's People to their Christian initiation, saying: "The baptized, by regeneration and the anointing of the Holy Spirit, are consecrated . . ." (LG, 10). In LG 11 it separates baptism and confirmation as distinct sacraments, but describes their effects in a way that emphasizes the continuity and progression of the process of initiation. Having said that the faithful are already incorporated in the Church and its worship by baptism, and are bound to confess the faith they have received, it adds: "By the sacrament of Confirmation they are more perfectly bound to the Church and are endowed with the special strength *(robur)* of the Holy Spirit. Hence they are, as true witnesses of Christ, more strictly obliged to spread and defend the faith by words and deed." This is the most decisive statement of the council about the meaning of confirmation. It has to be said that it relies on comparative terms to state the characteristic effects of confirmation ("*more perfectly* bound," "*special* strength," "*more strictly* obliged"), without explaining in what the "more" consists. The idea of witness and responsibility for the faith is further developed in LG 12, as a sharing in Christ's prophetic office. Although there is reference to "the whole body of the faithful who have an anointing that comes from the Holy One" and to their "appreciation of the faith aroused and sustained by the Spirit of truth," the sharing in the prophetic office is not linked with any sacrament. Indeed, when the text goes on to speak of the special charisms of the

---

13. Details in J. D. C. Fisher, *Confirmation Then and Now* (London: S.P.C.K., 1978; Chicago/ Mundelein: Hillenbrand Books, 2005), 142–152.

Holy Spirit it presents them as something additional to what the
Spirit does "through the sacraments and ministrations of the Church."
No special attention is given to confirmation in what the constitution
has to say in its Chapter 4 about the status and ministry of the laity;
and the Decree on the Apostolate of the Laity does not go beyond the
theological statements of *Lumen Gentium*.

There are passages about the Holy Spirit in the documents
of Vatican II which, although they do not refer explicitly to confirmation, must guide a Catholic theology of the sacrament. Chapter 7 of
*Lumen Gentium*, on "The Pilgrim Church," contains a fine statement
on the Holy Spirit in the Church of the eschatological age. It explains
how the work of Christ, now seated at the right hand of the Father, is
continued on earth:

> It is carried forward in the sending of the Holy Spirit and through him
> continues in the Church in which, through our faith, we learn the mean-
> ing of our earthly life, while we bring to term, with hope of future good,
> the tasks allotted to us in the world by the Father, and so work out our
> salvation (cf. Philippians 2:12). Already the final age of the world is with
> us (cf. 1 Corinthians 10:11) and the renewal of the world is irrevocably
> under way, for the Church on earth is endowed already with a sanctity
> that is real though imperfect ... So it is that, united with Christ in the
> Church and marked with the Holy Spirit "who is the guarantee of our
> inheritance" (Ephesians 1:14), we are truly called and indeed are children
> of God ... (LG, 48).

The missionary drive of the Church is very present in the
teaching of Vatican II and the Lucan tradition about the Holy Spirit
is well represented. It is well represented, along with the tradition
stemming from Paul and John, in the doctrinal section of *Ad Gentes
(AG)*, the Decree on the Church's Missionary Activity (end of AG 3,
continuing in AG 4):

> ... what was once preached by the Lord, or fulfilled in him for the salva-
> tion of mankind, must be proclaimed and spread to the ends of the earth
> (Acts 1:8), so that what was accomplished for the salvation of all men may,
> in the course of time, achieve its universal effect. (AG 4) To do this, Christ
> sent the Holy Spirit from the Father to exercise inwardly his saving influ-
> ence, and to promote the spread of the Church. Without doubt, the Holy

Spirit was at work in the world before Christ was glorified. On the day of Pentecost, however, he came down on the disciples that he might remain with them forever (cf. John 14:16); on that day the Church was openly *(publice)* displayed to the crowds and the spread of the Gospel among the nations, through preaching, was begun. Finally, on that day was fore-shadowed the union of all peoples in the catholic Church which speaks every language, understands and embraces all tongues in charity, and thus overcomes the dispersion of Babel . . . Throughout the ages the Holy Spirit makes the entire Church 'one in communion and ministry; and provides her with different hierarchical and charismatic gifts,' giving life to ecclesiastical structures, being as it were their soul, and inspiring in the hearts of the faithful that same spirit of mission which impelled Christ himself.

In the Apostolic Constitution on the sacrament of confirmation *Divinae consortium naturae* (1971) Pope Paul VI is mainly concerned with explaining and justifying decisions about the restoration of the sacramental rite (see Chapter 6, "History"). He does, however, offer some theological refinements of the teaching of Vatican II on confirmation. He says it is the rite "through which the faithful receive the Holy Spirit as a Gift." It is not the gift or gifts of the Spirit that are given but the Spirit himself, whose personal Trinitarian name is Gift. When Saint Thomas analyses this name of the Spirit in First Part, q. 38 he takes it to mean something total, irrevocable, final. Paul VI expounds the Gift as messianic, which comes to the same thing. He sees the apostles laying on hands "to complete the grace of baptism." He has a fine paragraph in which he situates confirmation within the three sacraments of initiation. He uses the Pauline notion of incorporation into Christ and into the Church to express the reality that he sees progressively brought to fullness in initiation. He uses the idea of character in both its christological and ecclesiological senses to state the effects of baptism and confirmation; and it is with the character that he associates what *Lumen Gentium* said about the faithful, when they are confirmed, being "bound more intimately to the Church" and being "more strictly obliged to spread and defend the faith both by word and deed as true witnesses of Christ."[14]

---

14. Text in *The Rites of the Catholic Church* (New York: Pueblo, 1976), 292.

## ECUMENICAL ISSUES

The theology of confirmation expounded by Paul VI would probably be accepted as a valid expression of the tradition of faith, if not the only one, by most Orthodox churches, by Anglicans, and by some Lutheran and Reformed churches. Evangelical churches and communities, however, would still refuse to accept confirmation as a rite that could be linked on any level of equality with baptism. In contemporary ecumenical dialogue the BEM text of the World Council of Churches (Chapter 2, "Ecumenical Convergence on Sacraments") attempts to build a consensus among Christians in a paragraph entitled "Baptism—Chrismation—Confirmation":

> In God's work of salvation, the paschal mystery of Christ's death and resurrection is inseparably linked with the Pentecostal gift of the Holy Spirit. Similarly, participation in Christ's death and resurrection is inseparably linked with the receiving of the Spirit. Baptism in its full meaning signifies and effects both. Christians differ in their understanding as to where the sign of the gift of the Spirit is to be found. Different actions have become associated with the giving of the Spirit. For some it is the water rite itself. For others, it is the anointing with chrism and/or the laying on of hands, which many churches call confirmation. For still others it is all three, as they see the Spirit operative throughout the rite. All agree that Christian baptism is in water and the Holy Spirit.[15]

Catholic difficulties with this text[16] come from its failure to identify confirmation as a sacrament. Underlying that failure is the less than satisfactory nature of BEM's understanding of sacrament already alluded to (see Chapter 2, "Ecumenical Convergence on Sacraments"). The issue for Catholic theology is not just one of discovering where "the sign of the gift of the Spirit is to be found" but whether or not the Spirit is actually given in and by the sign; and whether the sign thus understood is distinct from the sign of baptism; and whether it is an integral rather than an optional part of initiation.

---

15. *Baptism, Eucharist and Ministry, Faith and Order Paper 111* (Geneva: World Council of Churches, 1982), n. 14.

16. Text in M. Thurian (ed.), *Churches Respond to BEM: Official Responses to the "Baptism, Eucharist and Ministry" Text*, vols. I–VI, Faith and Order Papers 129, 132, 135, 137, 143, 144 (Geneva: WCC, 1986–1988).

# SYSTEMATIC THEOLOGY OF CONFIRMATION

## The Theological Question

A systematic theology of confirmation supposes much of what has been said about baptism in Chapter 5, "Systematic Theology of Baptism." In the early tradition baptism often stood for the whole process of Christian initiation, and in many ways the theology of baptism is a general theology of Christian initiation. And, of course, the general theology of sacraments offered in Chapter 3 must also underlie a theology of confirmation. The systematic questions about confirmation begin to emerge when, believing confirmation is a sacrament distinct from baptism, one looks for a way of defining its distinctiveness. As suggested in Chapter 5 "Regeneration in the Grace of the Holy Spirit," these questions have to be put as questions about the action of God in giving the Holy Spirit. As with all the sacraments, it is with the distinctive action of God that is signified in it that one ought to begin the specific study of confirmation. It is too late to start looking for what is specific to confirmation, and at how it differs from baptism, when one has come to discuss the effects of the sacrament. Effects that one would want to assign to confirmation will be found to have been already claimed for baptism. One will be left struggling to work out the difference between the two sacraments in terms of modalities and degrees of the same effect. Sacraments are signs: one must begin to look for what is distinctive about a particular sacrament, not on the level of its effects but in its symbolism; the effects follow on the symbolism (*efficiunt quod figurant*, as the Scholastics said). The originality of sacraments is not so much in what they do—God can do all that is needed for human salvation without them—but that they make what God is doing visible in a human symbol. What is symbolized first and foremost in a sacrament is the salvific action of God. Human prayer and human response is also symbolized, but that is always relative to the particular way in which God is believed to act in the rite.

As a sacrament of initiation confirmation must symbolize the salvific action of God through Christ and in the Spirit as it first takes hold of humans. From the tradition about the rite it is clear that it symbolizes in a particular way the action of God in giving the Spirit. The problem is that the living and life-giving waters of baptism already symbolize the divine action of giving the Spirit. The theological question then must be: is there anything in the divine giving of the Spirit that is not clearly symbolized in baptism and is important enough for human salvation to require symbolizing in another rite? If one can identify such a distinctive feature of God's salvific action, and show how it is well symbolized in the rite of confirmation, one will have a theological insight into the nature of the sacrament of confirmation and a reason for its distinction from baptism. The identification of a second sacrament of initiation does not postulate any new salvific action of God. It refers rather to something in that unique saving action that is manifested and communicated to humans in a ritual other than baptism. The theological question about confirmation is not just about the gift of the Holy Spirit but about *something distinctive in the gift of the Spirit that is made visible in the rite.*

## The Messianic, Eschatological Spirit

As God's People tell their story, God has been sending his Spirit upon his world from the first instant of creation. In the Old Testament the coming of the Spirit was often visible and palpable in things, events, and people (for example, in ecstatic prophecy and charismatic leadership). One of the lines of messianic hope developed by the prophets looks beyond these partial, provisional manifestations to a definitive, full outpouring of the Spirit in the day of the Lord at the end times. The prophets see the gift of the Spirit being experienced both in a perfect interiorizing of relations with God and in spectacular external manifestations of his power. The Spirit would be at the heart of the messianic transformation of all things. The New Testament tells how this promise is manifestly fulfilled. It is fulfilled visibly in Jesus himself. The Spirit is seen to come upon him in the form of a dove, and is seen to stay with him in the way he sets about preaching the good news that messianic salvation has arrived in his own person, and that the end times are at hand. He promises and visibly gives the messianic Spirit to his disciples, sending them to preach salvation to the ends of the earth. The events of the day of Pentecost are the most spectacular manifestation that the day of the Lord has arrived and that the eschatological outpouring of the Spirit has occurred. There are other manifestations recounted by Luke in Acts—prophecy, speaking in tongues, a house shaking, daring missionary enterprises undertaken—and the visibility of the coming of the Spirit is also associated with a rite of laying on of hands with prayer. As well as Luke's account of these colorful and noisy manifestations that the reality of the messianic Spirit has arrived, there is the other tradition, told by Paul and later by John, that pays more attention to the way the prophetic hope for an interiorizing of relations with God through the inner gift of the Spirit is seen to be realized: here the gift that has been given to those who believe in Jesus shows in the faith they profess, in the love they practice, and in their peace and strength and joy and prayer. There is no rite associated with the visibility of the messianic Spirit in John or Paul, but the images of anointing and sealing are there, even if only as metaphorical language, to describe what the gift of the messianic Spirit looks like. The use of these images, which can easily be turned into actual rites, as well as of the rite of laying on of hands described by Luke, entitles one to advance the suggestion that the rite that was eventually recognized as confirmation is a sacramental way of making visible the messianic, eschatological quality of the gift of the Spirit in the New Testament: it does in ritual form what the spectacular events of Pentecost, on the one hand, and the inner experience of ultimate salvation enjoyed by the first Christians, on the other hand, do in a prototypical way.

One can explore the suggestion further. With the coming of the messianic Spirit something changes radically in the relationship between God and his People. The giving of the messianic Spirit is the final salvific act of God in human history. No further divine act is needed for the salvation of the world. Only the Parousia remains, to close the series of "the wonderful works of God." The last times have arrived and the Parousia is at hand. In the time of waiting for it, people draw on the gift that God has already given. The world and the people who make its history are being transformed by a power of God that is already at work in it. The necessary resources are already in the world and in human hearts. The people on whom the Spirit has come visibly are made aware, by personal experience, of this radical change in the dispensation of grace. They are made aware that they have within themselves the full resources to complete the work of salvation. They can go public about salvation. They have what it takes. The Spirit is always an enabling gift. The eschatological Spirit enables people to do "the last things," to do everything necessary to make

themselves and their world ready for the coming of the Lord. They
do not have to look outside themselves, individually or as community,
for anything that might be needed for the day of salvation. The time
for pedagogues, for being led by the hand and for childish religion
is ended. The regime of grace has come of age. The adult phase of
salvation has arrived. It is not that the children of God are automati-
cally turned into adults. What Pentecost manifests is not immediately
something about people but something about the quality of grace. It
proclaims that the grace now available, because it is eschatological, is
adult grace, which, if taken on its own terms, will find expression in
adult attitudes toward God and his work in the world. It will be lived
with the self-confidence and maturity that comes from the experience
of having been given within oneself all that is required for salvation. It
will be a life of interiority, of self-motivation, of self-reliance, of freedom and creativity. It will have to cope with conflict and opposition
but will have the inner and outer strength and self-assurance to deal
with them. These qualities belong to the grace of the New Testament
because it is the grace of the messianic, eschatological Spirit. It seems
reasonable that those who are being initiated into grace should have
this messianic, eschatological quality of the gift of the Spirit manifested to them in a special rite, called confirmation, as it was manifested to the first Christians at Pentecost. An anointing with perfumed
oil has emerged as an appropriate rite. It has been recognized by the
Church as actually giving the grace that it signifies. It is a sacrament.

## For the Salvation of the World

The regime of grace inaugurated by Pentecost is for people whose
inner strength and adult behavior mark their relationship with other
people no less than their individual relationship with God. People
who are aware of receiving the eschatological fullness of the Spirit
are, of necessity, public people. The coming of the Spirit concerns all
peoples and all creation. It raises an issue that no one can ignore or be
neutral about. All people are caught up in the eschatological reality of
the Spirit, whether they know it or not. Sooner or later they must say
where they stand about Christ and the Spirit he has sent. Those who
have received the Spirit in some visible way cannot, then, confine their
lives to private issues and relationships, or allow their Church to be a

private club. They have responsibilities in the great public issue that
dominates the final stage of human history. The Spirit has, indeed,
been poured out on all flesh but the manifestation of the Spirit was
given from the first only to some. It is they who are to tell the rest of
the world what is happening in this final stage of human history. They
are spokespeople of the Spirit, gathering together those who accept
salvation, and standing firm against those who oppose it. They tell
how the Father has sent his Son, Jesus, to be the Savior of the world,
and how that salvation is being worked out through the action of the
Spirit who has been sent into the world. If they do not do the telling,
it will simply not be done.

    This is the missionary meaning of the gift of the Spirit,
the side of it brought specially to light by Luke in his account of
Pentecost, and all through Acts. It is another aspect of the coming-
of-age of the plan of salvation, of the mature adult phase of grace that
has been reached. God can now trust men and women to save the
world, because he has given them in this manifest way the resources
that match this responsibility. The gift and its responsibilities are made
visible in the tongues of fire seen at Pentecost, as well as in the behavior of the disciples on whom they came. Men and women who were
timidly minding their own business behind closed doors come out
compulsively into the streets and begin to talk to everyone they meet.
They find themselves suddenly strong enough in their convictions
and articulate enough in their speech to be able to proclaim publicly
the faith that is in them. They overcome the barriers of language in a
way that symbolizes the overcoming of all barriers of communication
that might impede the worldwide preaching of the message of salvation. They also overcome mockery, opposition, and persecution. They
become effective public people. The Lucan account of the manifestation of the Spirit is quite consonant with, and is very much enriched
by, the accounts of Paul and John. The power from on high that Luke
speaks about is a power that is also from within. The disciples take
a public stand from inner conviction and strength. They are not just
empty vessels being used by the Spirit. They act responsibly out of
personal faith and love, which is what Paul and John so emphasize.
The difference between the two traditions is not about the gift of the
Spirit, which is seen as messianic and eschatological in both, but about
its manifestations: in Paul and John the manifestations are connected

predominantly with personal salvation and the inner building-up of
the community of salvation; in Luke the main accent is on those that
show the bringing of salvation to the whole world. The tradition of
faith about what is sacramentalized in the rite of confirmation has
veered at different times and places towards one or other set of manifestations. It can be claimed that the steadying and unifying factor in
the tradition about confirmation is that what defines the sacrament is
not this or that manifestation of the spirit, but the messianic, eschatological quality of what is being manifested.

## Confirmation, Baptism, and Other Sacraments

In understanding confirmation as the sacrament of the messianic,
eschatological quality of the gift of the Holy Spirit, one has a good
basis for distinguishing it from baptism, and from other sacraments.
The specific distinction from baptism does need clarification. Some
of the words used about confirmation in the theological tradition can
give the impression that the difference between the two sacraments is
almost one of quantity or degree: confirmation adds more of the same
to what is already given in baptism; or at most it completes and rounds
off what is already there. Such words as "completion," "perfection,"
"fullness," "strengthening," "maturing," "increasing," "sealing," and even
"anointing" can lend themselves to an idea of giving more of the same
to something, even if it is to the highest degree. However, these terms
can have another, more absolute sense: they can stand for an ultimate,
definitive state of things that is qualitatively different from anything
that may have gone before. The Christian tradition has, in fact, even
outside the context of confirmation, given an eschatological flavor to
these words: they can describe a state of things that belongs to the end
times. When they are used about confirmation they can have this distinctive sense, rather than be simply describing further grades of what
is already given in baptism. It is true that baptism gives the Spirit, as
do all the sacraments. What is distinctive about a sacrament, however, is not what it gives but what it signifies, what aspect of the gift it
makes visible. The Spirit is shown forth in the water rite of baptism
as the principle of new creation and new birth. Although this Spirit
is none other than the messianic, eschatological Spirit, it is not shown
forth precisely *as* messianic and eschatological in the rite of baptism.

Because the recognition of this truth about the Spirit, with an appropriate response to it in faith, is necessary for Christian life, another rite is given to show it forth and to draw an appropriate response to it from those who are becoming Christians. Confirmation gives the same Spirit and the same grace as baptism does. But to the extent that it sacramentalizes an aspect of it that baptism does not, it gives a distinctive sacramental grace. It is a grace that should show in Christian life.

The specification proposed for confirmation can also help to clarify its relationship with the Eucharist. The Eucharist is the sacrament of the eschatological banquet, celebrated in the Church until the Lord comes. The Spirit is poured out in it, both on the bread and wine and on the assembled community. What the Eucharist symbolizes about the Spirit is its relationship with the Body of Christ, both as sacramental reality and as ecclesial unity. The Spirit is seen to transform people, and the things of their world, into the Body of Christ, uniting everything in him. This is the goal toward which all the action of the Spirit is directed. It is a goal that is now possible because the Spirit is present in the world in that final fullness given by Christ. The Eucharist sacramentalizes the return of all things to God: they are gathered together in the eschatological Spirit, made one with Christ their Head and High Priest, and presented by him to the Father. The people who make such a sacrament should be seen to have been initiated into a life that is not only of Christ but also of the Spirit that is poured out at the end of time. The people who can make the Eucharist be and be seen to be the anticipation of the eschatological banquet are people who have been both baptized and confirmed.

The rite of ordination also sacramentalizes the giving of the Spirit. It even uses the same ritual elements as confirmation—laying on of hands and anointing. Like confirmation, it is connected with mission. The distinction between it and confirmation is particularly important because it is the sacramental correlative of the ecclesiological distinction between hierarchy and laity. There is a kind of ecclesiology that instinctively puts hierarchy before People of God in its vision of the Church. When it thinks about the gift of the Spirit, it has a way of telling the story of Pentecost as the coming of the Spirit *on the apostles* (reading the "they" of Acts 2:1 as referring only to the apostles) rather than on the whole community gathered with the apostles. It then sees the Spirit being given to others by the apostles through

the laying on of hands and in other ways. When this ecclesiological model is transferred to the sacramental order it tends to see the Spirit being given in the first place to the ordained, who are successors of the apostles; they are then able to give the Spirit to others through their ministry. Among the consequences of this approach is that any responsibilities that lay believers are recognized to have for the building-up of the Church and for its mission will be seen as a participation in and concession from the power that the Spirit has given to the ordained.
A different ecclesiological model emerges when the story of Pentecost is told as the coming of the Spirit on the whole community, including Mary the mother of Jesus, as it came later on the whole community of believers at Samaria, on the household of Cornelius, and on the whole group at Ephesus. The community would not, of course, have been the community of believers without the apostles, because it would not have had a secure witness to the story of Jesus without them; it was gathered under their leadership and in a communion of which they were the foundations. But the eschatological Spirit, with everything that it stands for in the relationship of humans with God, was given to all believers. The special gift of the Spirit that the apostles received found its place within this eschatological community and the total gift of the Spirit that filled it. Those who were appointed to carry on in various ways the work of the apostles were given a special gift of the Spirit for particular ministries that were necessary for keeping the community, in its words and in its rites, faithful to the truth about Jesus that had been proclaimed by the apostles. This gift also took its place within the already gifted community, and was in keeping with the eschatological quality of its life. When one transfers this ecclesiological model, which is that adopted by Vatican II in its Constitution on the Church, to the sacramental order (as is done in LG, Ch. 2) one can understand the priority of confirmation over orders in the giving of the Spirit and how what is sacramentalized in orders is conditioned by what has already been sacramentatized in confirmation. Ordination is for people who are themselves already confirmed, and is for a particular service that only gets its meaning within the community of the confirmed. The quality of that service manifests the gift of the Spirit when it fully respects the status that has been given to the members of the community it serves by their confirmation in the eschatological Spirit.

## Necessity of Confirmation for Salvation

The claims being made for confirmation raise the question of whether it is necessary for salvation. It is a standard theological question about any sacrament. The answer depends on how one sees the relationship between confirmation and saving grace. Now that Christ has come and the Spirit has been poured out, only one kind of grace is salvific. It is messianic, eschatological grace. This is a statement about the objective definition of grace rather than about the people who live in it. They can still be childish and immature, as Paul told some of them in no uncertain fashion. But the grace they are living in is, by definition, adult grace, as is proper to the eschatological age. This quality of grace has to be proclaimed, if those called to salvation are to benefit from it; this is what they have to respond to in faith and sacrament. In the community of salvation it is proclaimed by word and by rite. As well as being a visible proclamation, the rite gives shape to the response of the one being saved: a confirmed person has been confronted with the messianic, eschatological quality of saving grace, has presumably said yes to it and is recognized in the Church as having the status that it confers. Perhaps in the early years of the preaching of the gospel the rite was less necessary. There may not even have been a consistent, distinctive rite other than something implicit in the water rite of baptism. The manifest fervor of the first communities and the charismatic gifts that were common could have given sufficient external visibility to the reality of the messianic Spirit; it would have left aspiring Christians in no doubt about the kind of grace they were being called to and the kind of response they would have to make to it in Christian initiation. When the rite of anointing/laying on of hands did become a distinctive part of Christian initiation it came to be recognized as a sacramental proclamation of this particular aspect of Christian grace. It required a particular response. Without that response people would not be opening themselves to the only kind of grace that now gives salvation. Nor would they be accepting the particular status and responsibility that is now required of those who are members of the community of salvation. On this basis one can say that confirmation, at least the desire of it, is now necessary for salvation.

Obviously, many people are saved without being actually confirmed. To make theological sense of this one has to appeal to the kind of distinctions that are made about the necessity of baptism for salvation. What saves in baptism is the reality *(res)* of the sacrament. It can be gained from the desire of the sacrament when the rite cannot be received (baptism of desire). When people know about baptism the desire includes the intention actually to be baptized. Were they to exclude it they could scarcely claim to have baptism of desire. One may also say that when they know about confirmation their desire includes the intention of being confirmed. What they desire is saving grace. This is messianic, eschatological grace, given through Christ and in the Spirit. It must be desired as such. Confirmation sacramentalizes this quality of it. Hence, to desire it is to desire to be confirmed. To exclude the intention of being confirmed would be to desire something other than Christian grace. It would be to do deliberately something like what the group that Paul came across at Ephesus did through ignorance: to desire a grace other than the Spirit-filled grace of Christ that alone brings salvation. The further distinctions that are made about baptism of desire (explicit and implicit, etc.) to account for the salvation of those who know nothing about the sacraments can also be applied to the necessity of confirmation. There are many ways in which the reality of the sacrament is gained apart from its actual reception. But the reality that is gained, and that saves, will always be the reality that needs confirmation in order to be adequately sacramentalized. To that extent confirmation remains necessary for salvation.

It has to be admitted that the tradition of faith does not affirm the necessity of confirmation with anything like the force that it shows in affirming the necessity of baptism. The obligation to be confirmed has not been stated with the same canonical decisiveness as the obligation to be baptized. The sacrament can at times seem to belong to those things that are good and desirable for Christian life rather than to what is absolutely necessary. Hence the desire for it is not cultivated with the same urgency or required with the same degree of necessity. Perhaps theological uncertainties about the nature of the sacrament also made it difficult to promote effectively the desire for it. The recovery of the best traditions about Christian initiation in the Church of Vatican II, and the accompanying pastoral insistence on confirming everybody who is baptized, including infants, when they are in danger of death, lends support to a theological position that regards the grace of confirmation, and therefore at least the desire of the sacrament (see

Saint Thomas in *Summa*, Third Part, q. 72, a.6 ad 1), as necessary for
salvation. There is also a theological teaching of Saint Thomas about
desire for the Eucharist that fits well with the necessity of at least
some desire for confirmation for salvation. Thomas sees the grace of
salvation coming ultimately through the Eucharist. The baptism that
is necessary for salvation includes within itself the desire for Eucharist
(Third Part, q. 73, a. 3). The tradition about the sequence and unity of
the three sacraments of Christian initiation suggests that the movement of desire from baptism toward Eucharist should pass through a
desire for confirmation; and that the one desire is not possible without
the other. There is only one saving grace. Those who desire it must
desire it as it is. If it takes three rites to sacramentalize it in an orderly
way, the desire for salvation might be reasonably required to include a
desire for all three of them.

## The Effects of Confirmation

In sacramentalizing the messianic, eschatological quality of the action
of God in Christ and the Holy Spirit, confirmation also sacramentalizes its own proper effects. It makes those effects visible and in doing
so actually causes them. The Catholic tradition has analyzed them on
the twin levels of character and grace. As has been explained (Chapter
2, "The Scholastics and Saint Thomas Aquinas"; Chapter 3, "Divine
Institution"; Chapter 5, "A Theology of Baptism—in and through
the Church"), this pattern reflects a sacramental ecclesiology: people
receive and give the grace of Christ by being qualified and empowered
to act in and for the visible community of the church; Christ makes
the actions of such qualified people to be his own salvific actions,
communicating to those who do them a share in his own messianic
offices of prophet, priest, and king: a Church made up of such people
becomes his sacrament; it remains so even when not all the people
who form it at a particular place and time are actually living in grace.
The character qualifies people to give and receive in a Church that
is the eschatological community of salvation. The Christ they are
empowered to represent is the One in whom the messianic Spirit has
been poured out. The baptismal character is a qualification to receive:
it marks and qualifies people to receive all the gifts of the Spirit
that are available in the Church; it is the badge of and title to total

receptivity in the grace of the end times. The character of confirmation has more to do with giving than receiving. The coming of the eschatological Spirit on the Church, and through it on the world, requires that the Church's members should be also empowered in Christ to be givers of the Spirit. They are signed and sealed as eschatological prophets, priests, and kings. They can be counted on to play an active part in the transformation of the world by the Spirit. There is an activity of giving that has to be exercised by all members of the Church, which is prior to those specific ministries that are exercised by some and provided for by the character of order. The carrying out of this activity manifests that the Church is both Christ-like and Spirit-filled. When all members of the Church are recognized as having something to give — toward their own salvation, toward the salvation of their fellow believers, toward the salvation of those who are to be evangelized — the Church is seen to be what the Spirit has made God's People to be. The character of confirmation is, then, a qualification and an empowering to be this kind of person in the Church. In confirming all its members the Church is saying that it has to be made up of such people. Its teaching spells out what it expects of its members. Its legislation structures their relationships with one another, lays down patterns of authority and obedience, and organizes the conduct of the Church's mission to the world. But all this has to reflect and be judged against the peculiar dignity and responsibility that belongs to every Christian because he or she is marked with the character of confirmation. If people do not treat one another within the Church itself with the respect due to those who are sealed with the messianic Spirit and participate in the come-of-age phase of grace, the Church cannot be recognized as the eschatological community of salvation.

The character of confirmation thus understood qualifies people for any activity that is required for the life of the Church. Attempts to link it exclusively with the prophetic role of the Church, or with the lay apostolate, have the value of highlighting certain aspects of what it is to be a Christian but perhaps at the expense of other aspects of Christian life that the tradition associates with confirmation. For example, the character of confirmation clearly comes into play in participation in other sacraments: it has a priestly as well as a prophetic function. It seems more helpful theologically to look for the specification of the character of confirmation, not in particular ecclesial functions that would be proper to the confirmed, but in that eschatological quality of Christian life that has to be found in all Christian activities. The character of baptism says that people have the power to be alive in Christ and to receive every gift that he offers. The character of confirmation says that such people belong to the end times, are empowered to take an adult, public part in everything that needs to be done for their own salvation, for that of their fellow Christians, and for that of the whole world. Their qualification to act is not a concession made to them by the hierarchy of the Church, still less a participation in the work of the hierarchy. The form it takes has, of course, to be regulated by the hierarchy for the sake of the common good of the Church. But in itself it is the right and the responsibility of fully initiated Christians, sacramentalized for them in confirmation.

The grace of confirmation, like the grace of every sacrament, is sanctifying grace. Those who have received grace in baptism receive an increase in that grace from confirmation. But that grace also receives a new set of virtualities that correspond to what is symbolized in the sacrament. They are a special richness of sanctifying grace that makes Christians do, in faith and love, what the character of confirmation calls them to do. With the tradition, this special richness of grace can be called "strength." It is the adult moral strength of those who act from inner conviction, who pray because the Spirit is welling up within them, who can deal with inner conflict, who trust their own spiritual gifts and the gifts of others and are neither embarrassed nor exalted if these should take spectacular charismatic form, who can take their place comfortably and maturely in the community life of the Church in obedience but not subservience to their ordained ministers, who are not afraid to be recognized in public as Christians and indeed are at ease and joyful and communicative about their Christian faith in public situations, who can be counted on to do whatever the community under the direction of its leaders judges good for the preaching of the gospel to the world, who will have the courage and ingenuity to overcome all forces that oppose the preaching of the gospel and, when necessary, be prepared to suffer and die under persecution. All this seems more than enough to justify the standard statement, that confirmation makes a person "a strong and perfect Christian." However, it needs to be understood that the fullness and perfection referred to in this phrase are distinctive qualities of the grace of confirmation rather than degrees in which grace is realized: it is full and perfect because it is definitive, eschatological grace. The actual degree of grace depends on the progressively fuller and more perfect human response that it produces. An infant who is confirmed has full and perfect grace, as have seven-year-olds and adult converts; but they only become fully and perfectly graced through exercising and appropriating the grace that they have been given. Each sacramental grace contributes to an overall growth in sanctifying grace. It is specified by the sacramental rite; it is operative as soon as it is desired; it is taken hold of bodily in the actual celebration of the sacrament; it continues to grow under the retrospective influence of the sacrament; and in doing so it enters into the growth of sanctifying grace toward the degree of fullness proper to each person. It is the Eucharist, rather than confirmation, that sacramentalizes this growth and this fullness. If it is true that each of the sacraments is directed towards the Eucharist it is also true that the growth potential of each of them is gathered into the sacramentality of the Eucharist. The completing of initiation by the Eucharist shows, with particular clarity, how it does this for the grace of baptism and the grace of confirmation. As the nourishment of life, the Eucharist is a constant call to the Christian to renew the original acceptance of life in Christ that was sacramentalized in his or her baptism. As eschatological banquet it is a call to accept once again the eschatological gift of the Spirit, with all its consequences, that was originally sacramentalized in confirmation. The proper grace of each sacrament grows, and grows repeatedly, within the comprehensive sacramental grace of the Eucharist.

## A Suitable Age for Confirmation

Confirmation can be received at any age. It is given today in the Church, as it has always been, to infants, to seven-year-olds, to teenagers, and to adults. Theology can make sense of confirmation at any of these ages. It can explain how it works differently according to the different stages of personal development enjoyed by those who receive it. In doing so it can suggest advantages and disadvantages in being confirmed at one age rather than another. However, the theological balancing of advantages and disadvantages will probably never yield a decisive argument favoring any one age. The best it can do is to give the theological criteria that should inform the judgment of pastoral prudence, which is what eventually decides when and how a person or group of persons ought to be offered confirmation in the Church.

The judgment about a suitable age for confirmation belongs within a judgment about Christian initiation. There are strong theological reasons in favor of initiating infants into Christian life. Although in Western theology they are usually given as arguments in favor of baptizing infants (Chapter 5, "The Baptism of Children"), most of them could also be used in favor of confirming infants and admitting them to the Eucharist; indeed, it would make sense to do so in view of the theological arguments that can be put forward in favor of maintaining the unity of the process of Christian initiation. There are satisfactory theological explanations of how any sacrament can sanctify infants. While they are generally worked out by Western theology in discussions about infant baptism, they hold just as well for confirmation and Eucharist.

Over against the arguments in favor of initiating people to Christianity in infancy there is another set of arguments for delaying initiation: they are based on the value of informed personal faith and decision on the part of the one being initiated. They can be put forward about the whole process of initiation but also about any of the three sacraments that make it up. The Eastern tradition has never accepted the weight of these arguments, neither for the whole of initiation nor for any of its parts. The Western tradition agreed for over a thousand years. However, its liturgical practice developed in a way that allowed it to think of the three sacraments of initiation as separate, if connected, issues. In the thirteenth century it began to accept the force of the arguments for delaying initiation with regard to confirmation; and soon also with regard to the Eucharist. The argument for delaying confirmation was not that those who received it should be adults; it was rather based on the general premise that sacraments could profit from being an exercise of personal faith, and that the kind of moral sense of discretion required for faith could be expected about the age of seven years. This argument was never accepted as a ground for delaying baptism. The way the necessity of baptism for salvation was conceived, especially for infants, made such a delay unthinkable for any reason. And yet, one concession has been always made to the argument about the need for personal faith and decision regarding baptism. If there is no assurance that, through Christian education, infants can be brought to personal faith as soon as they reach the age of discretion, their baptism will be delayed, except when they are in danger of death. The effectiveness of the sacrament is recognized as being bound up with the convictions and intentions of their parents and educators. If these are not faith-bearing for the child, they will negate the faith of the Church and baptism will not be given.

It is recognized that there is an element of risk in initiating an infant—the risk of sacramental nonsense and therefore of profanation. The Eastern tradition takes the risk with the whole process of initiation. The Latin does with baptism but, helped by its liturgical tradition, feels free not to take it with confirmation and Eucharist. Positively, it seems to be reasoning that there is more to be gained by having personal faith and decision in confirmation and Eucharist than there is to be lost in delaying the two sacraments and breaking up the unity of initiation. To delay the two sacraments is not to deprive the infant entirely of their grace. If the analysis given earlier (see "Confirmation, Baptism, and Other Sacraments") of the way in which baptism includes the desire for confirmation and for Eucharist is correct, the grace of both sacraments is already at work in a baptized infant, reaching forward through the process of Christian education to the expression it will receive in actual confirmation and Eucharist. However, there is a real loss of sacramentality involved in breaking up the unity of initiation. It is more than a matter of liturgical propriety. Baptism alone does not express sacramentally the full reality of Christian grace: it does not express its Pentecostal fullness. By separating it from confirmation one risks offering an inadequate sacramental statement about Christian life. The absence of the Eucharist is even more problematical: the full meaning of incorporation into the Body of Christ, which occurs in initiation, is left without its strongest sacramental expression. Of course, preaching and Christian education compensate for the diminished sacramentality of initiation by baptism alone. The Eastern practice also requires this preaching and education because the sacraments given to infants are only fully operative when they have been appropriated by personal faith and decision at the age of discretion. In both cases there is a waiting for personal faith to realize initiation. In putting all three sacraments of initiation at the beginning of the process the Eastern tradition strongly emphasizes the priority of God's action in it. The Western tradition does this, if a little less emphatically, by baptizing infants. It gives greater prominence to the role of personal faith in the process by delaying confirmation and Eucharist until the age of discretion.

In many parts of the Latin Church confirmation is delayed even beyond the age of seven years. One can argue in favor of this practice on the grounds that personal faith is likely to become more developed as the years of childhood go by. To this are sometimes added other arguments that associate confirmation with entry into adulthood. It has been claimed earlier that there is no real justification for seeing confirmation as a sacrament of entry into adult life: what confirmation sacramentalizes is the coming of age of the history of salvation, the arrival of the adult age of grace, with the gift of the Pentecostal Spirit, rather than the becoming adult of individual Christians. However, it is true that the kind of behavior proper to the adult age of grace can normally be exercised only by adults. On that ground one can make a theological case for delaying confirmation until children are entering adult age. There can be a real gain in doing so. The personal commitment to being an adult in an adult Church, which is the effect of the distinctive grace of confirmation, can be made in the celebration of the sacrament itself rather than worked toward as something to be fully entered into at some future date. There is some difficulty about deciding what criterion should be used for determining entry into adulthood. One could set the age by analogy with civic life, making it correspond to the age when young people begin to vote, or are free to marry, or can get a driver's license. However, young people are often forced to take a stand on matters of religious faith rather earlier in their teens, if not in a fully public way, at least among their peers. They are also confronted with choices about serious moral issues (for example, in attitudes toward their parents, or in dealing with the sexual factor in relationships) earlier than the age at which they are admitted to public civic responsibility. The appearance of such religious and moral issues are telling theological indicators about the age for confirmation. To be able to take an independent and even a public stand on such issues is characteristic of the confirmed.

The judgment about the appropriate age for confirmation is also affected by the need to get the best balance between divine gift and human response in the sacrament. If there is reason to believe that the sacrament will be more effective when God's action is highlighted, the sacrament will be put early in the years of discretion; subsequent catechesis and religious formation will be experienced as a development of the sacramental gift and directed toward an eventual fully adult response. If it is thought better to highlight the human response, catechesis will be a preparation for and a build-up toward adult response in the sacrament itself, which will therefore be delayed until the candidate is ready to make such a response. The decision about which aspect of the sacrament to highlight depends to a large extent on the religious climate in which the young persons are being educated and on the extent to which the Church is present in their lives through parents and school. Where Christian faith is strong and pervasive in the world of young people, and particularly in their schooling, it makes theological sense to confirm them early. Otherwise it seems better to wait until their personal decision can be beyond reasonable doubt.

The criterion of personal faith and decision might seem to suggest that ultimately the best age for confirmation is that set by the one to be confirmed for himself or herself: people are ready for confirmation when they ask for the sacrament, for the right reasons. There is something to be said for this point of view; those who prepare candidates for confirmation nowadays often require them to make a personal request for the sacrament. But educators and those who have a sense of how complex are the decision-making processes of young people hesitate to make too much of the criterion of personal choice in determining the age for confirmation. Theologically speaking they have some good grounds for preferring to set an age and to guide and form young people toward acceptance of confirmation at that time of their life. Confirmation is delayed in order to allow the candidate to accept it in an act of personal faith. Faith is a gift of God and of the community. No Christian community will let its respect for freedom of choice turn into indifference about the choice that one of its baptized members makes for or against being confirmed. It will have a view and a discipline about the best age for offering this gift to its members. It will educate young people toward and prompt their decision to be confirmed with the confidence that it is communicating a gift of God, in which human freedom is fully realized, rather than interfering with freedom of choice. It is, indeed, continuing to follow the same logic that led it in the first place to baptize this person as an infant.

A major theological difficulty about the Latin practice regard-ing the age of confirmation is that many children are not confirmed before they are admitted to the Eucharist. The problem is one of sacramentality. If, as has been argued (see "Confirmation, Baptism, and Other Sacraments"), the grace of confirmation is included in the grace of the Eucharist, children are not really (i.e., on the level of *res*) being deprived of grace by having their confirmation delayed, any more than catechumens are by having their baptism delayed until they are ready for it. But the reality of that grace is not being given sacramental visibility in the way the overwhelming tradition of Christian liturgy and doctrine has wanted. Concern for the correct sequence of the sacraments of initiation is not a matter of liturgical faddism. Grace is given in a sacramental order, which is of God's design. Sacramentally, the Eucharist is the eschatological, messianic banquet celebrated for and by those who belong to the final age of grace. It is brought about by the Holy Spirit who transforms bread and wine into the messianic body of Christ and those who receive it into the eschatological com-munity of salvation, which is the Body of Christ. The Eucharist is the food of the strong, not of the childish. Sacramentally speaking, it is for the confirmed. There is a real loss of sacramentality in not prepar-ing children for the Eucharist by confirming them. There is at least as much reason for confirming them as there is for submitting them to the sacrament of reconciliation. It is theologically encouraging to hear that in recent decades the pastoral decision has been taken in some dioceses of the Latin rite to confirm children before their First Communion, which is given at the age that is now customary in the Latin Church.[17] In these dioceses, confirmation is a central part of their preparation for First Communion, in which the sacrament of rec-onciliation also has its place. It is to be hoped that the pastoral fruits of this decision will confirm the theological good sense that it makes.

An alternative way of restoring the doctrinally correct sequence of sacraments of initiation in the Latin Church would be to return to the practice that was common before Pope Pius X opened the way to First Communion for children reaching the age of reason:

---

17. Information for dioceses of the United States given by S. M. Jeffrey, "Christian Initiation: A Pastoral Perspective on Restored Order" in *Antiphon* 9.3 (2005): 245–252; see also J. A. Wilde, *When Should We Confirm? The Order of Initiation* (Chicago: Liturgy Training Publications, Archdiocese of Chicago, 1989).

Confirmation was given to young people in their teens and their First Communion was delayed until they had been confirmed. It is a solution that would be unthinkable today. While one can give a reasonable, if not peremptory, theological justification for delaying Eucharist until the age of discretion, arguments for delaying it further would carry very little weight. What one is entitled to ask, though, is whether the decision made about First Communion at entry into the age of reason, and before confirmation, pays sufficient attention to the full theology of the Eucharist. Is the truth that the Eucharist has something in it that should be prepared for by a prior sacramentalization of the Gift of the Spirit properly appreciated? Decisions about a suitable age for confirmation are also decisions about the Eucharist. They will not be entirely wise if they are informed by a theology of confirmation that fails to consider its relationship to the Eucharist, and even more so the requirements of the Eucharist itself, within the sacramentality of Christian initiation.

# Chapter 8

# Eucharist: The Rite

## DESCRIPTION

The rite of the Eucharist is celebrated in the Roman liturgy in the form prescribed by the Roman Missal. The word "missal" is a reminder that the rite of the Eucharist has been called *missa* in Latin even from the Patristic period (Saint Ambrose speaks of *missam facere*), and it is from the Latin that words like mass have come into European and other languages. Mass is a term that became specially significant for Catholics due to the role it played in the Church's defense of its eucharistic faith and practice during the Reformation debates. It does not of itself have a great deal of theological resonance and its meaning is best conveyed by grounding it in the biblical and theological richness carried by the term Eucharist.

The current Missal for the Roman rite was promulgated by Paul VI in 1969, with the Apostolic Constitution *Missale Romanum*. A new edition of it, including a revised version of the *General Instruction of the Roman Missal* (GIRM) was published in Latin in 2002. The Missal has been available in English and other contemporary language translations since 1969. It is due to be published in a new translation, based on the 2002 Latin edition. The detailed ordering of the rite, called *Ordo Missae*, is preceded in the Missal by the *General Instruction*, which carefully explains the structure and parts of the rite, as well as giving some of the doctrinal and pastoral principles that underlie it. The study of this *Instruction*, as given in the 2002 edition, is indispensable for entering into the sacramentality of the eucharistic rite.

The rite is presented in the GIRM as a calling together or assembly of God's People in one place, under the presidency of a priest *(sacerdos)*: "The People of God is called together, with a priest presiding and acting in the person of Christ, to celebrate the memorial of

the Lord, the Eucharistic sacrifice" (GIRM, 27). The celebration has
two parts, called Liturgy of the Word and Liturgy of the Eucharist,
corresponding to the Eucharist being "the table both of God's Word
and of Christ's Body" (GIRM, 28). Before the Liturgy of the Word
begins there are some introductory ceremonies. They have to do with
the act of assembly and the kind of community that is being assembled. There is movement and singing and praying that create a
sense of being together as a community of Christian faith and repentance gathered in the presence of God. It is an ordered community.
There are formal entrances for those who have special ministries in
the celebration, and they are identified by the clothes they wear and
the places they occupy. The president of the assembly is clearly identified and wears the insignia of priesthood. He is the bishop or one
of the presbyters of the community. Nowadays there is no noticeable
restriction on attendance. But the rite is clearly meant for Christian
believers. They alone can take an active part in it. Those who believe
but have not yet been baptized can take an active part in the Liturgy of
the Word but, if they remain for the Liturgy of the Eucharist, do not
receive the consecrated bread and wine. There may be other members
of the assembly who, though baptized, do not receive from the table of
the Lord's body. Their abstention has some significance, but what that
is does not appear from the rite itself.

Once the community is assembled in an orderly way it listens
to readings from the scriptures and to a homily given by the president,
or someone designated by him who is another priest or a deacon. The
homily is an address about the significance that what has been read
can have for the present life and situation of the community; it is an
exhortation to live out the demands that the word makes on those who
celebrate it in the Eucharist. This Liturgy of the Word is a working out of the principle set out in the introduction to this book, that
word is always twinned with rite in the celebrations of God's People,
and relates the rite to life. It is God's word to his People, repeating
promises and guarantees of the covenant and stating the response they
require. It is the ongoing story of God's People, brought up-to-date for
the celebrating community in the preaching addressed to it, and projected forward in the prayers for their salvation and that of the whole
world that end the Liturgy of the Word. The whole Bible is meant to
be read at successive Eucharists, over a period of time (currently three

years). The movement of the story that the Bible tells is conveyed by having two or more readings, taken from different parts of the book. The final reading is always from the climax of the story as it is narrated in one of the four gospels. Sometimes the continuous reading of the Bible is interrupted and special passages are chosen in order to bring the word of God to bear on some particular event of salvation that is being celebrated by the community.

The transition from Liturgy of Word to Liturgy of the Eucharist can seem somewhat abrupt and the continuity may be obscured by the terminology; there may be an impression that the Eucharist proper only begins when the Liturgy of the Word has ended. But, in fact, the whole celebration, from the assembling of the community right through to its dismissal, is a unified action of word and rite, which in its totality is called Eucharist. The word obviously predominates in the first part and the distinctively eucharistic ritual elements are found in the second. A Liturgy of the Word can, indeed, be celebrated independently of the Eucharist or within the celebration of another sacrament. But when a community assembles to celebrate the Eucharist its Liturgy of the Word is already eucharistic and is being affected by the rite of which it is part. The rite, in turn, gets an essential element of its significance from its connection with the word. It becomes a response to the covenant word of God and as such a sacrifice of covenant renewal. The GIRM insists that the two parts of the Eucharist (Liturgy of Word, Liturgy of Eucharist) "are so closely interconnected that they form but one single act of worship" (GIRM, 28).

The "single act of worship" continues, then, with a taking and putting on the altar of bread and wine. These are seen as gifts made by members of the community for common use. They are taken from them in some symbolic way and received with prayer as gifts of God. Other gifts that the participants bring for the needs of the Church, including money, are gathered at this time, but only bread and wine are put before the presiding priest. What they are put on is called a table, because they are food for eating and drinking. It is also called an altar, because what will be done with the food by the presiding priest is an act of sacrifice. He does it in the form of a prayer of thanksgiving said over the bread and wine. He associates the community with the prayer by an introductory dialogue, by having them see and hear what he is doing, by inviting them to chorus their acclamation at various points and by drawing them to approve the prayer with a final Amen.

The eucharistic prayer nowadays follows a formula fixed and approved by the Church. It includes the following elements (GIRM, 79):

(a) *Thanksgiving*, which is the dominant note of the prayer and gives its name to the entire rite ("eucharist" comes from the Greek word for thanksgiving); the thanksgiving is for the gifts of bread and wine, because the prayer is said over them, but it broadens out to be for the total gift of God evoked by them, which is the giving of his own glory in the work of creation and redemption; sometimes a special work of salvation that is being commemorated and that has been proclaimed in the Liturgy of the Word is highlighted in the first phase of the thanksgiving, which has traditionally been called the Preface.

(b) *Acclamation*, by the whole assembly of the holiness of God, in a song taken from images of the heavenly liturgy, and of the blessedness of the one who comes in his name; to say God is holy is to proclaim the disinterestedness of God's giving, and the impossibility of giving him anything in return other than by making these gifts that have come forth from him return to him by being made holy with God's own holiness.

(c) *Epiclesis*, from the Greek word for "calling down," which calls down the power of God on bread and wine to make them holy; the transforming divine action called for is usually attributed to the Holy Spirit; the making holy or consecration that is called for is that the bread and wine would become the body and blood of Christ.

(d) *Narrative of Institution*, which authorizes the request made in the epiclesis and guarantees the efficacy of the eucharistic prayer; it proclaims that at the Last Supper Christ said that the bread and wine he was giving to his disciples was his body and his blood being offered for the salvation of the world, and that the disciples were to remember him by themselves doing this giving of his body and blood in bread and wine.

(e) *Anamnesis*, from the Greek word for "remembering," which is a bringing to mind of all that was done and will be done in the body and blood of Christ—death, resurrection, ascension, and second coming. Because of what the bread and wine now are, the thanksgiving for them has become real thanksgiving for the saving gift of God that is given in the body and blood of Christ.

(f) *Oblation*, in which the remembering community lets its thanksgiving (and the self-offering that thanksgiving implies) be taken over by the self-offering that Christ, its Head, makes in his body and blood, so that what it offers to God with thankfulness is the sacrifice of Christ; in that sacrifice the community offers itself, praying that the Spirit, who makes its bread and wine be the body and blood of Christ, will make it itself be one in his Body.

(g) *Intercession*, in which the solidarity that the assembled community enjoys in the Body of Christ reaches out to all those who form the Body of Christ, asking for a sharing with those who are already with Christ in glory, for the unity of all the communities that form the Church of Christ on earth, for the faithful departed that they may enter into eternal rest, and for all those who are being saved in Christ.

(h) *Doxology*, in which the prayer returns to the dominant mood of praiseful thanksgiving offered to the Father through Christ and the Spirit; the presence and action of Christ and the Spirit have been invoked throughout the prayer to transform the gifts of the Church and its thankful acceptance of them into a holiness that is the ultimate glory of God. The ritual gestures and the way of treating the bread and wine have shown the movement toward this holiness. What has been prayed over as bread and wine from the beginning is affirmed at the end of the prayer as the divine glory that it has become.

When the eucharistic prayer is finished preparations are made for the eating and drinking of the consecrated bread and wine. The Lord's Prayer is said: it resumes, in the Lord's own words, what has been said in the eucharistic prayer about the holiness of God, the bond between heaven and earth, the meaning of God's gifts and how they meet the needs of human life. The members of the community exchange a gesture of reconciliation and peace. The consecrated bread is broken into portions and given to the participants to eat. The cup of consecrated wine is given to them for drinking. The distribution and receiving of the Body and Blood of Christ is accompanied by prayers and gestures of reverence and song.

The rite ends with prayer and with a formal act of adjournment or dismissal by one of the presiding ministers. The people are sent out with a final blessing.

# HISTORY

The rite of the Eucharist is, even in its present form, highly complex. Its history is correspondingly complex. As every detail of the rite has some significance, so every bit of information about the history of the rite is valuable for understanding it. But even a less than meticulous history can throw a great deal of light on the rite. One can find certain patterns of worship in the Old Testament that recur in the Eucharist; one can see the form these patterns took at the Last Supper and in the "breaking of bread" of the apostolic communities in the New Testament; one can see the liturgical shape of the rite developing in descriptions of the Eucharist in the texts of the early centuries; and one can follow in broad terms the evolution of those first forms of the rite through the particular liturgical tradition of the Roman Church, in a way that throws light on how and why that tradition has been given the form it has today in the Missal promulgated by Paul VI.

## Rites of the Old Covenant

As the life of God's People has been dominated from its beginning by the covenant that God made with them, so their rites have been connected in one way or another with covenant making and covenant keeping and covenant renewal. Covenant making and renewal follow a consistent ritual pattern in the Old Testament: there is a summoning by God of certain chosen people to come into his presence; God speaks in some way, and his words are of promises, of guarantees of his fidelity, and of the behavior that God expects of those for whom the promises will be fulfilled; those who have been called accept the promise and guarantees, and undertake to fulfill its terms, and accept their identity as God's very own People; they give some tangible expression to their decision to let themselves be taken by God as his People, which is commonly some form of ritual sacrifice; by sharing in that rite they are affirmed as God's People and the inheritors of his promise. The pattern is already visible in the account of the covenant that God made with Abraham (Genesis, chapters 12 and 15): God calls Abraham, makes a promise to him and gives certain guarantees; Abraham believes and expresses his acceptance of God's covenant in various sacrificial rites, and all this is done within a palpable experience of the presence of God.

The pattern is more developed in the making of the Mosaic covenant at Mount Sinai during the Exodus (Exodus 19–24). God has summoned his People and, by the dramatic events of the Exodus, brought them out of Egypt and into his presence at this holy mountain. Their leader and prophet Moses goes apart and hears the word of God being spoken to him. He assembles the People. The act of assembly is itself significant for the whole history of covenant ritual. It is the original setting up of what is called the *qahal Jahweh*, the assembly of the Lord. The term *qahal* will be used regularly in the Hebrew Bible to designate God's People gathered formally to conduct the business of the covenant. It will be translated in the Greek Bible as *ékklèsia*, or *synagôgè*, and the first of these words will provide the disciples of Jesus with a term to describe themselves when they gather for events of the new covenant: they will be the new *qahal Jahweh*, the *ékklèsia tou Theou*, the Church of God.[1] Moses transmits the word he has heard from God to the assembled People: it is a word of promise, centered on the gift of being God's own People, from which all other blessings will flow; it is a word of command about how the covenant People should live; and it is a word that guarantees God's fidelity to his promise in the form of reminders of what God has already done for his People, from the time of their ancestors to the more recent events of the Exodus.

It is this covenant word that the People assent to: "Moses came and told the people all the words of the Lord, and all the ordinances; and all the people answered with one voice, and said, 'All the words which the Lord has spoken we will do'" (Exodus 24:3). Their acceptance of the covenant is not just verbal; it is also ritualized. The link between word and rite is facilitated by the fact that "Moses wrote all the words of the Lord" (Exodus 24:4). The word is now a book, which is called the Book of the Covenant. The hearing of the word of

---

1. See L. Bouyer, *Liturgical Piety* (Notre Dame: Notre Dame Press, 1956); published as *Life and Liturgy* (London: Sheed & Ward, 1956), Ch. 3.

God will from then on include listening to the reading of a book. The book itself is incorporated into the ritual making of the Mosaic covenant. An altar is set up and animals are sacrificed to God. Moses takes the blood of the sacrificed animals and sprinkles half of it on the altar. Then he takes the Book of the Covenant and reads it to the People. It tells them what they are committing themselves to. Their assent is put into words in Exodus 24:7: "All that the Lord has spoken we will do, and we will be obedient." This is the verbal equivalent of the rite of sprinkling the blood of sacrificed animals on the altar: to do so was to put one's life (symbolized by the blood of an animal that one had once owned) into the hand of God (symbolized by the altar, which consecrated to God whatever was put on it). It is the God-ward movement of the sacrifice. Once the People had agreed to the covenant, Moses could sprinkle the other half of "the blood of the covenant" on the assembled People. This is the human-ward movement of the sacrifice: it is the receiving from God, in ritual form, of the mark and the gift and the bonding of being his very own People.

When the second book of Kings tells, in Chapter 22, how King Josiah set about renewing the life of his People in accordance with the covenant, it sets the story in the framework of covenant ritual. First there is a new giving of the word of God through the discovery of the Book of the Covenant in the Temple and the interpretation of its significance, in which priests and prophets and king are involved. Then, in Chapter 23, the People are summoned to solemn assembly in the house of the Lord. The king "read in their hearing all the words of the book of the covenant which had been found in the house of the Lord." Then, standing by the pillar (a recognized place for performing solemn, official actions) he "made a covenant before the Lord, . . . to perform the words of this covenant that were written in this book; and all the people joined in the covenant." No ritual action is mentioned in connection with the making of the covenant at this point, but later, when the trappings of worship that were contrary to the covenant have been purged from the holy places the People are called to "keep the Passover to the Lord your God, as it is written in this book of the covenant." The Passover included the fundamental covenant sacrifice.

There is another covenant renewal at the beginning of the restoration after the Exile, described in Nehemiah, Chapters 8 and 9, which is ritualized according to the same pattern. There is an assembly of the People, led by Nehemiah the governor, and Ezra who was scribe and priest, and the Levites. There is a reading from "the book of the law of Moses which the Lord had given to Israel," which goes on from early morning until midday. The People weep at what they hear but are told by their leaders to "Go your way, eat the fat and drink sweet wine and send portions to him for whom nothing is prepared; for this day is holy to our Lord; and do not be grieved, for the joy of the Lord is your strength." The reading continues on successive days and the People keep feast for seven days and live in tents, as they did during the Exodus. On the eighth day there is a solemn assembly. The People fast and wear sackcloth and ashes; they separate themselves from foreigners and confess their sins. These are cultic preparations for entry into the presence of God. Once assembled, they listen again to the book of the law of the Lord. Then comes a new element: they pray ("for another fourth of it [the day] . . . they made confession and worshipped the Lord their God"). The text of the prayer said by Ezra the priest is given. It is a prayer of praise of God and of remembering the wonderful things he has done for his people in spite of their infidelity. It concludes with the words: "Because of all this we make a firm covenant and write it, and our princes, our Levites and our priests set their seals to it." There could be no sacrifice to ratify the covenant because the Temple had not yet been rebuilt. The prayer, however, takes the place of ritual sacrifice in ratifying the covenant.

There was already a connection between sacrifice and prayer in the Jewish ritual tradition. Among the sacrifices prescribed in the book of Leviticus is the *todâ*, which is variously translated as "sacrifice with or of thanksgiving" or "sacrifice with or of praise."[2] It is suggested that it was a kind of communion sacrifice accompanied by expressions of praise or thanks. Many of the psalms of blessing, praise, and thanksgiving are associated with the sacrificial worship of the Temple. Psalm 50 represents God as assembling his People "who made a covenant with me by sacrifice" (v. 5), and telling them that what really counts in his eyes is not the sacrifice of animals but the sacrifice of praise/thanksgiving (vv. 14 and 23; cf. Psalm 119:108). During the exile in Babylon the Jews were deprived of the Temple and the ritual

---

2. On forms of sacrifice in the Old Testament see J. J. Castelot and A. Cody, OSB, "Religious Institutions of Israel" in R. E. Brown, SS, J. A. Fitzmyer, R. E. Murphy, OCARM, eds. *The New Jerome Biblical Commentary*, 1268–1271.

sacrifices that could only be offered there. They developed in its place the synagogue form of worship. They assembled in groups (and it was the Greek word for "assembly" that gave the name "synagogue" to the kind of community they formed and the place where they met) to hear the word of God and to respond to it by prayer. The prayer of Ezra in Nehemiah, Chapter 9, is an example of the type of prayer that came to be used in synagogue services. It follows a fundamental Jewish prayer form that is called *berakah* and usually translated as "blessing." To pray is to bless and praise God for who and what God is. It is to bless God for his gifts. The prayer of blessing is also a prayer of thanksgiving. One of the Greek translations of the Hebrew words for this type of prayer is the word for "thanksgiving," *eucharistein*, from which comes "Eucharist." Thanksgiving is a form of praise. As in the prayer of Ezra the blessing of God can include remembering the wonderful things he has done for his People throughout their history. It expresses the experience of "making a memorial" (*zikkaron* in Hebrew, *anamnesis* in Greek) that is at the heart of Jewish worship. It can also be a remembering of the infidelities of the People, finding in them the reason for their present difficulties. The prayer of blessing is also a prayer about the present (see the typical transition to the present made with the words "Now therefore . . ." in v. 32 of the prayer of Ezra). It calls on God to repeat the wonders of the past here and now for a People who are pledging themselves once again to obey the covenant.

The prayer of blessing was also part of the ritual of all Jewish meals. It was the form taken by what would today be called Grace at Meals.[3] While all Jewish meals were religious events that, in various ways, affirmed the covenant and its blessings, it seems that in post-exilic Judaism there were special meals that were held for specifically religious purposes. Conjectures about the ritual form these meals might have taken and their eventual influence on the rite of the Christian Eucharist might not always be well founded.[4] But it might seem reasonable to assume that meals could provide Jewish people with a special experience of the presence of God. A phrase is quoted from the Talmud: "When they sit at table and the words of the

---

3. Texts in L. Bouyer, *Eucharist: Theology and Spirituality of the Eucharistic Prayer,* trans. from French (Notre Dame: Notre Dame University Press, 1968), Ch. 4.

4. See J. Jeremias, *The Eucharistic Words of Jesus,* Trans. from 3rd German ed. (London: SCM Press, 1966), Ch I.

Torah are the subject of their conversation, then the Shekinah comes down upon them."[5] It might also be suggested that a certain ritualizing of meals would lend itself well to the needs of those communities of people who were drawn together, as the disappointing years of postexilic Judaism went on, by a strong faith in the prophecies about the new covenant and who saw themselves as the poor, or remnant of Israel, with whom that new covenant would be made. The meal form could lend itself particularly well to messianic and eschatological hopes, and to the new assembling of God's People that it would bring. The image of a banquet in which people feasted together in a shared, God-given abundance was common in prophetic descriptions of the messianic age. Table talk lent itself to sharing the hopes and dreams and demands that different people were hearing in the word of God, especially as it looked toward the future. The blessing prayer lent itself to that more interior, spiritual worship that was to characterize the new covenant. It also lent itself to expressing the contrast between promise and present reality that is always the pain of prophetic people. The form of the blessing prayer allows for a passage from praise and thanks for the wonders God has done in the past to a consideration of the present misery and need of his People. At that point the community could put some of its own pain, especially what it was suffering because of its fidelity to God, into the blessing prayer. The prayer would give their situation something of that sacrificial value in the sight of God, which the great prophecies of Isaiah about the Suffering Servant of the Lord had seen in human pain that was accepted in dedication to God for the taking away of sin. That sacrificial view of present sufferings would give confidence to the petitions with which the blessing prayer ends for a new and definitive fulfillment of the promises of the covenant.

There is less need for conjecture about the ritual of the Passover meal, which was part of the official annual commemoration of the Exodus and the covenant. The basic rite is reflected in the account given in Exodus 12 of what the Jews were commanded to do at the original Passover in Egypt. The form of the rite that would have been in use in Jerusalem at the time of Jesus is known with reasonable

---

5. J. M. Nielen, *The Earliest Christian Liturgy.* trans. from German (St. Louis/London, 1941), 37.

accuracy.[6] A family or family-sized group gathered at table on the evening of the feast to eat the Passover lamb, as their ancestors had done on the eve of their liberation from Egypt. The lamb had been slaughtered ritually by priests in the Temple during the day. It was eaten with bitter herbs and with unleavened bread, and various ritual cups of wine were drunk. During the meal the head of the household explained, in response to questions from the younger members of the family or group, the meaning of the different kinds of food and drink that were being taken. There was also singing of psalms of praise. At the beginning of the meal—as of every Jewish meal at that time—the head of the household would break the loaf of bread into portions that he distributed to those at table. The action was accompanied by a prayer of blessing, such as "Blessed be thou, JHWH, our God, king of the universe, who bringest forth bread from the earth."[7] The blessing prayer said over the different cups of wine and over the bread when it was being broken were particularly solemn. A text that might have been used for the blessing said over the final cup of wine at the time of Jesus has been reconstructed from later sources. It can be found in Bouyer.[8]

## The Rite of the New Covenant

The meal that Jesus took with his disciples on the night before he suffered is presented by the Synoptics as a Passover meal.[9] There have been some hesitations among exegetes about accepting the historical accuracy of this presentation because of the chronology of the Passion given in the gospel of John. In John's account the official Jewish Passover meal should have been eaten on the evening of the day that Jesus died rather than the evening before (see John 18:28). His death would then have corresponded to the sacrificial slaughtering of the Paschal lamb in the Temple. Whatever the historical value of the different chronologies,[10] and the debate about the findings of Jeremias,

---

6. Details in Jeremias, *The Eucharistic Words of Jesus,* 84–88.

7. Bouyer, *Eucharist,* 8.

8. Bouyer, *Life and Liturgy,* 124–125; cf. also R. C. Jaspers and G. J. Cuming, *Prayers of the Eucharist: Early and Reformed,* 3rd ed. (New York: Pueblo Publishing Company, 1987), 7–12.

9. Jeremias, *The Eucharistic Words of Jesus,* Ch I.

10. See A. Jaubert, *The Date of the Last Supper,* trans. from French (New York: Alba House, 1965); Leon-Dufour, X., sj, *Sharing the Eucharistic Bread: The Witness of the New Testament,* trans. from French (New York: Paulist Press, 1987).

there seem to be adequate grounds for holding that the accounts of the Last Supper are to be interpreted against the background of Passover ritual and ideas. Remaining on the level of rite and reserving questions about the full theological meaning of the New Testament texts for Chapter 9, one can use the Passover background, and the general Jewish tradition about ritual meals, to appreciate what the evangelists understood Jesus to require of his disciples when he asked them to do what he did in memory of him. The meal represents Jesus *assembling* the nucleus and leaders of the new covenant people; it is the setting in which he speaks his final *word* to them to explain how his leaving them would be a new exodus; its solemn *prayer of blessing* over the bread and the cup is used by Jesus to put into words, words that are themselves a *sacrifice* of praise, the sacrifice that he would make on the following day as Suffering Servant, offering himself in his body and blood on the cross; the expression the meal gives to festive *togetherness* and sharing of food and drink is being established as the rite that would give assurance to the disciples of being already with Christ in the definitive kingdom of God.

When the accounts of the Last Supper were being written down, the Church already had some decades of experience of regularly practicing the rite of "the breaking of bread" in memory of Jesus. The accounts select those elements of the Passover meal that justify and explain the practice. What was being done in the first Christian communities was patterned on the distinctive words and actions of Jesus rather than on the full rite of the Passover meal that he had used. The Passover was a once-yearly celebration of the former covenant. The disciples of Jesus could meet every day to remember him and wait for his coming; they met at least on the first day of the week, which they celebrated as the day he rose from the dead. When they met they listened to the story about Jesus proclaimed in the testimony of the apostles. They were celebrating a new Passover and the making of a new covenant. They were doing it in the "breaking of bread," that is to say, in a meal that had a special significance for them because of the way the ritual breaking of bread, which was a normal feature of Jewish meals, had been done by Jesus.

The Last Supper was not the only meal that affected the meaning that the disciples found in their "breaking of bread" in memory of Jesus. Some of them had eaten with him regularly during his ministry of preaching and doing good. Once they had begun to recognize him as the Messiah sent by God these meals took on something of the character of the messianic banquet promised by the prophets. This impression had been confirmed by miraculous multiplications of their food, which had allowed them to share it with multitudes of people. They had also seen Jesus eat with people who were considered to be sinners and outcasts, and perhaps shared that experience with him. That must have brought it home to them that meals at which Jesus was present and accepted were events of reconciliation and fellowship that knew no human barriers. Some of them had also shared food with him after he had risen from the dead, which was a powerful reinforcement of the sense they had of his presence with them when they were gathered for the breaking of bread.

The Emmaus incident reflects, in a quite moving way, the paradigm of the eucharistic rite.[11] It happens away from Jerusalem, away from the Temple and its sacrality, to people who are on a journey. It begins with a conversation that grows, on the one hand, out of the lived experience of the two disciples—their hopes for salvation and their troubled reaction to the death of Jesus and the stories of the women that he was alive—and, on the other hand, out of the scriptures. The passages of scripture selected and explained by Jesus give the disciples new light on the death of Jesus and their own reactions to it, which makes their "hearts burn within them." Their acceptance of the word and of the one who has expounded it to them impels them to insist that he stay with them and share their meal. But it is he who becomes the host of the meal. He takes bread, says the prayer of blessing, breaks it and gives it to them. In these ritual actions they recognize Jesus for who he is. He then disappears from their sight, as if to say that as long as they can break bread together in the distinctive way that he had of doing it, they do not need his visible presence. The two disciples, powerfully confirmed in their faith in the resurrection, go back to join the community of disciples gathered with the Eleven in Jerusalem. They are able to confirm one another in their faith that Jesus is alive. Once again he appears to them, and once again he eats with them.

---

11. See J. Dupont, osb,"The Meal at Emmaus" in J. Delorme and others, *The Eucharist in the New Testament,* trans. from French (Baltimore/Dublin: Helicon Press, 1964), 105–121.

The nearest one gets to a description of what a Christian community actually did at the "breaking of bread" in memory of Jesus is in 1 Corinthians 11. Paul is describing what happens, or rather what ought to happen, "when you assemble as a church" (v. 18). Earlier in the chapter he had been laying down the discipline that should regulate praying and prophesying (v. 4) in the Christian assembly. Now he talks about the meal that is taken. It seems to be a full meal, at which people could eat and drink their fill. What Paul reproves them for is that in this meal "it is not the Lord's supper that you eat" (v. 20). The reason he gives for saying so is not a matter of ritual but of life: they do not share the meal together, but divide up into separate parties, at which some have too much to eat and drink and others do not have enough. Paul does not say that they should not eat together but simply that, if it is a private party they want, they should have it at home. Only if they are sharing their food in true fellowship can they be celebrating the Lord's Supper. But he then gives a reason drawn from the ritual that they should be following, and from its meaning. The ritual is the one given by the Lord at the Last Supper and handed on in the Church. If Paul repeats the traditional account of the Last Supper it is presumably to remind the Corinthians that at some point in their meal bread should be taken and a blessing said over it that proclaims it to be the body of Christ, and that it should be broken and distributed to all; likewise with the cup. He does not say who should do this or at what point of the meal it should be done. A community, the majority of whose members were likely to be Jewish converts, would hardly need to be told. When Christian communities moved farther from their Jewish roots it would be necessary to regulate these matters. Before the end of the first century the taking of bread and wine in remembrance of Jesus was being separated from the meal of fellowship (the *agapé*) and being celebrated as a distinct rite.

The prophesying and praying that Paul regulates before dealing with the Eucharist in 1 Corinthians 11 was a normal feature of the assemblies of the Corinthians. Paul deals with the subject in detail in subsequent chapters, but without connecting it explicitly with the Eucharist. He deals in those chapters with other matters that are subsequently associated with the Eucharist, including fellowship with other Christian communities and the collecting of contributions for the saints to be made on the first day of the week (Chapter 16), but again without mentioning the Eucharist. A connection between the word of God and "the breaking of bread" is, however, made in two texts from the Acts of the Apostles. In Acts 20:7–11 Luke recounts: "On the first day of the week, when we were gathered together to break bread," Paul talked with them ". . . and he prolonged his speech until midnight. . . ." And when Paul ". . . had broken bread and eaten, he conversed with them a long while, until daybreak." The capsule description that Luke gives in Acts 2:42 of the new life of those who had received the word, had been baptized and joined to the Christian community, puts together very neatly the elements that structure the eucharistic rite: ". . . the apostles' teaching (i.e., the word) and fellowship (i.e., communion with the Church of the apostles), the breaking of bread (i.e., ritual meal) and the prayers (i.e., a setting of worship that could not but have included the prayer of blessing over the bread and the cup)."

## The Second and Third Centuries

There are some indications in the documents of the second and third centuries that Christians took some meals together that were not modeled on the Lord's Supper. There are hints of meals taken with bread but without any particular attention to what was drunk, meals with bread and salt, and meals with fish.[12] Some of these practices have a basis in the New Testament. Then, there were meals of fraternal *agapé* that cannot be said with certainty to have included the rite performed by Jesus at the Last Supper. The *Didache* provides the most outstanding example of this ambiguity.[13] It prescribes prayers for "the eucharist," one "concerning the cup," another concerning "the broken bread." It follows these with a general prayer of thanksgiving to be said "after you have taken your fill of food" (9–10). Later (14) it prescribes: "On the Lord's own day, assemble in common to break bread and offer thanks; but first confess your sins, so that your sacrifice may be pure. However, no one quarrelling with his brother may join your meeting

---

12. O. Cullmann, "The Meaning of the Lord's Supper in Primitive Christianity" in *Essays on the Lord's Supper* (Richmond: John Knox Press, 1958).

13. Text in J. A. Kleist, SJ, trans. *The Didaché, The Epistle of Barnabas, The Epistles and the Martyrdom of St Polycarp, The Fragment of Papias, The Epistle to Diognetus,* Ancient Christian Writers 6 (Westminster, MD: The Newman Press, London: Longmans, Green and Company, 1948).

until they are reconciled; your sacrifice must not be defiled. . . ." The prayers of the *Didaché* are of the Jewish blessing type, with Christian content. They do not include the narrative of institution.

Traces of the kind of love feast/Eucharist represented by the *Didaché* can be found in some later liturgical traditions. But the separation of the eucharistic rite from other meal elements comes to predominate. The form is found in Saint Justin's descriptions of the Eucharist, written in his *First Apology* about AD 150. His first account (nn.65–66)[14] is part of his description of Christian initiation. After the newly baptized have been admitted to the assembly,

> Bread and a chalice containing wine mixed with water are presented to the one presiding over the brethren. He takes them and offers praise and glory to the Father of all through the name of the Son and of the Holy Spirit, and recites lengthy prayers of thanksgiving to God in the name of those to whom he granted such favors. At the end of these prayers and thanksgiving, all present express their approval by saying "Amen." This Hebrew word, "Amen," means "So be it." And when he who presides has celebrated the Eucharist, they whom we call deacons permit each one present to partake of the Eucharistic bread, and wine and water; and they carry it also to the absentees. We call this food the Eucharist, of which only he can partake who has acknowledged the truth of our teachings, and who has been cleansed by baptism for the remission of his sins and for his regeneration and who regulates his life upon the principles laid down by Christ.

There follows a theological explanation in which Justin appeals to the accounts of the Last Supper in order to show that the food called the Eucharist is "no ordinary bread" but the flesh and blood of Jesus. The term "Eucharist" has passed by now from being the kind of prayer said at the breaking of bread to being the name for the whole action, and specifically to being the word used to describe the bread and wine once they have been prayed over. There is no suggestion that the Eucharist is part of an ordinary meal. The fact that Justin, in the course of his explanation, thinks of a possible comparison with the Mithraic mysteries (only to exclude it; see Chapter 2, "The Mystery Religions") suggests he does see the Eucharist as a kind of cultic rite. His description of the Sunday assembly (n. 67) adds some

---

14. Text from P. Palmer, SJ, *Sacraments and Worship: Liturgy and Doctrinal Development of Baptism, Confirmation, and the Eucharist* (London: Longmans, Green and Co., 1957), 4–6, 59–60.

details. There is a Liturgy of the Word, including a homily and general intercessions: "On the day which is called Sunday we have a common assembly of all who live in the cities or outlying districts, and the memoirs of the Apostles or the writings of the Prophets are read, as long as there is time. Then when the reader has finished, the president of the assembly verbally admonishes and invites all to imitate such examples of virtue. Then we all stand up together and offer up prayers . . ." (n. 67). After repeating his description of what is done with the bread and wine he adds: "The wealthy, if they wish, contribute whatever they desire, and the collection is placed in the custody of the president. . . ."

The next oldest description of the Eucharist is in *The Apostolic Tradition* attributed to Saint Hippolytus (see Chapter 4, "History"). It describes the Eucharist that is celebrated at the ordination of a bishop (III, 4) and the Easter Eucharist that completes Christian initiation (XXIII). The structure is fundamentally the same as that described by Justin. Distinctive ministries are now assigned to the bishop, who presides and says the eucharistic prayer, to presbyters who assist the bishop and with him lay hands on the "oblation," and to deacons. The fullest description of the Eucharist is found in the description of the ordination of a bishop. The properly eucharistic part of the rite begins with the bringing of what is called the "oblation" before the bishop. This consists of bread and wine mixed with water, which are set apart from other foods that are to be shared. A prayer of thanks is said by the bishop over the bread and wine. The text given for this prayer is taken to be a model rather than a fixed and binding formula. It is in recognizable continuity with the Jewish form of blessing prayer but with a distinctively Christian content. The bishop begins his prayer by addressing the community:

> The Lord be with you . . . lift up your hearts . . . let us give thanks . . . , to which the responses still used in the Roman rite are given. He continues the prayer of thanks by recalling the events of the mystery of Christ (in a form that has been taken over by the Preface of Eucharistic Prayer II of the present Roman Missal). The evocation of Jesus' betrayal and acceptance of death leads to a recall of the words he said about bread and wine being his body and blood at the Last Supper. This is followed by an *anamnesis* of his death and resurrection, which leads to the words "we offer to Thee the bread and the cup making Eucharist to Thee because Thou

hast bidden us [or, found us worthy] to stand before Thee and minister as priests to Thee." Next there is an *epiclesis*, calling down the Holy Spirit on the oblation and on the faithful. The prayer ends with a Trinitarian doxology. The account of the Easter Eucharist does not give a text for the prayer of thanksgiving but simply says that the bishop will "eucharistize first the bread into the representation of the Flesh of Christ; and the cup mixed with wine for the antitype of the Blood which was shed for all who believed in him. (XXIII, 1)

In its description of the paschal Eucharist with the newly initiated *The Apostolic Tradition* tells about the ritual of communion: "And when he breaks the Bread in distributing to each a fragment he shall say: The Bread of Heaven in Christ Jesus. And he who receives shall answer: Amen. And the presbyters shall hold the cups and stand by in good order and with reverence . . . and he who receives shall say: Amen" (XXII, 5).

## The Roman Rite, Fourth to Fourteenth Centuries: Historical Influences

Even if *The Apostolic Tradition* in its present form were to date from the fourth century it can be thought to represent a particular form of eucharistic celebration that had begun to develop during the second century. Throughout the Church other forms were developing that can be documented from the fourth century onward. Notable differences have by then emerged between East and West; within both East and West several distinct traditions, associated with the great primatial sees, have emerged. It was accepted in the Church that each of these traditions was faithful to the apostolic tradition and that a common core was being maintained in the different ritual developments that allowed every Eucharist celebrated in the Church to be a bond of communion with those who celebrated elsewhere and otherwise. Acceptance of one another's Eucharist has always been a condition for communion between the churches. It is, indeed, an instance of a general pattern of rituality, in which a rite can maintain its distinctive influence over the course of time and space in forms that vary in different cultures.

The Roman rite of the Eucharist that emerges from the fourth century onward takes its core from the apostolic tradition.

Historical studies allow us to see how it took on, in the course of time, certain characteristics that were the fruit of its own creative energy and ability to adapt itself to patterns of life characteristic of its own world. Some of these became a permanent part of the self-expression of the Roman Church. But the studies also allow us to see that some developments were a response to transient historical situations. Some of these were discarded when the situation changed, but others were allowed to continue long after they had ceased to have any significance. History tells of moments of reform and renewal. It can tell how these entailed an effort to recover the best of the tradition of the Roman Church, to purge it of elements that had ceased to be useful to it, and to make its significance stand out more effectively in a new era that was marking the life of God's people.

What needs to be understood here, in the interest of doing a theology of the sacrament of the Eucharist, is how that apostolic core, which has been detected in the New Testament and in the writings of the Apostolic Fathers, has been maintained in the variations that have occurred over the centuries, how it is maintained in the form the rite now takes in the Missal of Paul VI, and why it takes the particular form it now has in that Missal. Historians of the liturgy establish the facts. As well as establishing the facts, they also attempt to explain why things developed the way they did. From the theological point of view these explanations are particularly interesting because they bring into play theological and human considerations that are essential to the theologian's own concerns. And to the extent that these considerations can be operative again today and in the future, even if in different forms, they help theologians to understand the present state of things and prospects for the future.

The factual history of the Roman rite of the Eucharist has benefited from excellent historical studies over the past seventy years. The work of J. A. Jungmann[15] is monumental and it has been added to and corrected by excellent scholars in recent years (see Appendix 2: Further Reading). Assuming that work, and recommending the study of it, what is being presented here is an exploration of the why and the wherefore of the various phases of development that have marked the

---

15. J. A. Jungmann, SJ, *The Mass of the Roman Rite: Its Origins and Development. (Missarum Sollemnia).* New revised and abridged edition of *Missarum Sollemnia*, published in 2 vols., in 1949 (New York: Benziger Bros., 1959).

Roman Rite of the Eucharist and a use that analysis as a way of gaining some theological understanding of the present rite and of how it can function today and in the future. What will be looked at are:
1. The cultural and sociopolitical factors that were at work in the world at various periods when significant developments occurred in the rite of the Eucharist; 2. The self-understanding that the Latin Church, under the primacy of the church of Rome, manifested in those periods of development; 3. Particular positions in theology and spirituality that influenced the way in which the Eucharist was being understood and practiced at different stages in the formation of the Roman rite.

*Cultural and political factors.*

The first people who were called together in the new covenant and who assembled week by week to ratify it in the eucharistic rite were Jews. Soon they were joined by Greeks and Romans and later by those they called "barbarians." The culture of each group that accepted the call of the new covenant left a mark on the rite. The original Jewish core remained, canonized forever in the New Testament. The Greeks took the rite from the biblical sources, which were already in their own language, and enriched it creatively out of their own literary and philosophical resources. They filled out the Jewish prayer forms and added new ones. They introduced their human conventions of reverence into the action of the rite. They built and decorated places of assembly suited to the Eucharist, according to their own artistic taste. Eventually, when the Greek world became predominantly Christian, the liturgy became one of the principal carriers of its culture.

      Rome drew on the Greek cultural tradition and its oldest known liturgies of the Eucharist are in Greek. When the Latin language came to be used, it carried with it into the rite the peculiar genius and values that characterized Latin culture. The people in the western provinces of the Roman Empire did not just translate the Greek liturgy into the Latin language: they Latinized it through and through. Texts and forms were not yet fixed authoritatively, so they had a good deal of freedom in composing their own texts and shaping their ritual forms. The most creative work of which there are records was done in Rome itself from the fourth to the seventh century.

The rite of the Eucharist has always been affected by the way
the community assembled, and particularly by the kind of building
chosen for the assembly. After the era of house churches, the church at
Rome chose for its assemblies the type of building that was commonly
used for public business, the basilica. They chose a "secular" kind of
building rather than a religious one, such as a temple. It was in their
being together that God was present to them, and not in any sacredness of the building. The arrangement of space in the basilica already
gave a certain shape to the way the rite of the Eucharist developed.
For example, it gave the ministers their proper place in the apse and
spatially defined their relationship to the faithful. The community was
no longer seated around a table. The act of assembling was solemnized with processions and movement, and enlivened with singing.
Special forms of dress, copied from civil life, were adopted to identify
roles; the conventions of reverence for persons (bows, kisses, genuflections, incense, lights) were introduced; arrangements were made for
an orderly reading of the scriptures and the actual reading was done
by special ministers and surrounded with ritual; the preparation of the
gifts became an elaborate ceremonial; the prayers, and particularly the
eucharistic prayer, came to be given fixed forms in a Latin that was of
the best literary quality available.

The form of eucharistic rite that was developed in Rome
itself was only one of several Latin liturgies that emerged during
those centuries. There was an African form that was very close to
the Roman; there were Gallican, Celtic, Spanish, and Milanese
types that were rather more different. However, the creation of new
liturgical families slowed toward the end of the patristic period.
Eventually it stopped altogether. New communities of Christians,
instead of creating a new form of liturgy suited to their own human
situation, simply copied the existing liturgies of other churches.
There were ecclesiological reasons for this halt to the growth of
new forms in the rite of the Eucharist. But there were also sociological and political ones. The effect of these was still to relate the
Eucharist to a given human situation, but one that was being controlled by various centralizing and standardizing forces. The development of the Roman rite was profoundly affected from the late
eighth century onward by the political decisions of Charlemagne.
One of the strategies he used to bring order and unity into his

turbulent territories was to require that the churches throughout his empire should reform their liturgy according to the rite of the church of Rome. Since the only Roman books available were those that described the rite of the Papal Mass it was that form of the rite that begin to have a dominant influence on the way the Eucharist was celebrated throughout Europe. However, the Frankish and Germanic peoples did leave their imprint on the Roman Mass. They added many prayers to the rite, which were quite different in character from the Roman prayers: they were individualistic, emotional, and repetitious. Several of them became a permanent part of the Roman tradition. The *Ordo Missae* that was codified in these Germanic and Frankish lands, sometimes called generically the Gallican form, was eventually taken back to Rome and was in use there by the eleventh century. It was the form in which the Roman rite was handed on to the medieval world.

### Self-understanding of the Church.

When a group of people "assemble as a church to celebrate the Lord's Supper," their way of doing it is bound to be affected by the way they understand what it is to be a church. There has been development in the self-understanding of the churches, and it is reflected in the way they have celebrated the Eucharist. The community of believers that gathered in Rome at the home of one of its better-off members during the centuries when Christianity was an unlawful and persecuted religion had a different self-image from the community that gathered in the basilica of Saint John Lateran around their pope and bishop in the century after the peace of Constantine. The difference is reflected in the different way they celebrated the Eucharist. The later community could be so much more self-confident in its belief that in the Church itself the world was being transformed and won for Christ. The world and its ways, and, best of all, its leaders were becoming members of the Church. Leaders of the church were being accepted as civic dignitaries. Assemblies of Christians were public events; their celebrations were celebrations of the public good. The eucharistic assembly had, from the beginning, been understood to be an earthly representation of the coming of God's kingdom. When those who formed it were no longer a persecuted minority but a dominant majority they could afford to

let their Eucharist be a triumphant celebration of the society in which
they lived.

As the Church came to see itself as the religion of a Christian
society it could begin to fill out its eucharistic rite with forms taken
from the cultic practices of society. There were already good reasons
for adopting forms of Roman culture. The fact that some of these may
have at one time been associated with the worship of the emperor or
with the mystery cults was no longer felt to be a threat to faith. More
importantly, there was a precedent in the Bible itself for this kind of
relationship between forms of worship and the state of society. In the
theocratic world of the Old Testament religious worship had reflected
the reign of God over every detail of life. There was total interaction
between the temple cult in Jerusalem and the social, political, and
economic life of the people. It is true that in the New Testament the
Christian way is contrasted sharply with the ritualism of the Old Law,
and during the first three centuries analogies between Christian liturgy
and the rites of the Old Testament are handled very discreetly. But
once the Church has an established position in a world that was predominantly Christian there begins to be a more conscious modeling of
Christian liturgical forms on the Old Testament. The Temple begins
to overshadow the Upper Room. Fixed forms of prayer and stylized
sacred actions take the place of calculated improvisation. There is a
sanctuary, with its holy of holies, there are priests and orders of priests
who do cultic things and wear priestly vestments. As the Church sees
itself mirrored more realistically in the relationship between religious
institutions and society that is described in the Old Testament, it has
a theological justification for the use of Old Testament images and
forms, and for giving an Old Testament interpretation to forms bor-
rowed from civil life, in its celebration of the Eucharist.

The development of ecclesiology in the Roman Church was
affected by the sheer size of the Christian community in a world that
had become Christian, and by the need to organize it internally and
in relation to civil authorities. The structures of ministry and authority received from the New Testament became more formal and the
distinction between clergy and laity more pronounced. The form of
eucharistic celebration that developed in the Roman Church reflected
an ecclesiology that gave prominence to the hierarchical structure of
the Christian community. When it was taken over by the churches of

the Frankish empire under Charlemagne it found itself being influenced by an ecclesiology that added a clerical character to the hierarchical: canon law regulated the holiness expected of the ordained ministers of the Church in ways that set them more and more apart from the lay faithful. For this and all sorts of sociological reasons, the Church came to be thought of as being adequately represented by the clergy. Acts of the Church were acts of the clergy. The celebration of the Eucharist reflected this ecclesiology. In the Middle Ages the rite was done by the clergy. The faithful could do little more than attend and watch what was being done for them. The clergy did their part in a Latin language that the people no longer understood and did much of it in a voice that was not supposed to be heard. The singing was done by choirs of clerics. The reading of the scriptures had become a formal exercise because the people could not understand what was being read. When the Reformers protested against Roman ecclesiology they protested particularly against what it had done to the celebration of the Eucharist. Their calls for a return to a simpler, biblical form of celebration were, simultaneously, calls for a return to a biblical ecclesiology and theology of ministry.

Another element of the ecclesiology of the Roman Catholic Church that came to be criticized by the Reformers had an important bearing on the development of the rite of the Eucharist. The Petrine ministry of unity given to the church of Rome is exercised by watching over the faith of all the churches and also over their celebration of the sacraments. In keeping with the nature of ritual the Roman Church had confined its care for the Eucharist of other churches to the essential core of the rite; the liturgical form given to the rite in particular churches was their own business. The liturgy of the Pope's own church did, indeed, have considerable authority among the churches of the Latin West, and the work of popes like Saint Leo the Great and Saint Gregory the Great had been accepted as normative. But when the Roman liturgy was imposed by Charlemagne as a standard for many churches of the West, the initiative seems to have come from the emperor himself, rather than from the Pope. Papal initiative in favor of liturgical reform and pressure toward standardization according to the usages of the Roman Church did become insistent as the Middle Ages went on. But up to the Council of Trent there was still no obligation on particular churches to conform their celebration of

the Eucharist to a form determined by the Pope. The authority of the
Pope to do so was generally recognized but it only became an undis-
puted part of Catholic ecclesiology after the Council of Trent. After
that council the rite of the Eucharist became increasingly standardized
and Romanized in the churches of the Latin West, in keeping with
Counter-Reformation ecclesiology.

### *Theology and spirituality.*

As well as being influenced by the general self-understanding of
the church that produced it, the Roman rite of the Eucharist was
influenced by particular theological teachings and spiritual experiences that flowered over the centuries in the Western Church. What
the Church thought about the grace of God, about the way it is
given in sacraments, and specifically about how it was given in the
Eucharist, affected the form given to the rite. The spiritual experience
that accompanied doctrinal developments, and was sometimes more
responsible than intellectual considerations for its moving in a particular direction, also molded the rite.

  The eucharistic prayer that a church uses is always a good
indicator of what it thinks about the mystery of grace, about sacramentality, and about the Eucharist. The way it is said and the rituals
that accompany it give a good sense of how the Eucharist is being
spiritually experienced and understood by the celebrating community.
Within the common Christian teaching about the grace of salvation
that is inherent in every eucharistic prayer, particular churches find
one or other aspect of the mystery more spiritually and intellectually congenial; they accent it accordingly in the text they develop. In
every eucharistic prayer, as in the Jewish *berakah* on which it is modeled, there is a sense that everything is grace from God: creatures are
there to bless and thank him. There is also in it a sense of the justice of
things: God is right to punish us for our sins, but at the same time he
ought now to show us his favor because we are committing ourselves
anew to obeying his covenant. It appears that a sense of justice was
something that appealed strongly to the people of the Roman world.
In the civil sphere they worked out a rather admirable system of law
and of procedures for the administration of justice. In theology the
churches of the Latin world developed a special interest in how that

sense of justice could be maintained within an understanding of the grace of God. Most of the early doctrinal debates about grace occurred in the West. Special attention was given in the theology of grace to the place of human action, and to the experience of give and take that marks human reception of God's gifts: how is it that we can do nothing to establish a claim on God's gifts, and yet we must do everything to please God and make ourselves worthy of his grace; what is the gift within us that allows us to be our human selves in receiving the gifts of God? The Scholastic theology of grace and justification came to give particular attention to these typically Western concerns.

The Roman Canon began to appear in Rome in the fourth century, has existed substantially as it is now since the sixth century, and was adopted by all Western churches between the ninth and eleventh centuries. While it embodies the classical tradition of eucharistic prayer, it has the distinctive Western accent on the give and take of grace. It is not afraid to speak of the offering that the faithful, and the priest on their behalf, make in the Eucharist as "these gifts we offer you in sacrifice," and to ask that they be accepted by God as were the gifts of Abel and the sacrifice of Abraham and the bread and wine of Melchizedek; it sees the taking of "this sacrifice to your altar in heaven" as connected with the faithful being "filled with every grace and blessing"; it offers "this sacrifice of praise for ourselves and those who are dear to us. . . ." The Eucharist is the sacrifice offered by God's people and they expect results from it. According to the intentions of a Western, and especially a Scholastic, theology of grace, the certainty that the only offering now acceptable to God is the sacrifice of Christ (which is a fundamental presupposition of every eucharistic prayer) is not in the least compromised by this attention to the human offering. The whole effort of Western theology was to understand how the work of salvation could be entirely the gift of God, realized by the sacrificial death of Christ, and communicated by the grace of the Holy Spirit, while being at the same time a genuinely human work that had meritorious, satisfactory (propitiatory), and intercessory value in the sight of God. That theology found a congenial expression in the Roman Canon. However, if that Scholastic theology were badly understood it could make the Roman Canon seem to be saying that the gifts of God were somehow the result of a claim that humans established by their sacrifice. The Reformers challenged the

Scholastic theology of grace on the basis of their understanding of the biblical doctrine of justification: they were convinced that to attribute any meritorious and satisfactory value to human action was to negate the grace of God given only in Christ. From their perspective the Roman Canon was not only uncongenial but un-Christian. It made the Eucharist to be a work of the law. In their attack on the Catholic doctrine of justification, they could hardly avoid raising the issue of the Roman Canon, because it truly does express the characteristic Roman Catholic theology of grace and justification.

The Western theology of grace is also at work in the way the Roman Canon prays for the consecration of the bread and wine so that they will become the body and blood of Christ. In most other eucharistic prayers, ancient and modern, this takes the form of a call-ing on God to send the Holy Spirit to sanctify the offerings (it is an *epiclesis*). The Roman Canon reflects a theology and a spirituality that is particularly sensitive to the created effect of God's sanctifying action, and does not always find it necessary to attribute it to one or other of the divine Persons. From the *De Sacramentis* of Saint Ambrose onward one can find explanations in Latin theology that such actions, although they may be attributed in some of their aspects to one or other of the divine Persons, involve a joint causality, a single sanctify-ing action of the whole Trinity.[16] The effect of the action involves some kind of real change in created reality (habitual or sanctifying grace in humans, transubstantiation in the bread and wine). The petition for consecration in the Roman Canon is simply that the offering itself may be "blessed, approved, acceptable . . . may become an offering in spirit and in truth." It is a prayer for sanctification that is more con-cerned with the effect of sanctification than with the personal identity of the sanctifier. It accords with a general reticence of Latin theology about the Holy Spirit and its volubility about the created effects of sanctification.

The theology of sacraments that was worked out in the Latin Church (see Chapter 2, "The Scholastics and Saint Thomas Aquinas" and Chapter 3, "Technical Questions about Sacraments") inevitably influenced the Roman rite of the Eucharist. The thesis

---

16. Ambrose, Sermon VI, 5 in E. Yarnold, sj, *The Awe-Inspiring Rites of Initiation. The Origins of the RCIA*, 2nd ed. (The Liturgical Press: Collegeville, MN, 1994), 147.

that each sacrament has an essential matter and form, for example, made it necessary to identify these two components in the Eucharist. Bread and wine were obviously the matter. The words of Jesus, "This is my body . . . this is the chalice of my blood," were identified as the form. The moment when these words were said was identified as the moment when the sacrament came into existence. The theology of the Eastern churches was less interested in defining the exact moment of consecration, but when it did ask the question it looked rather to the *epiclesis* than to the saying of the words of Jesus for an answer. The Latin theology made the moment of consecration be the climax of the celebration. Correspondingly, the rite came to surround that moment with special solemnity and gestures of reverence, such as genuflections, burning of incense, and ringing of bells. The theological analysis of how the consecration happened also had its effect on the rite. The relationship between the sacramental bread and the body of Christ was worked out in terms of substance and transubstantiation (see Chapter 9, "Medieval Theology"). It became clear to the Church that the consecrated bread was no longer substantially bread. It became clear, too, that every fragment of the consecrated bread is the body of Christ. This kind of theological clarification, allied to a deep reverence for the body of Christ truly present in the sacrament, had an influence on the practice of preparing special bread and wine for use in the Eucharist. White, wafer-thin bread, already separated into particles suitable for individual communion, gradually began to take the place of loaves of unleavened bread from the ninth century onward; "altar wine" eventually became a special commodity. The taking of bread from the faithful at the offering of the gifts and the breaking of the loaf for distribution in communion were no longer needed. The doctrine of what is called "concomitance"—which explained that, while sacramentally the bread becomes the body and the wine the blood of Christ, nevertheless the whole Christ, body, blood, soul, and divinity, is really present in the species of bread alone, as it is in the species of wine—gave a theological justification for the practice of giving the faithful communion only under the form of bread. A spiritual need to see and adore the body of Christ present in the consecrated species was met by introducing the elevation of the host and chalice at the consecration; the practice of exposing the consecrated host in a monstrance allowed this act of eucharistic devotion to be prolonged outside the celebration of the

Eucharist. A spirituality of the real presence brought to the Roman celebration of the Eucharist a distinctive quality of adoration and a sense of reverence for the wonder of God's coming to be present with his people. Later, during the Baroque period, this found expression in a way of celebrating the rite that had something of the theatrical about it. Even though the official rite still provided for participation of the faithful by sacramental communion and various responses, these were often sacrificed to the interests of a more solemn performance of the rite by the clergy, and by the choir and musicians who gave a splendor to the celebration worthy of the divine manifestation that occurred within it.

There were other theological and spiritual factors contributing to the acceptance of celebrations of the Eucharist in which the faithful did not partake of the body and blood of Christ. A case came to be made for expressing a sense of wonder at the gift of the Eucharist by abstaining from receiving it. The tradition of faith had recognized that a sense of unworthiness and a confession of sinfulness had its place in the celebration of the Eucharist. It had expected sinners who were not reconciled to God in and by the community to abstain from the Eucharist until they had been absolved from their sin. But only special kinds of sinful situations required this exclusion from the Eucharist. Indeed the Eucharist itself was recognized as expressing repentance, bringing God's forgiveness, and effecting reconciliation within the community. A confession of sinfulness and various prayers · for forgiveness had found a place in the Roman rite from the ninth century onward. The rituals of adoration that expressed Western devotion to the real presence accentuated feelings of unworthiness and an appreciation of the spiritual value of excluding oneself from receiving the Eucharist until one was really ready and worthy. The very abstention was reckoned to be a good way of improving the quality of one's participation in the Eucharist. Theology taught that one could receive the grace of the Eucharist by the desire of receiving it, without actual sacramental reception. Once ritual form was given in the Eucharist to a strong theology and spirituality of the real presence, acts of seeing and adoring the host could be treated as a form of spiritual communion that would do as much for one's growth in grace as sacramental communion. Saints no less than sinners regularly took part in the Eucharist without receiving communion, and it was not unknown from the late Middle Ages to have the Eucharist celebrated in the Roman rite without any provision for communion of the faithful.

There was another line of theological justification for celebrating the Eucharist without provision for communion, and even without provision for attendance by the faithful. The general tradition about the Eucharist, and the Roman tradition in particular, had always recognized the Eucharist as a sacrifice. Medieval theologians introduced a distinction between the effects that the Eucharist had as sacrifice and those that it had as a sacrament received in communion (Chapter 10, "The Reformers and the Council of Trent"). Late medieval preaching and practice made much of the fruits of the Eucharist as sacrifice, in a way that made them seem independent of the reception of communion. Not only that, but a theological case could be made in those terms for saying that reception of the fruits of the Mass as sacrifice did not depend on one's presence at it, or indeed on the presence of anyone but the celebrating priest. When an ordained priest performed the rite, using the essential matter and form, one had a real Eucharist with its sacrificial effects. The effects could be directed by the intention of the priest toward those for whom he was offering the sacrifice, whether they were present or not. Thus a Mass without an actual congregation could be given theological sense. The prescribed rite of Mass was not deprived of its communitarian features, but many of them were incongruous without an assembled community. These "private" celebrations of the Eucharist became more frequent and acceptable in the Roman rite through being associated with devotion to particular mysteries of the life of Christ, or to the saints (Votive Masses), and with promises of special favors that could be gained through various combinations of them, for the dead as well as for the living. They also became an important source of income for the priests who celebrated them. But there was some incongruity between the multiplication of "private" Masses (and of the reasons for which they might be celebrated, such as special intentions of benefactors, special devotional exercises, votive offerings) and the basic meaning that continued to be embodied in the rite that was the gathering together of an ecclesial community to renew the covenant that bound them together to God and to one another in the Body of Christ.

The offering of the Eucharist for particular intentions or in connection with needs of individuals not shared with the community also affected the relationship between the two parts of the eucharistic rite, which are nowadays called the Liturgy of the Word and the Liturgy of the Eucharist. The reading of the word was done with impressive solemnity in the original Roman rite. It became a somewhat formal ritual, however, when it continued to be done in Latin even where that was no longer the vernacular language of the communities who were celebrating. The choice of passages to be read was determined in the classical tradition of Roman liturgy by the intention of having the whole Bible heard, if not in all its pages at least in a representative selection, over a certain period of time. While that principle was never abandoned its effectiveness was gradually blunted by the many other criteria of choice that began to operate. Feasts of saints, votive celebrations, Masses for the dead, and many other particular occasions had their own proper readings that interrupted the continuous reading of the Bible. The result was that many Christian communities heard a quite haphazard selection of readings. They were not exposed to that full story of God's People in the Old and New Testaments that gave them their identity as God's Covenant People, and to which their Eucharist was a response in Christ. Their Eucharist was affected more by the occasions and intentions for which it was celebrated than by the pedagogy of God's word. The general neglect of the homily during the Middle Ages left the scripture readings often without controlled application to the life of the community, and left the community without direction as to how it should offer itself to God in the eucharistic part of the rite.

## The Missal of Pius v

It is undeniable that by the beginning of the sixteenth century many of the celebrations of Mass in the Western Church entailed a greater or less distortion of the rite that had been received from the apostles, had been given a classical Roman shape in the period from the fourth to the seventh century, and then adapted to the new Europe of the Middle Ages with a good deal of sensitivity to the culture and historical reality of its people. The Council of Trent knew all about the situation. It had before it detailed catalogues of ritual and other aberrations in the way the Eucharist was celebrated. A special commission was set up at the council to deal with what were called *abusus Missae*. However, before the Council of Trent met, the Protestant Reformers had been having their say about the abuses of Mass. They had fulminated against the Mass as they experienced it. The forms they knew were not always in the rite of Rome itself, because there was as yet no uniformity of rite in the Latin Church, but they were close enough to it to let Rome and its rite of Mass be the credible target of Protestant outrage.

The Reformers attributed the abuses they found in celebrations of the Eucharist to, among other things, bad theology: they saw them as the outcome of erroneous, unbiblical Catholic thinking about justification, about the relationship between faith and sacraments, about the Eucharist as sacrifice, and about the presence of Christ in the consecrated elements. That left the Council of Trent with a dilemma. It may have wanted to make some of the reforms in the celebration of the Eucharist that Protestants were proposing or already making. But the Protestants were giving theological reasons for their reforms that the Catholic Church could not accept. In their new liturgical creations they were doing some things that Catholics might have considered to be the right things, but doing them for what Catholics judged to be the wrong reasons. (They were also judged, of course, to be doing some wrong things for those same wrong reasons.) The Council of Trent believed it had to define Catholic doctrine unambiguously in the face of erroneous Protestant teaching and practice. If it made reforms in the celebration of the Eucharist that had already been preempted by the Protestants it risked giving the impression that the Protestants were right—not just about the reforms—but about the reasons for them. To give that impression would have been to obscure the firmness of the dogmatic positions that the council was taking. It could also have weakened the authority of the Church and of the Pope on which the dogmatic value of the teaching of the council depended. If popes and councils had been wrong about so many things in the celebration of the Eucharist ... then they might be wrong about other things. Hence the reforms in the celebration of the Eucharist enacted by the Council of Trent are modest and cautious. Its *Decretum de Observandis et Evitandis in Celebratione Missae* (1562) is a call for the elimination of obvious abuses stemming from "avarice, irreverence and superstition."[17] It does not provide for any changes in the rite itself. Neither did it take a decisive line on the much-debated question of whether the rite should be standardized and centrally controlled in the Western church.

The Council of Trent left the whole question of rites to be dealt with by the Pope. Work on the Mass was begun immediately after the council and it resulted in the promulgation of a *Missale Romanum* by Pope Saint Pius V in 1570. The arrangement of the rite *(ordo missae)*, the calendar and the selection of scripture readings that it contained was made obligatory for the Latin Church, but not for those dioceses and religious orders that could demonstrate they had been using a stable rite of their own for more than 200 years. The form of rite chosen was the one that was then in use in the Roman Curia. While the commission did make some attempt to examine the original sources of the Roman rite in such documents as were available to scholars at the time, and whereas the Pope stated in his Bull of Promulgation that the intention had been to restore the celebration of the Eucharist *ad pristinam sanctorum Patrum normam ac ritum* ("to conformity with the original norm and rite laid down by the holy Fathers"), what the compilers of the Missal settled for was, in fact, a well-established and distinctively medieval form of the Roman rite. (A passage in *General Instruction of the Roman Missal* (2002), [GIRM, 7] provides a good explanation of the reasons for and limitations of the choices made in the Missal of Pius V). Although it went beyond Trent in the degree of standardization and centralization it imposed on the Latin Church, the Missal did generally obey the intentions of Trent: it provided a good standard form of the rite according to which the celebration of the Eucharist could be restored; it retained medieval forms that corresponded well with the doctrinal definitions of the council; it refused reforms such as the use of vernacular languages and communion from the chalice for the laity, thus avoiding the doctrinal ambiguity to which they could give rise, as well as the pastoral risks that changes in well-established custom would have entailed at a time when the Church needed a strong defensive strategy.

---

17. Text in Tanner, *Decrees of the Ecumenical Councils*, vol. II, 736–737.

## The Missal of Paul VI

The Missal that was promulgated by Pius V in 1570, with a few very minor changes, remained binding on Catholics of the Latin rite, with a few exceptions, until it was replaced by the Missal of Paul VI in 1969 (see "Description"). The new Missal is presented in the apostolic constitution that introduces it as a revision of the old. The revision is said to be based on the experience of the liturgical movement and on scholarly research, and to complete "the adaptation of the Roman Missal to the new outlook and spiritual mentality of our own times," which was already begun by Pope Pius XII. While praising the Missal of Pius V as "universally acknowledged to be among the most useful of the many fruits which that Council [of Trent] brought forth for the good of the whole Church of Christ," Paul VI readily admits that it needed revision. He has no doubt that the revised form of the rite he is promulgating embodies one and the same tradition that is represented by the Missal of Pius V. The analysis of the development of the Roman rite given in "The Roman Rite: Fourth to Fourteenth Centuries" should help one to appreciate what the Pope means. The tradition received from the apostles has taken an ongoing variety of forms under the influence of cultural, ecclesiological, and theological factors. It was given a particular historical form in the Missal of Pius V. That form was not identical with the form in which the rite was celebrated at the time of Saint Gregory the Great. There is no reason why it should have been. Neither is there any good reason why it should not be subject to the same developments that produced itself. And there are many good reasons for it to be able to recognize itself in the Missal of Paul VI. As the GIRM 6 puts it: "... both Roman Missals, although separated by four centuries, embrace one and the same tradition. Furthermore, if the inner elements of this tradition are reflected upon, it also becomes clear how outstandingly and felicitously the older Roman Missal is brought to fulfillment in the new." It is not surprising that some people found the changes introduced in the Missal of Paul VI to be rather abrupt and to be upset by them. For one thing the very nature of rite calls for stability and a sense of the familiar; in ritual, any change is upsetting. But the changes made after Vatican II had to be particularly severe. There had been no change of any consequence

in the Roman rite since 1570. In other periods of history the factors
of change had been allowed to work gradually and almost impercep-
tibly. During the centuries after the Council of Trent, however, it was
judged better to maintain the rite in a rigidly fixed form. Inevitably,
when change could be allowed again, and a beginning was made in the
courageous reforms of Pius XII, a lot of ground had to be made up and
changes were experienced as abrupt and surprising.

The rite of the Eucharist in the Missal of Paul VI was
designed on the paradoxical principle that the best way to be progressive in reforming an institution like the Eucharist is to look back
toward its origins. The criterion of authenticity in relation to sources is
more fundamental than the criterion of relevance in liturgical reform.
The authors of the rite went back to the biblical and patristic sources
of the eucharistic rite and to the classical beginnings of what is distinctive about the Roman rite. They had better historical information
than did the compilers of the Missal of Pius V. They knew when and
why particular additions had been made in the past and why some of
these could now be omitted without prejudice to the wholesomeness
and simplicity of the rite. They preserved the main lines of the Missal
of Pius V. What they omitted from it was almost entirely from the
medieval stratum; what they restored to it came from the patristic and
early Roman level. They did not add contemporary new features to
the rite, but rather restored it to its essential, classical Roman shape.
However, in allowing for some choices and possibilities of adaptation, the restoration did make provision for letting the use of the rite
be affected by contemporary human culture, ecclesiology, and theology—those factors that have always influenced the development of
the eucharistic rite. Subsequent difficulties that have arisen about the
Church's celebration of the Eucharist according to the new rite have
been less about the rite itself than about the way these contemporary factors have been allowed to influence the way the rite is used.
Disagreements between conservatives and liberals about these matters are often projected on the "new liturgy." Judgments that are made
and proposals for alternatives to the rite of Paul VI often have little or
nothing to do with the liturgical merits of different rites. And they do
not always pay sufficient attention to the catholicity of the eucharistic
rite, which is intended for use, not just in settled, stable parts of the
world familiar with a cultural past that goes back to the Middle Ages

and Renaissance, but in new churches opening up in parts of the world that have little or nothing to do with that particular cultural past and are still being evangelized.

There are limits to the cultural adaptation allowed for in the present Roman rite. Here the ecclesiological factor begins to come into play. In Catholic belief the church of Rome is at the centre of the unity of the Church of God. Anything that helps its mission of unity is good for the whole Church. Toward the end of the apostolic constitution with which he introduces the Missal, Paul VI expresses a hope that, in spite of the variations that it allows for in obedience to Vatican II, "this book will be received by the faithful as an aid whereby all can witness to each other and strengthen the one faith common to all, since it enables one and the same prayer, expressed in so many different languages, to ascend to the heavenly Father through our High Priest Jesus Christ in the Holy Spirit—a prayer more fragrant than any incense."[18] Obviously this appeal for liturgical unity is addressed only to Catholics of the Latin rite, because the book is intended for them alone. Those who follow an Oriental rite of the Eucharist are not calling the unity of the Church into question by attachment to their own rite. One must take the Pope's words to mean that Catholics of the Latin rite will have a deeper experience of unity among themselves, and give a more effective witness of unity to the rest of the Church when their celebration of the Eucharist is in accordance with the prescriptions of the one Roman Missal. Dogmatically, it would be quite permissible for a local church to want to develop a new rite of the Eucharist according to its own cultural and ecclesiological perceptions that would go beyond the adaptations allowed for in the Roman Missal. There is no dogmatic reason why new rites should not emerge in the Church of today as they did in the early centuries, provided they respect the essentials of the common tradition of faith and the fundamental structure of the rite that comes from the apostles. The discipline of communion between the churches, and the special liturgical authority that the Roman Church has over churches that are historically of the Latin rite might, however, be put at risk by such a step. For a church that is historically of the Latin rite to want to opt out of it would

---

18. A. Flannery, OP, ed., *Vatican Council II. The Conciliar and Post-Conciliar Documents,* revised ed. (Dublin: Dominican Publications and Northport NY: Costello Publishing Company, 1996), 141.

put some strains on the bonds of communion. However, disciplinary requirements for communion have not always been the same in the Church. The hope expressed by Paul VI is expressed within the terms of a particular stage of the development of ecclesiology. Perhaps future refinements in the understanding of the disciplinary requirements of communion—affected, for example, by the reuniting of churches now separated—could result in greater flexibility in the forms the Latin rite might take. One could envisage their being other missals that draw enough from the Roman Missal to ensure their belonging to the Roman Rite but enrich the rite with new liturgical forms that are more in keeping with their own non-Latin cultures. The authorizing of a distinctive Missal for the churches of Congo-Zaire in 1988 is a move in that direction.[19]

The ecclesiology of Vatican II constructs the Christian community from the People of God, on the basis of the sharing that all its members have in the priestly and prophetic offices of Christ, before it puts in place the ordained hierarchy of ministers by which it is served. The rite of the Eucharist reflects this view of the Church. Its primary form is designed for participation by the full ecclesial community. It diversifies roles so that many persons can contribute to the rite according to the particular ministry and gift they have in the community. It highlights the special priesthood of the one who presides, and provides for concelebration by a number of priests in a single celebration; but this does not downplay the general priesthood of believers or the ministries of deacons, readers, acolytes, singers, etc. The structured hierarchical character of the eucharistic assembly is fully maintained, but the virtual monopoly of ritual action that clerics had in the former Roman rite is broken. The rite is an action of the whole church in the variety of its members (see GIRM, n.5).

The Preamble of GIRM gives special attention to the doctrinal issues about sacraments and about the Eucharist itself that affected the form of the rite standardized in the Missal of Pius V. It notes that Vatican II had made its own the definitions of the Council of Trent on the questions about the Eucharist that were at issue with the Reformers: the Eucharist is a sacrifice; Christ is really present

---

19. C. Egbulem, op, "An African Interpretation of Liturgical Inculturation: The 'Rite Zairois'" in M. Downey and R. Fragomeni, eds., *A Promise of Presence. Studies in Honor of David Power* (Washington, DC: The Pastoral Press, 1992), 227–250.

under the eucharistic species through transubstantiation of the elements; the celebrant is a ministerial priest who offers the sacrifice in the person of Christ (nn. 2–4). These truths are stated, however, in a way that draws on the renewed and ecumenically sensitive sacramental theology that had been adopted by Vatican II. It suggests that the caution required by the dogmatic disputes of the Reformation is no longer necessary. It was for dogmatic reasons that Pius V found it necessary to stand by the form that the Roman rite had come to take during the Middle Ages (n. 7). But now one can give liturgical recognition to the priesthood of all believers without compromising the ministerial priesthood of the ordained (n. 5). There is no longer a risk of casting doubts on the objective efficacy of the Eucharist by having it in the vernacular, by having the eucharistic prayer said aloud, and by other things that may be done to heighten the pastoral and catechetical value of the rite (nn. 11–13). One does not call the Tridentine doctrine of the real presence of the whole Christ under the appearance of bread into question by reintroducing communion under both kinds (n. 14). Nor, one might add, is transubstantiation put in danger by requiring that the bread used in the Eucharist should look like food and be in a form that allows it to be broken into pieces for distribution (GIRM, nn. 282–283). It must also be said that what has been done to restore sacramental communion as the normal way of participation by all the community in the Eucharist does not call its sacrificial values into question. The theology of salvation and grace inherent in the Roman Canon is, of course, affirmed and the prayer is retained in the Missal with only minor modifications. It has been relativized, however, by the introduction of new eucharistic prayers which, according to the apostolic constitution, "emphasize different aspects of the mystery of salvation."[20] All the new eucharistic prayers have an epiclesis of the Holy Spirit. Theological traditions other than the Roman and Scholastic are at work, then, in the rite, as they are throughout the teaching of Vatican II.

Vatican II has a theology of the Word of God and of its relationship to sacrament that puts the debate with the churches of the Reformation about the role of faith and sacraments in justification on a much more promising level. The liturgical reforms since Vatican II

---

20. Flannery, *Vatican Council II*, 139.

have done much to make the eucharistic action be experienced once again in the Roman rite as a response in faith to the great events of the new covenant as they are told in the Bible. The rearrangement of the calendar, the setting of limits to the number of feasts of saints to be celebrated, the control of celebrations for special and private occasions, as well as a new lectionary, have allowed the continuous reading of the scriptures to be reestablished, so that the history of salvation and its fulfillment in Christ is put before the covenant people in an orderly way. The celebration of the Word of God, read and sung and then applied to concrete situations of the community in the homily, gives meaning and reality to the covenant sacrifice of praise that God's assembled people make in Christ, in their meal of bread and wine that is his body and blood.

## Anthropological Considerations

### Ritual Meals

The rite of the Eucharist has precedents and parallels throughout human life. Ritual meals mark or recall significant moments in family and civil life. Sacred meals are celebrated in many of the world religions. Reflection on the human significance of meals can help to develop a sensitivity to the sacramentality of the eucharistic rite.

People eat because they need food to sustain life. They eat together because they usually do things better when they do them together, and the human quality of life is enriched by company. The food is likely to be better for being provided, prepared, and shared by several. When people are happy to be together it affects the way they eat. Their meals become festive. They use them to identify the things that make them happy. When, for example, they are particularly aware of one of their members because it is the anniversary of his or her birth they turn their meal into a birthday party. The party says that their life together is richer because that person is with them. When one of their group marries they have a wedding feast. It becomes a way of saying that they have a future as a family. Those who belong together in professional associations, sports clubs, and business firms have their annual dinner. It is good for morale and fellowship and dedication to a common purpose. On a more intimate scale people invite friends, or those they want to have as friends, to their home for a meal; or friends go out to eat together. People eat together, eventually, because they have some life-giving common bond, which is important to them and which they want to last. The meal renews the bond, deepens it, and becomes a promise that it will continue. When they are happy about the bond their meal becomes a celebration.

## Sacrifice

Because they entail the giving and taking, not just of food but of friendship and solidarity, meals lend themselves readily to the religious instinct to offer sacrifice. To sacrifice is to give to another who in receiving ratifies a bond of togetherness. In the religious history of humanity doing something with food, vegetable or animal, is an almost universal way of giving ritual expression to sacrifice. Food is something that one can possess as "fruit of the earth and work of human hands." It is something one can give to others and take satisfaction and joy from the giving. One gives it away and it becomes life-giving for others. To sacrifice is to decide to surrender, to set apart for another's use, to share with another and to create a bond with that other. There is something of sacrifice in every giving of food. In it people give themselves to each other. When the other is God, what is set aside for God is said to be made holy, to be consecrated. It is consecrated because it expresses the self-giving of a person and their desire to be one with God. That Christ should want to ritualize the sacrifice he made of himself to the Father on the cross in a meal of bread and wine fits easily with the anthropological meaning of sacrifice, and with the way sacrifice has been expressed for centuries in the religion of the Old Testament. A proper understanding of the relationship between food and sacrifice shows how unfounded are the warnings sometimes given by theologians about the need to separate consideration of the Eucharist as meal from consideration of it as sacrifice.

## Occasions and Roles

Meals, and especially festive meals, easily become ritualized. Special food and drink are used to give a sense of occasion. In the Western world there has to be a cake at a birthday party or wedding, and champagne is a recognized festive drink. Sometimes the food is chosen to stir memories and maintain continuity. Americans eat turkey at their Thanksgiving meal because the Pilgrims supposedly did so and their descendants have been doing it ever since. Roles become ritualized. Because food has to be provided and prepared by someone, and a table has to be set, those who give the meal are distinguished from those who are invited to receive it as a gift. The host, the "breadwinner" and the cook are easily recognized as gift-givers. Guests are receivers, although they may also bring gifts of food or other things to a meal. Then there is conversation and even speeches and toasts at meals. There is something there that can help one to understand the place of the Liturgy of the Word in the rite of the Eucharist. The scripture readings and homily can be experienced as the kind of family speeches and conversation, and messages from absent friends that are listened to at festive meals. At family festive meals speech usually takes the form of conversation. The meals of less personally intimate groups are inclined to ritualize words in the form of speeches and toasts. The speeches will proclaim what the group stands for, tell of its origins, boast of its successes, thank those who have contributed, express hopes for the future. The toasts are more specific and personal. They are often associated with the taking of the distinctive festive food and drink—with the cutting of the cake and the opening and pouring of the champagne. Indeed the significance of the meal tends to be concentrated in such moments. They can provide an analogy for understanding features of the eucharistic prayer said over the bread and wine and followed by their distribution for eating and drinking.

## The Hungry of the World

People do not take festive meals just because they are hungry. And yet hunger, even the hunger of the world, is an issue in every meal, be it festive or just functional. No meal is entirely private. Having a table to sit down to goes along with being in a family, having friends, belonging to a socially productive group. Each of these circles provides some guarantee that one will not go hungry. Good people who eat together with joy and thankfulness think readily enough of those who have no table at which they are welcome and who therefore go hungry. They must feel some responsibility for feeding the hungry and welcoming the stranger. There is a built-in will to hospitality in a humanly good meal. In many cultures there had to be always a place at table for a traveler and extra food was prepared for the poor. Nowadays one expects those who eat well to have a certain social conscience about their responsibility to work for a society in which everyone would have a table at which they could feel at home and no one need go hungry. There are, of course, those whose meals are a celebration of their own selfish successes, and of values and events that actually make others be outsiders and go hungry. Their meals can become a flaunting of food in the face of the hunger of others. The meals of the generous, on the other hand, are symbols of human hope and hospitality. The meals of the selfish may be festive to them but they can be an outrage to the hungry.

## Sacramentality

The human values of ritual meals were incorporated in the Jewish and Christian tradition out of which our present rite of Eucharist comes (see "The Rites of the Old Covenant" and "The Rite of the New Covenant"). It has to be recognized that the expression of them is today rather formalized. If they are to function sacramentally ways must be found of giving those who take part in them a credible experience of eating and drinking together. For this it is not necessary that the Eucharist should become an imitation of one or other of the festive meals that are experienced in family or civil life. That could make the human communion seem to be the very purpose of the Eucharist rather than a part of the sacramentality through which more profound communion is achieved. Ritual elements should indeed produce some real human experience. But they are meant to work on other levels of significance besides the obvious and immediate. They normally work better when they are somewhat formal and exotic. By being formal they allow people to manage emotions that might otherwise be rather overpowering; by being exotic they allow them to recognize that something special is happening. Champagne and cake might not be as real as tea and toast but they work much better as rituals. To try to make the Eucharist like any other meal, and to think that any food and drink would do just as well as bread and wine, would be, apart altogether from strictly theological objections, to weaken its ritual power. The sacramental sign is a ritual meal and must be experienced as such. It helps to have the bread and wine look and taste like the food and drink they are. But they need to be presented as establishing continuity with the food and drink that Jesus used at the Last Supper, and that Christians have used always and everywhere since. Eating and drinking them is to be likened, not to the hearty consuming of the main course, but to the nibbling of the wedding cake and the sipping of champagne that comes at the end.

The fact that the food is given, and that it is given by a priest who represents Jesus Christ, the one who said that his giving of bread and wine would have within it the sacrifice he would make in his own body and blood, makes the meal ritualize his sacrifice. It makes it be a sacrificial meal. Its model, however, is not the sacrificial meal of religions, even of Judaism. The eating of the Passover Lamb is not described in the accounts of the Last Supper, and early Christians were very careful to distance their rite of the Eucharist from the cultic practices of the religions of their day. The model is a simple experience of human togetherness enjoyed in a meal of bread and wine. The taking of that food is a taking of something that has been consecrated to God by being identified with the sacrifice of Jesus. In that spirit, the ritualized human experience of communion and of the self-giving that it entails becomes that communion with God that is realized through the sacrifice of Christ.

# Chapter 9

# Eucharist: The Word from the New Testament to Aquinas

Because the Eucharist is the climax of Christian initiation, and the regularly repeated celebration of Christian living, the word that accompanies it in the Church is uniquely comprehensive. Indeed, no word of the Church is out of place in the celebration of the Eucharist and every word that is truly of the Church must sooner or later be spoken there. The entire Bible is read, the whole tradition of God's People is remembered in feasts and anniversaries, the full range of human experience is dealt with in preaching and in prayer. The Liturgy of the Word is designed specifically to bring this comprehensive word of God and this breadth of human life right into the midst of the eucharistic rite. The eucharistic prayer is a celebration of all that is proclaimed in the Word and it draws the entire People of God—on earth, in heaven, and on the purifying journey of grace between death and heaven—into the final reality that is proclaimed in that word, which is the saving sacrifice of Christ realized in his body and blood, and given as bread of life in communion; it draws this community into the mighty doxology that the whole universe sings to the Father in Christ and the Holy Spirit.

While the totality of the Word of God and of its power to give life to the whole world is present in the celebration of the Eucharist, there are within that word specific theological words about the Eucharist itself that have to be heard. These words deal with the sacramental reality of the rite itself and with the way it gives life to God's People. They explain why it is that the Eucharist embodies the fullness of God's saving action and the full taking hold of it by his People. These are the truths that let the Christian community understand how it can find in the Eucharist a sacramentalizing of all the gifts of God and of its own entire life. But it is important not to isolate words that have to be spoken on particular theological issues about the Eucharist itself from the full richness of the Word of God that is actually spoken in the celebration of the Eucharist. The theology of the Eucharist needs to be a fully liturgical theology.

It is important to establish this perspective when one is embarking on a theology of the Eucharist in the Catholic Church. Historically, catholic theology has had to deal with two critical issues about the Eucharist—real presence and sacrifice. They are questions about the Eucharist itself. One cannot understand the Eucharist without getting at the truth about them. But if they are the only issues dealt with in a theology of the Eucharist, or if they loom so large that everything else seems accessory, the impression may be given that the Eucharist exists for what it is in itself and not for the sake of the life it gives to God's People. A theology of the Eucharist has to be about the Eucharist, about the Eucharist as it realizes the presence of the body and blood of Christ in bread and wine, about the Eucharist as the sacrifice of Christ, but about all this as it is the sacrament of the fullness of eternal life for the Church of God. It has to be a real sacramental theology that appreciates the place of this particular rite in the whole sacramental economy. The real presence and the presence of Christ's sacrifice make it possible for the Eucharist to be at the centre of the sacramental economy, but the purpose and finality of these gifts is to bring God's People to the fullness of life through listening to the entire word of God and consecrating themselves to him in the ongoing course of their daily life. A theology of the Eucharist must keep this broad perspective. It must not reduce its examination of the scriptures and of the patristic and other witnesses to the tradition of faith to a search for material on real presence and sacrifice—although these will inevitably present themselves as major issues. And when it comes to systematic constructions it must attempt to find a framework for thinking about the Eucharist that will situate these two questions within a full, life-centered theology of the sacrament.

# The New Testament

## Accounts of Institution

Scriptural material from the Old and New Testament was examined in Chapter 8 with a view to understanding the form that the rite of the Eucharist takes in the Church. The passages that had the most immediate bearing on the rite are the accounts of the institution of the Eucharist that are found in the Synoptics and in Paul. Even while holding that they are a historical record of what happened at the Last Supper, one must recognize that they are inevitably also a theological statement about the Eucharist. They reflect what the Church had been thinking about the place of the Eucharist in its life during the years that passed between the resurrection and the writing of the accounts of the Last Supper in the form they now have in the gospels and in Paul. Christians had been living as the People of the new covenant, gathered under the leadership of the apostles of Jesus, saved from the slavery of sin by a new passover in his blood, already enjoying a place in the eschatological banquet of his kingdom while they waited for him to come again. All the scriptural words in which they describe their experience belong to a full biblical theology of the Eucharist. The great themes of salvation that resonate in the eucharistic words find their clearest expression in passages that deal with the death, resurrection, and coming again of Jesus. Those passages provide the immediate context for the eucharistic words. The accounts of institution are saying, in the language of covenant, passover, salvation, and ultimately of the cross, what the Church believes God is doing for his world in the Eucharist. The Eucharist is what it is because of all that God has been doing, is doing, and will do for the salvation of the world.

At the core of the Synoptic accounts of the Last Supper, and highlighted by Paul's resumé of what happened at it, are the words that Jesus spoke about the bread and wine that he took and gave to his disciples (Matthew 26:26–29; Mark 14:22–25; Luke 22:19–20; 1 Corinthians 11:23–27). He said that the bread was his body and the wine in the cup was his blood. There is no convincing reason for not taking his words literally. Jesus can be presumed to have spoken in Aramaic, or, if not, in Hebrew.[1] Although there would have been

---

1. J. Jeremias, *The Eucharistic Words of Jesus*, trans. from 3rd German edition (London: SCM Press, 1966), 196–198.

no verb corresponding to "is" in the phrases about the bread and the wine in either of these languages, the simple juxtaposition of the words bread and body, wine and blood was sufficient to affirm identity between "this (bread)" and "my body," between "this cup (of wine)" and "my blood." The Greek of the New Testament text makes the "is" explicit with the verb *estin*.[2] Given the Semitic idiom and ideas being employed, "body" in the context means something like "me in my concrete personal reality." "Body" stands not just for part of a person (to be distinguished from "soul") but for the whole person in the reality of physical existence and presence. Jesus is saying in effect, "what I am giving to you is myself." When he adds that the cup of wine that he is passing around is his blood he is still talking about himself. Blood is the life of the body. A person's life is in his/her blood. In the cup, Jesus is with his disciples in the reality of his life. He is a living person for them. But if he is living he is also capable of dying. In Luke and Paul the bread is said to be not just "my body" but "my body that is given for you." One gives one's life by dying; one can do it by shedding one's blood. The blood that the cup of wine is said to be in the texts is "my blood of the (new) covenant, which is poured out for many for the forgiveness of sins" (Matthew 26:28).

The words of Jesus that come to be translated "body" and "blood" in the accounts of institution are thought to be a pair of words, *bisra/dama* in Aramaic or *basar/dam* in Hebrew, drawn from the vocabulary of ritual sacrifice.[3] They evoke the Passover Lamb.[4] The word "given" that accompanies them is likewise sacrificial. The blood is "poured out" as it was in the ritual sacrifices of animals in the Temple. It is the "blood of the covenant," likened to the blood of sacrificed animals that Moses sprinkled on the people and on the altar when the covenant of Sinai was being ratified (Exodus 24:8). Jesus is presenting himself as one who, like the Suffering Servant foretold by Isaiah (Isaiah 53:4–5), gives himself in sacrifice for many, bringing the forgiveness of sins and the coming of the kingdom.[5] The Aramaic word that Jesus is thought to have used about the bread could be translated

---

2. P. Benoit, OP, in J. Delorme and others, *The Eucharist in the New Testament,* trans. from French (Baltimore/Dublin: Helicon Press, 1964), 65.

3. Jeremias, *The Eucharistic Words,* 198–201.

4. Ibid., 220–225.

5. Benoit, in Delorme, *The Eucharist,* 54–58.

"flesh" and as such could evoke the dead flesh of animals slaughtered in sacrifice. But the Greek text translates the word used by Jesus about the bread as "body" *(soma)*, not "flesh" *(sarx)*. The Jesus who is present in the Eucharist is alive, in the body. And that life is in the blood, which, although it is poured out in the death of Jesus, becomes living and life-giving in the resurrection.

The words of institution in Luke (22:19) and Paul (1 Corinthians 11: 24) contain the phrase "Do this in remembrance of me." Those who did what Jesus had done would be remembering him as he had presented himself in what he said about the bread and wine. They would be remembering him in his dying for the salvation of many. The custom of remembering in a ritual meal those who had died was common in the Greek and Roman worlds of the first century. However, it seems certain that the remembering of Jesus that was done in the Christian Eucharist was an exercise of a much more profound kind, that came out of the Semitic and biblical experience of God in prayer and in ritual. To make a "memorial" *(zikkaron* in Hebrew, *anamnesis* in Greek) of the events in which God had acted in human history for the benefit of his covenant People was somehow to call on and allow God to do that wonder again in a new, present situation that had some similarity with the past. When Christians did the eucharistic rite in memory of Jesus they were making a memorial of the event in his life in which God had performed the definitive work of human salvation. They were remembering the death and resurrection in which his life reached its climax. In their remembering, he was present with them in the reality of his body and blood, in which he had died and was now risen. In that presence God is even now realizing the forgiveness of sins and the making of the new covenant in the blood of Jesus for those who are celebrating the Eucharist. The bread that is his body and the wine that is his blood are life-giving for the assembled community and their fellowship is in that life.

## Saint Paul

Because of the literary form they were using, the Synoptics had to keep their theological reflection about the Eucharist within the literary limits of a narrative about the Last Supper. Paul is also faithful to the narrative method when giving his account of the Lord's Supper in his first letter to the Corinthians. However, the literary form of an epistle allows him to add some explicit theological thinking about the relationship between the Last Supper and actual celebrations of the Eucharist. He does it in Chapter 11, but also in other places in the letter. First Corinthians Chapter 11 has already been discussed for its significance in general sacramental theology (Chapter 1, "Rite, Word, and Life in the New Testament") and for the information it yields about the rite of the Eucharist (Chapter 8, "The Rite of the New Covenant"). Here it needs to be examined, along with other passages of the letter, for the theology of the Eucharist they contain.[6]

Paul's theology of the Eucharist in 1 Corinthians is the fruit of his concern for the relationship between participation in the Eucharist and Christian life. He argues that the realism of what occurs in the rite has definite imperatives for Christian living. He bases the realism of his thinking about the Eucharist itself on the account of institution that has been handed on to him. If he adds the strong phrase "For as often as you eat this bread and drink the cup, you proclaim the Lord's death until he comes" at the end of the account, it is to make quite explicit something that is already stated clearly in the words of institution; it is also to support his theological reflection about what participation in the Eucharist means for Christian life. Paul sees the Lord's Supper touching life on different levels. It is a community celebration in the form of a meal. It therefore touches the level of life that is nourished by taking food and that is offended against when people are left hungry or eat and drink too much (v. 21–22, 33–34). It is also about the level of life that is nourished by people being together in community (vv. 2–16: each one knowing and keeping his or her place; vv. 21–22, 33–34: sharing resources and "waiting for one another"), and therefore it is flouted when people are "contentious" (v. 16) about roles and divide into factions (v. 19). But ultimately the Supper touches the level of life that corresponds to its being the commemoration and proclamation of the saving death of Christ until he comes again. What the Corinthians are doing, then, is not just being selfish and contrary to the spirit and order of Christian assembly. Because what they are doing occurs in an event that puts them in the presence of the dying of

---

6. C. K. Barrett, *A Commentary on the First Epistle to the Corinthians* (London: Hendrickson, 1993), 258ff.

Christ, they are behaving just like those who condemned and crucified him, and hence they are "guilty of . . . the body and blood of the Lord" (v. 27). If they are not measuring up to the reality that is given in their eating and drinking, the Supper itself condemns them (v. 29). Indeed, the Lord himself, whose Supper this is and who is therefore its real host, condemns them (v. 32). Instead of drawing life from the Supper they are left prey to illness and death (v. 30).

Paul had already used the line of reasoning that he follows in Chapter 11 to instruct the Corinthians on another issue of Christian life. How were Christians to relate to the world of pagan worship that surrounded them? In 10:14 he tells them to "shun the worship of idols." The reason he gives is not moral but sacramental (Chapter 1, "Rite, Word, and Life in the New Testament"). He tells the Corinthians that they ought to be able to see the point for themselves if only they remembered the reality that was inherent in their own assemblies: "The cup of blessing which we bless, is it not a participation in the blood of Christ? The bread which we break, is it not a participation in the body of Christ? Because there is one bread, we who are many are one body, for we all partake of the one bread" (1 Corinthians 10:16–17). His argument appeals to the significance of drinking from a single cup and eating from a single loaf. It is, on one level, a demand for loyalty toward those with whom one shares the table of the Lord. But the force of the argument comes from the reality communicated by that cup and that loaf. The reality is the body and blood of Christ. The body and blood of Christ, given in a loaf that is broken among them and a cup that is shared, brings with it the reality of Christian fellowship ("we who are many are one body, for we all partake of the one bread"). The body of Christ is found in Christian fellowship. If one belongs there one does not belong at the table of demons (v. 21). If Paul had spoken only about the body of Christ in this passage, without mentioning the blood, one might wonder if the reality he was arguing from was simply the fellowship and solidarity that is experienced in a common meal and expressed by calling the Christian community a body. However, the twinning of body and blood, loaf and cup, and the reference to the blessing of the cup, make it clear that it is the Eucharist as body and blood of Christ that is at the heart of his argument. The community is the body of Christ because it eats of a loaf and drinks of a cup that are his body and blood. This eucharistic realism makes much more sense of the way Paul presents the Christian community as body of Christ in 1 Corinthians 12.[7]

There is already a hint of the connection between partaking of the Eucharist and membership of the body of Christ in 1 Corinthians 6:12–20, where Paul argues against sexual immorality on the principle that "your bodies are members of Christ." He says: "The body is not meant for immorality, but for the Lord, and the Lord for the body. And God raised the Lord and will also raise us up by his power. Do you not know that your bodies are members of Christ? Shall I therefore take the members of Christ and make them members of a prostitute? Never" (v.15). While he does not mention the Eucharist explicitly in this passage there must be a real possibility that the ideas about being united to and in the body of Christ that he expounds later in the epistle are already present in his mind. The model of reasoning is the same: because one is joined to the body of Christ one ought not to have any part with behavior or institutions or persons who are contrary to what Christ stands for in his dying and rising. To know what the Eucharist is, is to know what one is oneself, and what kind of company one should keep. Here, as in the phrase about "eating and drinking without discerning the body" in 1 Corinthians 11:29, there would be a two-sided discernment corresponding to the two-sided meaning of "body." The eucharistic act makes the bread to be the body of Christ and at the same time makes the community to be his body. If one is not seeing oneself and one's fellow Christians as members of the body of Christ one can hardly claim to be recognizing the truth of the word of Jesus that the bread and wine are his body and blood given for the salvation of others.

Paul does not speak about the Eucharist in any of his letters other than 1 Corinthians. And there his teaching about it is almost incidental: it occurs within a teaching about Christian life. He is clearly more interested in life than in rite. And he was a man of the word, a preacher, before being a man of rites (see 1 Corinthians 1:17). The fact that Paul does not refer to the celebration of the Eucharist in his letters to other churches does not mean they did not have the rite, or did not understand it in the way Paul did, nor does it mean

---

7. Benoit in Delorme, *The Eucharist*, 72–73; Boismard, ibid. 97–99.

that Paul considered it unimportant. But it does suggest that he was much more aware of the reality that was within the rites than of the rites themselves. He talks much more often, then, about what Christ did and is in the body, and what Christians are and do in the body of Christ, than he does about the bread that is his body. The rite, in fact, must have been a rather ordinary and unself-conscious act of life for the earliest Christians. It was an exercise of that simple, familiar worship in spirit and in truth that distinguished the new covenant from the old. It was surely dominated by the sense of the reality and influence of the risen Christ that marked the life of the first Christian communities. Their rites of worship must have had a kind of transparency that allowed faith to go right through them to the reality of Christ himself, present in his own body, and in his body that was the living Christian community. The fact that it was being celebrated with a strong sense of waiting for the coming again of Christ ("until he comes" in 1 Corinthians 11:26) increased the transparency. The captivity epistles never mention the rite of the Eucharist. But they are full of the reality of the Eucharist that was expounded in 1 Corinthians. They are about the mystery of what God does in Christ, of how Christ has become life-giving and Spirit-giving in the body in which he died and rose again, of how he is joined as head to his body that is the Church, of how that Church is life-supporting through the diversity of ministries and gifts with which it is endowed, and of how Christians ought to live in this Church and in the world as they wait for the coming of the Lord.

## Saint John

If Paul does not feel the need to draw attention explicitly to the rite of the Eucharist each time he addresses a Christian community, John seems to want to avoid doing so altogether. He tells the story of the Last Supper without describing the meal rite or giving the "words of institution" that are so central to the Christian Eucharist. There are allusions to the rite in the discourse on the bread of life in Chapter 6 of the gospel, but in the form of hints that would only register with people who already knew about the rite. The reticence about the rite has to find its explanation in the purpose and character of the Fourth Gospel and the other Johannine writings. The general position of

R. Brown seems to offer a reasonable explanation of how these writings deal with the sacraments (see Chapter 1, "New Rites for a New Covenant"). The author of John was, it suggests, primarily concerned with the truth about Jesus, with his origin as preexistent Word from the Father, with his being made flesh, with the divine works (signs) that he performed, with his glorification and the consequent sending of the Spirit from him. Life comes to the world from Jesus and is received by faith in him. There is reason to believe that the author of John thought that some of the institutions of the Church—teaching ministries and rites among them—were developing in a way that could obscure the centrality of Jesus himself. He was concerned to overcome this danger by showing that it is the divine power of Jesus alone that is saving and life-giving, and that the life that he gives is the life that he himself receives from the Father. Belief in him and in the truth about him is the only way to receive life. In Brown's view there are no solid grounds for saying that John is antisacramental. What he wants to ensure is that the ministerial structures and rites that Christian communities have (notably baptism and Eucharist) do not obscure the centrality of Jesus and the profound truth about his relationship with the Father. He speaks about sacraments but in the language of symbolism rather than of ritualism. By this he invites believers to raise their minds to the divine realities that are signified by familiar rites and institutions that may have become settled and formal, or may have remained weighed down by a residue of Old Testament ritualism among those Christians who retained some allegiance to Judaism. He wants to tell them how life can be found in these activities by telling them how Jesus can be found in them through faith.[8]

If John does not tell about the institution of the Eucharist at the Last Supper, he does tell about Jesus washing the feet of the disciples (13:1–20). The story of the washing of the feet may have some ritual references, particularly in relation to baptism. However, what is interesting about it for a theology of the Eucharist is not any reference to rite but what it says about Jesus and about the life of those who would "have a part in him" (v. 8). Jesus takes an initiative that shows the kind of life he wants to give to his disciples. They were to

---

8. On Eucharist, see R. E. Brown, ss, *The Community of the Beloved Disciple* (New York: Paulist Press, 1979), 74, 78–79, 88, 157.

be together in a fellowship of service to one another. Their service was to be of the kind Jesus gave to them. He, though Lord and Master, became the servant of all, by washing their feet. In that service he was acting as host, providing the courtesies of hospitality to those he had invited to his table, but doing it himself rather than having a servant do it. He humbled himself before them. By accepting his service they "had a part in him." People who associated the Eucharist with the Last Supper should have been able to see the message. When they gather for the eucharistic meal the real host is not the one who presides at their table but Jesus himself. He gives people a "part in him" by an act of becoming their servant, which he did preeminently by giving himself to death on the cross for their sake: in the Eucharist he is remembered in this humiliated, servant state of dying. Those who partake of the Eucharist must live together in a fellowship of mutual service in imitation of Jesus: not to do so is to have oneself judged by Jesus who gave himself for others (which is precisely what Paul said in other terms to the Corinthians).

One can find further teaching about the Eucharist in John's account of the Last Supper. There is something about the place of the word in it. John puts a long discourse and a prayer on the lips of Jesus. The rite of bread and wine is accompanied in the Eucharist by words of discourse and of prayer. They are not just about the bread and wine but about the whole gift of life that the Father gives through Christ and the Spirit to those who believe and live together in his love, waiting in the midst of the world until he comes again. These are the themes of the last discourse of Jesus in John. There may even be a eucharistic reference (through a symbolic evocation of wine) in the parable/allegory of the vine.[9] It is not that the discourse and prayer provide a model for a liturgical celebration of the Eucharist, but they do expound the great truths and hopes that the words and prayers of the Eucharist must be about if the rite is to be life-giving and bread of life.

Jesus is presented as the bread of life in Chapter 6 of John's gospel. What has been said about the purpose and character of the Fourth Gospel, and about the distinctive way that John has of talking about rites and institutions, entitles one to read the whole chapter as

9. See R. E. Brown, ss, *The Gospel According to John,* Anchor Bible 29, 29a; 2 vols. (Garden City, NY; Doubleday, London: Chapman, 1966, 1971), vol. II, 672–674.

a theology of the Eucharist. Later dogmatic disputes about the relationship between faith and sacrament in justification have sometimes been projected on this chapter of John. Attempts have been made to establish that all of it is about receiving Jesus by faith in the word, which is what bread would stand for, so that there is nothing in the chapter about the sacrament of the Eucharist. There have been other attempts to divide the discourse that makes up most of the chapter into sections, some of which deal exclusively with the word and others with the sacrament. However, theology, least of all the theology of the New Testament, does not require one to choose between faith and sacrament: all receiving of Jesus is by faith, and faith is always in response to the word of God; but when God makes that word concrete in a rite such as baptism or Eucharist, faith of necessity takes the form of receiving him in that rite. A case can, indeed, be made for saying that the chapter is a putting together of different literary units, some of which might not have been originally eucharistic. But as the chapter, and particularly the discourse on the bread of life, now stands there is good reason to think that it is all directed towards a Christological understanding of the Eucharist.[10] The chapter, then, can be read from the beginning as being about Jesus and about recognizing and receiving him for who he is; as being about the life he has come to give, about how he gives it to those who receive his word in faith, and about how that word is food; about how receiving that food requires eating the flesh and drinking the blood of Jesus in what can only be the rite of the Eucharist; and finally about recognizing that what Jesus is saying is not understood by everyone: those who understand the rite in the way Jesus has explained remain with him in the fellowship of his disciples and there receive from him the gift of eternal life.

The eucharistic theology of John 6 is worked out with an extraordinary richness of detail. The author sets the events he is describing at the time of Passover (v. 4), thus giving them an Exodus and covenant and ritual flavor. He presents Jesus as the one who works signs (v. 2). These signs identify him as the Messiah, in the

---

10. See Brown, *The Gospel*, vol. I, 284ff; note his suggestion on p. 290 "that the juxtaposition of the sapiential and the sacramental themes is as old as Christianity itself. The two forms of the Bread of Life Discourse represent a juxtaposition of Jesus' twofold presence to believers in the *preached word* and in the *sacrament* of the Eucharist. This twofold presence is the structural skeleton of the . . . Roman Mass."

specific Johannine sense of the one sent from heaven by the Father and endowed with power to do things that only God does. The sign that Jesus performs is the feeding of a multitude with five loaves and two fish (vv. 5–14). The miraculous giving of food to the people wandering in the desert is an Exodus theme. Jesus gives food, not because he has been reminded by the disciples that the people are hungry (which was how the Synoptics told the story) but on his own initiative (v. 5). The formula used to describe what he did with the loaves echoes descriptions of what he did with the bread at the Last Supper and what Christians do at the Eucharist: he "*took* the loaves, and when he had *given thanks*, he *distributed them* . . ." (v. 11). What Jesus provided is recognized as a kind of messianic banquet by the people (vv. 14–15). If, as Brown suggests, John sees Christian sacraments as a prolongation of the signs that Jesus worked while on earth, this messianic banquet given by Jesus can be a symbolic statement about the Eucharist: the one who is at work in the Eucharist is the one sent by the Father and manifested in signs and works. After another incident that symbolically manifests his divine power and identity (walking on the water as an evocation of the power that brought the Israelites safely across the Red Sea, and the words "It is I" evoking the name "I am who I am" revealed to Moses), Jesus provokes a discussion about food with the people who had followed him, which allows him to explain the real significance of the sign he had worked (vv. 22–26). He wants them to think of "the food which endures to eternal life" (v. 27). There follows an extended discourse on "the bread of life." It is a Christology in which Jesus is presented as coming from the Father to give eternal life. It uses the imagery of bread and the typology of the Exodus to describe what the Father is doing in Jesus. The Father gives true bread from heaven. The bread is true by comparison with the manna that Moses gave in the desert, which gave life but not eternal life. When Jesus got his hearers to the point of asking (v. 34) "Lord, give us this bread always" (John had Jesus provoke a similar request for water from the Samaritan woman in a passage of Chapter 4 that evokes Baptism), he announces that he himself is the bread from heaven that gives eternal life: "I am the bread of life" (v. 35). Those who believe in him, recognizing that he comes from the Father, will never hunger or thirst; they will receive eternal life and Jesus himself will raise them up on the last day. He can do so because he comes from the Father (vv. 35–50).

If the discourse on the bread of life ended at v. 50 it would
be a statement of profound Christological truth but not necessarily
have a bearing on the theology of the Eucharist. Verse 51, however,
carries the thought forward in a way that allows all that has preceded in Chapter 6 to be taken as part of a theology of the Eucharist.
John wants Christians to understand the rite of the Eucharist in a
Christological and theological way: by developing his Christology in
terms and images of bread, he has prepared it for use in a theology
of the Eucharist. The first half of verse 51 is a résumé of what he has
already said: "I am the living bread which came down from heaven; if
anyone eats of this bread he will live forever"; the second half of the
verse opens up the question of the Eucharist: "and the bread which I
shall give for the life of the world is my flesh." The incredulous reaction of the Jews, described by John in v. 52, leaves no doubt about how
the statement is to be understood. To their question "how can this man
give us his flesh to eat?" Jesus answers: "Truly, truly, I say to you, unless
you eat the flesh of the Son of man and drink his blood, you have no
life in you; he who eats my flesh and drinks my blood has eternal life,
and I will raise him up on the last day. For my flesh is food indeed,
and my blood is drink indeed. He who eats my flesh and drinks my
blood abides in me, and I in him" (vv. 53–56). Jesus is now talking
about drinking as well as eating, about blood as well as flesh. Unless
the intention is to refer to the Eucharist it is hard to see why drinking
should now be mentioned along with eating. If people do not eat the
flesh of Jesus and drink his blood they will not have life. This is how
the "bread of life" who is Jesus has now to be received. What is taken
as food is the flesh of Christ, what is taken as drink is his blood. John
uses the Greek *sarx* (translated "flesh") rather than *soma* (used by Paul
and the Synoptics and translated "body"). "Flesh" is a key word in the
Christology of the Johannine writings. "The Word became flesh . . ."
(John 1:14). In eating his flesh Christians are receiving the one sent by
the Father in all his reality, and they are recognizing him for who he
is. When "flesh" is twinned with "blood" the words evoke the cross. In
19:34 John will describe how blood and water came from the pierced
side of Jesus; 1 John 5:8 talks about the threefold witness of the Spirit,
the water, and the blood. It is because he died in obedience to the
Father's will that Jesus can give life, can give the Spirit. The life that

he gives is the life he himself receives from the Father. It is eternal life, and those who have it will be raised up by Jesus on the last day. Already by eating his flesh and drinking his blood they abide in him and he in them. This is the deep meaning and purpose of the eating and drinking that Christians do in the rite of the Eucharist.

The final section of the discourse on the bread of life in John 6 deals with the fact that not everybody accepts what Jesus has been saying about the bread of life (vv. 60–71). It has a statement of Jesus that can cause some difficulty for the eucharistic interpretation of the whole discourse: "It is the spirit that gives life, the flesh is of no avail; the words that I have spoken to you are spirit and life. But there are some of you that do not believe" (vv. 63–64). Brown thinks these words refer not to the specifically eucharistic part of the discourse but to what Jesus had been saying about the bread of life in vv. 35–50. He claims that vv. 60–71 originally formed a single literary unity with vv. 35–50.[11] The final editor of John inserted the eucharistic material of vv. 51–59, drawing out the eucharistic implications of vv. 35–50, but without adjusting the final section to eucharistic doctrine. If one does not accept Brown's hypothesis one can still understand the words of Jesus in a way that does not call into question the realism of what he had been saying about the Eucharist in vv. 51–59. Jesus prefaces his words about the flesh being of no avail with the words: "what if you were to see the Son of Man ascending where he was before?" (v. 62). If John is writing for people who may have been celebrating the rite of the Eucharist but missing its full Christological meaning, the words of Jesus would be telling them that it was no good remembering Jesus as he was in the flesh during his earthly life if one does not believe that he is the Son of Man who came from the Father and is now glorified and sending the Spirit: it is this Jesus who gives life in the Eucharist. The eucharistic reference is possibly confirmed by the final verses of the section, which evoke the Last Supper. The twelve remain with Jesus because, as Peter confesses, He has "the words of eternal life; and we have believed and come to know that you are the Holy One of God" (vv. 68–69). But among the twelve is Judas (vv. 70–71). The reference to the twelve and to the betrayal by Judas seems to be intended

---

11. Brown, *The Gospel*, vol. I, 229–303.

as a link between what Jesus has been saying, and indeed the whole of Chapter 6, and the Last Supper.

## The Letter to the Hebrews

There is no explicit reference to the Eucharist in Hebrews. However, the doctrine of the letter about the priesthood of Christ has a profound bearing on the theology of the Eucharist. If the rite is to be of any value for the salvation of God's People, it must come from some kind of identification with the high priestly offering that Jesus made in his own blood, by which the new covenant is established. Priesthood, altar, sacrifice, and liturgy are unique and "once for all" in the new covenant. The use of covenant and sacrificial language about the rite of the Eucharist, which has been noted in the Synoptics, and in Paul and John, can never contradict the primary reference of that language, which is to Christ's own priestly person and work.

The author of Hebrews assumes that those he writes to have already been instructed in "the elementary doctrine of Christ," and that they know about the practices of Christian life such as "ablutions, the laying on of hands" with the eschatological flavor these carry under the influence of "the resurrection of the dead and eternal judgment" (6:1–2). But he does require Christians to assemble together, and the passage in which he explains why they should must say something about what they do when they assemble:

> Therefore, brethren, since we have confidence to enter the sanctuary by the blood of Jesus, by the new and living way which he opened for us through the curtain, that is, through his flesh, and since we have a great priest over the house of God, let us draw near with a true heart in full assurance of faith, with our hearts sprinkled clean from an evil conscience and our bodies washed with pure water. Let us hold fast the confession of our hope without wavering, for he who promised is faithful; and let us consider how to stir up one another to love and good works, not neglecting to meet together, as is the habit of some, but encouraging one another, and all the more as you see the Day drawing near. (10:19–25)

All of these motives that require Christians to "meet together" in assembly are, in fact, given ritual expression in the Eucharist. The same evocation of the reality, if not the rite of the Eucharist can also be sensed in the final exhortation of the letter, beginning with, "Remember your leaders. . . ." and ending ". . . through Jesus Christ; to whom be glory for ever and ever. Amen" (13: 7–21).

# The Fathers

Beginning with the *Didaché*, there is regular reference to the Eucharist in the earliest literature of Christianity. Early Christian art also represents it. There are texts that describe the celebration of the Eucharist, and soon there are homiletic and catechetical commentaries on it. It is in these that theological reflection on the Eucharist begins and develops. Theological reflection on the Eucharist also begins to appear in discussions about the incarnation and about the Church. In the patristic age the theologies of the Eucharist are the fruit of spontaneous reflection on the experience of faith rather than a deliberate discussion of technical questions. There are few if any intellectual problems about the Eucharist. One has to be careful, then, not to expect clear answers in these texts to the theological and dogmatic questions of later ages. And yet one may be surprised at how many of the questions and insights that might seem to belong only to the controversies of the Reformation are already appearing in the Fathers, and at how the tradition of faith is already pointing toward later Catholic teaching. One can, for example, find witness to belief in the real presence and in the sacrificial character of the Eucharist in those early texts, although not in the theological terms of a later debate. But the theology of the Eucharist in the Fathers, as already in the scriptures, is more comprehensive than a theology of real presence and sacrifice. It deals with these questions and with other aspects of the Eucharist within broader questions about the work of God in Christ and in his Church.

## The Apostolic Fathers

It is within a theology of the incarnation, directed against Docetists who deny the reality of the flesh of Christ, that Ignatius of Antioch speaks about the Eucharist in the letter *To the Smyrnaeans*.[12] Belief

---

12. Translated in J. A. Kleist, sj, *The Epistles of St. Clement of Rome and St. Ignatius of Antioch*, Ancient Christian Writers 1 (Westminster, MD: The Newman Press; London: Longmans, Green and Company, 1948).

"that the Eucharist is the Flesh of our Savior Jesus Christ, which suffered for our sins, and which the Father in His loving-kindness raised from the dead" (n. 7) is so bound up with belief in the incarnation (nn. 3–4) and in "the Passion which effects our resurrection from the dead" (n. 5), and with "faith in the blood of Christ" (n. 6) that those who deny those truths inevitably deny the truth about the Eucharist. This is Johannine Christology brought into explicit relationship with Eucharistic realism, as John himself had done in the discourse on the bread of life. Ignatius speaks more explicitly about the rite than John did. He calls it "the Eucharist," which from the beginning of the second century comes to be used as a technical term for what the New Testament calls "the breaking of bread" or "the Lord's Supper." In his letter *To the Philadelphians* Ignatius relates the Eucharist to ecclesiology. Those who believe in Jesus are gathered into unity in the Church around the Bishop (nn. 1–3). The Eucharist expresses and guarantees this unity: "Take care, then, to partake of one Eucharist; for, one is the Flesh of Our Lord Jesus Christ, and one the cup to unite us with His Blood, and one altar, just as there is one bishop assisted by the presbytery and the deacons, my fellow servants" (n. 4). The same thought is found in *To the Smyrnaeans*, n. 8. Ignatius has several other references to the Eucharist that show its bearing on Christian life. The most beautiful expression of this is in the way he speaks about his own coming death, where one can read: "I have no taste for corruptible food or for the delights of this life. Bread of God is what I desire; that is, the Flesh of Jesus Christ, who was of the seed of David; and for my drink I desire His Blood, that is, incorruptible love"(*To the Romans*, n. 7).

Saint Justin follows up the description of the Eucharist that he gives in his *First Apology* (see Chapter 8, "The Second and Third Centuries") with an explanation of why the Eucharist is different from ordinary food and drink. He uses an analogy with the incarnation to show how the prayer said over the bread and wine make them be the flesh and blood of Christ:

> We call this food the Eucharist, of which only he can partake who has acknowledged the truth of our teachings, who has been cleansed by baptism for the remission of his sins and for his regeneration and who regulates his life upon the principles laid down by Christ. Not as ordinary bread or as ordinary drink do we partake of them, but just as, through the word of God, our Savior Jesus Christ became Incarnate and took upon

Himself flesh and blood for our salvation, so, we have been taught, the food which has been made the Eucharist by the prayer of His word, and which nourishes our flesh and blood by assimilation, is both the flesh and blood of that Jesus who was made flesh. (n. 66)[13]

In his *Dialogue with Trypho* Justin argues that those who believe in God, have their sins taken away in the name of his Son and are called by his word "are now of the true priestly family of God." As priests they offer everywhere those pure and pleasing sacrifices foretold by the prophet Malachi. Justin identifies these sacrifices as those "which Jesus Christ commanded to be offered, that is, in the Eucharist of the Bread and of the Chalice, which is offered by us Christians in every part of the world" (nn. 116–117). He explains how the sacrifice is offered in the form of a prayer: "Now, I also admit that prayers and thanksgiving, offered by worthy persons, are the only perfect and acceptable sacrifice to God. For Christians were instructed to offer only such prayers, even at their thanksgiving for their food, both liquid and solid, whereby the passion which the Son of God endured for us is commemorated . . ." (n. 117). The Christian Eucharist takes the form of a prayer said over bread and wine, at the command of Christ, in commemoration *(anamnesis)* of his passion, on behalf of the true priestly people in whom the promises made in the old covenant are fulfilled.

Saint Irenaeus also sees the prophecy of Malachi fulfilled in the Eucharist (*Adversus Haereses*, IV, 17, 4). The pure offering that God wants from people is "faith and obedience and justice for their own salvation," not burnt offerings and sacrifices. And yet, Irenaeus argues, this does not exclude the things of creation from the worship of God. In being received with thanks they are offered to God. This is what Jesus wants done in the Eucharist:

And yet, when counseling His disciples to offer to God the first fruits from among His creatures—not as if He needed them, but lest they themselves should be unfruitful and ungrateful—He took that which is from creation, bread, and gave thanks, saying: "This is my body." And likewise the cup, which is of the same creation as ourselves, He confessed to be His blood, and taught a new oblation of the New Testament. This the

---

13. Trans. from P. Palmer, sj, *Sacraments and Worship: Liturgy and Doctrinal Development of Baptism, Confirmation, and the Eucharist* (London: Longmans, Green and Co., 1957), 196–197.

Church receives from the Apostles and offers [it] to God throughout the world, to Him who gives us nourishment, as the first fruits of His own gifts in the New Testament. In reference to this oblation, Malachias, in the twelve Prophets, attached the following meaning in advance.... (Malachi 1:10–11)[14]

That passage is part of Irenaeus' ongoing argument about the goodness of the material world against the Gnostics. He is particularly concerned with affirming that, in the human make-up, flesh is as much the creation of the goodness of God as spirit, and that it shares in eternal life by resurrection. He argues this point on the basis of a very realistic understanding of what the Eucharist teaches about human flesh and blood because it is itself the flesh and blood of Christ:

How can they [the Gnostics] say that the flesh yields to corruption, and does not partake of life, that flesh which had been fed on the body and blood of the Lord? ... But our doctrine is in perfect accord with the Eucharist, and the Eucharist in turn confirms our doctrine. For we offer to God that which is His own, and in so doing we proclaim the union of flesh and spirit, and confess our belief in the resurrection of both flesh and spirit. For just as bread from the earth, receiving the invocation of God, is no longer common bread but a Eucharist consisting of two elements, an earthly and a heavenly, even so, our bodies, partaking of the Eucharist, are no longer corruptible, possessing as they do the hope of resurrection unto life eternal. (*Adversus Haereses*, IV, 18, 6)

In a further argument about the flesh against the Docetism of the Gnostics, he appeals again to the realism of the Eucharist and has a beautiful explanation of how it fits into the creative action of the Spirit and of the Word of God in the world of matter and flesh:

When, therefore, the mixed chalice and the bread that is made receive the word of God and become a Eucharist, the body of Christ, by which the substance of our flesh grows and subsists, how can they [Docetists] deny that the flesh is capable of the gift of God, which is life eternal, seeing that it is nourished with the body and blood of Christ, and is His member? ... And just as a cutting from the vine, planted in the earth, bears fruit in due season, and a grain of wheat, falling on the ground, therein dissolves, and rises again with large increase by the Spirit of God who sustains all things, and thereafter, by the Wisdom of God becomes fit for

---

14. Trans. from Palmer, *Sacraments and Worship*, 273–274.

man's food, and at last receives the Word of God and becomes a Eucharist, which is Christ's body and blood, so too our bodies, nourished by the Eucharist, and laid in the earth there to suffer dissolution, will in due season rise again. (*Adversus Haereses*, V, 2, 3)

The description of the paschal Eucharist given in *The Apostolic Tradition* of Hippolytus[15] (see Chapter 8, "The Second and Third Centuries") includes remarks that indicate some theological reflection on how the bread and wine are made to be the flesh and blood of Christ. He uses a verbal form that Dix translates "eucharistize" to describe what is done by and in the eucharistic prayer over the bread and wine. It is not the last of the strange words that will be coined throughout the history of theology to define this unique action! What the bishop does is to "Eucharistize first the bread into the representation of the Flesh of Christ; and the cup mixed with wine for the antitype of the Blood which was shed for all who believed in Him" (Dix, *Apostolic Tradition*, XXIII, 1). The words translated "representation" and "antitype" are an attempt to explain the relationship of the bread and wine to the body and blood. They come from the language of symbolism and imaging, from a thought pattern that accepts that some obvious things are not really what they seem to be but stand for deeper, hidden realities. Some such analysis of the Eucharist has to be done sooner or later, because on the level of sense-experience the body and blood of Christ will still look and taste like bread and wine. The language of *The Apostolic Tradition* is a recognition of what later theology will express by saying that the flesh and blood of Christ are taken in the Eucharist *sacramentally*. It is in no sense a denial that the Eucharist is the body and blood of Christ. That is confirmed by the evident difference there is between the "blessed bread," that features along with other foods that are blessed in the celebration, and the Eucharist (i.e., bread that has been "eucharistized" to be the body of Christ), and also by the care that he expects people to take of the Eucharist when they receive it in their homes, precisely because it is the body of Christ (XXVI, XXXII).

*The Apostolic Tradition* uses the word "oblation" several times to talk about the bread and wine and other gifts brought to the bishop

---

15. Translation in G. Dix, *The Apostolic Tradition of St. Hippolytus of Rome*, 2nd ed., intro. H. Chadwick (London, 1968).

in the Eucharist. It indicates the spiritual attitude in which Christians meet for the Eucharist and share their gifts. In the text that he gives for a eucharistic prayer the words of institution are followed by this *anamnesis*: "Doing therefore the *anamnesis* of His death and resurrection we offer to Thee the bread and the cup making eucharist to Thee because Thou hast bidden us [or, found us worthy] to stand before thee and minister as priests to Thee" (IV, 11). The putting together of "anamnesis," "offering," "making eucharist," "ministering as priests" in this text says something profoundly revealing about the mystery of the Eucharist. The connection between the ideas is not articulated; but taken together they leave little doubt about the sacrificial quality being attributed to the Eucharist.[16] The final passage of the prayer expresses the effect of the Eucharist as union with God and the outpouring of the Holy Spirit (the words in square brackets may be a later addition):

> And we pray Thee that [Thou wouldest send Thy Holy Spirit upon the oblation of thy holy Church] Thou wouldest grant to all Thy Saints who partake to be united to Thee that they may be fulfilled with the Holy Spirit for the confirmation of their faith in truth, that we may praise and glorify Thee through Thy Beloved Child Jesus Christ through whom glory and honor be unto Thee with the Holy Spirit in Thy holy Church now and for ever and world without end. Amen.

## The Eastern Fathers

It is in liturgical catechesis and occasionally in scriptural commentaries that the Fathers of the Eastern churches deal with the Eucharist. There were no real dogmatic problems about it during the patristic age, nor any issues on which churches were divided. True to their catechetical and exegetical methods, Origen and Clement of Alexandria give a highly spiritual and mystical interpretation to the eucharistic words and rites. But there is enough evidence in their writings to reassure one that they also gave them a realistic meaning, in accordance with the general faith of the Church of their time.[17] Teaching on the Eucharist is still being expressed in predominantly scriptural and

---

16. L. Bouyer, *Eucharist: Theology and Spirituality of the Eucharistic Prayer,* trans. from French (Notre Dame: Notre Dame University Press, 1968), 177–179.

17. J. Quasten, *Patrology*, 3 vols. (Westminster, MD: Spectrum Publishers, 1950, 1953, 1960), vol. II, 28–31, 85–87.

liturgical terms into the fourth century. However, there are theological developments. Some are derived from the more refined theologies of the incarnation that were worked out during those centuries. Others arise from catechetical reflection on the Eucharist itself. It is noted, for example, that if what was bread and wine at the beginning of the celebration is later the body and blood of Christ it must somehow have been changed. People were entitled to ask why and how. A fragment from a sermon of Saint Athanasius (d. 373) notes the fact of change and attributes it, as Irenaeus did, to the coming of the Word on the bread and wine (PG 26, 1325).[18] Saint Gregory of Nyssa (d. 394) deals with the question of change in his *Oratio Catechetica Magna*, chs. 37ff. (PG 45, 9–106): to the idea that the change is brought about by the coming of the Word in the eucharistic prayer he adds a peculiar theory that Christ somehow "digests" the bread and wine to make it his own body and blood. Sermons 4 and 5 of the mystagogical catecheses of Saint Cyril of Jerusalem[19] are a quite full statement of the tradition of faith about the Eucharist. They raise some theological issues and offer explanations. It is to reassure the newly initiated that they themselves "are now 'of the same body' and blood of Christ" that Cyril insists on the realistic meaning of Christ's words "this is my body . . . blood" (Sermon 4, 1). He argues that if Christ could change water into wine it is credible that he could change wine into his blood (Sermon 4, 2). He is thinking about the Eucharist, then, in terms of some kind of miraculous change. But immediately he recognizes that, in one sense, nothing is changed. The "body has been bestowed on you in the form of bread and his blood in the form of wine" (Sermon 4, 3). "Form" *(tupos)* here belongs to the language of symbolism.[20] Symbols, in the mind of Cyril, are not opposed to reality. The symbol allows the reality to be received and to transform the receiver: "So let us partake with the fullest confidence that it is the body and blood of Christ. For his body has been bestowed on you in the form of bread and his blood in the form of wine, so that by partaking of Christ's body and blood you may share with him the same body and blood" (Sermon 4, 3).

---

18. Quoted in Quasten, *Patrology*, vol. III, 79.

19. Relevant texts in E. Yarnold, sj, *The Awe-Inspiring Rites of Initiation. The Origins of the R.C.I.A.* 2nd ed. (The Liturgical Press: Collegeville, MN, 1994).

20. On this terminology of Cyril see Yarnold, *The Awe Inspiring Rites*, 93, note 23.

Sermon 5 of the mystagogical catecheses is a commentary on the rite of the Eucharist and particularly on the eucharistic prayer. Cyril attributes the change of bread and wine into the body and blood of Christ to the Holy Spirit invoked in the *epiclesis*: "for clearly whatever the Holy Spirit touches is sanctified and transformed" (Sermon 5, 7). He introduces the petitions that are made in the eucharistic prayer with the remark: "When the spiritual sacrifice—this worship without blood—has been completed, we beg God over the sacrifice of propitiation for . . ." (Sermon 5, 8); and he later describes these prayers for the living and the dead as being made "while the holy and most awesome sacrifice is being offered" (Sermon 5, 9). When he is justifying praying for the dead in the eucharistic prayer he says that it is effective because "we offer Christ, who has been slain for our sins, and so we appease the merciful God on their behalf and on ours" (Sermon 5, 10). His commentary on the words "Taste and see that the Lord is good," which are used to invite the faithful to come forward to receive the body and blood, is: "Entrust this judgment not to your bodily palate, but to faith which knows no doubt. For those who taste are bidden to taste not bread and wine but the sign *(antitupos)* of Christ's body and blood" (Sermon 5, 20).

Cyril's description of how the body and blood of Christ are actually received is full of a sense of "homage and reverence" (Sermon 5, 22): one must be careful not to drop a particle of the body for "to lose any of it is clearly like losing part of your own body" (Sermon 5, 21). But worse still would be to cut yourself off from communion, "deprive yourselves of these holy and spiritual mysteries through stain of sin" (Sermon 5, 23).

The last two of the Catechetical Homilies of Theodore of Mopsuestia (d. 428) deal with the Eucharist. They are numbered IV and V in the translation of the properly mystagogical ones given by Yarnold.[21] Homily IV begins with some reflections that connect the Eucharist with baptism. The new birth of baptism is an anticipation in a symbol of the real new birth of resurrection when "you will eat another kind of food which is wonderful beyond description; you will feed upon the grace of the Spirit, which will make your bodies immortal and your souls unchanging" (Homily IV, 2). The symbolic

---

21. Yarnold, *The Awe-Inspiring Rites of Initiation*, 168–250.

anticipation is a real "advance payment" of that life of the resurrection. To nourish it while we wait for the resurrection "we need a food which is suitable for our life in the world to feed us symbolically with the grace of the Holy Spirit" (Homily IV, 3). The Eucharist is this eschatological food. Theodore makes this thesis the cornerstone of his theology of the Eucharist.

The food that nourishes us in the life of the resurrection comes from the risen Christ. He entered into resurrection through his death. The Eucharist becomes the food of resurrection in proclaiming the death of Christ. Theodore interprets Christ's words about the bread and wine as meaning "that by his death he will give us the world to come where our sins will be forgiven." From this he concludes: "It is our duty to take part in the sacrament and symbolically proclaim his passion, which will procure for us the possession of the future blessings, together with the forgiveness of our sins" (Homily IV, 7).

Theodore explains why this should be done in sign and symbol (Homily IV, 8–9; cf. 13–14 for the symbolism). At the same time he insists that the bread and wine really are the body and blood of Christ, not merely symbols: "When he gave his apostles the bread he did not say, 'this is the symbol of my body'" (Homily IV, 10). As symbols they represent another reality, which they become by the grace of the Holy Spirit. Christ "wanted us to turn our attention from the nature of the bread and the chalice once they received the grace and the presence of the Holy Spirit and to receive them as the body and blood of our Lord" (ibid.).

In spite of the well-known ambiguities of Theodore's Christology,[22] his theology of the Eucharist is enriched by an analogy he finds between the Eucharist and the Incarnate Word. Unlike other Fathers, who use as an analogy for the Eucharist the uniting of Word and flesh in Christ, Theodore finds the analogy in what happens to the humanity of Christ in his death and resurrection. In Homily IV, 11 he interprets the words of Jesus "It is the Spirit that gives life, the flesh is of no avail" (John 6:63) in relation to what Jesus has just said about "seeing the Son of Man ascending where he was before." He comments: "He would undergo this change [the 'ascending'] . . . by the nature of the life-giving Spirit, which would transfer him to this state

---

22. See Yarnold, *The Awe-Inspiring Rites*, 173 and 216, note 11.

in which he would become immortal himself and confer immortality on others." He applies this to the Eucharist:

> But if the life-giving Spirit gave our Lord's body a nature it did not possess before, we, too, who have received the grace of the Holy Spirit by sacramental symbols should not regard the offering as bread and chalice any longer, but as the body and blood of Christ. It is the descent of the grace of the Holy Spirit that transforms them, obtaining for those who receive them the gifts which we believe the faithful obtain by means of our Lord's body and blood.

Theodore's explanation of how the Eucharist is "a kind of sacrifice we perform" tries to balance the truth that it is a memorial of the passion of Christ, and as such is his unique sacrifice, with his conviction that it is a sacrifice offered by the priestly Church. He begins his rather extended treatment of the subject in this way:

> The most important point to grasp is that the food we take is a kind of sacrifice we perform. It is true that we commemorate our Lord's death in food and drink, believing that these are the memorials of his passion, since he said himself: "This is my body which is broken for you." But it is evident also that what we perform in the liturgy is a kind of sacrifice. The duty of the High Priest of the New Covenant is to offer this sacrifice which revealed the nature of the New Covenant. It is clearly a sacrifice, although it is not something that is new or accomplished by the efforts of the bishop: it is a recalling of this true offering. (Homily IV, 15)

Sacrifice and priesthood go together. Theodore explains how the bishop, who presides at the liturgy, represents Christ the High Priest. The bishop is related to Christ as the earthly to the heavenly. What he does on earth is a symbol of what is done in heaven: "Since the bishop performs in symbol signs [*sic*] of the heavenly realities, the sacrifice must manifest them so that he presents, as it were an image of the heavenly liturgy" (Homily IV, 15). Christ exercises the true (in the Platonic sense) high priesthood in heaven, where he "is High Priest of the heavenly things, and will bring us all up there when the right time comes" (Homily IV, 17). In the meantime, we receive the food of immortality by approaching the first fruits of these blessings, the risen Christ, in the symbols of the liturgy (Homily IV, 18). Theodore argues that the relationship of the eucharistic liturgy to the high priestly work of Christ is ensured by the fact that it is presided over by ordained priests, and in the course of his argument gives a remarkable statement of the relationship between the kind of sacrifice that the Eucharist is and the sacrifice of Christ:

> It follows that, since there needs to be a representation of the High Priest, certain individuals are appointed to preside over the liturgy of these signs. For we believe that what Christ our Lord performed in reality, and will continue to perform, is performed through the sacraments by those whom divine grace has called to be priests of the New Covenant when the Holy Spirit comes down on them to strengthen them and ordain them [literally, "establish them as sons of the sacrament"]. This is why they do not offer new sacrifices, like the repeated immolations prescribed by the Law . . . For there is only one sacrifice which was offered for us all, the sacrifice of Christ our Lord. (Homily IV, 19)

It has to be noted that, in all this development about the Eucharist as sacrifice, Theodore is relying on his basic thesis about the Eucharist being the food of immortality, symbolically anticipated in bread and wine. That is its essential relationship to the risen Christ, who became food of immortality by giving himself to death in his body and blood. It is what makes the Eucharist be the symbolic, earthly representation of the sacrifice of Christ. Being a sacrifice in this sense, it gives access to the heavenly reality that is the fruit of the priestly action of Christ.

After working out his theoretical theological explanations, Theodore proceeds to apply them in a step-by-step commentary on the rite of the Eucharist. Among the points he makes one can note how, to the idea that the bishop is minister of Christ, he adds the idea that the bishop acts on behalf of the whole community: "For although it is the bishop who stands up to make the offering [i.e., by saying the eucharistic prayer] he is only acting as the tongue on behalf of the whole body" (Homily IV, 41). He calls the Eucharist "the community sacrifice," saying: "For the ceremony which is about to take place is a community affair. The community sacrifice is immolated and the community offering is presented on behalf of all, for those absent as well as those present, in as much as they have shared the faith and been numbered as members of God's Church and lived out their lives in it" (Homily IV, 44). He comments about the breaking of the bread: "When we receive one little mouthful we each receive Christ whole," and has a fascinating analogy by way of explanation of this: "When we kiss, we ordinarily do so with the mouth; it is a small part of the body, but by means of it we intend to embrace the whole body. We often walk in pairs hand in hand, taking this part of the body as a sign of our fellowship" (Homily V, 19). He sees the receiving of "the divine food" as communion both in the sense of union with our Lord's body and blood and in the sense of making us part of the community of the baptized, that is, the body of Christ (Homily V, 24). He seems to be complaining about people who abstain from communion although present at the Eucharist when he says: "Our Lord showed by his words that the efficacy of the sacrament lay in the eating and drinking: 'He who eats my flesh and drinks my blood will live forever.' He does not say 'He who celebrates,' but 'He who eats'" (Homily V, 25). He explains at length the spiritual and moral attitudes expected of those who receive the Eucharist. But he insists that those who sin through human weakness, far from abstaining from communion, should find forgiveness and strength to overcome sin by receiving it. However, he recognizes that: "If we have committed a serious sin of any kind which implies the rejection of the Law once for all, we must abstain from communion, but we should not allow ourselves to stay away from it indefinitely" (Homily V, 39). The penitential discipline of the Church is available to bring such sinners back to the Eucharist (Homily V, 39–44).

Saint John Chrysostom (d. 407) deals with the Eucharist frequently in homilies and scriptural commentaries.[23] His teaching about how the Eucharist is related to the once-only sacrifice of Christ resembles that of Theodore (they studied together in Antioch). He joins the sacrificial action of Christ in the Eucharist to the action by which he makes the bread and wine become his body and blood, attributing a permanent actuality to the words he said at the Last Supper:

> It is not man who causes what is present to become the Body and Blood of Christ, but Christ Himself who was crucified for us. The priest is the representative when he pronounces those words, but the power and the grace are those of the Lord. "This is my Body," he says. This word changes the things that lie before us; and as that sentence "increase and multiply," once spoken, extends through all time and gives to our nature the power to

---

23. References in Quasten, *Patrology*, vol. III, 480.

reproduce itself, even so that saying "This is my Body," once uttered, does at every table in the Churches from that time to the present day, and even till Christ's coming, make the sacrifice complete.[24]

The Alexandrian tradition of eucharistic theology reaches a high point in Saint Cyril of Alexandria (d. 444). He brings his theology of Trinity, of the Incarnation, and of grace as divination to bear on his understanding of the Eucharist. In his commentary on the gospel of John, for example, he discusses the return of those who were once sinners to union with God through Christ and the Holy Spirit. Having recalled how oneness is realized in the Trinity and in the Incarnation he continues:

> That we might attain to union with God and with one another, and that we might he made one despite that fact that we differ so peculiarly in both body and soul, the Only-begotten, with the wisdom that is proper to Him and with the counsel of the Father, devised a kind of plan. With one body, and that His own, He blesses through mystic communion those who believe in Him, and makes them one body with Himself and with each other. For who shall separate those who are joined through that sacred body in union with Christ; who shall detach them from the natural union that they have among themselves . . . United then as all of us are to Christ through His sacred Body—since we receive the one and indivisible Christ in our own bodies—we owe the service of our members more to Him than to ourselves. . . . (PG 74, 553–561)[25]

## The Latin Fathers

One can find witness to the basic faith of the church of Africa about the Eucharist in Saint Cyprian (d. 258), as already before him in Tertullian (d. c. 225). It is in Cyprian's Letter 63 *Ad Caecilium*,[26] where he is arguing against a practice of using not wine but only water in the Eucharist; it is in his commentary on the Lord's Prayer,

---

24. Homily I *'de proditione Judae'*, PG 49, 380 and 389, quoted in Quasten, *Patrology*, vol. III, 481.

25. Trans. from Palmer, *Sacraments and Worship*, 220.

26. R. B. Donna, csj, *St. Cyprian, Letters (1–81)*. The Fathers of the Church. A New Translation, vol. 51 (Washington, DC: The Catholic University of America Press, 1964), 202–216.

where he gives a eucharistic interpretation to "our daily bread";[27] and it is in various discussions about the unity of the Church. However, there is little by way of theological development in these passages. In Africa that will only come with Augustine. Meantime, Saint Ambrose (d. 397) contributes some important ideas to the Latin tradition. One can study them especially in his catechetical sermons collected in *De Sacramentis*.[28] There, after explaining baptism and the sealing with the Spirit in the rite of Christian initiation, he creates a dramatic build-up, at the end of *Sermon* III and the beginning of *Sermon* IV, about approaching the altar: "You went there [to the baptismal font], you washed, you came to the altar, you began to see what you had not seen before: that is to say through the font of the Lord and the preaching of the Lord's passion your eyes were opened. Before, you seemed to be blind of heart; but now you began to perceive the light of the sacraments" (Sermon III, 15). The term "altar" is explained by means of types from the Old Testament and a reminder that the baptized are a priestly people (Sermon IV, 3). What they see on the altar is the sacraments, i.e., bread and wine, things common and familiar in themselves but with a symbolism more ancient and profound than the sacraments of Judaism, because derived from Melchizedek and actually established by Christ who is a priest according to the order of Melchizedek (Sermon IV, 8–13). There is something of a theology of the Eucharist as sacramentalizing the priesthood of Christ in these allusions.

There is a more straightforward piece of theological explanation in the answer that Ambrose goes on to give to a supposed objection, that the Eucharist is just ordinary bread: "Perhaps you say: 'the bread I have here is ordinary bread.' Yes, before the sacramental words are uttered this bread is nothing but bread. But at the consecration this bread becomes the body of Christ. Let us reason this out. . . ." (Sermon IV, 14–15). Ambrose invites his hearers to do something that Latin theology will subsequently love to do about this question, to "reason things out." There is no reasoning about the fact that the bread and wine are the body and blood of Christ. That is a given of faith. The reasoning is that if they were not the body and blood from

---

27. R. J. Deferrari, ed. and trans., *St. Cyprian, Treatises*, The Fathers of the Church. A New Translation, vol. 36 (Washington, DC: The Catholic University of America Press, 1958), n.18.

28. Yarnold, *The Awe-Inspiring Rites of Initiation*, 98–149.

the beginning, then they must have become it. That becoming he calls a "consecration": to be made the body and blood is to be made holy. A becoming has to have some cause. Ambrose assumes that the cause must have something to do with the words said by the priest, "this is my body . . . blood." These are the words that consecrate and bring the sacrament into being. The question then is, how can words do such a thing? The answer of Ambrose is that these words are the words of Christ. He proves that by noting that the priest speaks them, not as his own words as he had been doing up to that point, but as the words of Christ. Ambrose then makes a theological identification between words *(sermones)* of Christ in the plural and word *(sermo)* in the singular. This is the principle that allows him to argue that the words of consecration can make bread and wine become the body and blood of Christ because they have within them the power of the Word by which all things were made. The Word that gave existence to all things can very well change what already exists into something else. Western theology of the Eucharist will make much of this idea of changing what already exists into the being of something else.

Indeed, the whole line of reasoning followed by Ambrose in this text became standard in Western theology up to the time of the Reformation. Sometimes the final part of it (connecting the words with the Word) would be forgotten and the words of consecration would seem to be given a power of their own. At other times, when a predominantly juridical judgment was being made about the Eucharist, it would seem that their power was thought to consist simply in their being the fulfillment of a command: if one said the words one was supposed to say, the Eucharist would be valid and the consecration would follow. For Ambrose, however, as for the Fathers generally, the words consecrate because the divine, creative Word of God is present and acting in them. The Eucharist truly is a mystery. Ambrose is not particularly concerned about identifying the exact moment of consecration. He pays attention to the whole eucharistic prayer in the sermon (Sermon IV, 21–29). However, his argument does, in fact, link the consecration with the saying of "the words of consecration." This becomes a standard position in Western theology, and later puts it in some conflict with the Eastern tradition that came to associate the consecration with the invocation of the Holy Spirit on the gifts more than with the saying of the Lord's words.

Having affirmed the reality of the change in the sacrament, Ambrose has to face the difficulty that the bread-made-body and the wine-made-blood do not look like body and blood. His explanation is that "I do not see the appearance *(species)* of blood. No, but the likeness *(similitudo)* is there" (Sermon IV, 20). This is his way of saying that the blood is received in a symbol, "in order that nothing of the horror of blood may be there and at the same time that the price of our redemption may become operative" (ibid.). He returns to this theme in his final homily where, having recalled what he had said about the power of the word of God "to change and transform *(convertere)* the fixed natural species *(genera instituta naturae)*," he shows how the realism of body and blood, that is required in order to preserve "the grace of redemption" in the Eucharist, can be maintained without provoking the natural "horror of blood": "you receive the sacraments in symbolic form *(in similitudinem)* but you receive the grace and efficacy of Christ's real . . . nature *(verae naturae)*" (Sermon VI, 3).

Finally, one may note that Ambrose is satisfied to let the liturgy of the Eucharist speak for itself about its being a sacrifice. In Sermon IV, 27 he quotes the prayer of offering that follows the *anamnesis* of the death, resurrection, and ascension, in a form that is almost identical with the corresponding part of the Roman Canon, and contains the words *hostiam* (victim), *incruentum* (unbloody) and *oblationem* (offering). He explains how the eucharistic offering heralds the remission of sin because it heralds the death of the Lord, and what it heralds it actually does:

> What is it the apostle says about every time you receive it? "As often as we receive it, we herald the death of the Lord." If we herald his death, we herald the remission of sins. If whenever his blood is shed, it is shed for the remission of sins, I ought always to receive him so that he may always forgive sins. Since I am always sinning, I always need the medicine. (Sermon IV, 28)

At the risk of over systematizing the rich and abundant material about the Eucharist that can be found in the writings of Saint Augustine,[29] one can deal with it successively in relation to

---

29. Texts in H. Lang, *Aurelia Augustini. Textus eucharistici selecti.*, Florilegium Patristicum fasc, 35 (Bonn, 1933) and in Palmer, *Sacraments and Worship*, 208–213, 215–216, 281–288.

his Christology, to his soteriology, to his ecclesiology, to his general sacramental theology, and finally to his theology of sacrifice. Much of what Augustine says affirms the general tradition of faith and need not be repeated. What needs to be looked at are the points on which he showed some theological originality, and those that had a significant influence on later Latin theology.

Since Christology teaches that Christ is the divine Son of God who took flesh for our salvation, it requires that he be adored in that flesh that is given to us to eat for our salvation. In a complicated commentary on Psalm 95, verse 5, "And adore his footstool because it is holy," he says:

> For He assumed from earth—since flesh is of the earth, and from Mary's flesh He took flesh; and because in His very flesh He walked on earth, and because His very flesh He gave us to eat for our salvation—and no one eats that flesh unless he has first adored it—we find how that footstool of the Lord may be adored, and not only do we not sin by adoring, but we sin by not adoring. (*Comm. on Ps. 98*, PL 37, 1264)[30]

Soteriologically, Christ is mediator between God and humans; he is a priest who offers himself in sacrifice: "... He is also priest, the very one who offers and the very offering. And He willed that the sacrifice of the Church should be the daily sacrament (*signum*) of this. Since she is the body of this head, through Him she is taught to offer herself ... To this supreme and true sacrifice all false sacrifices have given way" (*The City of God*, 10, 20: PL 41, 281ff.).

Christ is now risen, and for Augustine that is the key to understanding what he means when he says "unless you eat my flesh and drink my blood you will not have life in you." Among the many commentaries that Augustine made on this text is this characteristic passage:

> Do you think that I am speaking of this body which you see, as though I were about to make it into pieces by cutting up my members and giving them to you? "Then what if you shall see the Son of Man ascending to where He was before?" Surely He who can ascend in His entirety cannot be consumed. Thus He gave us His body and blood for our salutary refreshment and at the same time solved in a few words the great problem of His own integrity (wholeness). Therefore, let those eat who eat, and drink who drink; let them hunger and thirst: life let them eat, life let them drink. To

---

30. Trans. from Palmer, *Sacraments and Worship*, 209–210.

eat thereof is to be remade; but you are remade in such a way as not to
unmake that by which you are remade. To drink thereof, what else but to
live? Eat life, drink life; you will have life, and life remains whole and entire.
Then shall it come to pass that the body and blood of Christ will be life
to each one, when that which is received visibly in the sacrament is in very
truth spiritually eaten, spiritually drunk. (*Sermon* 131: PL 38, 730)[31]

Augustine's ecclesiology ensures that when he thinks about
the body of Christ that is given in the Eucharist he is thinking at
the same time of the body of Christ that is made by the Eucharist.
His ecclesiology—which is worked out predominantly in terms of
the body of Christ—pervades his eucharistic theology. "Body" draws
together Christ, the Church, and the Eucharist in his thinking:

... the whole redeemed city, that is to say, the congregation and community of the saints is offered as a corporate sacrifice through the great Priest,
who also offered Himself in his passion for us, in the form of a servant,
that we might be the body of so glorious a head ... Now therefore the
Apostle, having exhorted us to present our bodies a living sacrifice, holy
and acceptable to God, our spiritual worship ... says, " ... so we though
many are one body in Christ, and individually members of one another ..."
(Romans 12:5). This is the sacrifice of Christians: we the many are one
body in Christ. And this also is the sacrifice which the Church continually
celebrates in the sacrament of the altar—which is known to the faithful.
In it the Church learns that in the offering which she makes she herself is
offered. (*The City of God*, 10, 6: PL 41, 281ff.)

The Eucharist is the source of unity, especially when seen in
continuity with baptism and confirmation:

In this bread you are reminded how you ought to love unity. For is that
bread made from a single grain? Were there not many grains of wheat? But
before they came to be bread, they were separate. By water and a process of
pulverization *(contritionem)* they were united. For unless wheat is crushed
and sprinkled with water, it can in no way take on that form which is
called bread. In like manner, you too were first crushed under the humili-
ation of the fast and the sacrament of exorcism. Then, baptism in water
was added. You were, as it were, wetted down that you might take on the
shape of bread. But until there is fire there is no bread. Where then is the
symbol of fire? It is in the anointing. For oil is the sacrament of the Holy

---

31. Trans. from Palmer, *Sacraments and Worship*, 212.

Spirit, our fire . . . After water, then, the Holy Spirit is added, fire; and you become bread, which is the body of Christ. In this way, so to speak, unity is symbolized. (*Sermon* 227: PL 38, 1099–1100)[32]

Augustine makes much of the symbolism of bread and wine—of their being made and of the eating and drinking of them. That, combined with his repeated insistence that one must eat "spiritually," can give an impression that he thinks the Eucharist to be only a symbol of the body of Christ. Later theology, during the Middle Ages and at the Reformation, was able to quote him on both sides of the debate about what had then become the issue of the real presence. It is on this point that one needs to interpret his theology of the Eucharist in the light of his general sacramental theology (see Chapter 2, "The Latin Tradition and Saint Augustine"). The rites of the Church do belong to the world of sign and symbol. To call them sacraments is to say so. But it is also to say that they hold within themselves a reality *(res)* that they bring about. The *effect* of a sacrament is complex. Augustine had to establish against the Donatists that a sacrament can bring about a certain reality—and therefore be a real, true sacrament—even when it does not bring about its ultimate effect, which is the grace of the Holy Spirit. While he worked out that theory mainly with reference to baptism, there is also room for it in his understanding of the Eucharist. In the celebration of the Eucharist there is a level of sheer symbolism: it is exploited freely by mind and imagination. Underlying this, and brought about by the celebration, there is a level of sacramental reality: the Eucharist really is the body and blood of Christ. Because this level is not yet itself the ultimate reality of the Eucharist but points forward to it, Augustine can still call it the sacrament (medieval theology will call it the *res et sacramentum*): it is the real body and blood of Christ, but acting, in the form of bread and wine, as a sign of an even deeper reality. That deeper reality is still the body of Christ, but now uniting to itself in a single body those who are receiving the grace of the Holy Spirit: the ultimate reality *(res)* of the Eucharist is the unity of the Church as body of Christ. It is to this body of Christ that most of Augustine's attention is directed in his eucharistic theology. He is interested in the sacramental body and blood as a sacrament of the unity of the ecclesial body, more than as a reality to be thought about

---

32. Trans. from Palmer, *Sacraments and Worship*, 215–216.

in its own right. To eat only of the sacrament (which sinners can do) profits nothing. One must eat spiritually. To eat spiritually is to eat in faith and love, recognizing and accepting the reality of the unity of the body of Christ that is signified and brought about by the Eucharist.

There is nothing novel about Augustine's clear statements that the Eucharist is a sacrifice or about the way he identifies it with the one true sacrifice of Christ. What is distinctive, and had considerable influence on later Western theology, is the general theory of sacrifice he applied to the Eucharist and the way his idea of sacrament affects the application. Augustine develops a teaching on sacrifice in Book 10 of *The City of God*. He is contrasting the beliefs and practices of Christians with those of the pagan world. In Chapters 4 and 5 he stresses the interiority and spirituality of what Christians understand by sacrifice. In a phrase that will be much used in medieval theology he says that "visible sacrifice is a sacrament, that is to say a sacred sign of invisible sacrifice." Another definition of sacrifice that will be prized in the Middle Ages appears at the beginning of Chapter 6: "Now, a true sacrifice is every work done that we may cleave to God in holy fellowship, a work that is related to that supreme good in which we can find our true beatitude." This definition allows him to explain how Christians offer true sacrifice by living in the service of God, how all these sacrifices are offered to God by Christ the High Priest who offered himself in his passion to make us members of his body. It is this reality of Head and members, offering and being offered together, "which the Church continually celebrates in the sacrament of the altar." The Eucharist is a sacrifice because it is the sacrament or sacred sign of that one reality, which is the self-offering of Christ, head and members. The Eucharist can be a sign of Christ's sacrifice because it has some similarity with it:

> Christ was immolated in himself only once, and yet sacramentally *(in sacramento)* he is immolated not only in every celebration of Easter but every day for the people: if one is asked about it one will not lie in saying that he is immolated. If sacraments did not have some similarity with the things of which they are sacraments they would not be in any way sacraments. (*Letter* 98: PL. 33, 363)

Thus, while Augustine uses a technical analysis of sacrifice, drawn from the meaning the word has in general religious language, to talk about the Eucharist as sacrifice, he transforms it profoundly by working into it his concept of sacrament.

## Medieval Theology to Aquinas

There is reciprocal influence between theological thinking about the Eucharist and its liturgical celebration. Some of the features of liturgical practice that go hand in hand with theological development in the Latin church during the Middle Ages are: an increasing passivity of the lay members of the congregation, who tended to look on the Eucharist as something that the clergy did for them rather than as something in which they joined actively with the clergy; the gradual silencing of the word component of the celebration, because of the continuing use of a Latin language that was less and less understood, and also because of the use of a subdued tone of voice in the saying of many of the prayers, including the eucharistic prayer; the gradual disappearance of communion from the chalice for the faithful, and the substitution of loaves of bread by wafers of unleavened bread already divided into particles; increasing abstention from communion by those who were present at the Eucharist; the development of forms of devotion to the reserved sacrament, and a spiritual fascination with Christ present in it; the multiplying of Masses celebrated without a congregation for private intentions and occasions.

The theological questions that got the most attention during the Middle Ages reflected these features of liturgical practice, and the theological answers proposed influenced practice. The question of the relationship between the body of Christ and the bread that was consecrated and eaten and reserved in the Eucharist was debated at length. There were also some questions about the use or reception of the Eucharist and about how it produces its effects. The tradition that the Eucharist is a sacrifice got some attention in that context (it produced effects as a sacrifice even for those who did not receive it sacramentally) but was not really a major issue in theology until quite late in the Middle Ages. The questions that were asked about the body of Christ and its relationship to the bread of the Eucharist had, obviously, also to be asked about the blood of Christ in relation to the wine, and answers had to be along the same lines. But quite frequently the discussion was just about body and bread. To some extent this was a form of theological shorthand: if one said something basic about body and bread one was not expected to repeat it each time about blood and wine. But it must also have reflected a certain concentration on the body of Christ apart from the blood, both in theology (*corpus Christi* was by itself a bridge with ecclesiology and Christology in a way that *sanguis Christi* was not) and in devotion (when communion was taken only under the form of bread and the reserved *corpus Christi* became an object of devotion in the way *sanguis Christi* did not). The concentration on certain questions does not mean that the broad tradition of faith about the Eucharist was altogether absent during the Middle Ages. It continued to be carried by the scriptures, by the liturgy itself, and by the writings of the Fathers that were known. It sometimes found expression in allegorical commentaries on the liturgy which, for all their lack of discipline, transmitted a sensitivity to the mystery of the Eucharist that the better medieval theologians never lost, for all their stern reasoning.

## Ninth to Twelfth Centuries

The first questions about the Eucharist arose when the scholars of the ninth century began to apply the rules of grammar and logic to statements about the sacrament that were to be found in the scriptures and in texts of the Fathers, particularly of Augustine. There were texts that said quite simply that the bread taken in the Eucharist is Christ's body and that the wine is his blood. On the other hand there was John 6:63: "It is the spirit that gives life, the flesh is of no avail." Augustine had commented enthusiastically on that text, saying that in the Eucharist the body of Christ was eaten spiritually, or sacramentally, or *in figura*; it was not eaten carnally or "capharnaitically" (a word coined from Capharnaum where, according to John 6:59, the carnal, almost cannibalistic caricature of what was meant by "eating the flesh" of Jesus was first put forward and ridiculed). What was meant by these contrasting statements? Did the "body of Christ" that they spoke of refer to the flesh-and-blood body that was born of Mary and is now glorified in heaven? Or was it some kind of spiritual body that was being received spiritually? Or was it the body of Christ that is the Church, which was coming to be designated increasingly in those centuries by the term *corpus mysticum*, "mystical body"—a term that had originally

referred to the Eucharist? Questions of this kind were launched by
Amalarius of Metz (d. 850) in the course of a commentary on the
Mass. They were taken up by Paschasius Radbertus (d. 860) in his *De
Corpore et Sanguine Domini* (PL 120, 1267–1350). He takes what has
been called a "realist" position (in contrast to the more symbolical, if
not allegorical, position of Amalarius). He affirms that the body that
is said to be eaten in the Eucharist is identical with the body born of
Mary, because that is the only body that can give salvation and that
can be head of the body of the redeemed, which is the Church. The
Eucharist is the *veritas* (truth, reality) of the body of Christ, whereas
the rites of the Old Testament were simply its *figura*. However, this
real body of Christ is present in the Eucharist in signs; it is eaten
mystically (in *misterio*) and not in a way that is perceptible to the
senses. There is nothing "capharnaitic" about the eating. But realism
verges on the realistic in the thinking of Paschasius. When he wants
to explain how the body of the risen Christ could be present within a
host, and in so many hosts, he postulates a miraculous multiplication
of the flesh of Christ analogous to the multiplication of the loaves
recorded in the gospels. He seems to suggest that the bread is replaced
by the flesh of Christ: the *veritas* (reality) of the Eucharist is the body
of Christ; the bread is only an appearance, serving as a *figura* of the
body of Christ. He attributed this change of reality in the bread to the
miraculous work of the Holy Spirit, putting it in line with his work of
uniting the divine to human flesh in the incarnation, and seeing it as
preparing humans for the final miracle of their transformation in the
resurrection.[33]

The position of Paschasius seemed novel and exaggerated
to Rabanus Maurus (d. 856). He had no doubts that the bread consecrated in the Eucharist is really the body of Christ. But he and
others questioned the simple identification of what was eaten in
the Eucharist with the historical body of Christ. He thought, for
instance, that this would suggest that Christ actually died each time
the Eucharist was celebrated. The opponents of Paschasius distinguished between the historical body of Christ, the ecclesial body, and
the eucharistic body. Although these three were *naturaliter* identical
they were *specialiter* distinct. That meant for these grammarians and

---

33. Text from Paschasius in Palmer, *Sacraments and Worship*, 223.

logicians that one could not talk about one the way one talked about the other. They thought Paschasius was confusing different kinds of language and so saying things that were false.[34] Ratramnus of Corbie (d. 868) was one of those who opposed Paschasius. In his *De Corpore et Sanguine Domini* (PL 121, 125–170) he tries to work out what can and cannot be said about the Eucharist by introducing a type of analysis that today might be called epistemological. He takes the common Augustinian terminology of *veritas/figura* as referring to the way things are known rather than to what is known: *veritas* is what is attained in direct perception; what is known in *figura* is what is known through the symbolism of what is directly perceived. According to this terminology the *veritas* of the Eucharist is bread; the body of Christ is in the bread *in figura*, because it is perceived through the symbolism of the bread. The *veritas* of the body of Christ is now in heaven. That body is present in the Eucharist, not *corporaliter* or in *veritate* (i.e., not precisely as a body) but *in figura*. In the terms proposed by Ratramnus this presence *in figura* is the only way that the body of Christ could be present and life-giving in the Eucharist. He thinks that the explanation of Paschasius, in affirming that it is the risen body of Christ, which was born of Mary, that is truly present in the Eucharist, is affirming a corporeal presence of the sort that the tradition of faith, especially as expounded by Augustine, said was of no avail. The *veritas* of the body of Christ is what was present on earth during his life, on the cross in his dying, and is now in heaven; it is a body animated by physical, biological life. It is not that corporeal life that is communicated in the Eucharist, says Ratramnus, but spiritual life. The presence of the body of Christ in the Eucharist is spiritual, the eating of it is spiritual, the life that it gives is spiritual. The eucharistic body, like the ecclesial body, is, indeed, identical with the body born of Mary, but not with the corporeal form that it took on earth and now takes in heaven.[35]

The approach of Ratramnus was taken up with even greater dialectical rigor two centuries later by Berengarius of Tours (d. 1088) in his *De Sacra Cena*.[36] For his pains he has the distinction of being the

---

34. Text from Rabanus in Palmer, *Sacraments and Worship*, 226.

35. Text from Ratramnus in Palmer, *Sacraments and Worship*, 224–226.

36. See W. H. Beekenkamp. ed., *Berengarius of Tours, De sacra coena adversus Lanfrancum* (The Hague, 1941).

first theologian to be condemned, by a Synod of the Roman Church, for a teaching on the Eucharist. The question he raised was, once again, the relationship between the consecrated bread and the body of Christ. His thinking on the question was founded on faith but was affected by certain elements of philosophical analysis that were then being introduced into theology by the dialecticians. In particular, he assumed that the reality of a thing was known by its appearances, and therefore that a thing must really be what it seems to be. If what was on the altar seemed to be bread it must be bread.[37] Berengarius believed that what is received in the Eucharist is the body of Christ. He took from the Augustinian tradition that it was received and eaten spiritually. For Berengarius the qualification "spiritually" meant that the body of Christ was there not in a bodily way, not materially, not as an object of sensation. His philosophical position would not allow for any change in the bread: if it seems to be bread then it is bread, not merely its appearance. Nor did he see any reason why it should change. In his view what happens at the consecration is that, while continuing to be what it is, the bread begins to be the sign of the life-giving body of Christ that is thus present and eaten spiritually. Neither does this involve any change in the body of Christ. It does not come down from heaven, nor is it multiplied in many hosts as Berengarius understood the proponents of the realist position to be saying. It is active and life-giving in the Eucharist, but present only spiritually and in the sign of bread.

The opponents of Berengarius, the most prominent of whom was Lanfranc, Archbishop of Canterbury (cf. his *De Corpore et Sanguine Domini*: PL 150, 407–442), argued that his theory denied that the bread really became the body of Christ at the consecration; he was not therefore, they argued, confessing the faith of the Church that what is eaten in the Eucharist truly is the real body of Christ. They claimed that his theory said no more than that the bread is a sign through which the heavenly Christ is believed to be active and life-giving.[38] That, too, was the judgment of two Roman Synods that devised professions of faith that Berengarius was required to make by way of renouncing his errors. The way the faith is expressed in these

---

37. J. M. Powers, sj, *Eucharistic Theology* (New York: Herder & Herder, 1967), 28.
38. Texts from Lanfranc in Palmer, *Sacraments and Worship*, 229–231.

texts shows the uncertain state of theological thinking and language
about the Eucharist at that time. The first formula, imposed by a
Roman Synod of 1059, states the faith of the Church in a language
of rather extravagant realism that leaves little place for sacramentality: "... the bread and wine ... are not only the sacrament but the
real body and blood ... and in a tangible way *(sensualiter)*, not just
sacramentally but in truth, are handled and broken by the priest
and chewed by the faithful ..." (DS 690). It is a formula that Saint
Bonaventure would later criticize as *nimis expressa* (IV Sent. d. 12, I,
3, 1), and Saint Thomas would feel the need to explain away (Third
Part, q. 77, a. 7 ad 3). The second formula, which the recalcitrant
Berengarius was required to sign by a Roman Synod of 1079, is more
carefully worded. It avoids the epistemological ambiguities associated
with *sensualiter* and *in veritate*, and the use of "handling, breaking,
chewing" in relation to the body of Christ. It uses language that allows
it to state what the Eucharist is objectively rather than in terms of our
perception of what it is; it is more metaphysical than epistemological.
The profession of faith is:

> I, Berengar, believe in my heart and confess with my lips that the bread
> and wine which are placed on the altar are, by the mystery of the sacred
> prayer and the words of the Redeemer, substantially changed *(substantiali-
> ter converti)* into the true and proper and life-giving body and blood of
> Jesus Christ our Lord; and that, after consecration, they are Christ's true
> body, which was born of the Virgin and hung on the cross, being offered
> for the salvation of the world, and which sits at the right hand of the
> Father; and Christ's true blood, which was poured forth from His side;
> not only by way of sign and by the power of the sacrament *(non tantum per
> signum et virtutem sacramenti)* but in their true nature and in the reality
> of their substance *(in proprietate naturae et veritate substantiae)*. (DS 700;
> ND 1501)

The suggestion that this text marks a concentration on the
ontological reality of the Eucharist, and a shift away from the more
epistemological concerns that were prominent in the debates of earlier
medieval theology, is borne out by the appearance of the word *substantia* in it. The body of Christ is no longer said to be there *in veritate* but
*in veritate substantiae*. The previous history of the word "substance"
had prepared it to serve in discussions about the ontological reality of

the Eucharist.[39] It had been in Latin theological language from the beginning. It appears in Latin versions of the scriptures: in Hebrews 11:1 ("faith is the *substantia* of things hoped for, the conviction of things not seen"), and in Matthew's version of the Lord's Prayer, where what is nowadays rendered in English as "our daily bread" is *panis super-substantialis* (Matthew 6:11). It played a prominent part in dogmatic debates about the Trinity (cf. *consubstantialis* in the Nicene Creed) and about the Incarnation. While the word was given technical overtones and some philosophical honing in these debates, it continued to be used in a general nontechnical sense for what is solid and permanent in a given reality, for the abiding nature of a thing that holds steady when its appearances change, for the "real thing" as distinct from what something might seem to be. It is found in a text, thought to be from the fifth-century Faustus of Riez (*PL* 30, 272),[40] which speaks of a change of bread and wine into the *substantia* of the body and blood of Christ. But it does not seem to have gained a significant place in the vocabulary of eucharistic theology until the time of the condemnation of Berengarius. From then on it is the key word in medieval theological discussion about the reality of the Eucharist. It was there, then, before the introduction of Aristotelian philosophy into the medieval universities. The meaning given to it was eventually influenced by that philosophy; but it always kept a certain theological independence. In the profession of faith imposed on Berengarius it is used in a phrase that states the genuineness and realness of the body of Christ that the consecrated bread becomes. It is not yet strong enough to carry the meaning all by itself, but requires the support of other words: *in proprietate naturae et veritate substantiae*. But it has already been used in an adverbial form earlier in the text and it is this use that really makes its fortune in theology: the bread and wine are said to be "substantially changed" *(substantialiter converti)* into the body and blood of Christ by the mystery of prayer, i.e., the eucharistic prayer of consecration and the words of institution. The change from bread to body is put on the level of substance.

The idea that bread and wine are changed into the body and blood of Christ in the Eucharist was already present in the Fathers

---

39. See E. Schillebeeckx, OP, *The Eucharist* (London and New York; Sheed & Ward, 1968), 70ff.

40. Schillebeeckx, *The Eucharist*, 73.

(see "The Tradition of the Fathers"). The change was variously attributed to the Holy Spirit and to the Word of God, and likened to what happened to human flesh in the incarnation. The Greek tradition developed various words beginning with *meta-*, corresponding to Latin words beginning with *trans-*, and to their English equivalents "transform," "transfigure," "transmute," etc., to describe the change.[41] The theological and philosophical horizon in which the Greeks used these terms was not quite the same as that in which the Latins used "transubstantiation," especially after Aristotle had become a force in Western theology.[42] Although they affirmed the change every bit as strongly as the Latins they were not very much concerned about whether or how the bread ceased to be bread when the change occurred. For the Latins, however, that became a critical question. Berengarius thought the bread did not, and could not, cease to be bread and simply remain an appearance. The profession of faith required him to affirm that the bread was "substantially changed." That was not yet an explicit statement that the bread ceased to be bread. There is no direct reference in the text to the substance of bread. However, the qualification of the change as substantial, and the use of substance to affirm the kind of reality that the body and blood of Christ have in the Eucharist inevitably required reflection on the substance of bread. It is into that kind of reflection that the word "transubstantiation" fits. It appears in the works of Etienne de Baugé (*PL* 172, 1291–1293), around 1140, and somewhat later in the *Sententiae* of Roland Bandinelli, later Pope Alexander III.[43] It defined the change of bread and wine into the body and blood of Christ that is confessed in the tradition of faith as a change of the substance of bread into the substance of Christ's body, and of the substance of wine into the substance of Christ's blood. It measured up to the realism about the presence of the body and blood of Christ in the Eucharist required by the profession of faith of Berengarius. It also offered some explanation of how what seemed to be bread was no longer so, because it said that the substance under the appearances was no longer that of bread but of the body of Christ. It became a standard term in medieval theology

---

41. Schillebeeckx, *The Eucharist*, 65–67.

42. Schillebeeckx, *The Eucharist*, 67–69.

43. J. Gietl, ed., *Roland Bandinelli, 'Sententiae'* (Fribourg: Editions Universitaires, 1891), 231.

of the Eucharist from the middle of the twelfth century onward. It found its way into the *magisterium* at the Fourth Lateran Council in 1215 (DS 802; ND 21).[44] At first it had no technical philosophical connotations, other than the general sense derived from what the word "substance" meant in the Greco-Roman thinking adopted by the Church of the Fathers. When the philosophy of Aristotle won its way into Catholic theology in the thirteenth century it offered an analysis of reality in which the category of substance played an important part. That analysis was found useful by some theologians who wanted to push the understanding of transubstantiation to its intellectual limits with a view to a better understanding of the Eucharist. It was also found useful by them as a protection against a certain grossness that the employment of a badly understood notion of substance could leave in people's perception of how the body and blood of Christ were present and received in the Eucharist.

## Saint Thomas Aquinas

There is much more to the eucharistic theology of the Middle Ages than a doctrine of transubstantiation. While the question of the sense in which bread and wine become the body and blood of Christ at the consecration was pivotal from the beginning, and remained so right to the end, it was not dealt with in isolation from the broad tradition of eucharistic faith and practice that the medieval world inherited from the Fathers. Earlier writings on the subject may be somewhat one-sided because they are occasional and controversial. The controversies and special interest remain noticeable even in the more systematic works and Summas that come to be written later, but there is in them, nevertheless, a better sense of balance. The treatment of the Eucharist in the *Summa Theologiae* of Saint Thomas Aquinas is a fine example of medieval systematic theology. Apart from its intrinsic worth as theology it also has to be studied because of its historical influence on the distinctively Catholic tradition about the Eucharist.

Thomas' principal study of the Eucharist is in the Third part of the *Summa*, within his treatment of the sacraments of the Church. In his general discussion on sacraments he establishes that

---

44. N. P. Tanner, sj, ed., *Decrees of the Ecumenical Councils*, vols. I and II (London and Washington: Sheed & Ward and Georgetown University Press, 1990), vol. I, 230.

Eucharist is the most important *(potissimum)* of the seven and that all the others are somehow directed toward it (q. 65, a. 3). He deals with it after baptism and confirmation, showing sensitivity to the liturgical appropriateness of following this order (cf. q. 72, a. 12 ad 3). He organizes his thinking in a sequence of questions that is dictated by his general theory of the sacramental economy (see Chapter 2, "The Scholastics and Saint Thomas Aquinas"). First, he asks whether and how the Eucharist is a sacrament (q. 73); then he analyses it in terms of the essential "matter" (qq. 74–77) and "form" (q. 78) that must come together in it to constitute the sacramental sign; then he looks at the effects produced in and by this sign (q. 79), and at the sacramental action and attitudes of the people who take these effects to themselves (qq. 80-81); finally, he asks about the minister of the Church who leads the making of the sacramental sign (q. 82) and about the full liturgical rite in which the Eucharist is celebrated (q. 83).

The first of this series of questions (q. 73) is crucial. In establishing there that the Eucharist is a sacrament in the technical sense Thomas identifies the special kind of reality that it is and the peculiar categories that must be used to understand it. As with all the sacraments, it is being a sign that makes it be a sacrament. He builds his case for this sacramentality/sign of the Eucharist from the outside inward, going from the symbolic action to what is symbolized: the symbolic action is the taking of food and drink in a meal; what it symbolizes is the nourishing of that spiritual life that the whole sacramental economy is meant to cultivate (a. 1–2). In relating the Eucharist to life and seeing it as nourishment, Thomas is drawing on the Johannine tradition about the Eucharist as bread of life. Next, he asks if the Eucharist is necessary for salvation: it has to be so in some way in order to be recognized as a sacrament of the Church. In establishing its necessity for salvation he introduces the ecclesial symbolism of the Eucharist and the Pauline tradition about the body of Christ. As a meal of bread and wine the Eucharist sacramentalizes a life of unity with others in the mystical body of Christ, outside which there is no life or salvation.

The third step Thomas takes to establish the sacramentality of the Eucharist is to show that it has the threefold significance for past, present, and future that is characteristic of the sacramental economy. He finds that reflected in three names that the tradition had given to the Eucharist—sacrifice, communion, and viaticum (a. 4). First, the Eucharist looks to the past by commemorating the passion of Christ: the passion was a sacrifice; as the sacrament of that sacrifice the Eucharist is itself called *sacrifice*. From this early stage of his discussion on the Eucharist, Thomas is seeing sacrament and sacrifice as interwoven: it is a sacrament because it symbolizes, among other things, the life-giving sacrifice of Christ; it is a sacrifice because it is a symbolic commemoration of the sacrifice of Christ. Thomas has no treatment of the Eucharist as sacrifice apart from his treatment of it as sacrament. He has no treatise on the Mass. All that he has to say about the Mass, and about its sacrificial nature, is said under the heading of the sacrament of the Eucharist and in the language of sacramentality. The Eucharist is a sacrifice because it is a sacrament of the cross. Second, the Eucharist as a meal looks to the present by signifying and being called *communion*, that is, the unity of the Church. Thomas leaves the word open here to its full biblical and patristic meaning. Third, as a banquet the Eucharist looks to the future in which God is enjoyed in heaven. Here the tradition about the eschatological significance of the Eucharist is integrated in its sacramentality. The name *viaticum*, which Thomas appeals to here, has not yet come to mean the last communion before death. It refers to a quality there is in every Eucharist: it is always food for the journey, sustaining those who wait for the coming of the Lord and anticipating the joy of his coming.

The final step taken by Thomas to establish the sacramentality of the Eucharist is a discussion about its scriptural origins (a. 5–6). It meets the requirements for institution as sacrament, in that it is rooted in the scriptures of the Old and New Testaments. Thomas is not concerned with canonical institution here but with showing how the sacramentality of the Eucharist takes its origin from what was said and done by Jesus at the Last Supper, and how this was prepared for by the classical Old Testament types: Melchizedek, ritual sacrifices of expiation, the manna, and, preeminently, the Paschal lamb.

The theological method of Thomas in this first question 73 about the Eucharist—one of giving intelligible shape to the tradition of faith about the Eucharist by applying the technical categories of sacramentality to it—has to be kept in mind for understanding all the rest of his eucharistic theology. Otherwise one will get things like his theory of transubstantiation and some remarks he makes about

sacrifice quite out of perspective. His discussion about transubstantiation comes in the course of his study of the "matter" of the Eucharist,
that is to say, of the material element that, in the sense defined by the
words with which it is used (the "form"), carries the sacramental symbolism. In Thomas' view, transubstantiation serves the sacramentality
of the Eucharist, and it is in doing so that it gives it its reality. In the
medieval analysis of sacramentality, which is derived from Augustine,
there is a level that is found in the symbolism of the "matter" and
"form" in themselves: this is the level of the *sacramentum tantum*.
There is a further level that arises when the "matter" and "form" are
actually used in a liturgical celebration: something real is produced (a
sacramental character or some other such ecclesial reality), which has
a significant role in bringing about the final effect of the sacrament.
It is called the *res et sacramentum*. It can exist and signify even if the
final reality is for some reason blocked. It can do so because a sacrament is always an act of the Church, exercising its role as sacrament of
Christ. The third level of a sacrament is its final effect, which is grace.
It is called the *res tantum*. In q. 73, a. 1 ad 3 Thomas notes that the
Eucharist differs from the other sacraments in that its *res et sacramen-*
*tum* is in the "matter" of the sacrament rather than in the person who
receives it, as is the case in other sacraments. What he proposes is, in
fact, that the *sacramentum tantum* of the Eucharist is bread and wine;
the *res et sacramentum* is the bread and wine consecrated to be the body
and blood of Christ by the Lord's words spoken about them; the *res*
*tantum*, or proper grace effect of the Eucharist, is unity in love between
baptized Christians in the Body of Christ (q. 73, a. 6), in other words
the Church. The bread and wine are consecrated when the Eucharist
is properly celebrated, even if those for whom it is being celebrated do
not accept the proper grace of the sacrament (as the baptismal character is caused even when the recipient puts some obstacle in the way of
the grace of the baptism). But the whole purpose of the consecration
of bread and wine, according to this analysis, is to signify and eventually cause the grace of the Eucharist. The Eucharist does bring about
the "real presence," but that is not its ultimate reality. Its ultimate reality is the nourishing of the life of love for the baptized in the oneness
of the body of Christ.

Thomas carries his study of the sacrament of the Eucharist
forward, then, by considering how bread and wine are suitable symbols

of all that he has discovered the Eucharist to be in his q. 73 (life, life for humans made of body and soul, life in the community of the Church, life coming from the passion of Christ, life that reaches fulfillment in the eternal enjoyment of God). In q. 74 he explores this symbolism in the liturgical usages of bread and wine in the Church as he knew it. Then he moves on to the level of the *res et sacramentum*, studying the bread and wine as they are consecrated to be the body and blood of Christ. He takes up the patristic idea of the changing *(conversio)* of the bread and wine to become the body and blood of Christ: in q. 75 he explains how the reality of Christ's body and blood in the Eucharist is brought about by this change; in q. 76 he examines the kind of presence that the change gives rise to; in q. 77 he considers what ontological status the bread and wine have after the change; and then in q. 78 he studies the words that, as sacramental "form," bring about and give meaning to the change. In the thirty articles he needs to deal with these questions, Thomas dutifully discusses the problems that medieval theology had been raising about the Eucharist since Amalarius, and the liturgical and devotional practices of his time that called for theological reflection.

Thomas's theology of what will come to be called "the real presence" (which is a term that Thomas does not use and will not come into general use until around the time of the Council of Trent[45]) is grounded on the faith of the Church (q. 75, a. 1). The magisterial authority he appeals to is the profession of faith required of Berengarius. He does not cite the Fourth Lateran Council, nor does he use the word "transubstantiation" to state the basic faith of the Church. He works toward it as a suitable theological term for explaining the kind of change in bread and wine that makes them be the body and blood of Christ. He argues that, to maintain the faith of the Church, one must hold that the substance of bread does not remain after the consecration, and that it is, in fact, changed into the substance of Christ's body (q. 75, a. 2). The tradition of faith was not decisive about whether or not the bread remained bread after the consecration, and earlier medieval theologians had disagreed on the question. But Thomas now puts the question not just about bread but about the

---

45. L. G. Walsh, op, "The Presence of the Mystery of Christ in the Broken Bread" in J. McEvoy and M. Hogan, ssc, eds., *The Mystery of Faith. Reflections on the Encyclical Ecclesia de Eucharistia* (Dublin: Columba Press, 2005), 140–160.

*substance of bread*, and he is giving the word "substance" a precise technical sense. Put this way the question requires a more definite answer.
The word substance had been used for some centuries in the theology
of the Eucharist to refer to the fundamental, stable, distinctive reality
that was present in the sacrament. Taking it in that sense one could
make a good, but not overwhelming, theological case for saying that
the substance of bread did not remain in the Eucharist after the consecration: a thing cannot be two different realities at the same time; if it
becomes the reality of the body of Christ it surely ceases to be the reality of bread. However, with his particular understanding of the terms
of the question, Thomas comes up with a much more decisive argument, and goes so far as to say that it would be heretical to say that the
substance of bread remains (q. 75, a. 2). The reason for his dogmatism
is that he is taking "substance" in a precise metaphysical sense, which
he has worked out philosophically under the influence of Aristotle.
In Aristotelianism a substance is that which exists independently of
anything else. The substantial components of a reality are those that
give it independent existence as a particular kind of reality. It may have
other components that can come and go without changing its substantial nature. These are called its accidents. Of special importance for the
theology of the Eucharist is that, epistemologically, substance and substantial components can only be perceived by intelligence and affirmed
by the judgments of intelligence; they cannot be the immediate objects
of sensation. What a thing is (its substance), as distinct from what
it appears to be, can only be reached by mind. Putting the question
about bread as a question about its substance, understood in this sense,
Thomas can see no possible way that the consecrated bread could truly
be judged to be the body of Christ if the substance of bread continued
to be present. If the independent existent that one is talking about is
bread it cannot at the same time and on the same level be the body
of Christ. It is not as if Thomas wants to get rid of the bread to make
way for the presence of Christ. He rejects the hypothesis of some kind
of local movement that would bring Christ down from heaven into
the bread, as being as contrary to the faith of the Church as a purely
symbolic theory of presence would be. He refuses the hypothesis that
the bread is annihilated. What he wants to show, in fact, is that it is
precisely in allowing itself to be changed on the level of substance that
the bread makes it possible for the body of Christ to be really there in

the sacrament of the Eucharist, and likewise with the wine. This is the positive theological worth that he sees in the idea of transubstantiation. The bread and wine lend their symbolism to make the Eucharist a sacrament; they also lend their reality to being changed so that the Eucharist can be the reality of the body and blood of Christ.

At the risk of trivializing what is a profoundly metaphysical discussion one may offer the following hints toward a theological reading of Thomas' teaching on transubstantiation. Christ is an independent existent, and therefore a substance. This substance is personal, because Christ is an existent endowed with mind and freedom (Thomas would define "person" as "a substance of the thinking sort"—*rationalis naturae individua substantia*). Christ is now present in his total personal reality, with all the attributes of his being, at the right hand of his Father. If he is to be really present in the sacrament of the Eucharist, as Christian faith confesses, it must be this independent existent who is present; not, however, with the visibility and tangibility of his risen body, but in a sign of bread and wine. Bread and wine are independent existents—substances. The theory of transubstantiation invites one to think that they are changed on the level of what gives them independent existence into Christ on the level of what gives him independent existence. This allows one to understand how he, not they, is present where they had been before their consecration to be his body and blood. The "being there" of them, their substance, is now the "being there" of him, his substance. God, because he acts on created reality at the most profound level on which things are, can bring about such a change. The divine power, acting through the Word and the Spirit in the eucharistic liturgy, changes the substance of bread into the substance of Christ's body, and the wine into the substance of his blood.

The change being postulated in the doctrine of transubstantiation is not the making of one thing out of another: obviously the body of Christ is not being made out of the bread, and in any case the body that is made present in the Eucharist is the body of Christ that already exists. What is claimed to happen is that the existent that was once substantially bread is made to be substantially the body of Christ. There is not a common subject of change that is carried over from one substance to the other. It is not the kind of change that occurs when one material substance has its substantial form changed and becomes something else of the material kind: the change that is postulated by transubstantiation is a change of the total substance of bread, not just of its substantial form. But there is continuity or succession in existence between the substance of bread and wine and the substance of Christ that justifies speaking of a passing (*trans-*) from one substance to another. There is always something there, which once is bread and then is body. That the bread and wine continue to look and taste like bread and wine is coherent with the explanation that it is only their substance that is changed so that Christ can be there in his substance. The accidents of bread and wine remain to give sacramental access to Christ. They also give a certain continuity in the process of change from one substance to another. The change being postulated has to be the work of God, which is what one must expect in a mystery such as the Eucharist is. Only God can operate change in the total substance of something; creatures always require a subject, or matter, to work on when they change things. In the Eucharist God changes the entire substance of the bread, making the ongoing act of existence that substantiated itself in bread become the act of existence that substantiates itself in the body of Christ. This is the change that is called *trans-substantiatio*.

Thomas has to explain that in the Eucharist the appearances *(accidentia)* of bread and wine remain in existence by divine power, unchanged in themselves but no longer being given existence by their proper substance. Because of the change, and because it has been done for the sake of making a sacrament, these appearances become the symbols of, and at the same time the point of presence and contact with, the independent existent who is Christ. Christ is not in any way changed in such a transition. He becomes, on the level of his substance, the term of a change worked in the bread and wine, as a result of which their accidents are now related to him and consequently he to them (in q. 76, a. 6 and ad 3 Thomas says he has a *habitudo* to them). Anything related to these accident/symbols is therefore related to Christ. Specifically, anyone who eats and drinks what they now contain is related to the substance of Christ, i.e., to Christ as person. When that eating is a personal act, done in faith by people endowed with mind and freedom, it gives them personal contact with Christ, as really as if they were seeing and touching him. Yet Christ is not touched, nor seen, nor moved around; he is present in the fullness of his personal being, but in the way that substance is present (*per modum substantiae* is Thomas' expression), since it was his substance that was the term of the change in the substance of bread and wine. Christ is only one substance, but the humanity in which he subsists has component parts, like body and soul and blood, which can be distinguished. In the interests of sacramentality *(vi sacramenti)* the substance of bread has been changed into the substance of his body, that of wine into the substance of his blood. This makes it possible for the appearances of bread to symbolize his bodiliness, in which he worked human salvation and gave himself in love to the Father and to his brothers and sisters. The appearances of wine symbolize his life's blood, which he gave for the sacrificial ratification of the new covenant. But as body and blood are now substantially one in the living divine person of Christ, wherever the body is there also *(vi concomitantiae)* is the blood and everything else that belongs to the personal reality of Christ; likewise with the blood. The division of bread and wine into parts for eating and drinking by many does not divide anything of Christ. Since each divided part is still the same substance as what was divided it is the substance of Christ, i.e., his full personal reality.

Thomas seems to think that transubstantiation is the only good explanation of the Church's faith that the Eucharist really is the body and blood of Christ. It meets the needs of realism and of sacramentalism. It protects against crass and fanciful ways of understanding how Christ is in the Eucharist (q. 76, aa. 5–8; q. 77, aa. 3–8). It respects the mysteriousness of the eucharistic presence and its accessibility to faith alone because it sees it as brought about by an action of God that works through the sacramental words of Christ, and that can only be affirmed on the authority of those same words. The sacramental presence of Christ is, in fact, brought about by the "form" of the Eucharist, which is Christ's own words spoken in his person by the ordained minister; it gets its significance from those same words. Thomas' discussion on the form of the Eucharist in q. 78 completes his doctrine of transubstantiation and confirms that his thinking about the presence of Christ in the Eucharist is, for all its realism, entirely sacramental.

Thomas follows up his discussion on the consecration of the bread and wine with a question on the effects of the Eucharist (q. 79). It is the standard movement of sacramental theology from the *sacramentum*, through the *res et sacramentum*, to *the res tantum*. However, there is a complication in the case of the Eucharist. Thomas had noted it in q. 78, a. 1: other sacraments exist only when they are in actual use; the Eucharist already exists *(perficitur)* before it is used (i.e., before the individual Christian receives it by eating and drinking). The sacrament of the Eucharist exists once the bread and wine have been consecrated to be the body and blood of Christ. One may be tempted to find here a theological justification for that separation of Mass from Holy Communion that so blighted the eucharistic life of the Church during the later Middle Ages. If one says that the Eucharist is complete once the consecration has taken place, one can be giving the impression that sacramental communion is something of an appendix to the celebration of the Eucharist as Mass. It is a historical fact that the kind of analysis that Thomas is doing here (and it was done by other medieval theologians as well) was used at times to justify such a separation of Mass and Communion. But this was hardly the intention of Thomas' theology. He continues to assume that, in the Eucharist, the *usus sacramenti*, and therefore the distinctive purpose for which it is designed and celebrated, consists in the eating and drinking of the body and blood of Christ by the faithful (q. 74, 3; q. 80).

What Thomas is accounting for in making the distinction between the *perfectio* of the Eucharist in the consecration of the matter and its *usus* in communion is, in fact, something that lies deeper in the tradition of faith than the peculiarities of medieval practice. It is a sense that the celebration of the Eucharist responds to the reality of the Church itself, rather than simply to the demands of individual Christians for communion. While late medieval Catholicism multiplied Masses without much reference to a celebrating, receiving community, and Protestantism, in reaction, directed the celebration of the Eucharist immediately toward the needs of actual communicants, the main Christian tradition surely is that wherever there is a church (i.e., an ecclesial community) the Eucharist is celebrated regularly, especially on the Lord's Day. It is celebrated even if all the members do not assemble or if some of those who do so may not, for one reason or another, receive communion. The Eucharist is celebrated for the benefit of the Church: the ecclesial reality that is expressed in it and affected by it is wider than those who actually receive communion. Sacramentally, that ecclesial reality is ensured by the presence of at least some members of the community, some if not all of whom communicate; and by the ministry of an ordained priest who always communicates. But it is ensured above all by the fact that, when such a community celebrates and consecrates the Eucharist, Christ is present in the consecrated bread and wine as head of the Church and as its priest. He continues to be present in the bread that is reserved by the Church for the benefit of its members who are ill or absent for some other reason, and who may want to receive the Eucharist later. This presence of Christ, sacramentalized in these different ways by the presence and action of the Church, is the sacrament of the Eucharist. The reality of the Eucharist, then, does not depend, as Thomas notes, on the use of the Eucharist by the faithful, in the way that, for example, the reality of baptism depends on there being someone to be baptized. By the consecration of the Eucharist Christ is present and acting and available as the giver of the specific grace of building-up the Church as his body. The people who take part in the Eucharist are already the body of Christ through baptism. They are this, and can become it more fully in the Eucharist, even if not all of them actually receive the body of Christ sacramentally. Many other people who are not even present at the Eucharist are remembered there, as belonging to the body of Christ. There is an ecclesial reality in the Eucharist, therefore, that is not coextensive with those who actually receive communion. This is the tradition that Thomas is allowing for when he says that the Eucharist is realized in the consecration of the matter rather than in its use by the faithful (q. 78, a. 1; q. 80, a. 12 ad 3). At the same time it is clear from his treatment of the effects and the *usus* (i.e., receiving) of the Eucharist that he is also fully aware of the central truth of the tradition, which is that the Eucharist is made for reception by the faithful; that the building-up of Christians in the body of Christ is done by eating his body and drinking his blood.

The effects of the Eucharist are presented by Thomas in q. 79 as grace, charity, and the taking-away of sin. His teaching organizes the great themes of the patristic tradition. In the course of it he works out a distinction between the Eucharist as sacrament and as sacrifice that builds upon what has already been noted in connection with *perfectio* and *usus* of the sacrament. It is an important distinction in eucharistic theology, but one that has sometimes been badly used. Thomas introduces it in q. 79, a. 5 to explain how the Eucharist

takes away the punishment due to sin. He says the sacrament of
the Eucharist is both sacrifice and sacrament. The distinction is not
between two different parts of the sacrament but between two different aspects *(ratio)* of it. One and the same Eucharist is a sacrifice
precisely as offered *(offertur)* and is a sacrament as consumed *(sumitur)*.
In the Eucharist, as in every sacrament there is a double movement,
from humans to God in worship, and from God to humans in sanctification (see Chapter 2, "The Scholastics and Saint Thomas Aquinas").
The word "sacrament" has, indeed, tended to be more associated with
the sanctification movement (the giving of grace) than with the worship movement. When, in the context of the effects of the Eucharist,
Thomas contrasts sacrifice with sacrament he is using "sacrament" in
this more restricted sense: he is setting it over against sacrifice, which
is the specific upward movement of worship proper to the Eucharist.
But the object that is being analyzed as both sacrifice and sacrament is,
in Thomas' own language, the sacrament of the Eucharist. In this sense
the sacrifice is an aspect of the sacrament. It is, in reality, the passion
of Christ, which is offered sacramentally in the Eucharist. Thomas
takes the distinction up again in q. 79, a. 7, where he asks whether the
Eucharist benefits others besides those who receive the sacrament.
His answer begins with the observation that the Eucharist is not only
a sacrament but is also a sacrifice. What he explains now is that it is a
sacrifice in so far as it represents the passion of Christ; it is a sacrament
in so far as grace is given in it through symbols. Thomas has already
explained that it is as a sacrament that the Eucharist represents the
passion of Christ (q. 73, a. 4). Therefore he cannot mean that sacrament and sacrifice are two separate things in the Eucharist: the whole
reality of the Eucharist is sacramental, including its sacrificial reality;
the sacrament, for its part, draws from the sacrifice, because all grace
comes from the passion of Christ.

In Thomas' view the sacrifice of Christ is sacramentalized in
the twofold consecration, which sacramentally separates Christ's body
and blood, thus representing his death (q. 80, a. 12 ad 3). It is sacramentalized, too, in that it is offered by the Church in the Eucharistic
Prayer, which makes Christ really present as victim. The prayer of
offering includes intercession for those for whom it is being offered.
Christ's body and blood were offered for everyone and everything on
the cross. They are offered in the Eucharist in that same general way,

but also for specific persons who are mentioned in the eucharistic prayer. Thomas quotes from the Roman Canon in q. 79, a. 7 to show that the first ones prayed for are those who receive the sacrament by eating the body of Christ and drinking his blood. Their grace is, therefore, the effect of the Eucharist as both sacrament and sacrifice. Others who are prayed for in the eucharistic prayer, but who do not communicate sacramentally, receive grace from that particular Eucharist as sacrifice but not as sacrament. Here Thomas is using the word "sacrament" in the restricted sense of something that sanctifies through being actually "used." In his general sacramental theory grace is said to come from a sacrament when it is given in the application of the matter and form of a sacrament to a particular individual. In this sense it is true to say that only those who eat of the bread and drink of the cup receive grace sacramentally. However, the terminology does carry the risk of setting up two independent ways in which the Eucharist gives grace. It would be so used later to justify multiplication of Masses without communicants and even without congregations. This could happen when the distinction was taken out of the context in which Thomas made it. He never suggests anything like an *usus* of the Eucharist purely as sacrifice. The Eucharist is a sacrifice within its sacramentality, nor independently of it. The sacrament has eventually to be received, if by nobody else than the priest. And those who receive grace from the Eucharist considered as sacrifice have at least a desire for eucharistic communion, as all must have in order to be saved (q. 73, a. 3; q. 79, a. 1 ad 1). No one receives grace from the Eucharist as sacrifice, no matter how much their welfare is intended and prayed for, without their having at least this desire for communion, and without actually receiving the reality of it when they can, on earth or in its consummation in heaven.

In q. 80 Thomas discusses reception *(usus vel sumptio)* of the Eucharist. He deals with the requirements for fruitful reception and with the obstacles to it, especially sinfulness; and he discusses how often and in what form one should communicate. While his theology is well grounded in the patristic tradition, it is marked by a certain apologia for new liturgical practices that were developing in the Middle Ages—for example, that of not giving the faithful communion from the chalice. It is the kind of judicious theological reasoning that tries to make the best of pastoral practice, even while recognizing that it is not always ideal (cf. q. 80, a. 12 regarding communion from the chalice). Even if this kind of theology was sometimes used to justify liturgical vagaries of the late Middle Ages it is principled enough in Thomas to have served to justify the cautious reforms of the Council of Trent, and most of it can sit quite comfortably with contemporary liturgical standards. A good example of its strengths and weaknesses is the distinction that Thomas draws between spiritual and sacramental eating of the Eucharist (q. 80, a. 1). To receive the sacrament in faith and love, and therefore to accept its grace, is to receive it spiritually; to receive the sacrament, but without its spiritual effects, is to receive it (merely) sacramentally. It is a distinction that can be traced back to the Fathers, especially to Augustine. But it is also possible to use the term spiritual for a desire for the Eucharist without actual sacramental eating, because that can also give the grace of the Eucharist. Thomas allows for this in q. 80, 1 ad 3. If that is what spiritual reception of the sacrament is taken to mean, spiritual can become an alternative to sacramental, rather than the perfection of sacramental. That makes it easier to justify Mass without sacramental communion: one can have the grace of the sacrament by a "spiritual communion." The distinction between spiritual and sacramental communion, made by Thomas for other reasons, came to be used in that sense during the late Middle Ages and subsequently.

The final questions devoted to the Eucharist in the *Summa* deal with the minister (q. 82) and the rite (q. 83). They are a systematic reflection on the liturgical practice and discipline of the Eucharist as Thomas knew it, in the light of the tradition of faith. He argues the need for a priest to consecrate the Eucharist from the dignity of the sacrament: the reality and the form of the Eucharist require that it be done *in persona Christi* (i.e., the words of consecration are Christ's own words and what is consecrated is his body and blood); to act *in persona Christi* in this way one must receive a special power from Christ, through ordination to priesthood; one must be put on the level of those to whom the Lord said at the Last Supper, "Do this in memory of me." Thomas does not, then, derive the priesthood of the consecrating minister from the sacrificial reality of the Eucharist, but from the need for someone to act *in persona Christi* in the sacrament. He correlates the power of the priest to consecrate the Eucharist with the power the baptized have to receive it. And he sees the distribution of communion as being integral to the power of the priest to act *in persona Christi* (q. 82, a. 3). Behind his thinking lies the tradition that there is a giving and taking in the Eucharist that has to be sacramentalized; there is a host at the meal and there are guests. Christ does the giving and that has to be sacramentalized in his priestly minister. Christ is the head of the body that he is nourishing in the Eucharist: acting in his person the minister is sacramentalizing his headship.

The sacramental giving in the Eucharist includes an act of sacrifice. This sacrificial movement of the Eucharist gets its clearest development in q. 83. There Thomas explains how Christ is immolated in the Eucharist (the sacrament ritually represents his passion and applies its fruits). The perspective is entirely sacramental. The sacrifice that is in the Eucharist is sacramental; and the sacrament is sacrificial. There is a giving to God *(oblatio)* and a receiving from God *(sumptio)*. The giving, or offering, is a sacrifice because it represents the sacrifice of Christ. What is received is the fruit of this sacrifice. The offering is done sacramentally in the eucharistic prayer. The prayer also sacramentalizes the receiving because those who will receive communion, and others who will benefit from the Eucharist, are interceded for in it. The sacramentality requires that at least the one who says the eucharistic prayer should eat and drink the consecrated bread and wine. It requires that those who are present, and on whose behalf he says the prayer, should be brought, as far as is possible, to sacramental and spiritual eating and drinking. It allows that those of the congregation who are impeded from receiving communion, and others not present who are prayed for, can receive the fruits of the Eucharist without sacramental eating, provided they are living in faith and charity and thus united to the body of Christ (q. 79, a. 7 ad 2), and, it may be added, are by that very fact desiring eucharistic communion (see q. 73, 3).

# Chapter 10

# Eucharist: The Word from the Reformers and Trent to Vatican II and Beyond

## THE REFORMERS AND THE COUNCIL OF TRENT

The main positions of medieval theology on the Eucharist were established by the early fourteenth century. They were carried on toward the controversies of the Reformation by commentaries on the *Sentences* of Peter Lombard, by the works of the masters like Thomas and Bonaventure and Scotus, and also by pastoral manuals and a more popular kind of theology. Such development as occurred in this later period of Scholastic theology was by way of logical analysis of texts of the earlier masters. In such a method, what was clear and commonplace got less attention than what was difficult and controversial. As a result, technical philosophico-theological issues were sometimes made to seem more theologically important than the great themes of the scriptural and patristic tradition that filled the eucharistic theology of a master like Thomas. Nominalism did a critique of this kind of theological speculation, but the alternative it offered was inspired by a new set of philosophical and logical principles more than by a recovery of the biblical and patristic tradition. Indeed, its logical radicalism uncontrolled by tradition produced some strange variants of Scholastic theories about the Eucharist. The Reformers seem to have often judged Scholastic theology by the nominalist form of it that was prominent in the fifteenth and early sixteenth centuries.[1]

---

1. See F. Clark, SJ, *Eucharistic Sacrifice and the Reformation*, 2nd ed. (Baltimore: Helicon Press, 1965), Ch. XIV.

Speculative developments in the theology of the Eucharist in the later Middle Ages were mainly on the question of the reality of Christ's presence in the sacrament and the explanation of it by transubstantiation. There was little theological speculation about the Eucharist as sacrifice. That was not a disputed issue. The biblical and patristic traditions about it, formulated in terms like those noted in Thomas, were routinely repeated. This may seem surprising when one considers the violence of the Protestant opposition to Catholic teaching on the Eucharist as sacrifice, but it can be documented from a study of Catholic theologians of the pre-Reformation period.[2] What is harder to document is the way Scholastic theology of the Eucharist, for all its rectitude, was being used popularly in relation to the abuses that there undoubtedly were in Catholic eucharistic practice during the century before the Reformation.[3] At its best this theology could have kept liturgical practice on secure lines. At its worst, in the minds of people for whom distinctions easily justified separations, and possibilities thought about readily became permissions presumed, Scholastic theology could go hand in hand with decadent liturgical practice. There seems good reason to believe that the Reformers judged the theory to be saying what the practice was doing. Thus the Catholic theory of the Eucharist as sacrament and sacrifice was, for all its good intentions, judged to mean that there was nothing wrong with separating the Mass from communion, with multiplying Masses celebrated for private intentions without communicants or congregation, and with promising extravagant fruits from such Masses without much reference to the way the people for whom the offering was made participated sacramentally and spiritually in the Eucharist. The preponderant and possessive role that ordained priests had in Catholic practice of the Eucharist was thought to be underpinned by the theological theory. The Catholic theory of transubstantiation was judged in relation to abuses by the way priests employed the power they alone had to consecrate the

---

2. Clark, *Eucharistic Sacrifice*, Ch. V; M. Lepin, *L'Idée du Sacrifice de la Messe d'après les théologiens depuis l'origine jusqu'à nos jour* (Paris: Beauchesne, 1957), 213–240.

3. J. A. Jungmann, sj, *The Mass of the Roman Rite: its origins and development. (Missarum Sollemnia)*, new revised and abridged ed. of *Missarum Sollemnia*, published in 2 vols., in 1949 (New York: Benziger Bros., 1959), 96–101; Clark, *Eucharistic Sacrifice*, Ch. IV; D. N. Power, omi, *The Sacrifice We Offer: The Tridentine Dogma and Its Reinterpretation* (Edinburgh: T. & T. Clark, 1987), Ch. 2.

Eucharist, and by forms of devotion to the reserved sacrament. The doctrine of sacrifice was judged by the way priests used the power it gave them to produce and distribute fruits of the Eucharist and to be rewarded economically for so doing. The Reformers were prophets of the renewal of eucharistic celebration before they were theologians of the Eucharist.

## The Reformers

The teaching of the Reformers on the Eucharist fits into their general theology of the justifying grace of God and its acceptance by faith, and of the way this is realized in sacraments. Their general sacramental doctrine, and particularly the prominence they gave to word in relation to rite, has been discussed already (see Chapter 2, "Reformation and the Council of Trent"). Here attention is drawn to the more specific issues they raised about the Eucharist. Because it is a sacrament of the Lord, attested in scripture, they were much more positive about the Eucharist than they were about other rites of the Church that were claimed to be sacraments but did not have a clear biblical warrant. The biblical texts that were at the center of its celebration made it already a proclamation of God's word. Some of the eucharistic theology of the Reformers was a recovery of elements of the biblical tradition of faith about the Lord's Supper that were not very operative during the later Middle Ages. More of it, however, was reformist and polemical, concerned with eradicating Roman "superstitions" and "idolatries." The doctrine of sacrifice, with all the practices that seemed to depend on it, was the primary target. The doctrine of transubstantiation, as an explanation of the presence of Christ in the Eucharist, was the second major target. The liturgical form and manner of celebrating the rite—the Roman Canon, gestures of adoration made to the consecrated bread, neglect of the proclamation of God's word, the refusal of the chalice to the laity, Masses said without congregations and merely because a stipend had been offered for some private intention—were a third target, since they reflected a sacrificial understanding of the Eucharist and a doctrine of transubstantiation. While the critique was made on the authority of Scripture, it inevitably produced new theological positions that were offered as alternatives to the Scholastic doctrines, and new liturgical forms.

John Wycliffe (d. 1384) had already rejected the doctrine of transubstantiation a century and a half before the Reformation. He had philosophical as well as theological difficulties with it, and he blamed it for fostering a worship of the consecrated host that he considered idolatrous. Drawing on Augustine, he thought that one should understand the presence of Christ in the Eucharist as being spiritual and in a sign, and that the substance of bread remained in it along with the substance of Christ (*consubstantiatio* rather than *transubstantiatio*). The theology of Wycliffe was summarily condemned at the Council of Constance in 1415 (DS 1151–1153).[4] Transubstantiation was already being taken as a touchstone of eucharistic orthodoxy. However, it is worth noting that in the Papal *Bulla* of 1418, in which Martin V carried forward the work of the council against the followers of Wycliffe and Jan Hus, he does not use the term *transubstantiatio* in formulating the questions that were to test their orthodoxy about the Eucharist (ND 1507).

The historical leaders of the Reformation (notably Luther, Zwingli, Calvin, Cranmer) gave particular attention to the theology and to the rite of the Eucharist. They wished to restore in the Church a scriptural understanding and practice of the Eucharist as the Lord's Supper. They read what the scriptures had to say about the Lord's Supper in the light of what they understood it to say about justification by faith. Ultimately, it was their doctrine of justification, and their understanding of the role of sacraments in it, that required them to deny that the Eucharist is a sacrifice, in the sense they understood Catholic theology to be saying it was. The *ex opere operato* effectiveness (see Chapter 2, "Reformation and the Council of Trent") that was being claimed for the Mass seemed to them to set it up as a "work" which had some independent value for justification. They were particularly opposed to the idea that the Eucharist had any of the propitiatory value that they thought sacrifice must have. They had a deeply felt sense of human sinfulness and of faith in the redeeming value of the cross of Christ as being the only way of forgiveness. Anything that seemed to claim that the forgiveness of sin could be gained for oneself or others by a human work (i.e., a sacrifice) was an intolerable denial

---

4. N. P. Tanner, SJ, ed., *Decrees of the Ecumenical Councils*, I (London and Washington: Sheed & Ward and Georgetown University Press, 1990), 41–416.

of the all-sufficiency of the cross. In the theological development of this position of the Reformers, Melanchthon had an important role. He argued that, since the Eucharist could not be propitiatory (only the cross was) it could not possibly be a sacrifice, because sacrifice in the strict sense is propitiatory and requires *immolatio* or the shedding of blood.[5] His argument set a challenge that Catholic theologians took seriously, both at the Council of Trent and in subsequent eucharistic theology.

What the Reformers contested, then, was something deeper than any eccentricities there may have been in late medieval theology about the Eucharist as sacrifice.[6] They wanted to affirm beyond any doubt that the Eucharist is a gift of God, not a work of man (in Luther's words a *beneficium* rather than a *sacrificium*).[7] The salvific movement it sacramentalizes is entirely from God to humans. It has some God-ward movement, in the sense that it has elements of praise and thanksgiving in it, and so can be metaphorically called a "sacrifice of praise." But the real business of the sacrament is the giving of the grace of God, in the face of which humans have nothing to offer but acceptance of justification in faith and repentance. What the rite does is to proclaim and pledge that this grace is being given, for the forgiveness of sin, in the bread and wine that Christ gave as his body and blood at the Last Supper. The Eucharist is a *testament*, or promise of what believers will inherit from the death of Christ. The words of institution that are the center of the rite are a gospel proclamation that Christ died for sinners. The bread and wine are the sign or pledge of the promise of salvation proclaimed in the words. Given as body and blood of Christ, they call forth faith from those who eat and drink and in that faith their sins are forgiven. There is no room for offering by humans in this view of the Lord's Supper. All words suggesting it must be eliminated from the prayer said over the bread and wine. It was for this reason that the Roman Canon, which has so much about the oblation being made by the Church, was so scornfully rejected by the Reformers. And with the rejection of a sacrificial canon went the

---

5. Lepin, *L'Idée du Sacrifice*, 245–248.

6. Clark, *Eucharistic Sacrifice*, Ch. V, VI.

7. See B. Thompson, *Liturgies of the Western Church* (Cleveland/New York, 1962; Philadelphia: Fortress Press, 1980), 100.

rejection of any special priesthood for the one who said the canon. Ministers of the Eucharist did not make a sacrifice. They proclaimed God's word of promise, which was confirmed by the body and blood of Christ that they distributed to those who believed. In this view, a silent canon, or a canon said without a congregation, made no sense. The Reformers did affirm strongly that the Supper is a memorial of the sacrifice of Christ. But it is a remembering of the sacrifice of Christ, not as something that is being offered but as something from which the fruits of salvation are now being drawn.[8]

The three principal leaders of the Reformation wanted to maintain the truth of the Lord's words that the bread and wine given in communion are his body and blood. They differed about the sense in which they were true. For Zwingli they meant that Christ was present in his body and blood to those who received the saving proclamation of his passion by faith: the bread and wine strengthened the proclamation and helped faith, because as used in the Lord's Supper they are signs of his body and blood. In this view there is no question of bread and wine being changed into Christ's body and blood: to say so would be to materialize Christ in the Eucharist, whereas what faith and philosophy call for is a spiritual, life-giving presence; transubstantiation is unthinkable. Luther had more realism in his understanding of how bread and wine are the body and blood of Christ. He argued rather vehemently against Zwingli on the subject. However, he rejected transubstantiation as an explanation of how the presence came about. He blamed Aquinas, schooled in the rationalism of Aristotle rather than in the faith of the scriptures, for introducing it. He would have seen, too, how closely the theory was bound up with the doctrine that the Eucharist is a sacrifice. It concentrated attention on the act of consecration by which, according to medieval theology, the priest, and he alone, brought the sacrifice into existence. Transubstantiation was also, of course, the principal theological reason given for worship of the reserved sacrament. Luther provided an alternative theology of the presence, using an analogy with the incarnation, something that many of the Fathers had done. He took up a

---

8. Texts of the Reformers on the Eucharist as sacrifice in P. Palmer, sj, *Sacraments and Worship: Liturgy and Doctrinal Development of Baptism, Confirmation, and the Eucharist* (London: Longmans, Green and Co., 1957), 293–304; Lepin, *L'Idée du Sacrifice,* 241–252.

form of the theory that had already appeared in the Middle Ages and goes by the name of "impanation." As the Word took flesh to himself in the in-carn(=flesh)-ation, so in the Eucharist Christ, through his words, takes bread to himself in an im-pan(=bread)-ation. The bread, in Luther's view, remains bread, while becoming the body of Christ; the two substances coexist; instead of *transubstantiatio* there is what was called *consubstantiatio*. He also speculates that Christ can be present in many Eucharists at one and the same time because of his divine ubiquity, which is communicated to his body in the incarnation. Luther did not accept Zwingli's idea that consecrated bread and wine that is not consumed in the Eucharist simply reverts to being ordinary bread and wine. Reservation of the sacrament was, indeed, rejected by Lutheranism, as it was by Calvinism; but the care taken in both traditions to consecrate only as much bread and wine as was needed, and to consume any that remained, was a way of avoiding the extreme position of Zwingli about the duration of the presence.

Calvin's teaching about the presence of Christ in the Eucharist draws from both Zwingli and Luther, while being critical of both. He criticizes Zwingli for not giving sufficient force to the presence, by treating the bread and wine merely as symbols. He criticizes Luther for being still too close to what he thought was the crude realism taught by the proponents of transubstantiation. Calvin's own contribution to the theology of the presence was to see it as the power *(virtus)* of the heavenly Christ being made active in the bread and wine that are received in the eucharistic celebration. This power is the real substance of the sacrament. It is not something exercised from afar but constitutes a real, mysterious presence of Christ in the bread and wine. He even writes in his *Short Treatise on the Lord's Supper*: ". . . the internal substance of the sacrament is joined with the visible signs . . . we have good reason to be satisfied when we realize that Jesus Christ gives us in the Supper the real substance of his body and his blood, so that we may possess him fully, and, possessing him, have part in all his blessings."[9]

It was Calvin's teaching more than that of Luther that influenced the Protestant current in the Anglican Reformation. It is in

---

9. J. Calvin, *A Short Treatise on the Lord's Supper*, trans. from French by J.K.S. Reid, Library of Christian Classics XXII (Philadelphia, 1954), 148.

the thinking of Cranmer, in the liturgy of the Lord's Supper that he designed and in the Articles of Religion that deal with the Eucharist.[10]

## The Council of Trent

The doctrinal and disciplinary decrees of the Council of Trent on the Eucharist are the reaction of Catholic orthodoxy to the theology and ritual practice of the Reformers. Catholic doctrine is presented in a way that will protect the faith of the Church from what are considered to be untraditional and divisive doctrines. The dogmatic canons attached to the decrees are direct condemnations of what are judged to be the heresies of the Reformers. Theologians had prepared summaries of the doctrine of the Reformers, documented by extracts from their works, for use by the Council Fathers. These had an important influence on the agenda of the council, and on its decrees and condemnations. The council considered the Eucharist in two phases. During the first, which lasted from 1547 to 1551, it dealt with errors concerning the real presence. The outcome of this work was the approval, in Session XIII (October 1551), of the *Decretum de ss. Eucharistia*; and the *Canones de ss. Eucharistiae sacramento* (DS 1635–1661; ND 1512–1536).[11] Work began immediately afterward on the question of the Eucharist as sacrifice, but the council was interrupted in 1552 and did not reassemble again until 1562. What amounted to a new beginning was made on the Eucharist. The results were a document, approved in Session XXI, on communion under both kinds and communion by children and, in Session XXII (September 1552), the *Doctrina de ss. Missae sacrificio*, with accompanying canons (DS 1725–1762; ND 1537–1563).[12] The separation of sacrament and sacrifice, in treatment and in time, reflects the way the issues were seen at the Reformation: the Mass as sacrifice was one issue; the real presence understood as brought about by transubstantiation was another. The separate dogmatic treatment had the effect of giving a

---

10. Texts of the Reformers on eucharistic presence in Palmer, *Sacraments and Worship*, 240–250; liturgical texts with introduction in B. Thompson, *Liturgies of the Western Church*; also in R. C. D. Jasper and G. J. Cuming, *Prayers of the Eucharist: Early and Reformed*, 3rd ed. (London: SCM Press, 1966), Part II, 177ff; analysis in Y. Brilioth, *Eucharistic Faith and Practice, Evangelical and Catholic*, trans. from Swedish (London: SPCK, 1930, 1965).

11. Tanner, *Decrees*, II, 693–698.

12. Tanner, *Decrees*. II, 726–741.

methodological and even a kind of dogmatic justification for a separation of the two issues in Catholic theology.

The doctrine on the Eucharist as sacrament is about the
reality of the sacramental presence, about the worship due to the
sacrament, and about its reception. It is presented in a rich setting
of scriptural texts. The texts are interpreted in a sense and with a
language that was considered to be justified by the tradition of the
Church and necessary for the unambiguous affirmation of the faith
at that point in time. Using the language of medieval sacramental
theology, Chapter 1 states that in the Eucharist after the consecration Christ is "truly, really and substantially . . . contained" under the
appearance *(species)* of bread and wine. There is no contradiction,
it is explained, between the natural way of existing that Christ has
at the right hand of his Father and his being present sacramentally
*(sacramentaliter)* by his substance to us *(nobis)* in many other places.
Sacramentality qualifies the mode of the eucharistic presence in a
way that does not call its reality into question. The special quality of
Christ's presence in the sacrament of the Eucharist "as distinct from
the other sacraments" is indicated by saying he is present there "in his
substance." This doctrine is said to be the plain meaning of the scriptural texts about the institution of the Eucharist, and the way they
have traditionally been understood in the Church. Chapter 2 presents
the reasons why Christ gave this sacrament to the Church: they are
the commonly accepted values and effects of the Eucharist, including
that of being a memorial of the death of Christ, but without any use of
the term sacrifice. Chapter 3 explains that the Eucharist surpasses the
other sacraments in that the author of holiness exists in it before it is
used *(ante usum)*, whereas the others only become sanctifying when in
actual use. What is present in the Eucharist is the entire Christ, now
risen, uniting in himself body, blood, soul, and divinity. He is present
under the appearance of bread and wine in the consecrated host and
chalice and in every portion of them when they are divided. A distinction worked out by medieval theology is used to explain why, nevertheless, it is his body that is present under the appearance of bread
and his blood under that of wine. His body is present in the bread "by
virtue of the words" *(vi verborum)*, while his whole person is present
"in virtue of the natural connection and concomitance *(vi . . . concomitantiae)* by which the parts of Christ the Lord, who has already risen

from the dead to die no more (cf. Romans 6:9), are united together."
(This distinction is important for a sacramental understanding of how
the Eucharist is a sacrifice, but Trent makes no reference to the sacrifice at this point.)

Chapter 4 introduces transubstantiation, saying: ". . . this holy
Council now again declares that, by the consecration of the bread and
wine there takes place a change of the whole substance of bread into
the substance of the body of Christ our Lord and of the whole substance of wine into the substance of His blood. This change the holy
Catholic Church has fittingly and properly named transubstantiation"
(see the corresponding canon 2). The concept of change *(conversio)*
that Trent is using is well attested in patristic teaching about the
Eucharist, whereas its description of the change as being of "the whole
substance of bread into the substance of the body of Christ. . . ." comes
from medieval Latin theology. One is entitled to think that Trent was
assuming that the medieval teaching is in faithful continuity with the
patristic teaching. It wanted to say what the Fathers said. It wanted
to say it clearly and unambiguously, in the language of its own time.
Like their medieval masters, the Council Fathers of Trent knew of no
way in which the issue of the full reality of Christ's presence in the
Eucharist could be stated other than in terms of substance. The only
kind of change they knew that would bring about the real, sacramental
presence that they had defined in Chapter 1 was a conversion of substance to substance. That is how they explained the change that occurs
in the Eucharist, and they added that such a change was appropriately
called "transubstantiation" by the Catholic Church. Transubstantiation
is, then, (a) a term that is approved, for (b) an explanation that is
required, for (c) maintaining the truth of the real presence. The three
levels of definition are interconnected, but obviously the fundamental
truth of faith that is being defined is the reality of the presence.

The remaining chapters (5–8) of the Decree on the Sacrament
of the Eucharist deal with consequences of what has been defined in
the first four: worship and veneration of the sacrament, its reservation
and communion of the sick, and its reception *(usus)*. Oddly, it is in a
paragraph of Chapter 5 that defends solemn public processions of the
Blessed Sacrament that the idea of availing of the Eucharist to represent the triumph and victory of Christ's death is put forward. The two
ways of receiving the Eucharist distinguished by Thomas and others as

*sacramentaliter* and *spiritualiter* had by the time of the council become three, with the addition of a reception that was *tantum spiritualiter*. Trent approves this threefold distinction in its Chapter 8, understanding the *tantum spiritualiter* to refer to " . . . those who, receiving in desire *(voto)* the heavenly bread put before them, with a living faith 'working through love' (cf. Galatians 5:6), experience its fruit and benefit from it." Spiritual communion can thus be presented as an alternative to sacramental communion. The Decree, however, concludes with an exhortation to frequent sacramental communion, that is at the same time a moving plea for the restoration of unity among Christians in the Eucharist (DS 1649; ND 1524).[13]

Finally, Trent proceeds to "add a series of canons so that all, already knowing the Catholic doctrine, may also realize what are the heresies that they must beware of and avoid." The first two of these condemnatory *(anathema sit)* texts need to be quoted: "1. If anyone denies that in the sacrament of the most holy Eucharist the body and blood, together with the soul and divinity, of our Lord Jesus Christ and, therefore, the whole Christ is truly, really and substantially contained, but says that He is in it only as in a sign or figure or by His power, *anathema sit*. 2. If anyone says that in the holy sacrament of the Eucharist the substance of bread and wine remains together with the body and blood of our Lord Jesus Christ, and denies that wonderful and unique change of the whole substance of the bread into His body and of the whole substance of the wine into His blood while only the species of bread and wine remain, a change which the Catholic Church very fittingly calls transubstantiation, *anathema sit* (DS 1651/2; ND 1526/7).[14]

The Doctrine on the Sacrifice of the Mass is introduced in the Foreword as being about "the great mystery of the Eucharist . . . as true and unique sacrifice." Although the Eucharist is spoken of as "mystery" it is never called "sacrament" in this Decree. Indeed, it is called Eucharist only once more, when reception of communion is being dealt with in Chapter 6. Otherwise it is spoken of as "Mass," or "sacrifice," or "the sacrifice of the Mass." The question dealt with in Chapter 1 is, nevertheless, a typically sacramental one—that of institution. The

---

13. Tanner, *Decrees*, II, 697.
14. Tanner, *Decrees*, II, 697.

institution is established by an analysis of what Christ did at the Last
Supper (which is how the institution of the Eucharist as sacrament
had been established in the earlier Decree). The chapter begins with
a Christological statement about the priesthood of Christ, based on
Hebrews. This sets the perspective for the discussion: sacrifice is to be
seen as an act of priesthood. The action of Christ at the Last Supper
is analyzed in what is, in Latin, one long, elaborately constructed
sentence. The first clause presents a kind of Christological imperative
for what Christ did: the priesthood that he would exercise by offering himself once for all to the Father on the altar of the cross was not
to be extinguished by his death. It takes several clauses to get to what
he actually did to perpetuate his priesthood: he offered his body and
blood under the appearances *(sub speciebus)* of bread and wine to the
Father. The sacramental fullness of what he did is conveyed by saying that, as well as offering his body and blood, he gave them to his
apostles under the same signs *(sub earundem rerum symbolis)* to consume. He did this, by his own claim, as "a priest according to the order
of Melchisedech." The reason he did so was to leave to his beloved
spouse the Church a visible sacrifice, such as is required by human
nature. It is a visible sacrifice of a very particular kind because it is one
in which the bloody sacrifice that would be carried out once only on
the cross would be represented *(representaretur)*, its memory *(memoria)*
preserved until the end of time, and its saving power applied *(salutaris
virtus applicaretur)* for the forgiveness of the sins that we commit every
day. In offering his body and blood and giving them to his apostles to
consume, Christ is said to have established them as priests of the new
covenant. He commanded them, and their successors in the priesthood, to offer his body and blood, which he had given them under the
appearance of bread and wine, by telling them "Do this in memory of
me." This is how the Church would have its visible sacrifice, in which
the priesthood of Christ would be perpetuated, because what was to be
done by the apostles and their successors would represent and remember and apply the fruits of his once-for-all sacrifice of the cross.

   Although it does not use the word "sacrament," the text of
Trent is giving what can legitimately be called a sacramental explanation of how the Eucharist is a sacrifice.[15] The reality of it is Christ

---

15. Power, *The Sacrifice We Offer*, 130.

offering his body and blood to his Father; the symbolic representation, memorial, and application of it is done in bread and wine that have become the very body and blood of Christ that is being offered. The sacramental view is confirmed by the parallel that the text goes on to draw between the Eucharist and the Passover. Christ is said to have "instituted a new Pasch, namely Himself to be offered by the Church through her priests under visible signs *(sub signis visibilibus immolandum)* in order to celebrate the memory of His passage from this world to the Father when by the shedding of His blood he redeemed us . . . ." The sacramental tradition right back to the Fathers had not hesitated to see Jesus symbolically immolated in the Eucharist, because of the representative, memorial, and application relationship of the Eucharist to the Cross. This is what Trent is affirming here. If it says that those who do the offering on behalf of the Church are priests, their priesthood can only be some kind of sacramental participation in the unique priesthood of Christ, which is what the Eucharist is meant to perpetuate. The offering/immolation is done under visible signs, which is what general sacramental theory means by a sacrament. The chapter ends with another typically sacramental concern: the sacrifice has its own intrinsic value, "which cannot be defiled by any unworthiness or malice on the part of those who offer it." This is established by identifying the Eucharist, as the tradition had done since Justin Martyr, with the "clean oblation" promised by the prophet Malachi, and then by an argument from 1 Corinthians. One sees something of the dilemma created by the separation of sacrament and sacrifice in the way Paul's words are used. A clear argument is available in 1 Corinthians 11:23–29 for the "objective" reality of the Eucharist in relation to the death of Christ. But the accent there is on eating and drinking ("sacrament" in the Tridentine sense) rather than on offering (Trent's "sacrifice"). So instead 1 Corinthians 10:21 (about those who partake of the table of the Lord not partaking of the table of the devil) is used: its language is unmistakably cultic and sacrificial. Just to be sure that "table" would not be misunderstood in a Protestant sense, Trent qualifies its reference by adding: "By 'table' he understands 'altar' in both cases." Finally, the Eucharist is said to bring to fulfillment and perfection all the sacrifices of the Old Law, which is what a sacrament of the New Law is expected to do.

Chapter 2 of the Doctrine on the Sacrifice of the Mass takes up a critical issue between Catholics and Protestants: was the Eucharist not just a sacrifice but a propitiatory sacrifice? Propitiatory meant having value for the expiation and taking away of sin in oneself and in others. Many questions of theory and practice turned on the propitiatory value of the Eucharist. The doctrine of justification was involved: to say the offering of the Mass was propitiatory was to say that humans could do something that had meritorious and satisfactory value in the giving of grace and the forgiveness of sin. The practice of offering Mass, and having Mass offered for oneself and others, for the living and the dead, relied on it. The right of a priest to apply the fruits of the Mass to those from whom he had received a stipend depended on it. The issue of propitiation was being debated at the time of the Reformation with the help of two theological ideas: immolation and oblation. Oblation is the moral act of offering inherent in the very notion of sacrifice; immolation is the shedding of blood or other destruction of the victim in a sacrifice. The terms can be found in the Fathers, and they were used by medieval theologians in discussion about the Eucharist as sacrifice. They were not, however, given much technical definition in Scholastic theology before the Reformation. Paradoxically, it was the Protestants who forced Catholics to develop a theology of the Eucharist as sacrifice in terms of them. They were arguing from the scriptures that there was no propitiation for sin without the shedding of blood; the shedding of blood in sacrifice is immolation; hence there could be no propitiation where there was no immolation; since there is no immolation in the Mass it cannot be propitiatory; it cannot, therefore, be offered (oblation) as a sacrifice of propitiation. The Fathers of Trent had no ready-made Catholic theology of the Eucharist as sacrifice that would answer these arguments precisely in the terms set by the Reformers. There was nothing comparable to what the doctrine of transubstantiation had been able to provide for dealing with the question of real presence. One can see the theology of sacrifice being worked out in the debates of the council itself.[16] On some points (e.g., on whether there was an immolation of the body and blood of Christ at the Last Supper) the theological effort could not provide a sufficiently clear or convincing answer to be of any

---

16. Analysis of the debates in Lepin, *L'Idée du Sacrifice*, 297–326.

use for the formulation of conciliar teaching. The theological debate would continue long after the council. But meanwhile the council did find a way of stating the essential tenet of Catholic faith about the Eucharist being a propitiatory sacrifice, and the way it did so gave some direction to future Catholic theology.

The essential teaching of Chapter 2 is that "the divine sacrifice which is celebrated *(peragitur)* in the Mass . . . is truly propitiatory." It is so because "the same Christ who offered Himself once in a bloody manner (cf. Hebrews 9:14, 27) on the altar of the cross is contained and is offered *(immolatur)* in an unbloody manner." The one who is offered was immolated in a bloody manner *(cruente)* on the cross; he is immolated "in an unbloody manner" *(incruente)* in the Mass. It is taken as given that Christ's offering of himself on the cross is propitiatory; the Mass is propitiatory because it is that very offering that Christ made of himself on the Cross. The realism of the identification is ensured by the realism of Christ's presence in the Eucharist (he is "contained" and thus immolated). The sacramental quality of the real presence (i.e., that it occurs in the signs of bread and wine) is not, however, invoked to explain how the Mass realizes the identification. There was a lot of theological debate at the council about how what is done with the bread and wine constituted an immolation, about how such an immolation satisfied the definition of sacrifice, and about how it makes the sacrifice propitiatory. Melanchthon had criticized the Catholics for not defining clearly what they meant by sacrifice. The theologians at Trent tried to work out such a definition and to make immolation part of it.[17] They seemed to have been looking for a general definition that would be applicable both to the cross and to the Mass. They failed to agree on one. The Fathers of the council eventually decided that the challenge of Melanchthon should be answered in another way. Their text does not adopt any definition of sacrifice, or any theory about how what is done with the bread and wine constitutes an immolation. Rather, it proceeds descriptively, comparing the Mass with the cross, and showing that it has the elements that make the cross be a sacrifice: Christ himself is offered and immolated in it, and Christ himself is the one who offers. The sacrificial nature of the Mass is not established, then, from its verifying of any moral or cultic

---

17. Lepin, *L'Idée du Sacrifice*, 312.

definition of sacrifice, but simply from its identification with the sacrifice of the cross. The only difference stated between it and the cross is that the oblation/ immolation of Christ is done in an "unbloody manner." From the dogmatic point of view Trent is saying what essentially needed to be said at that time: the Mass is a real propitiatory sacrifice because it is really, though not realistically, the sacrifice of Christ on the cross. A theological question remains about how this "not realistically" can be put into more positive terms. In Chapter 1 the council related the Mass to the cross as its "representation, memorial, and application." Theology ought to be able to identify what there is in the Mass that makes it a representation, memorial, and application of the cross. Trent leaves the question to the theologians.

A propitiatory sacrifice has the effect of taking away sin and giving grace. Protestants charged that the Catholic teaching was giving the impression that the Mass itself forgave sin and conferred grace, and that it did so without faith and conversion on the part of those for whom it was offered. The text of Trent replies with an application of the Catholic doctrine of justification. It says that the propitiatory effects of the Mass are for those who "draw near to God with an upright heart and true faith, with fear and reverence, with sorrow and repentance." The assumption is that these dispositions are themselves the fruit of grace. Grace is given in the Eucharist on one ground only: that God is pleased by the offering since it is of the same victim and by the same priest as was the cross, only the manner of offering being different. Understood thus, as the application of the fruits of the sacrifice of the cross, the sacrifice of the Mass could not, says Trent, possibly detract from the all-sufficiency of the cross. It is, therefore, "rightly offered according to apostolic tradition, not only for the sins, punishments, satisfaction, and other necessities of the faithful who are alive, but also for those who have died in Christ but are not yet wholly purified."

Chapters 3–8 of the Doctrine on the Sacrifice of the Mass apply the doctrine of the first two chapters to issues that had been raised by the Reformers: Masses in honor of Saints (Chapter 3); the Roman Canon (Chapter 4); the ceremonial of Mass (Chapter 5); Masses at which only the celebrating priest communicated (Chapter 6); the mixing of water with the wine (Chapter 7); the use of vernacular languages (Chapter 8). Chapters 6 and 7 are quite sacramental, and there is an exhortation to the faithful to receive communion at every Mass, "so that they may derive more abundant fruits from this most holy sacrifice." Chapter 8 recognizes the need for instruction *(eruditio)* that is inherent in the Eucharist and "orders that pastors and all who have the care of souls must frequently, either by themselves or through others, explain during the celebration of Masses some of the readings of the Mass, and among other things give some instruction about the mystery of this most holy sacrifice, especially on Sundays and feast-days." It is a careful concession to something the Protestants were insisting on, but it is quite some distance from their theology of the Eucharist as proclamation. The use of the vernacular is not excluded as a matter of principle but is not considered expedient as a general practice. Each church was to maintain its own rite, including the traditional language of the rite. The council was cautious about liturgical innovations and defensive about Catholic practice. Even if some reforms had seemed desirable, the fact that they had been preempted by the Protestants on the basis of an unacceptable sacramental and Eucharistic theology discouraged the council from adopting them.

The final chapter on the Doctrine on the Mass formulates the condemnatory canons against Protestant errors. They state the doctrines and practices of the Church that Protestants were thought to be rejecting.

## From Trent to Vatican II

The two dogmatic texts of the Council of Trent, about the sacrament and the sacrifice, dominated Catholic systematic theology of the Eucharist during the centuries of what came to be called the Counter-Reformation. The broad tradition of faith about the Eucharist continued to be studied in the scriptures, in the Fathers and in the medieval masters. But the material was organized systematically around the questions of real presence and sacrifice. It became common to present two separate treatises: one on the Eucharist as sacrament, which dealt with the real presence, communion, reservation, and veneration of the Eucharist outside Mass; the other on the Eucharist as sacrifice, or on the sacrifice of the Mass. The agenda of these treatises was influenced very much by the agenda of the Council of Trent. The dogmatic material on which the various theses were constructed were the canons of the council. Apart from the profession of faith imposed on Berengarius and a few references to transubstantiation in some medieval councils they were the only dogmatic texts available about the Eucharist. The reason it was the canons rather than the doctrinal expositions of Trent that were given the status of dogma was methodological. It was held that when Trent condemned a proposition attributed to the Reformers it was dogmatically defining the opposite of the condemned proposition: what the heretics were condemned for denying was what Catholics were bound to believe. It would not have been claimed that the dogmas of Trent so understood exhausted Catholic teaching on the Eucharist. But when Catholic theology was conceived as an exposition of the dogmas of the Church it was difficult to justify giving a major place to other questions about the Eucharist that did not have the credentials of dogmatic definition. The dogmas also determined the categories and language of Catholic theology. Since what Protestants had been denying were generally the positions of medieval Catholic theology, their negative judgments were often formulated in Scholastic terms. The condemnation of their views by Trent was necessarily formulated in the same terms. When the canons were turned around to become dogmatic definitions their language was also canonized for dogmatic usage.

There were developments in Catholic theology of the Eucharist during the centuries after Trent. Some came from a better grounding of Catholic dogmatic positions on the tradition of faith through a more informed use of the scriptures and the Fathers. Others came from systematic analysis and philosophical refinements of key concepts. These speculative developments occurred regarding both the sacrament and the sacrifice. The metaphysical niceties of transubstantiation were studied thoroughly. The theology of the Eucharist as sacrifice was worked at even more intensely and the developments are noteworthy. Trent had defined the tradition of faith quite clearly but had left many open theological ends. Catholic faith in the Eucharist as propitiatory sacrifice was intellectually vulnerable until an appropriate theology was worked out. A definition of sacrifice was sought that would be verified in the Mass but in a way that allowed for its being the same sacrifice as the cross. Explanations had to be given of how the immolation of Christ on the cross was represented, remembered, and applied in the Mass, which would at the same time show the Mass to be a real sacrifice and not merely a representation or memorial. The relationship between Christ's offering and the offering made by the priest-minister, by the whole Church and by individual Christians, had to be unraveled. Proper distinctions had to be made between the fruits of the Mass that were available to different persons who offered the Mass or had the Mass offered for them. Reasons had to be given for these fruits being limited even though the cross from which they all flow in the Mass is infinite in value and efficacy. Because consideration of the Eucharist as sacrament usually belonged to a different theological treatise, questions about the Mass were rarely dealt with in the categories of sacrament. Use was made rather of the kind of theology of sacrifice that Scholastic masters like Thomas Aquinas had worked out in their analyses of the virtue of religion—something which, it is interesting to note, Thomas himself did hardly at all in his theology of the Eucharist.[18]

The Counter-Reformation model of eucharistic theology remained dominant among Catholics until the various movements that led up to the Second Vatican Council began to make their presence felt. From the end of the nineteenth century the renewal of general sacramental theology (see Chapter 2, "From Trent to Vatican II") was particularly at work in the theology of the Eucharist. The Mass began to be experienced in a different way under the influence of the liturgical movement. The tradition of faith about the Eucharist began to sound richer as the independent voices of biblical and patristic scholars came to be added to those of the neo-Scholastic theologians. While the renewal of eucharistic theology was a complex process, one of the key transforming factors must certainly have been the more profound understanding of the word sacrament and the sense given to it when applied to the Eucharist. The image of a key was, in fact, used by Dom Ansgar Vonier, osb in the title of a remarkable book about the Eucharist that he published in 1925.[19] The key he offers is the concept of sacramentality. Vonier took the concept from Saint Thomas. He

---

18. Lepin documents and analyses these developments in post-Tridentine authors in *L'Idée du Sacrifice*, 335–758; Clark deals with the way they are presented by more recent Catholic authors in *Eucharistic Sacrifice*, 249–268.

19. A. Vonier, osb, *A Key to the Doctrine of the Eucharist*, original edition 1925; revised edition in *The Collected Works of Abbott Vonier*, vol. II (London: Burns, Oates, 1952; Westminster, MD: Newman Press, 1992).

was, as the editor of his collected works notes, writing in the context of "a good deal of controversy on the relation of the Mass to Calvary."[20] The controversy was being carried on by Catholic theologians in mainly Scholastic terms, with frequent appeal to Saint Thomas. Vonier believed, says his editor, that "some of the protagonists, in spite of their elaborate display of scholarship had departed from the traditional concept of the Eucharist." He considered that concept to be "the essentially sacramental character of the Sacrifice of the Altar." Vonier demonstrates his thesis from the text of Thomas and finds confirmation of it in the teaching of Trent about the Eucharist as sacrifice. He sees sacramentality as the key not just to the question of sacrifice but also to the question of presence. It is a unifying idea that requires that the ideas of sacrament and sacrifice should interpenetrate rather than go their separate ways. Other authors besides Vonier had been giving sacramentality a richer sense when applied to the Eucharist. Billot has it in his theology of transubstantiation; De la Taille has something of it in *Mysterium Fidei* (1921) and *Esquisse du Mystère de la foi* (1925). However, both these authors maintain the standard Counter-Reformation division of the treatment of the Eucharist into sacrifice and sacrament. The methodological distinction can probably never disappear entirely from the Catholic way of doing the theology of the Eucharist, but the separation of the two ideas can be overcome.[21] The studies of Odo Casel and his school posed questions for systematic theology about the relationship between mystery/sacrament and cult/sacrifice, and about the presence in mystery of the Passover sacrifice of Christ, which required the drawing together of sacrament and sacrifice in the theology of the Eucharist.[22]

The controversies and schisms of the Reformation set up independent traditions of Eucharistic theology in Lutheran, Calvinist and Anglican churches. They continued to reflect the battles of the Reformation for almost as long as Catholic theology did. Without the firm dogmatic framework that Catholics accepted from the

---

20. *The Collected Works*, 226.

21. See for example E. Masure, *The Christian Sacrifice*, trans. from French (London: Burns, Oates & Washbourne, 1944), and *The Sacrifice of the Mystical Body*, trans. from French (London: Burns, Oates & Washbourne, 1954).

22. See T. Filthaut, *La théologie des mystères. Exposé de la controverse* (Paris and Tournai: Desclée, 1954).

decrees of Trent, theologians of these other traditions often felt freer to explore approaches to the Eucharist that might go beyond their own confessional statements. They were, of course, also vulnerable to reductionist tendencies when historical and psychological studies on the Eucharist from the standpoint of comparative religion became common in the nineteenth century. But from the beginning of the twentieth century one begins to get important biblical and patristic theologies of the Eucharist from all the churches, which contribute to a recovery of the full tradition of faith and to the possibility of a theology that might approach the controversies of the Reformation in a new and reconciling way. Significant works of this kind from the Anglican tradition are C. Gore, *The Body of Christ* (1901) and E. L. Mascall, *Corpus Christi* (1953). From Lutherans came the important work of the Swedish scholar Y. Brilioth, *Eucharistic Faith and Practice. Evangelical and Catholic* (1926; English edition 1930). An influential study from the Reform traditions was that of O. Cullmann, "The Meaning of the Lord's Supper in Primitive Christianity" (1936); this was published in English in 1958, along with F. J. Leenhardt, "This Is My Body," under the title *Essays on the Lord's Supper*. Cullman's essay was a critique of another study from the Protestant side that had raised troublesome theological issues about the Eucharist: H. Lietzmann, *Messe und Herrenmahl* (1926; English trans. 1953). Leitzman's studies of the early liturgies of the Eucharist led him to the hypothesis that Saint Paul's teaching on the Lord's Supper, which relates the fraternal meal of Christians to the death of Christ by interpreting it in the light of the Last Supper, was distinct from another New Testament tradition that saw the fraternal meal of Christians as a joyful, eschatological remembering of the fellow-ship the original disciples enjoyed when they ate with Jesus during his lifetime on earth, in meals that were messianic but had no con-nection with his death. Cullmann shows from the New Testament, using especially the accounts of the sharing of food that Jesus did with his disciples after the resurrection, that the Eucharist as a joyful meal of Christian fellowship was also and at the same time a com-memoration of the Passover death of Jesus which, in the light of the resurrection, is the source of that fellowship. His demonstration has important theological consequences for understanding the Eucharist as a sacramental meal and how that very sacramentality makes it be a real commemoration of the sacrificial death of Christ.

The study of Leenhardt that accompanies Cullman's essay is an ecumenical attempt to interpret the doctrine of transubstantiation in a way that, while doing justice to the Catholic dogma, would also be acceptable to Protestants. The effort became associated with, if it was not actually the inspiration of, attempts by some Catholic theologians to restate the doctrine of transubstantiation in personalist, phenomenological terms. The effort produced, in the years around 1960, theories of "transfinalization" and "transignification" as explanations of the real presence of the body and blood of Christ in the Eucharist. In simplified terms, the theories suggested that the "final reality" of anything is determined by the finality intended for it by its maker, rather than by what it is made of. Bread and wine are made for the purpose of giving human nourishment and promoting human fellowship in a meal. In the Eucharist God changes the finality which, as Creator, he gave bread and wine, making it have the finality of the body and blood of Christ given for the salvation of all. The change in finality brought about by God is a change in the reality of bread and wine into the body and blood of Christ. One can thus speak of a "transfinalization." The theory expressed by the term is claimed to be a faithful rendering of the Catholic dogma of transubstantiation, having the advantage of avoiding various philosophical and theological difficulties that the word "substance" and the Aristotelian philosophy associated with it, have in a theology of the Eucharist. Another form of the same basic theory went by the name of "transignification." It sees the reality of the things that eucharistic theology is concerned with in their signification or meaning. The reality of things is the significance or meaning that they have for human existence. In profane use bread and wine have a given human signification. In the Eucharist that signification is changed: what is signified now is all that is meant by the body and blood of Christ. The trans-signification is a change of reality because the reality of things at issue in the Eucharist is the signification they have in human life.

Some versions of "transfinalization" and "transignification" advanced in the early 1960s were quite superficial. They employed a simplistic reading of what the tradition of faith said about presence in sign to justify treating the eucharistic presence of Christ as a matter of signification; they gave careful enough attention to the anthropological process by which the meaning of things changes, but less thought to the action of God and its consequences for the reality of things, that has always been the primary referent of the words sacrament and sign in the tradition of sacramental theology. Transubstantiation was sometimes dismissed as being an "outdated" concept, without much reflection on the difference between being "dated" and being "outdated." But there were other theologians who did the kind of hard intellectual work that was needed to establish a serious theory of transignification. The texts of Trent were examined hermeneutically to discover the historical sense given to transubstantiation by the Fathers of Trent and the extent to which a contemporary grasp of that same meaning required the continued use of the term transubstantiation. The philosophical value and limits of the concept substance were examined (particularly in view of its associations with Aristotelian physics and philosophy of nature), and the ontological status of an analysis of reality in terms of meaning was defended.[23] Pope Paul VI intervened in the debate in 1965 with the encyclical *Mysterium Fidei* to remind Catholics of the faith that had been defined at Trent and to warn about limitations in theories of transignification and transfinalization. He did not condemn these theories but set the conditions under which they might be incorporated into Catholic theology. He writes, for example: "It is not allowable . . . to exaggerate the element of sacramental sign as if the symbolism, which all certainly admit in the Eucharist, expressed fully and exhausted the mode of Christ's presence in this sacrament . . . As a result of transubstantiation, the species of bread and wine undoubtedly take on a new meaning and a new finality, for they no longer remain ordinary bread and ordinary wine, but become the sign of something sacred, the sign of a spiritual food. However, the reason why they take on this new significance and this new finality is because they contain a new 'reality' which we may justly term ontological" (ND 1577, 1580).[24]

---

23. See for example, E. Schillebeeckx, OP, *The Eucharist* (London and New York: Sheed & Ward, 1968).

24. See C. E. O'Neill, *New Approaches to the Eucharist* (Dublin: Gill & Son, 1967), 110.

# SECOND VATICAN COUNCIL

Vatican II confirmed the dogmatic positions of the Council of Trent
on the Eucharist (Constitution on the Liturgy, *Sacrosanctum Concilium*,
nn. 6, 7, 55). It is, however, sparing in its use of Tridentine language
and of technical categories of the post-Reformation Scholastic theology that had for so long interpreted Trent for Catholics. It prefers
the biblical and patristic language that had been earning its place in
eucharistic theology in the halfcentury preceding the council. It is
not that the council is itself doing a new kind of systematic theology—such is not the business of a council—but, nevertheless, the way
in which it expresses the faith of the Church about the Eucharist has
inevitable consequences for theology. The council is telling the world
about the mystery of the Eucharist rather than telling Catholics how
to defend their faith against heresy on particular points. It is telling
Christians of other churches what the faith of the Catholic Church is
with a view to bringing about the union of Christians in the Eucharist,
rather than with a view to condemning the views of others about the
Eucharist. It is telling Catholics, then, to develop a theology of the
Eucharist that would reflect the full biblical and patristic tradition in a
balanced way rather than concentrate on the dogmatic issues settled by
Trent against the Reformers.

      There is no separation of sacrament and sacrifice in the for-
mulations of Vatican II about the Eucharist. There are inevitable distinctions between offering the sacrifice and eating the Lord's Supper
(SC, n. 10; LG, n. 11) but the aspects so distinguished are not dealt
with apart from one another. Chapter 2 of the Constitution on the
Liturgy is entitled "The Most Sacred Mystery of the Eucharist,"
and deals in a unified way with material that Trent separated into
sacrament and sacrifice. Attention was drawn (see Chapter 2, "Life,
Word, and Rite in the Texts of Vatican II") to the richness of the
idea of sacrament used by Vatican II, and to the way it recovers the
biblical and patristic tradition of *mysterium/sacramentum*. It is a
conception that expects an interaction between word and rite in the
celebration of sacraments; it leads the council to say in the chapter
on the Eucharist: "The two parts which in a sense go to make up
the Mass, viz. the liturgy of the word and the Eucharistic liturgy, are
so closely connected with each other that they form but one single

act of worship" (SC, n. 56). In presenting the Eucharist as mystery/ sacrament the council is putting it in series with the mystery of Christ and with the mystery of the Church as universal sacrament of the salvation Christ is sent to give to the world in his human flesh. The Christological reality of the Eucharist had been defined in its essentials by Trent. Vatican II gives more attention to the ecclesiological reality that is present in it. All that is said about the liturgy in Chapter 1 of the constitution is verified preeminently in the Eucharist. All that will subsequently be done, in the redesigning of rites and in pastoral strategy, to make the Eucharist be a real expression of the life of the whole Church community is grounded on the doctrinal statements made in the chapter on the Eucharist, particularly in its opening numbers 47 and 48.

Postconciliar documents on the Eucharist, and particularly the *General Instruction of the Roman Missal* (Chapter 8, "Description" and "The Missal of Paul VI"), spell out the doctrinal and pastoral orientations provided by the council. A theology of the Eucharist that lets itself be prompted by these texts will take a sacramental approach to the Eucharist; it will relate the rite of the sacrament to the word that is proclaimed within it; it will see the Eucharist as an action of the whole Church; it will consider the realism of Christ's presence in the consecrated species in relation to the manifestations of his presence that are given in the assembled community, in the word that is read and preached, and in the ministry of the ordained; it will see the sacrificial reality of the Eucharist as a unique (because sacrificial) realization of that movement of worship that corresponds to the movement of sanctification in the whole sacramental system; it will take full sacramental participation, climaxing in the eating and drinking of the body and blood of Christ (i.e., with communion under both kinds) to be the normal practice according to which the Eucharist has to be understood; it will refuse to see communion as a sacramental extra for which one has to give added explanations, considering that what needs the added explanation is rather the incongruity of Christians not receiving the body and blood of Christ when they assemble as Church to take part in the Eucharist; it will take account of the eschatological dimension of the Eucharist as the Church celebrates it within a world that is working out its salvation while waiting for the coming of the Lord.

# ECUMENICAL CONVERGENCE

The kind of eucharistic theology patronized by Vatican II has made it possible for Catholics to have productive ecumenical dialogue with Christians from other ecclesial and theological traditions. Theologians of all churches have been drawing on the same general sources and using a similar methodology to think out the Church's faith about the Eucharist. Scriptural and historical studies are done ecumenically. The patristic theology of the Eucharist maintained in the Eastern churches is increasingly well known and appreciated in Western theology. The theology of the great Reformers is being looked at with a new appreciation for what it did to restore and transmit the tradition of faith and to challenge certain limitations of medieval theology. The work of the Council of Trent can be presented more persuasively in view of a general willingness to recognize exaggerations and omissions in the theology of the Reformers that needed correction. At the same time the historical situating of the decrees of Trent allows them to be used without that absoluteness that was commonly attributed to them in Counter-Reformation theology.

The Eucharist is considered a central issue in most of the bilateral and multilateral dialogues that have been held between the churches since Vatican II fully engaged the Catholic Church in the ecumenical movement. The Anglican–Roman Catholic International Commission (ARCIC) dealt with it at the very beginning of its work and produced *An Agreed Statement On Eucharistic Doctrine* (Windsor, 1971),[25] which set a headline for many of the dialogues between the Catholic Church and churches issued from the Reformation. The statement claims to represent substantial agreement on the issues that once divided Catholics and Anglicans. It is not meant to provide a comprehensive theology of the Eucharist but at the same time its authors consider that their text has not omitted anything essential. It uses the idea of *mystery* to state the most basic truths about the Eucharist; it uses the idea of *memorial/anamnesis* to state the relationship between the Eucharist and the cross in a way that would meet Catholic dogmatic requirements about the sacrificial character of the Eucharist and Anglican concern about maintaining the all-sufficiency

---

25. H. Meyer and L. Vischer, eds. *Growth in Agreement. Reports and Agreed Statements of Ecumenical Conversations on a World Level* (New York: Paulist and Geneva: WCC, 1984), 68–77.

of the cross; in speaking of the presence of Christ it says that "Communion with Christ in the eucharist presupposes his true presence, effectually signified by the bread and wine which, in this mystery, become his body and blood. The real presence of his body and blood can, however, only be understood within the context of the redemptive activity whereby he gives himself, and in himself reconciliation, life and peace to his own" (n. 6); it uses the concepts of sign and sacrament to affirm both the reality of the presence and its being ordered to communion (nn. 8–9); it also relates the consecratory prayer *(anaphora)* to communion by saying that "Through this Prayer of thanksgiving, a word of faith addressed to the Father, the bread and wine become the body and blood of Christ by the action of the Holy Spirit, so that in communion we eat the flesh of Christ and drink his blood" (n. 10); "transubstantiation" is described in a footnote as a word "commonly used in the Roman Catholic Church to indicate that God acting in the eucharist effects a change in the inner reality of the elements. The term should be seen as affirming the fact of Christ's presence and of the mysterious and radical change which takes place. In contemporary Roman Catholic theology it is not understood as explaining *how* the change takes place." The ARCIC issued a series of elucidations on the intentions and meaning of its Windsor and other statements in 1979, by way of response to comments it had received on its texts. The fact that the commission did not revise its original statement shows the continued confidence that its members had in their formulation. However, the fact that the text of the elucidations is longer than the text of the statement is an indication of the complex process of critical reception that has to go on in the churches before effective agreement is reached. Obviously, the authorities responsible for doctrine in both churches have a decisive role to play in the process. A resolution of the Lambeth Conference of 1988 welcomed the Agreed Statements on Eucharist and Ministry as "consonant in substance with the faith of Anglicans" and saw them as offering "a sufficient basis for taking the next step forward toward the reconciliation of our Churches grounded in agreement of faith."[26] The Holy See has responded positively but

---

26. Full text in J. Gros, E. R. Elder, and E. K. Wondra, eds., *Common Witness to the Gospel. Documents on Anglican-Roman Catholic Relation 1983–1995* (Washington, DC: United States Catholic Conference), 66–68; and in C. Hill and E. Yarnold, sj, eds. *Anglicans and Roman Catholics: The Search for Unity* (London: SPCK/CTS, 1994), 153–155.

cautiously to the Final Report of ARCIC I, which contains the statement on the Eucharist.[27] It approves a great deal of what is said about the Eucharist. But concerning a few points on which the formulations circumvent the language of Reformation controversies and Catholic dogmatic language is not used, there is a hesitation about recognizing that the fullness of Catholic teaching is being expressed. However, the ARCIC's Windsor Statement on the Eucharist remains an essential document for the contemporary theology of the Eucharist. It is a kind of prophetic statement along lines that theology will certainly want to pursue.

Among other important ecumenical texts on the Eucharist are the statement of doctrinal agreement on the Eucharist produced by the interchurch group of theologians called the "Groupe des Dombes" in 1972,[28] and the *Final Report on the Eucharist* issued by the Joint Roman Catholic/Lutheran Commission in 1978.[29]

A theological effort to develop a common statement of Eucharistic faith was begun by the Faith and Order Commission of the World Council of Churches as far back as its first conference in Lausanne in 1927. The study, along with parallel studies on baptism and ministry, was carried on by commissions made up of Protestant, Anglican, Orthodox and, in due course, Roman Catholic theologians, through various consultations and meetings of the Faith and Order Commission. The work eventually produced a text called *Baptism, Eucharist, Ministry*, commonly known by its acronym BEM, which was approved at the Lima Assembly of Faith and Order in 1982 (Chapter 2, "Ecumenical Convergence on Sacraments"). The Eucharistic theology of BEM is sacramental. It begins with the institution of the Eucharist by Jesus at the Last Supper, as a "sacramental meal which by visible signs communicates to us God's love in Jesus Christ, the love by which Jesus loved his own 'to the end'" (n. 1). The meaning of the Eucharist is expounded as it is discovered through its sacramentality, for "The eucharist is essentially the sacrament of the gift which God makes to us in Christ through the Holy Spirit" (n. 2). Five aspects are considered: in 3–4, Thanksgiving to the Father (this includes a state-

---

27. Text of official response in Gros, *Common Witness,* 69–77 and in Hill, *Anglicans and Roman Catholics,* 156–166.

28. Text in H. R. McAdoo, *Modern Eucharistic Agreement* (London: SPCK, 1973).

29. Text in Meyer and Vischer, *Growth in Agreement,* 190–212.

ment of the sacrificial movement of offering); in 5–13, Anamnesis or Memorial of Christ ("living and effective sign of his sacrifice . . . effective proclamation of God's mighty acts and promises," "sacrament of the unique sacrifice of Christ," "the sacrament of the body and blood of Christ, the sacrament of his real presence"); in 14–18, Invocation of the Spirit (by whose power, along with the living word of Christ, "the bread and wine become the sacramental signs of Christ's body and blood" and "remain so for the purpose of communion"·); in 19–21, Communion of the Faithful ("demonstrates and effects the oneness of the sharers with Christ and with their fellow sharers in all time and places . . . inconsistent if we are not actively participating in this ongoing restoration of the world's situation and the human condition . . . responsible care of Christians for one another and for the world . . ."); in 22–26, Meal of the Kingdom ("Reconciled in the eucharist, the members of the body of Christ are called to be servants of reconciliation among men and women and witnesses of the joy of resurrection . . . participation of God's mission to the world . . ."). The final section is about the liturgical rite and actual celebration of the Eucharist.

The theology of the Eucharist in BEM is an attempt by contemporary theologians from all the major ecclesial traditions to state the full apostolic faith about the Eucharist in a way that will help divided Christians to come together in full communion. It draws on the biblical and patristic scholarship of the twentieth century and organizes it in a classical framework of economic trinitarianism. It avoids using the dogmatic and confessional language in which the churches have historically defined their differences, not in order to avoid the issues about the Eucharist that divide the churches but to try to resolve them by dealing with them differently. The Commentary that accompanies the main text notes these difficulties and gives some suggestions about how they might be overcome.

There has been much that is positive in the reactions of the churches to the statements about the Eucharist in BEM.[30] The general reserves expressed by the Catholic Church about BEM (Chapter 2, "Ecumenical Convergence on Sacraments") hold for the section on

---

30. Texts of official responses in M. Thurian, ed., *Churches Respond to BEM: Official Responses to the "Baptism, Eucharist and Ministry" Text*, vols. I–IV, Faith and Order Papers 129, 132, 135, 137, 143, 144 (Geneva: WCC, 1986–88).

the Eucharist. They bear on ambiguities and inadequacies of expression rather than on anything that is actually affirmed. Among the inadequacies singled out are reliance on the notion of intercession as a way of stating the sacrificial reality of the Eucharist, the optional status given to belief that there is a change in the elements in which the body and blood of Christ are made present in the Eucharist, the noncommittal position adopted about the continuing presence of Christ in the eucharistic elements after the celebration. However, there is nothing in the official Catholic response to BEM concerning the Eucharist, nor indeed in its response to the fruits of other ecumenical dialogues, that would deter Catholic theologians from giving a serious place in their study of the Eucharist to the work being done in ecumenical circles.

# Chapter 11

# Systematic Theology of the Eucharist

The theology of the Eucharist has to be eminently about *life*, because the *rite* that it reflects on is a rite of the giving of life, and the *word* spoken about it in the tradition of faith is all about the gift of life that come to humans from the body and blood of Christ given in sacrifice for the salvation of the world. That life is received on a journey through time and place toward the banquet of heaven. Systematic theology relates the Eucharist to that life in its general terms. Pastoral theology will bring together this general reflection and the individual life experiences of those who actually celebrate the Eucharist and receive life from it.

A good case can be made from the tradition that has been presented in Chapters 9 and 10 for saying that a theology of the Eucharist does best when it is a theology of sacrament. What is offered here is some systematic sacramental thinking about the Eucharist. It supposes the theology of sacrament that was worked out in Chapter 3 and later used to think systematically about baptism (Chapter 5, "A Systematic Essay") and confirmation (Chapter 7, "A Systematic Essay"). The Eucharist builds on and completes what is begun in baptism and confirmation. A theology of it can profitably take up where the theology of baptism and confirmation left off and follow the same lines. In the categories of sacramentality it should be able to draw together in an orderly way and bring to light the intelligibility of the rich tradition of faith about the Eucharist that has been narrated throughout Chapters 8, 9, and 10. In doing so it will be giving the celebration of the eucharistic rite a word that can help it to get in touch with life, a word coming from a mind that thinks out the truth of things.

## A Sacramental Meal

What baptism and confirmation sacramentalize is God's giving of life to his People through Christ and the Spirit. They sacramental-ize that giving of life at its beginning—the passage from death to life (baptism) and the special adult quality of the life that is being entered into because it is to be lived in the final, eschatological phase of salvation history (confirmation). What the Eucharist sacramen-talizes is the solid and continuous possession of the life begun in baptism and confirmation. One is fully initiated only when one has taken part in it for the first time, and shown oneself able to take nourishment from the bread of life. Thereafter this same bread is the regularly repeated nourishment that ensures survival and growth. Ritually the Eucharist is a community meal of bread and wine that are taken as food and drink after a prayer of thanksgiving has been said over them. The meal ritual should be the starting point of all theological reflection about the Eucharist. From the time of the Reformation until quite recently, Catholic theology was some-what reluctant to think of the whole Eucharist as a meal; at most it would admit that one aspect of it could be called a meal. There seemed to be a fear that the idea of Eucharist as meal led inevita-bly to the Protestant view of the sacrament as a nonsacrificial Holy Communion service. Present day sacramental theology ought to be able to speak about the Eucharist as a meal without generating such fears. The Eucharist is a meal in the sacramental sense, as baptism is a bathing in the sacramental sense. It is a reality (body and blood of Christ, sacrifice, communion, viaticum, thanksgiving . . .) that is contained, conveyed, acted out, symbolized in and by a meal. The meal is the sign, not the reality. It is not just the bread and wine that are signs in the Eucharist but the bread and wine given and taken in a meal. The host of the meal is as much part of the sign as the food he gives, and the guests who receive the food contribute to its signifi-cance. There would be no Eucharist without an ordained minister to represent Christ in his role of host who gives himself as food, and without some believing people (at the very least the minister himself) to eat and drink the food that is prepared and given.

To give a meal to people is to give them life. Any giving of food is recognized as life-sustaining. The first drops of mother's milk given to a child and accepted by it are an effective sign of the mother's desire to keep the newborn child alive and of the child's ability to go on living: one cannot be sure that a newborn child has a hold on life until it begins to take food. It is in this sense that the Eucharist enters into the sacramentality of Christian initiation. As the first giving and taking of food it is a sign that initiation into the life process is really complete. To continue giving food is to make life continue and grow. To give it in a meal is to give life in its distinctively human dimension. Taking a meal is more than just taking food. Humans cultivate food and prepare it, as well as just gathering it: it is "fruit of the earth and work of human hands." They prepare it together and give it to one another. To prepare food and invite someone to come and sit down at one's table is to express one's intention of being life-giving for them in a distinctively human way: it is to offer them food of the body but also of the spirit in the form of companionship and conversation; it is to be ready to draw life from them in return. To make the meal a festive one is to express the joy of host and participants in some shared life experience, and in doing so to intensify their shared life. Meals are taken to remember people and events that have contributed to the life of those who eat and drink together. A special kind of food associated with the person or event being remembered may be used to reinforce the remembering. Meals are an occasion for remembering God the life-giver when food is recognized as God's gift. People pray at meals and express their awareness that all life comes from God. It is all of this that gives the Eucharist its sacramental richness and lets it bind into human existence the reality it bears within it.

## Sacrament of the Gift of Eternal Life

What the eucharistic meal ritualizes is God's giving of eternal life to his People and their receiving of it. The first Eucharist that is received as part of initiation manifests and ensures that the initiate has a stable hold on eternal life and is ready for nourishment and growth toward the full enjoyment of it. When people continue to take part in the

Eucharist in a regular rhythm, what is being sacramentalized is God's continuing care to maintain the life he has given and bring it to fullness, and their own acceptance of that growth. Every Eucharist, but particularly that which is received as a preparation for death, is a viaticum, sacramentalizing the fact that eternal life cannot be enjoyed in its fullness by those who live in time, so that what manifests and nourishes it on earth is always a looking forward to its fullness in heaven.

In sacramentalizing God's giving of eternal life and human reception of it, the Eucharist sacramentalizes Christ: he is the full, definitive giving of divine life to humanity and its perfect reception by humanity. It sacramentalizes Christ in his resurrection, by which his body was made fully alive and life-giving by God. It does so by sacramentalizing him in the death by which he gave his earthly life in witness to his acceptance that eternal life comes only from the God who is his Father: it was because of the way he died that he became totally open to receive that life from his Father at the resurrection. In sacramentalizing the Father's gift of life through, with, and in Christ, the Eucharist sacramentalizes the Holy Spirit, who is given from the risen Lord as the transforming pledge of eternal life in the midst of the world. It is as a Spirit-filled meal that the Eucharist does its sacramentalizing. The meal serves as a symbolic way of remembering Christ in his death and resurrection. It can do so because of what the Christian story tells about the meals Jesus shared with his disciples, after his resurrection as well as during his earthly life, and particularly about the solemn way he shared a Passover meal with them just before he went to his death. The Eucharist reproduces significant details of that Last Supper that Jesus took with his disciples. It is a meal of bread and wine. The bread and wine are prayed over, broken, and distributed by the one who presides and acts as host at the meal, just as Jesus did at the Last Supper. He says the same words that Jesus said about the bread and wine: "this is my body . . . my blood." These words define how Jesus is being remembered in the Eucharist. He is being remembered in his body and blood, because what he is giving in the Eucharist is his very body and blood. That means he is being remembered as a person of flesh and blood, real and alive, as he was at the Last Supper and as he showed himself to his disciples after the resurrection, still capable of sharing a meal with humans. It also means that he is being remembered in the events that brought him to this state. Jesus died violently. His blood flowed from his body. Giving bread as his body ("flesh") and wine ("blood of the grape") as his blood is a powerful reminder that he died on the cross. What is remembered is not just the fact that Jesus died but the meaning he himself gave to his death. This is conveyed sacramentally by the way the words of his that are repeated in the Eucharist evoke the Jewish Passover, with its sacrifice of the lamb, and the covenant, which was ratified by a blood sacrifice. Jesus is being remembered as offering himself in sacrifice on the cross for the salvation of the new covenant People. It is being recognized that it was in so offering himself in sacrifice that he became life-giving in his body and blood at the resurrection.

Thus the Eucharist sacramentalizes eternal life for humans by sacramentalizing Jesus becoming the source of eternal life in the sacrifice he made of himself to the Father in his body and blood, in his receiving of that life in his own flesh and blood at the resurrection, and as risen Lord sending that life into the world in the gift of the Spirit.

## For the Forgiveness of Sins

The Eucharist sacramentalizes the taking away of sin. The world that Jesus brought life to was a world in which death was reigning. There was death because there was sin. To give life Jesus had to take away sin. Sin was present in the behavior of humans: in their individual lives and in the institutions in which their world pursued sinful goals. It cut people off from God and divided them from one another. Instead of accepting the common Fatherhood of God people worshipped racial, political, or ideological gods that they invented to justify their own sinfulness. Instead of being able to sit down together to share God's life-giving gifts, individuals isolated themselves, or grouped together in selfishness, building up hostilities to others that were always, in one way or another, death dealing. People set about becoming rich in ways that inevitably made others poor; they provided food for themselves in ways that left others hungry; they embarked on forms of self-indulgence that required others to be abused in body and spirit. . . . Only God could take away the sin of the world, by forgiving and healing it. In his merciful design, revealed throughout the Old Testament, the taking away of sin was to be realized and manifested in the life of a representative of humanity who would proclaim the truth about God in the face of human sinfulness, and suffer the consequences. Jesus was put to death by a sinful world because he made the ultimate challenge to its sinfulness. He accepted his death, giving in it the supreme proof of love that allowed God to forgive human sinfulness. God raised him from the dead, showing that in him sin and its consequences had been forgiven and overcome. People who unite around Jesus receive the forgiveness of their sins; they are given life and become life-giving for one another. Baptism is the sacrament of the initial and radical taking away of sin. But the struggle against sin and its consequences is lifelong. The reality of it and the victory gained in it are sacramentalized again and again in the Eucharist. What people are initiated to once for all in baptism is worked out day-by-day in the eucharistic celebration of the reconciliation brought about by Jesus. People who forgive and are forgiven in him sit down together at a common table, at which they receive life from God and become life-giving for one another and for the world. They represent a new order of things in which there is no longer place for selfishness and self-indulgence, for divisions, oppressions, and the feeding of some through making others hungry. The eucharistic table offers hospitality to everyone who is open to the life that comes from the death and resurrection of Jesus. It is a meal of reconciliation, as were the meals Jesus shared with publicans and sinners. It is a meal where the poor and hungry of the world are remembered, and where those who eat together are pledged to take away the hunger of the world and all the sinful forces that cause it. It is the sacrament of the taking away of sin that Jesus did once for all in his death and resurrection, and that is being worked out day-by-day in the lives of those who are remembering him.

## Presence of Christ in the Sacrament

To say that the Eucharist sacramentalizes Christ in his dying and rising is already to state that he is present in the Eucharist. A sacrament by definition makes the action of God in Christ present in a rite. The fact that the Eucharist realizes a unique presence of Christ, in the consecrated species, is no reason for forgetting how the general presence that is realized in every sacrament occurs in it. All that the word sacrament has come to say about divine presence in human affairs must be fully realized in the Eucharist. Stirred by the "theology of mystery"

proposed by Odo Casel (see Chapter 2, "From Trent to Vatican II"),
twentieth century systematic theology devoted a good deal of attention to the analysis of sacramental presence, or "mystery-presence."
The effort needs to be continually made. To say that the presence is
"in mystery" is not to say that it is unintelligible. If it is real it must
be subject to some kind of thoughtful verification. It must be seen to
be consonant with what is known otherwise about reality, and seen to
make sense in real terms.

Along with making an effort to understand how the community, its ministers, the word of God and the general liturgical setting
of the celebration enfold the presence in the species and with it manifest the personal saving action of God, most recent theologies give a
foundational place to the biblical and patristic teaching on "memorial"
and "mystery" in their attempts to understand the eucharistic presence.
Thomist and neo-Scholastic theologians generally have made strenuous efforts to provide a metaphysically tenable theology that would
sustain and give some clarity to the affirmation about the mystery-
presence that Casel recovered from the Fathers.[1] Other theologians,
working out of other philosophical presuppositions (see Chapter 2,
"Theology of Sacraments Today"), propose other explanations. The
need for such theological clarification shows itself in a particular way in
ecumenical theology. The idea of memorial, and also that of mystery/
sacrament, have proved very useful in ecumenical statements about the
Eucharist. However, when texts couched in these terms are interpreted
in particular churches they are inevitably subject to the influences of
different confessional traditions and of more or less conscious philosophical assumptions. Different interpretations of memorial and mys-
tery/sacrament can arise. If there has not been some shared measure
of theological understanding about the way terms like memorial and
mystery/sacrament are being used in agreed statements, the different
interpretations they receive can undermine ecumenical agreement.

The question about presence in memorial and mystery is
fundamentally one about how God is present and acts in and on the

---

1. For an account see T. Filthaut, *La théologie des mystères. Exposé de la controverse* (Paris and
Tournai: Desclée, 1954); for examples see E. Schillebeeckx, OP, *Christ the Sacrament of Encounter
with God* (London/New York: Sheed & Ward, 1963), 64–109; C. E. O'Neill, OP, *Meeting Christ
in the Sacraments* (New York: Alba House, 1964), 63–95.

created world, and about how that presence/action occurs in Christ. Thomas Aquinas asks these sorts of questions in the First Part of the *Summa* (e.g., in q. 8 on the existence of God in things; in q. 105, on how things [and people] are changed by God). He uses the principles worked out in these metaphysical discussions to understand God's presence and action in the history of salvation, and specifically to understand how Christ in his humanness is present as the instrument of God in the grace of the New Testament. Even if one finds the answers of Thomas unsatisfactory one has to face in some form or other the questions that he asks. Otherwise, one cannot claim to be thinking theologically (i.e., on the level of the divine) about Christian belief that the saving act of God realized in the death and resurrection of Christ is present when that act is ritually remembered in the Eucharist. On the Christological level one has to understand how the Incarnation gives a divine dimension to all Christ's human actions. One also needs to have some reasoned explanation of how the moral choice of Christ to offer himself in sacrifice for his Father, which found expression in his body and blood on the cross, is still present and finding expression in the ritual remembering of the cross that is multiplied through time and space in the Eucharist (see Chapter 3, "Christ, the Sacrament of God"). It was in that choice that Christ realized his vocation of being a priest forever according to the order of Melchizedek, and entered into the heavenly sanctuary where he is "ever living to make intercession for us." Theology has to try to provide some explanation of how this priestly action of Christ is present in each Eucharist. Some Thomists have sought to find the explanation in Thomas' theory that Christ enjoyed the beatific vision during his earthly life, but that is not one of the more reliable of Thomas' theological positions. A solution can be sought in an analysis of the comprehensiveness of the final option that Christ made in death and in the way that final option was given a timeless permanence in his passage into glory. It can be argued that his final option, already made at the Last Supper, bore not alone on the giving of his body and blood in historical death but on the ritual remembering of the giving of his body and blood that his disciples would do in the future while they waited for him to come again. In that case his human intention, fixed forever at the moment of his death, would be as really present and expressed in the bread and wine that is made his body and blood in the Eucharist as they were in his body and blood on the cross. His presence thus understood would be a real presence of his priestly action, through which the divine action of giving eternal life is mediated.

## PRESENCE OF THE BODY AND BLOOD OF CHRIST

The Eucharist sacramentalizes the giving and receiving of eternal life through the priestly mediation of Christ by making his body and blood be really and abidingly present as the food of immortality. The bread and wine that are prayed over and shared in the rite of the Church are proclaimed to be the body and blood of Christ. The specific sacramentality of the Eucharist requires that this statement be taken in its literal truth. What is sacramentalized in other rites of the Church are specific actions of God sanctifying different moments of passage in the journey of members of the Christian community toward eternal life. What is sacramentalized in the Eucharist is the giving of an abiding hold on eternal life during that journey—the state of being alive, of staying alive, of enjoying the growth that is inseparable from living, of being part of a community in which life can be lived to the full. What gives people an abiding hold on eternal life can only be the body and blood of Christ. Because they are the direct and permanent object of his priestly offering (he offered himself in offering his body and blood), only in them can the priestly act of sacrifice and intercession of Christ that gives eternal life be contacted. This is the body and blood that became life-filled and life-giving at the resurrection. Wherever the body and blood of Christ are, there, and only there, is eternal life being offered as an abiding possession to those who are open to receive it. To have eternal life is to be joined to the living body of Christ and to continue drawing life from him until one is permanently transformed into his likeness at the resurrection. The Eucharist, then, is a sacrament only when the bread and wine have become the body and blood of Christ. The "matter" of the sacrament is, indeed, bread and wine. These together are the sign of everything that is realized in the Eucharist. But they do their symbolizing and are a sacrament precisely in becoming the body and blood of Christ. The "form" that determines their symbolism in a specific way is a divine word proclaiming in the Church that they are the body and blood of Christ, and it is a word that does what it says. This is the sacramental context in which the question of the real presence has to be discussed.

Before there were heresies about the real presence, the theology of the Eucharist did not give extended treatment to the question. The controversies that eventually came to a head in the condemnation of Berengarius earned the question quite a lot of attention in Western theology. At the Reformation it became one of the two major areas of debate. One hopes that the ecumenical climate of contemporary theology is making it possible to scale down the treatment somewhat within a more broadly based understanding of the Eucharist. Nevertheless, the question of the real presence of the body and blood of Christ in the eucharistic bread and wine has to be dealt with thoroughly. Theologically the issue is not just a matter of fact: it is also a matter of understanding the fact affirmed by faith. Accepting the affirmation of faith already requires a measure of understanding of what is being affirmed. It also requires a readiness to think about any reasonable questions that the fact raises for an enquiring mind. One cannot discount the questions simply by saying that they would never have occurred to the writers of the New Testament—because of their Semitic mentality or whatever. Nor can one discount all questions simply by pointing to a number of silly questions that have been asked about the real presence in the course of the history of theology. It is wishful thinking to claim that Christians will find it easier to agree about the Eucharist if they rely on simple formulas and do not ask too many questions about what they mean. Formulas, no matter how simple, are inevitably interpreted. If the interpretation of one person differs in some significant way from that of others, what seemed to be agreement may turn out to have been based on a misunderstanding. A theology of the real presence would want to clarify what is meant by the affirmation of faith at least to the point of eliminating basic misunderstandings.

Among the critical debates that can clarify what one means by real presence, the one about change must be the most urgent. The affirmation of faith in the real presence is about something that, before it is prayed over eucharistically, is clearly bread and wine and nothing else. After the prayer it is, in the judgment of faith, something else. Something in, or about, the bread and wine has changed. The patristic tradition was never afraid to affirm the real presence by affirming change in the bread and wine. When the hesitations came at the Reformation they were more about the kind of change than about the fact of change. The kind of change that is postulated must be in keeping with what the tradition of faith says about the kind of presence of the body and blood of Christ that is brought about in the change. What the tradition says is that the presence is both real and sacramental. Because it is real it is not merely symbolical, as Christ might be said to be present in a crucifix being used to bless people, or in an actor who plays the part of Christ in a passion play. Because it is sacramental it is not realistic, as was the presence of Christ in Peter's boat or with Mary when she embraced him after the resurrection; it is somehow a presence in bread and wine.

The best way to go about understanding the kind of change that reconciles realism with sacramentality would seem to be to distinguish between what changes and what does not change in the Eucharist. Something of what is there must remain bread and wine because it has to serve as the symbol in which the sacramental presence is realized; something of what is there must no longer be bread and wine on a level of reality that is sufficiently profound to allow the body and blood of Christ to be really and truly what is there. This is the kind of affirmation and explanation of change that one finds in the teaching of the Council of Trent about transubstantiation. Trent affirms the faith of the Church that the body and blood of Christ are really and sacramentally present in the consecrated bread and wine; it teaches that this requires a real change in the bread and wine, so that after the consecration what is present is no longer the reality of bread and wine but only their appearances; it uses the word "substance" to describe the level of being on which the change occurs and teaches that the substance of bread is changed into the substance of Christ's body and that of wine into his blood; it says that this change is fittingly called "transubstantiation," and all of this is said in order to confess in faith that what is eaten and drunk sacramentally under the appearances of bread and wine is truly, really, and substantially the body and blood of Christ.

# Theologies of the Real Presence

A Catholic theology of the Eucharist that wants to develop within the dogmatic teaching of Trent might turn spontaneously to a theology of transubstantiation, such as was worked out by Scholastic masters and developed by their disciples. That was the kind of theology that was on the mind of most of the Fathers and theologians of Trent. However, a critical hermeneutic of Trent can establish that what is affirmed there as being of faith does not require the acceptance of any particular Scholastic theology of transubstantiation, nor of the Aristotelian or other philosophical categories that might be used by it. Since Trent, the faith of the Catholic Church in the real presence cannot be stated without reference to the *dogma* of transubstantiation. But it is possible to do a Catholic explanation of the real presence that would not use transubstantiation as a *theological category*. It may even be necessary to do so. There are philosophical difficulties about the way the categories of substance and accident are used in the theory, and about the meaning of change on the level of substance. Some would argue that substance cannot cover and relate two such disparate realities as material bread and the personal reality of Christ: to say Christ is present as the substance of bread was present would be to give that carnal, local meaning to his presence that was rejected so decisively in the patristic tradition, especially by Augustine. Others point out that the postulate of the accidents of bread and wine subsisting without a substance in which to inhere is something of a *deus ex machina* solution that is metaphysically untenable. Others still wonder how one substance can change into another already existing substance, and whether the idea of transubstantiation does not eventually come to something like the changing of water into wine, which obviously does not yield an adequate explanation of the sacramental presence of Christ in the Eucharist. If a theology of transubstantiation has these weaknesses it could, paradoxically, have the effect of obscuring the very truths that Trent affirmed by the dogma of transubstantiation. In any case, even if the philosophical and theological difficulties are overcome, there could still be an ecumenical reason for avoiding the concept substance in a theology of the eucharistic presence. The rejection of the term in the theology of the Eucharist is so deeply lodged in the traditions of the Protestant churches that to claim one cannot explain the mystery of the real presence theologically without it would be to put a major block in the way of a common understanding of the Eucharist.

Theories of transignification and transfinalization (see Chapter 10, "From Trent to Vatican II") avoid many of the difficulties of transubstantiation. Perhaps nowadays they offer the best way to begin thinking about the kind of change that brings about the real presence. They give a good account of the sacramentality of the presence, and of how it is experienced and responded to by humans. They draw attention to the personal quality of Christ's presence in his body and blood, and to the personal significance for humans of eating his body and drinking his blood. They affirm a real change in the bread and wine, and a real presence of the body and blood on a level corresponding to the change. The theological difficulty that arises at that point, however, is whether or not the level of reality at which the change and presence are postulated is the deep, ontological level at which the tradition of faith affirms the presence. Does transignification affirm unambiguously that what is eaten and drunk in the Eucharist really is the body and blood of Christ? A convinced phenomenologist will say that it does, because the theory is talking about the ultimate level of being: existentially there is nothing more profound in bread than the meaning it has in the world of humans. Here the debate has to move beyond philosophy, into the realm of philosophical theology. What is at stake is not just the ontological issue but the issue of how things depend in their being on God. In the tradition of faith it is the word of God, not just the word of man that changes the bread and wine in the Eucharist. The word of God is creative: it makes things be what they are said to be; it gives them their ultimate reality. From the theological point of view things are significant in human life because of what they are by God's making, not the other way around. Theologies of transignification recognize this and make much of it. However, it is questionable whether the philosophy they employ gives an adequate basis for distinguishing the ontological effect of the creative word of God from the effect of merely human changes of meaning. Like Christologies "from below" (with which they have many affinities) in relation to the incarnation, they leave one wondering if they have said the last word about what God is doing in the mystery of the Eucharist.

Scholastic theories of transubstantiation certainly give priority to the action of God and its effects over human giving of meaning—sometimes, it has to be admitted, to the point of practically ignoring the human mediation of meaning. It is worth looking at such a theory again to see if it cannot give a better account than transignification of the level at which the change to the body and blood of Christ occurs; to ask if it can do so without sacrificing the valuable explanations of the sacramentality of the presence that are offered by transignification; and to speculate if it can do all this without running into insuperable philosophical contradictions. Even in the modest presentation of Thomas' theory of transubstantiation given earlier (Chapter 9, "Saint Thomas Aquinas") one can see that the change being postulated as bringing about the eucharistic presence is the work of God, who alone can reach things on the level of substance. Substance is not being used here in a physical sense. Its meaning is not conveyed by the images or concepts that the term evokes when used in physics and chemistry. The term is not, in fact, inevitably tied to and compromised by these images. A glance at the variety of meanings given to the word substance in any comprehensive dictionary of the English language is enough to confirm that it is often used in ways that have nothing whatever to do with analyses of physical reality, and still less with Aristotelian forms of it. In a theology of transubstantiation the "substance of bread" means the ultimate level of its reality, at which it exists independently as a piece of bread and as nothing else. "Accidents" mean its shape and size and taste and other characteristics of it, which can be changed without the thing of which they are shape, size, taste ceasing to be bread. The term substance is taking the mind beyond the physical. Transubstantiation as a theological theory postulates that God acts on bread in a way that leaves the characteristics of bread unchanged (allowing them to serve sacramentality) but changes the substance of bread into the substance of the body of Christ in such a way that what used to exist as bread, and was recognized as such by its accidents, now exists as body of Christ and is recognized as such by faith, and only by faith. Faith in the real presence of the body and blood of Christ is grounded on the word of God, heard in the words of Christ that have been spoken about the bread and wine by the priest, who is authorized to speak them in the name of Christ. Faith accepts the life-giving reality of the body and blood of Christ by an act of eating that is made possible by the accidents of bread and wine, to which Christ has become sacramentally related by the act of change. The substance of what is there and taken as food and drink is no longer bread and wine but the life-giving body and blood of Christ. The ontological assumption of transubstantiation is that if Christ is not there in his substance he is not really there at all. He is there as substance because the bread and wine yield to him by being changed in their substance into him.

Christ becomes present in the Eucharist according to the theory of transubstantiation, not because anything happens to him but because of what happens to the bread and wine. Christ in his substance becomes the term of a metaphysical movement of the bread and wine toward him. The term of the change of bread is his body, and that of wine is his blood. Metaphysically Christ is one living substance, so that where his body is substantially there also is his blood, with his soul and divinity, and everything else that makes him be who he is. His substantiality, however, can be predicated separately of those two life principles that are body and blood. Different aspects of his substantial existence were expressed in them during his life. They need to be expressed sacramentally in the Eucharist if it is to make him present as life-giving. Hence the sacramental act of transubstantiation changes the substance of bread into his body as substantial, and the substance of wine into his blood as substantial. Sacramentally (*ex vi sacramenti*, as the Scholastics said, or *vi verborum* as the Council of Trent preferred to say) the bread is his body and the wine his blood. But because of the substantial unity of Christ, where the substance of his body is there also is his blood and all the other components of his substantial existence. This is the presence of the *totus Christus, ex reali concomitantia*, which the Scholastics and the Council of Trent affirmed as the correlative of the presence *ex vi sacramenti* or *verborum*.

If the term of the change postulated by transubstantiation is the substance of Christ, his presence in the Eucharist must be of the kind proper to substance. This would explain how everything that makes him be this individual person (including his shape, appearance, sound of voice, etc.) is present in the Eucharist, but not in the natural mode of existence that these have in heaven. This concept of presence "by way of substance" *(per modum substantiae)* is the feature

of the theory that would eliminate any suggestion of the presence
being carnal or spatial, or the result of some local movement of Christ
toward where the Eucharist is being celebrated. Substance is the object
of mind, not directly of sense. One only knows what something is on
the level of its independent existence by thinking about it and judging what it is substantially. Furthermore, the substance of the body
and blood of Christ that is made present in the Eucharist can only
be known by a mind whose thoughts and judgments are enlightened
by the word of God. The presence of Christ in the Eucharist *per
modurn substantiae* is the object of a judgment of faith. Contact with
the physical, tangible aspects of Christ's bodiliness is on the level of
mind not of sense. What (i.e., the substance that) one eats and drinks
is truly Christ who is a person of flesh and blood. But one does not
have sense-contact with his flesh and blood as such. The sense-contact
is with the accidents of bread and the accidents of wine in eating and
drinking. As that sense-contact formerly put one's mind in touch with
the substances of bread and wine (and made one judge: "I am eating
bread and drinking wine and being nourished by them"), so now that
same sense-contact puts one's mind in touch with Christ and what he
is in his body (known in the eating of bread) and blood (known in the
drinking of wine): as one eats and drinks one is judging in faith: "I am
drawing from Christ the eternal life that he gained for me in the body
and blood in which he offered himself on the cross and now offers
to me in this same body and blood of his in which he is risen from
the dead." Life is given to humans—even the highest levels of spiritual life—in and through their bodies. Christ shares the life of grace
that resides uniquely in his body by making contact with his disciples
through their bodily actions of eating and drinking, and in that contact
their life is transformed into his life. It is this judgment of faith that
is being offered intelligibility in the claim that the substance of bread
and wine have been changed into the substance of Christ's body and
blood. By the change the accidents of bread and wine are related now
to Christ present as substance, that is to say as person. They do not
become his accidents but they do become his sacrament. They allow
him to offer humans a human contact, of sense and spirit, with himself. Christ exists in flesh and blood in heaven. Persons who are not
in heaven can contact him really and in a way that makes him present

and known as a person of flesh and blood in a sacrament of bread and wine. The act of faith in which this contact occurs is not just general faith in Jesus. It includes a very concrete judgment that the bread and wine that one is eating and drinking in faith are Christ really giving himself in his body and blood in a celebration of his Church at this particular point of place and time.

The philosophical difficulties about transubstantiation have to be answered philosophically. If it were demonstrated that the doctrine involves some metaphysical contradiction it would become untenable. But because the doctrine was developed, and is currently sustained or opposed, in discussions about a reality that is experienced only in faith, it is more likely that the difficulties come from a sort of philosophical awkwardness about what is being postulated theologically rather than from what are seen to be outright contradictions that are demonstrated on purely philosophical grounds. The theologian would want to meet the philosopher as far as possible on the philosopher's own ground. But he/she would also want to remind the philosopher that the reality being analyzed in the theory of transubstantiation is something unique and not verifiable by reason alone. It is hardly surprising that it stretches the categories of rationality. The theory is also appealing to the creative action of God, who alone can act on creatures on the level of substance. The act of creation is something about which philosophy is notoriously tentative. Transubstantiation is also assuming that the frontiers of being are stretched in that new creation that has been begun by the pouring out of the Spirit in the world. The theologian could argue that it is not unreasonable to expect some philosophical surprises when the things of this world, like bread and wine, are already caught up, by the power of the Spirit, in that transformation that makes the world of things become more and more the world of persons, and makes material things become more and more means of contact between persons rather than barriers between them. Philosophy might be interested also in exploring the suggestions that come out of the debate on transubstantiation about the connection between the ontological and the phenomenological. The theology of transubstantiation expounded here would claim to be a complement and deepening of theologies of transignification. It would claim to be so because it pushes a phenomenological analysis of the Eucharist that accounts well for the sacramentality of Christ's presence toward an ontological analysis that accounts better for its realism.

One would hope that the ecumenical difficulties of the term substance would be softened and eventually overcome by the kind of theological analysis of it that has been presented here. In ecumenical dialogue Catholic theologians will always need to explain what this word, that is so much part of their own tradition, really means in eucharistic theology—and transubstantiation is only one of its usages, and not the most fundamental. And all theologians must eventually face the fact that the word has been in the language of faith since the Lord's Prayer was formulated in the gospel of Matthew (see Chapter 9, "Ninth to Twelfth Centuries"). It was well established in theology before Aristotelian philosophy began to leave its mark on the way it was used in the theology of the Eucharist. Over many centuries it has put minds in touch with a level of reality that Christian faith has constantly to bring to the attention of humanity: that is, the level on which the creative, formative, and sustaining action of God occurs, and on which the ultimate transformation of reality in the new creation is being worked out. Such a well-defined concept of substance might manage to earn a degree of ecumenical toleration in the theology of the real presence, and eventually might even be found useful for equipping theology to deal with the ultimate level of reality on which the mystery occurs.[2]

## SACRAMENT OF THE CHURCH

As a community meal at which those who believe in him take the body of Christ for eating and his blood for drinking, the Eucharist sacramentalizes the Church: it gives visibility and reality to the mystical body of Christ that draws its life from his personal body and makes that life available in the world. The Church is the fruit of the Eucharist. It is also the maker of the Eucharist. The Eucharist is, indeed, the supreme instance of the ecclesiological principle that the

---

2. See L. G. Walsh, OP, "An ecumenical reading of Aquinas on the Eucharist" in *Liturgia et Unitas*, eds. M. Klöckener and A. Join-Lambert (Fribourg: Universitätsverlag, 2001).

Church "is both community of the redeemed and redeeming institution" (see Chapter 3, "The Church, Sacrament of Christ"). God builds up the Church through the Eucharist; at the same time God uses the Church as his instrument to make the Eucharist be the body and blood of Christ. In gathering people together for a community meal the Church is setting up a sign of the way that God gives life to humans by uniting them with one another in the body of Christ. In human terms the fellowship of a meal gives the participants access to the company and gifts of others, the stimulus of their conversation, the enjoyment of their friendship; it raises individuals to higher planes of life; it gives a sense of belonging that promises security and a future. It is in such a community meal that eternal life coming from the body and blood of Christ is given. The church gathers and is gathered by the Holy Spirit. The Spirit joins those who believe in Christ in a community of love, which is equipped with all the spiritual gifts needed to make it alive and life-giving. These are the gifts that make them be a prophetic and priestly people. Some gifts allow them to hear and proclaim the word of God. Others are "anointings with the Spirit," or priestly sacramental characters and other relationships with Christ, that allow them as his members to represent him and do things that he will recognize as his own. These gifts contribute in various ways to the celebration of the Eucharist. Some of them are indispensable for it. There can be no Eucharist without people who can proclaim and receive God's word authentically: the Eucharist requires prophets. Neither can there be a Eucharist without the baptized and the ordained: the Eucharist requires priests. The Church employs all its resources in the celebration of the Eucharist. Conversely all these resources are given ecclesial status through the Eucharist. Although the Eucharist is a family celebration of the Church, restricted to those who have been properly initiated and live in accordance with the Gospel, it is also a sacrament of the mission of the Church in the world. The word that is proclaimed in it is the prophetic word that is for the salvation of all. The poor and hungry are reached out to in charity. Prayers are said for the salvation of the whole world. The Church is sent forth from it to bring the reconciling message of the Gospel to all. The Eucharist is an open table awaiting all who receive the word and are baptized.

# Through the Ministry of Priests

To constitute a eucharistic community the prophetic and priestly people must be gathered under the presidency of a bishop or presbyter who is ordained to the ministry of priesthood. The fundamental reason is sacramental. To be the Eucharist a meal must sacramentalize not just the body and blood of Christ but Christ himself as priest, giving life to those gathered at table by giving his body and blood for them and to them as food. Christ the Priest is the real host of the eucharistic meal. While all those present have a share in his priesthood, which allows them to receive his sacrifice as their own, they do not represent him in his priestly action of giving himself to and for others by giving them his body and blood. The representation of Christ as he who gives to others is done by the one who presides at the Eucharist, acting as head of the community and host of the meal in the role of Christ *(ex persona Christi)*. This person is a priest in a distinctive sacramental sense because he is appointed by God to take the initiative and signify the giving in sacrifice and communion, without which the Eucharist can never be made. (The use of masculine pronouns to speak about ordained priests from here on reflects the actual discipline of the Catholic Church.) The faithful receive the gift from him that activates their own priesthood. The special sacramental relationship of the ordained priest with Christ is manifested liturgically in the fact that it is he who proclaims the narrative of the institution: he does so in a way that allows the words of Christ about the bread and wine being his body and blood to be heard again by the community as Christ spoke them at the Last Supper. He also says the sacramental prayer for the coming of the Holy Spirit on the bread and wine. He does these two things within the eucharistic prayer, in which he leads the thanksgiving of the community for the bread and wine that Christ makes to be the sacrifice of his body and blood.

There is also an ecclesiological reason why the Eucharist is presided over by an ordained priest. To be the body of Christ each particular community of Christians must be in communion with the whole Church, both in the present time and in that historical continuity that goes back to the Church of the apostles. While continuity and communion are ensured by all the members of a Christian community, it is signified and made effective in the continuity of ministry. The ordained ministers of the Church continue that part of the ministry of the apostles that ensures the internal unity of Christian communities and their bond with other communities; the derivation of their ministry from the apostles allows them to authenticate the faith and sacraments celebrated in the churches as coming from Christ, the ultimate centre of unity.

## SACRIFICE OF THE CHURCH

As sacrament of all that the Church is, the Eucharist sacramentalizes the Church's participation in the sacrifice of Christ. The sacrifice of Christ is present in the Eucharist because he is offering his body and blood in it. His body and blood are the permanent expressions of his self-offering to the Father for the salvation of sinful humanity: they became so on the cross and remain so in the resurrection. When they are made sacramentally present in bread and wine in the Eucharist, in an act of the Church that has within it the action of an ordained priest, they bring with them Christ's priestly act of oblation. This is the unique sacrifice that brings the forgiveness of all human sin, ratifies the new covenant, and assembles the Church as the new People of God. It is now the only sacrifice that is pleasing to God. It is made sacramentally present in the Eucharist so that its effects can be applied to those whom God gathers into the Church throughout the course of time and across the reaches of space. The theological question—which is inevitably marked by the disagreements of the Reformation—is about the sense in which the act by which the Church lays hold of those effects might itself be an act of sacrifice. The forgiveness of sin and a growing hold on life in the body of Christ that are the effects of the Eucharist are pure grace. The receiving of them, in human freedom, is also the effect of grace. The question is whether this grace of God moves those who are receiving the effect of Christ's sacrifice to an act that can itself be called sacrifice and, as such, play some part in bringing about the fruits of salvation. The answer depends on how one sees the relationship between God's action and human freedom in the working out of grace. A radically Protestant theology of grace would deny all value to human action in relation to the gift of justification. Applied to the Eucharist this would mean that the sacrifice of Christ produces its effects in it without any morally valuable action that might be a form of identification with Christ's sacrifice on the part of those receiving grace: the Lord's Supper, as Holy Communion, would be seen as proclaiming the descending mediation of Christ that is the application of the fruits of his sacrifice on the cross, but not in any way as a sacramentalizing of his upward mediation in the actions of those who receive grace. Radical Protestantism would allow that there is an upward movement of praise and thanksgiving for gifts received in the Eucharist, which could be called a sacrifice of praise, but would not allow that this enters into the sacramental giving of grace. The Catholic tradition is that, under the grace of God, humans make free acts of acceptance that are meritorious in relation to the gift of grace and are satisfactory (propitiatory) in relation to the taking away of sin. It can, therefore, see a God-ward movement in the Eucharist in which Christians unite themselves with the upward mediation of Christ, and specifically with his sacrifice of himself to the Father. It sees the sacramentality of these actions ensured by the characters of baptism, confirmation and ordination which are, in different ways, sharings in Christ's priesthood. By such priestly actions Christ's sacrifice is offered sacramentally in and by the Church. The gifts of grace received from the sacrifice of the cross in the Eucharist are seen to be simultaneously, and without any derogation from the uniqueness and all-sufficiency of Christ's sacrifice, fruits of the Eucharist itself. The liturgical form in which the Eucharist was universally celebrated up to the time of the Reformation, as well as the sacrificial language widely used by the Fathers about the Eucharist, are believed to require this Catholic doctrine.

A theological penetration of the Catholic confession of faith about the Eucharist as sacrifice requires one to explain the meaning that the term sacrifice has when applied to the Eucharist. It will not do to simply take an ethical or anthropological definition of sacrifice from studies of religious behavior, and show that it is verified in the Eucharist. The Eucharist must be a sacrifice in the sense that the cross is a sacrifice. When the epistle to the Hebrews uses the category of sacrifice to explain the saving value of the death of Christ it gives more attention to the way it differs from other sacrifices than to what it has in common with them: it is God himself who takes the initiative in it, rather than human pleading, sending his Son as definitive covenant word and eternal High Priest; it is valuable for all humans, and not just for those of one people or epoch, because of the solidarity that the High Priest has in flesh and blood with the whole human family that needs to be saved from sin; it is offered by Christ the High Priest in loving self-dedication to the will of the Father and accomplished in the shedding of his own blood, rather than in any formal ritual action; it is seen to be accepted once and for all, to the absolute discounting of any other sacrifice, by Christ's entry into the heavenly sanctuary where he lives forever pleading efficaciously for the salvation of those who believe that God's promise is fulfilled in him. The conclusion must be that technical elements that form part of anthropological definitions of sacrifice can he used in Christian theology only if they are rethought in line with the sense given to them by the unique sacrifice of Christ. The idea of oblation can express the inner heart of sacrifice, provided it is seen as the total dedication of self to God the Father in an obedience that is "better than sacrifice." Immolation can be used to describe the consecration, or setting apart for God of something in sacrifice, provided what is set apart is the only victim that is now pleasing to God, which is the body and blood of Christ. Propitiation can be used to talk about the way sacrifice takes away sin, provided it is understood that the only thing that takes away sin is the death and resurrection of Christ. Priesthood can be attributed to those who make and offer sacrifice, provided it is understood that the only priesthood now operative is that of Christ. Once these technical terms, and any definition of sacrifice constructed from them, are used in the meaning they have been given by the cross of Christ, they can be applied to the Eucharist without the risk of making it seem a sacrifice that would be somehow independent of the cross.

Before applying the idea of sacrifice to the Eucharist, one has to see how it was verified in the Last Supper. What Jesus did at the Last Supper was a ritual anticipation of what he did on the cross. The sense of self-oblation to the Father that marked his whole life was fixed, on that night before he suffered, on the end that would be made of his life on the cross by people who were already preparing his death. He knew at the Last Supper what giving his life to the Father was going to cost him. The thought of death was a thought about his body and blood: what happened to them on the cross and afterward was to be the ultimate test of his dedication to the Father and of the Father's acceptance of him. The food that was being eaten at the Last Supper was already a reminder of the Passover sacrifice that brought liberation to the People of the Mosaic covenant and of the sealing of that covenant in blood. When Jesus took bread and wine, gave it to his disciples and said it was his body and blood given for the remission of sin and the ratifying of the new covenant, he was anticipating the immolation of his body and blood on the cross for the forgiveness of sin and the sealing of the new covenant. What he did with the bread and wine was an act of symbolic immolation that expressed his oblation. In giving his body and blood as food and drink to his disciples he was proclaiming that his sacrifice was life-giving for them. When he told them to go on doing the same thing in memory of him, he was assuring them that it would go on being life-giving. It would be life-giving in being a memorial of his sacrifice.

The traditions about the Last Supper were written down by Paul and the evangelists to help Christians understand what Christ meant their "breaking of bread" to be. What they wrote surely tells the Church that Christ offers himself sacrificially in the Eucharist, as he offered himself at the Last Supper. He does so through the whole complex of persons, actions, and words that make up the Eucharist. The people who form the Christian community are people whose whole life is meant to be a sacrifice (Romans 12:1: ". . . present your bodies as a living sacrifice, holy and acceptable to God, which is your spiritual worship"). Their daily sacrifice is modeled on the sacrifice that Christ made in his body. It is made in the strength of the grace drawn from his sacrifice. It is worked out in the relations they have with one another in the Church: as members of Christ they give themselves to one another, sharing their life and their goods to the extent that this is necessary for the life of the community; out of that Christian solidarity they are also ready to give themselves for the life of the world, even if that means being made to suffer by the world. When they come together for the Eucharist the sacrificial sense of their life is heightened and focused. They are assembled as the People of the new covenant called together to hear again the covenant word proclaimed in Christ and to renew the ratification of it that he made in his blood. The symbolism of the meal lends itself to the expression of covenant sacrifice. The people are sharing their food and drink, giving what they have to one another as they give themselves. They are recognizing that their food, like their fellowship, is a gift of God and want to say so in an act of worship, which takes the form of a prayer of thanks said over bread and wine. The prayer of the community is said by the one who presides over the meal. He can represent all and signify their unity by reason of a special role he has been given to represent Christ as head and spokesperson of those who form his body. The sacramental likeness of the ordained minister to Christ also consists in the way he represents Christ as host of the meal, who gives his very self as food. Without this representation of Christ the giver, the food taken and shared could not be recognized as bearing the divine gift of eternal life. In being said by one who is consecrated in this special representational likeness of Christ by ordination and in being assented to by the Amen of the whole community, the eucharistic prayer is an act of the Church formally constituted as Body of Christ. It fully sacramentalizes his priestly worship.

The eucharistic prayer is made in that attitude of offering and readiness to give oneself in sacrifice that pervades Christian life when it is lived in imitation of Christ. It thanks God for his gifts and in doing so recognizes that anything it has to offer is already his gift. It makes a petition about the bread and wine that the community has set aside for sharing and for being a symbol of the spirit of giving and receiving in which its members are gathered. It asks that they should become, through the power of God's Spirit, the body and blood of Christ, and it grounds the petition on the promise of Christ's own words at the Last Supper. This is a petition for consecration, that is, for the setting aside of a gift of God and all it symbolizes, so that God can take it to himself again and use it exclusively for uniting people to himself in holiness. The consecration that is asked for—bread and wine becoming the body and blood of Christ—is the identification of what is being prayed over with something that already belongs totally to God, because it was given to him in sacrifice on the cross, and that it exists totally for the uniting of humanity with God in holiness. What the Church asks is that the sacrifice of Christ become its own sacrifice, so that the expression of its own self-offering to God would be none other than that body and blood in which Christ offers himself eternally to the Father. The eucharistic prayer becomes an act of faith that the worship being offered by the Church is the sacrifice of Christ, having as victim Christ himself, whose real immolation on Calvary is made present sacramentally in the consecrated bread and wine. The worship of the Church is sacrifice because it is the sacrifice of Christ. The eucharistic prayer passes from the consecrated bread and wine to a remembering *(anamnesis)* of the death and glorification of Christ and from this Passover mystery of his it expects the grace of the Holy Spirit to be given for the building up of the Body of Christ. In its act of sacrifice, which is already the fruit of Christ's sacrifice, the Church is opening itself further to the life that comes from the sacrifice of Christ. The Eucharist has, then, the double movement, of sanctification and worship, which is found in every Christian sacrament: grace is received from God in an act of worship of God that is itself his grace. The Eucharist differs from the other sacraments in that the act of worship made in it is an act of sacrifice.

## EFFECTS OF THE EUCHARIST

Like every sacrament, the Eucharist effects what it signifies. The reality signified in it is God's giving of eternal life as a stable, growing possession. This grace is given to those who are being gathered together in the Church by the death and resurrection of Christ and the sending of the Spirit, and are being sent, as members of that Church, to bring God's life to the world while it waits for the coming of the Lord. Participation in this reality is the special grace effect, or sacramental grace of the Eucharist. It is the grace of the Holy Spirit. Its specific eucharistic quality is defined by the tradition in categories drawn from the general theology of grace. It will be analyzed here as (a) *charity*, (b) *ecclesial charity*, or communion in the Body of Christ, and (c) *eschatological charity*, that anticipates and prepares the world for the coming of the Lord. But before examining the grace of the Eucharist according to these three dimensions of charity, there are four general observations that need to be made.

First, the grace of the Eucharist is absolutely necessary *(necessitate medii)* for salvation. There is no salvation without charity, without membership of the Body of Christ, and without being in the world in a way that reflects the "already" and "not yet" of the kingdom. Corresponding to this ontological necessity of the grace of the Eucharist there are ecclesiastical precepts binding people to take part in the Eucharist regularly enough to receive its grace (normally every Sunday and with full sacramental participation at least during the Easter season). The fulfillment of the precepts is subject to all the normal qualifications. If one cannot do what is required in fact, one must do it in desire. The desire of the Eucharist is, indeed, already included in baptism and confirmation and its grace is operative in them (see Chapter 7, "Necessity of Confirmation for Salvation" and "A Suitable Age for Confirmation"). Even in the baptism of desire that is postulated in the salvation of those who are saved by a moral choice of goodness that is not specifically Christian or perhaps even religious, there must be a desire for the Eucharist. People who choose salvation choose the kind of things that the Eucharist stands for: they find ways of celebrating life and fellowship and joy, and the transformation of the world by good people. It is easier to find the desire requisite for salvation in celebrations of this sort than it is to find it in the more cerebral choosing of abstract values like goodness or even God. Most ethical or religious systems within which people work out their salvation outside historical Christianity have rites or images that express these human values. These can serve as secular or religious pointers toward the Eucharist, and help one to understand how all salvific grace is eucharistic.

Second, a general observation needs to be made about the universal range of the effects of the Eucharist. Every Eucharist sacramentalizes the giving of all saving grace, at all times and all places! Other sacraments ask for and give grace only to those who are actually present and participating in the celebration. The Eucharist asks for and gives grace to a limitless range of persons. It can do this because it embodies the sacrifice of Christ and the Church's universal mediation of his grace. The eucharistic prayer expresses this universal intention and effectiveness of the Eucharist. It asks that the sacrifice of Christ that it makes sacramentally present may have its effect on an ever-widening circle of people. It gives pride of place to those who are present and taking part by sacramentally eating the body of Christ and drinking his blood. It also asks for and gives grace to those who are present but not communicating. It does likewise for others who are not present but are being prayed for (in that the Mass is being offered for them), to all those who are remembered as being joined to the Church through the bonds of ecclesial communion, to the faithful departed who are still in need of some purification before they are ready to enter the heavenly liturgy, and eventually to all people who are open to the grace of salvation. There is a theological tradition that describes the grace given by the Eucharist to those who do not communicate as an effect of the Eucharist considered as sacrifice, and contradistinguishes it to the grace given to communicants, which is described as the effect of the Eucharist as sacrament (see Chapter 9, "Saint Thomas Aquinas"; Chapter 10, "The Council of Trent"). The distinction is valuable for explaining an aspect of the Eucharist that makes it different from the other sacraments of the Church. But it is one of those distinctions that should be used, almost before it is made, to unite what it divides. Failure to do so has had unfortunate consequences for Catholic theology in the past. Because the Eucharist is a sacrament, the grace that it gives as a sacrifice is already sacramental. The sacrificial effects, in all their extension, are sacramentalized by the "matter" of the Eucharist within which the sacrifice is realized, because the table of bread and wine is open to all and the body and blood are given for all. The effects are sacramentalized in the eucharistic prayer, which as "form" of the Eucharist makes the sacrifice and directs the grace that comes from it toward its recipients.

Among the petitions that are expressed in the eucharistic prayer are those of the celebrating priest. Because of his ministry his intentions in offering the Eucharist are wide-ranging. They are directed in the first place to the faithful gathered with him in the celebration, of whom he is always, in one way or another, the pastor, and especially to those to whom he will be giving sacramental communion. But he can also be expected to remember in a special way those who by their alms and offerings support him and his ministry. He will want to make his own any petitions they may commend to him. He can make those petitions be the petitions of the whole eucharistic assembly by including them, at least by intention, in the eucharistic prayer. This is the theological ground for what are called "Mass intentions," and for the custom of linking such special intentions of the priest to the acceptance of a gift, called a "stipend," from a benefactor. It is a practice that has a long tradition behind it in the Catholic Church. It is, without doubt, open to misunderstanding and abuse. The Church has regulated it by law and practical moral teaching. Sometimes this discipline has been accompanied by a theology that suggests that the giving of a stipend is some kind of legal transaction based on the give-and-take of justice. Mass intentions and stipends must, however, be seen and judged above all as an exercise of eucharistic charity. A Christian community is grateful to any of its members who support its ministers and make it possible for them to live in the service of the Church. Its thankfulness is felt in a special way in the celebration of the Eucharist. The priest is particularly sensitive to the needs and wishes of those who contribute to his support and to the well-being of the Church. If he should choose to single out and pray for the intentions of one or more of those benefactors at a particular Eucharist, and to commend their intentions to the Church, his choice is adopted by the community, so that the intention of priest and benefactor is taken up into the Church's eucharistic sacrifice. The benefactor has the comfort of knowing that his or her gift and intention, in becoming the intention of the Church, is offered to God with the unique love and thanksgiving that the Eucharist realizes. The effect of that offering will occur according to the normal process of eucharistic grace: it will be received by those who open themselves to grace and let themselves be caught up in the charity that flows from the Eucharist. If the gift sought is of a material sort (rain, a good harvest, peace, etc.) it can only be considered an effect of the Eucharist to the extent that it draws people in grace to thankfulness and love. There is no way of measuring the grace or the gift against the stipend offered. The issue is not one of justice. Questions of justice may arise because of the discipline of the Church regarding Mass stipends, which, obviously, has to be conscientiously obeyed. But they do not prevail over the fundamental reality of gift giving and gift receiving, measured only by the bonds and responsibilities of love, which is the give and take that belongs intrinsically to the Eucharist. People can have the full benefit of the Eucharist, and a priest can direct it to whomsoever he wishes, quite independently of the practice of giving and receiving stipends.

Third, it needs to be noted that the grace that is given as fruit of the eucharistic sacrifice is not just generic grace; it is specifically eucharistic. Its eucharistic quality is obvious for those who actually eat and drink the body and blood. But it is also there in the grace given to those who do not communicate. What is offered to them as fruit of the sacrifice is a reaching out of the charity of the Church drawing them into its communion. If they are Christians, the grace offered will meet and correspond to the desire for eucharistic communion that they must have, and will be confirmed and increased when they actually do receive communion at another Eucharist. The effects of the Eucharist as sacrifice, or "fruits of the Mass" as they have often been called in the Catholic tradition, are eucharistic for the faithful departed: they draw them into the ultimate communion of saints in the heavenly banquet. They are eucharistic for all those who, as a result of prayers offered for them in the Eucharist, are saved without becoming Christian, because they draw them into various expressions of fellowship and peace and service of the world that reflect the Eucharist. Correspondingly, it must be recognized that what has been called the grace of the Eucharist as sacrament is always the fruit of the sacrifice. It is obviously so for those who receive the body and blood of Christ in the course of a full eucharistic celebration. It is so for the sick to whom the sacrament is brought when they are unable to be present at the Eucharist, or for people who receive it "outside Mass" for any other reason. The attitudes that the grace of the Eucharist provokes in them are precisely those expressed in the sacrificial movement formulated in the eucharistic prayer. The Lord's Prayer expresses these same attitudes, and is well used as a preparation for receiving the sacramental body and blood of Christ in any circumstances.

Fourth, a general remark needs to be made about the measure and frequency in which the grace of the Eucharist is given. The reality signified by the Eucharist is of limitless saving worth and power. Because of the limited capacity of the human heart, however, it is received in limited measures. And yet, because it can be repeated again and again there is no end to the receiving of it. The multiplication of it is not done mathematically. To say that nine Masses are better than one is really to say nothing: if one is talking about the objective worth of the Mass, nine times infinity is not any more than infinity; if one is talking about the subjective laying hold of the grace that comes from the Mass one has to qualify the statement with reference to the capacity of those for whom the Eucharist is being celebrated before it makes any sense. The Eucharist is a sacrament for human life. As there are rhythms for taking food that suit human life and nourish health and growth, so there are rhythms for taking part in the Eucharist that suit the life of grace. They suit the celebrating community and the individuals who belong to it. They can vary at different stages of the life of grace and from one community to another. To upset them, either by excess or defect, is to do a certain violence to life. The rhythm set by the main liturgical traditions is of weekly celebration, on the Lord's Day, for the living of a full Christian life; more frequent, even daily, for a more intense level of waiting for the coming of the Lord; and an annual celebration of special solemnity at Easter as a necessary minimum for life. There may be virtue in a certain modest abstinence from the Eucharist (there are examples of renunciation of daily Eucharist in the liturgical tradition, and it has been used with effect in some forms of spirituality) and in an occasional "over-indulgence" (like the three Masses on Christmas Day and All Souls' Day) but the criterion is never mathematical. One does not deprive others of grace by measuring the celebration of the Eucharist according to the rhythms of the life of the celebrating community and its members. A Eucharist well and truly celebrated according to the rhythms set by the liturgical tradition reaches out to others more realistically, and is therefore more grace-bearing, than a numerically multiplied Eucharist that does a kind of violence to the body of Christ because it does not respect the rhythm of its life.

It was proposed at the beginning of this section to use the theological categories of (a) charity, (b) ecclesial charity or communion, and (c) eschatological anticipation, to analyze the specific grace of the Eucharist.

(a) Charity: Life is realized to the full in love. In giving eternal life the Eucharist gives that special kind of love that Christians call charity. Everything about the Eucharist promotes charity. It is the supreme expression of God's love, which Christ made his own: the only response to that love is love. It breaks down the barriers to love by taking away sin. People are reconciled to one another in being reconciled to God by Christ. They can sit down at table together because they are being brought together by the body of Christ. The joy of love is promoted by the joy of a common festive celebration. Gifts are shared because they are being recognized with thanks as being from God and are being consecrated to him. The charity that is the effect of the Eucharist is experienced first and foremost within the celebrating community. But it is no inward-looking coziness. Because it is the charity of God it reaches out to the whole world. It reaches out in the prayer that is offered but also in a readiness to act. It is concerned with the needs of the poor in a realistic way, and especially with the divisions and lack of care that poverty manifests within the human family.

A practical readiness to help the needy is part of the sacramentality of the Eucharist. One can document it from the tradition, although there have been periods when little enough was made of it in the Church. The courage to take the social and political action that the real care of the poor always requires is present in the charity given by the Eucharist. So is the firmness of love and even the anger of love toward those who deprive the poor of the gifts of God and so contradict the Eucharist. But eucharistic charity has the passion to reconcile rather than to further divide. It is always an invitation to people to sit down together at the Eucharist itself and become life-giving rather than death-dealing for one another in the body of Christ. The prayer for peace that is made in the Eucharist is not only a prayer that Christians will be left in peace by the world but that the whole world will be given the fruit of Christ's sacrifice in the form of a just and reconciling love that brings peace.

(b) Ecclesial Charity: The charity caused by the Eucharist is intrinsically ecclesial. The relationships that it forms and in which its fidelity is proved are those of the Body of Christ. The Body is, first and foremost, the community of those who accept the word of God in faith and are baptized, who live in accordance with the gospel, who accept the ministry of those who have been ordained in the apostolic succession, and who accept the canonical discipline of communion. These institutional bonds of unity are recognized in the eucharistic rite. The Eucharist supposes them, reinforces them, and fills them with the life of love. It is in giving charity within this community that the Eucharist brings about the unity of Church. And it is that very unity that gives the Church the power to change the world and draw it into the Body of Christ by its witness and practice of love.

In making the Church grow in unity, charity has to overcome sin. All sin is a failure to love God and a breach of unity with those who are together in God's love. No Christian community or any member of it is perfect in love or fully faithful to the bonds of communion that have been set up in baptism and confirmation. Eucharistic charity brings growth in unity by overcoming the daily sins of Christians and reconciling them in love. The rite itself signifies ecclesial reconciliation in many ways, and most of all by letting those who are reconciled eat and drink together the body and blood of Christ. There are, however, some sins that the Church attempts to overcome by a discipline of temporary exclusion from full participation in the Eucharist. They are especially the sins that break the unity of the Church. Those who are judged to have broken the unity of faith by heresy or the union of love by schism, those who are judged to have seriously transgressed the law of Christ that Christians are agreed to live by, those whose baptism has made them members of a church that is judged to be outside Catholic communion—all those are excluded in various degrees from the Eucharist. Initially the exclusion is self-imposed. Those who culpably refuse the love of God and the bonds of Christian communion cannot mean what the Eucharist signifies or be open to its grace. Their sin is incompatible with full sacramental participation in the Eucharist. Subsequently, when the original culpable action is no longer being deliberately chosen (as can be, for example, the situation of people born and baptized into schismatic churches), the exclusion becomes a matter of discipline, administered by the pastoral authorities of the Church, who can determine some of its modalities and conditions.

It is important to understand the fundamental meaning of this exclusion, before going on to consider how it is applied in practice. It is not a punitive process, as if the Eucharist were a reward for good behavior that could be taken away as a punishment. The discipline of exclusion is for the reconciliation of sinners. It takes as its model Jesus, who went to eat with sinners because "it is those who are sick who need the physician." The purpose of exclusion is eventually to draw sinners back into full eucharistic communion. The charity of the Eucharist is endlessly forgiving. The judgment of the Church is that in excluding someone from the Eucharist for a specific reason it is proclaiming to them and to the whole Church the impor-tance of the bond that they are transgressing for their relationship with God, for the internal unity of the Church and for the credibility of its mission to the world. It is saying that the sin that has given rise to their separation is incompatible with the Eucharist. It is chal-lenging them to recognize this, to repent, and offering them a joyful welcome back into full eucharistic communion. That proclamation is believed to strengthen all the members of the Church in their own fidelity to the bonds of love. Christians generally recognize the value of this discipline of exclusion. Those who have sinned seriously will not take full sacramental part in the Eucharist until the grace of God has moved them to repentance and they have been reconciled with the Church in accordance with its penitential discipline. Christians who are cut off from communion with a church will not normally want to take part in its Eucharist until the situation that is responsible for their exclusion has been resolved. They may draw grace from the Eucharist by being prayed for in it and by feeling the charity of the Church that reaches out to them in reconciling love, but not by sacramental communion.

Because the discipline of exclusion is itself an exercise of eucharistic charity it has to be implemented with great delicacy. Very special care is needed when those who are being excluded are, in fact, living in a faith and charity that already unites them in a deep way to the eucharistic community. This is the situation of repentant sinners who have not yet fulfilled the canonical requirements of sacramental confession, penance, and absolution. The discipline of exclusion is not absolute in this case. It allows that repentant sinners can take full part in the Eucharist before fulfilling the requirements of reconciliation, if they are prevented from doing so for a reasonable cause. They are, however, required to make confession and receive absolution as soon as possible afterward. The thinking would seem to be that the power of the Eucharist to strengthen charity and take away sin by uniting a repentant sinner to the body of Christ and in it to his members (who are, all of them, also repentant sinners) is too valuable at that moment to be denied by a strict enforcement of the discipline of exclusion. The obligation of subsequent confession shows that what brought about the original exclusion has not been treated lightly.

A similar care is called for when the exclusion is due to the absence of communion between churches. There are Christians who share the faith of the Catholic Church and live in a charity that unites them deeply to its members, but are excluded from its Eucharist because they belong to a church that is not in communion with it. The discipline is not absolute here either, because Christians from other churches are, in fact, admitted to the Eucharist of the Catholic Church in certain circumstances. The charity that the Eucharist causes will always strive to use the discipline of exclusion in a way that will contribute to the unity of all Christians in the Church. It will find itself torn between two lines of theological reasoning about what is best for Christian unity, and will try to find a practical solution to the dilemma generated by the contrasting conclusions that may emerge. It can be argued, on the one hand, that Christians who, although they do not belong to the Catholic Church, are already united with its members in faith and love and are actively committed to Christian unity have, in fact, already overcome the fundamental barrier to eucharistic communion; their participation in a Catholic Eucharist can be a precious uniting grace for them as well as for the Catholic community. It can be argued along this line that, because such Christians are actively working for full institutional communion between the churches, their present lack of full communion cannot be culpable and will be repaired as soon as possible—as would be the case with repentant sinners who have not been able to have sacramental absolution. One may argue that to waive the discipline of exclusion in particular cases of this sort, for the sake of letting the uniting grace of the Eucharist be fully availed of, is to be faithful to the reconciling grace of the Eucharist: the grace of unity is being made available both to those being received to eucharistic communion and to the Catholic community that receives them. One will add that Catholics are well enough informed about ecumenical issues nowadays to be protected from unnecessary scandal by such a practice.

The same eucharistic charity, however, and the sense of responsibility that goes with it, especially in those whose ministry makes them responsible for the unity of the Church, will argue along another line and reach a different conclusion. The principle will be that a Eucharist that is readily open to those who are not in full communion with the celebrating Church contradicts itself, because it professes a unity that does not in fact exist. It will be pointed out that many Christians do not appreciate the importance of full ecclesial communion and will see in the practice of "intercommunion" an encouragement to believe that it does not matter very much what church one belongs to, or whether churches are in communion with one another or not. It will be argued that a strict enforcement of the discipline of exclusion is more honest and ultimately does more for promoting real Christian unity. Those who exercise pastoral authority in the churches have to decide between the conflicting claims of these two lines of arguments in the way they regulate the discipline of exclusion in ecumenical relations between the churches. In the Catholic Church they will be guided by the teaching of Vatican II, in its *Decree on Ecumenism*, n. 8, and by the *Directory for the Application of Principles and Norms on Ecumenism,* Vatican, 1993, nn. 122–136. They will be implementing a discipline that is an essential feature of the respect the Church owes to the truth of the Eucharist. At the same time they will be taking account of the truth that the Eucharist, while being a sign and anticipation of the perfect communion of heaven, is also the food of a pilgrim people, giving them the kind of love that must survive and even grow amidst the strains and accommodations forced on those who travel.

(c) Eschatological Charity: The charity that is the effect of the Eucharist, and which builds the Church as communion in the body of Christ, is eschatological. It is already a possession of eternal life and an anticipation of heaven. It looks to the resurrection and to being with Christ beyond the veil of sacramentality. The Eucharist is the food of immortality for body and spirit. Those who are nourished by it live forever. In the eucharistic prayer they make their own the "Holy, Holy, Holy" that is sung eternally before the transcendent majesty of God. They touch there the high point of contemplation. They celebrate communion with Mary and all the saints in the heavenly liturgy. At the same time, because those who celebrate the Eucharist are not yet in full possession of eternal life their access to the transcendent mystery of the All-Holy God is an act of contemplation of the earthly kind, needing to be nourished by and nourishing dedication to the practice of contemplative prayer. Communion with Mary and the saints includes an appeal to their intercession and a desire to follow their example. The eucharistic prayer, and the prayers and songs that are used on the feasts of Christ and the saints, are the words of people who are at home with the Lord and yet still on the way to their heavenly home. Because those who take part in it are still in the body, the Eucharist gives a charity that is appropriate to the present age of the world and to what has to be done there by those who are waiting for the coming of the Lord. Every Eucharist is a viaticum, that nourishes the body in nourishing the spirit. It gives Christians the grace to live in love in their bodies in view of the resurrection. Both Christian marriage and Christian celibacy are caught up in the heavenward movement of eucharistic charity. So is people's management of property and their exercise of social responsibility. So are other experiences of bodiliness, such as health-care and healing, asceticism, and all the arts in which the body becomes joy and celebration. The eschatological charity of the Eucharist transfuses bodiliness in all its forms with faith and hope in the resurrection.

The eschatological quality of the effects of the Eucharist would seem to be particularly valuable for understanding the practice of reserving some of the consecrated bread after the celebration, and also the various forms of devotion to the reserved host that are practiced in the Western Catholic tradition. If the Eucharist is the sacrament of life for those who are waiting for the Lord, there are advantages in having it always available: it gives perfect readiness for meeting the Lord. A full celebration of the Eucharist cannot be arranged for every Christian who is ill or dying; but they can be given communion from hosts reserved for this purpose. This is the historical and theological reason for reservation. That the reserved sacrament should be adored is a natural consequence of belief in the real abiding presence of Christ in it. For those who are meant to be at all times waiting for the coming of the Lord, it is quite in keeping with the sacramentality of the Eucharist to use adoration of the reserved sacrament to prolong the sense of the mystery celebrated in the Eucharist, to revive the grace of the sacrament, and to practice the kind of contemplation that the Eucharist offers to those who long for the vision of the All-Holy God. It is, no doubt, possible that those who practice such devotions are making of them a substitute for or distraction from the primary act of eucharistic devotion, which is the liturgical celebration of the sacrament itself with sacramental eating and drinking of the body and blood of the Lord. But it does not have to be so. One can quite well find the essential effect of the Eucharist in its liturgical celebration and then find a prolongation of it in other exercises of eucharistic devotion. At the same time, it cannot be said that those who do not practice such additional forms of eucharistic devotion are, by that very fact, rejecting the essential values of the sacrament or neglecting its grace.

As a grace of the time of waiting for the coming of the Lord the grace of the Eucharist is a sending on mission. It equips Christians for the task of preparing the whole world for its final destiny, which will be revealed when Christ comes to judge. In building itself up as Body of Christ through the Eucharist the Church is becoming the instrument that proclaims the Lordship of Christ to all people. The Eucharist makes it do so with the love that Christ himself showed, and also with a readiness to suffer for the sake of love that made the cross the supreme expression of his love. The Church's word to humanity is always a call to the kind of unity that it itself experiences in the Eucharist. It calls people unashamedly to faith in Christ and baptism. In doing so it also calls them to the Eucharist. It dares to hope that, even if they do not join with the Church in the sacrament that is celebrated in this time of waiting, they will so live as to join it in the reality of the Eucharist that is celebrated in heaven.

# Chapter 12

# Epilogue: Celebrating Initiation

## THEOLOGY AND PASTORAL PRACTICE

Every Christian initiation is a unique, unrepeatable event. So is every celebration of the Eucharist. Persons who are initiated are addressed by name; there is warrant in the tradition for naming the person who is being given the body and blood of Christ in communion. The rite is personalized by the word; the word is spoken uniquely to the person for whom the rite is being celebrated. If they are to be life-giving, rite and word must touch and transform the individual life of a person in all its particularity. Humans have only one life which, although it can be analyzed on different levels, is all of a piece. This is what Scholastic theologians were saying when they talked about grace building on nature. If the grace life given in a sacrament is not in continuity with the full range of life forces that are at work within the participant it will be rootless and die like the gospel seed thrown on stony ground. Obviously there is a sameness about the word and rite that are used in every sacramental celebration. There are certain things that the Church, as bearer of God's grace, must always do and say in baptism, confirmation, and Eucharist. But what is done for individuals in their baptism, confirmation, and Eucharist is always more than can be written in rituals or theologized about in books. It is an event of the Church, individualized and personalized by the participants and by the care that ministers of the Church give to each one of them, in preparation, celebration, and pastoral follow up. Individual celebration is the province of pastoral ministry rather than of theological programming. It is a work of art rather than a construct of science. People who write books about the theology of sacraments need to be constantly reminded that the reality of sacraments goes beyond what can be written in a book. The last word does not lie with the theologian. The people who are described generically by the theologian as participants and ministers are named individuals, each with a personal life story and with personal gifts and skills. A theology that has not somehow grown out of experience of this pastoral reality, and made itself open to being translated into a realistic, life-connected word in an actual celebration, will be a poor theology of sacrament.

The theologian can look with wonder and respect on the pastoral gifts of those who make good sacraments: on their skills with words and their skills with rites; on their ability to make the sacrament be so much part of the life of the participants that its life-giving, life-transforming potential can be released in them. These are the teachers and catechists, the liturgists and ministers, and the presiding pastors, who together make sacraments happen for people. They are the prophets and the priests who have always been present in the community of God's People, to make the word relevant to life and to keep the rites real and God-centered. The theologian is something of a prophet, but he or she also has the role of a scribe. The pastors and priests need their scribes. If they do not know the tradition of God's People they may invent stories and manipulate rites in a way that seems to correspond well with the life situation of their people, but may be empty of the life that comes from God. In telling the story of sacraments, of how they have been done and what has been believed and thought about them in the Church, and in making some systematic sense of them in terms of a contemporary human wisdom, the theologian is offering the catechist and the liturgist an invitation. It is an invitation to hear the whole story about sacraments: to develop a feel for the tradition of words and rites that lies behind present-day teaching and liturgical forms; to evaluate them critically and systematically; to have reliable intellectual criteria for judging how well any given insertion of a sacrament in an individual life situation is being true to the divinely given reality of the sacrament.

A theology of sacraments can be heard as an invitation by catechists and liturgists only if it is open to real, contemporary life situations. The theologian must have verified his or her thinking by some experience in actual sacramental practice, or at least have a proven ability to listen to and learn from those who do. A theology can be recognized as having this relevance to life while being fully technical and scientific. Some such theologies remain on a quite general level, developing those universal aspects of the tradition of faith that are shared by all Christians and that unite them in a common level of human experience in the Body of Christ. Other theologies already begin to direct the reading of the tradition toward the life situations of people within a particular culture or within a particular historical moment of cultural change. These can be technical and scientific theologies. They can develop a sociological, psychological, and philosophical analysis of the life situation of a particular group of people and, on the basis of it, do a hermeneutically sound interpretation of what the Christian tradition about sacraments means for that group of people. The result can be a distinctive set of words and ideas to explain and accompany sacraments, with proposals for distinctive ways of celebrating them. Latin American theologians, for example, have been doing such a theology of sacraments in recent years, and they have been followed by theologians from other areas of the Church where a life situation distinct from that in which classical Western theologies of sacraments were formed is being recognized. A theology of this sort may see the need to distance itself from certain features of an established European sacramental theology. Indeed, so too must a contemporary contextual theology of Europe itself and of North America: the life situations they address are as dramatically new in many ways as are those of Latin America. Theologies done in this way are a precious support for pastoral practice. It has to be added, however, that contextualized theologies sometimes diminish their value by setting up oppositions between their positions and those of the classical Western theologies of the sacraments. Such supposed oppositions can hide the fact that the tradition of faith that is embedded in classical theologies are being ignored, or listened to selectively. The apostolic faith witnessed to in the Bible and in the writings of the Fathers has been transmitted through the traditions of the churches of Eastern and Western Europe. There is no serious sacramental theology that does not listen appreciatively to the theologies that have emerged from them. The rereading done by contextual theologies has always to be of the complete tradition, not merely of the parts of it that are found to be congenial.

Christian communities draw on the sacramental theologies that are available to them under the influence of the life situation that they share with those who are being initiated into membership and brought to participate in actual sacramental celebrations. Sacramental theology and the rituals of today's Church want the whole community to be active in this pedagogy of life. There is a range of liturgical ministries provided for in every celebration of initiation: bishop, presbyters, deacons, readers, sponsors, parents, and choirs each have their roles. There is also a range of catechetical responsibilities. The bishop is the first catechist of his church: presbyters, deacons, parents, schoolteachers and those who are formally recognized as catechists by the community each play a part. While sacramental theologians will always need to relate to the liturgical ministers of the sacraments, they will want to have an even readier relationship with catechists. The reappearance of catechists, the status given to them and the training they receive, is undoubtedly one of the graces given to the Church of Vatican II. That there are fully trained and full-time catechists is a grace. That there are part-time catechists—laypeople in every sense of the word—who, with training from those qualified, give their service to the community in the work of preparing candidates for initiation is an added grace. If sacramental initiation and practice is from life to the fullness of life it cannot but gain from having as wide a range as possible of life experience introduced into its catechesis.

## THE UNITY OF INITIATION IN THEOLOGY AND PASTORAL PRACTICE

It takes three sacraments to initiate a person into full Christian life. If pastoral practice, and the catechesis that is central to it, is to help human life to grow into the fullness of life through these sacraments, it must keep the unity of the process of initiation clearly before it. To confront human life with one of the sacraments of initiation in isolation is to run the risk of giving a misleading view of the gift of life that God offers. It is easier for theology to maintain a sense of the unity of initiation than it is for catechesis. Theology can choose, as has been done in this book, to do its primary study of the sacraments of initiation on the form they take when celebrated in a continuous rite for the benefit of adults. It can then add the necessary qualifications that have to be made for understanding the sacraments as celebrated for children, or any one of them when it is celebrated apart from the others.

The pastoral worker, however, rarely has that ideal candidate for initiation that the theologian can make the subject of his/her reflection. The life situation that catechesis has to take into account includes the age of the candidate and the sequence and time-lapse between the different sacraments. It also has to allow for the fact that it will sometimes be preparation for a sacrament yet to be received, and at other times, or perhaps at the same time, retrospective reflection on a sacrament already received. The complexities of the task call for a keen sense of the relationship between the three sacraments of initiation.

Meeting the concerns of theology about the unity of initiation should come easiest to the pastoral worker who is dealing with the preparation of adults for full initiation. It should also come easily in the retrospective catechesis that is the required follow up to initiation (*RCIA*, nn. 234–241 1235–2391). That catechesis will want to center in a special way on the Eucharist, not only because it is the fullness of initiation but because the newly initiated are taking part in it regularly as the stable consequence of their initiation. But it will be a catechesis that draws explicit attention to the dependence of the Eucharist on baptism and confirmation.

When children who have reached the age of discretion are being fully initiated (*RCIA*, Part II, nn. 242–306 1306–3691), the catechetical requirements for maintaining the unity of initiation will be the same as for adults, although there will be obvious pedagogical adjustments. When children have already been baptized in infancy the catechesis of initiation will be directed to confirmation. The theological concern would be that this catechesis should also be a retrospective catechesis of baptism. It is being given at the stage of life during which the promises made on behalf of the child at baptism have to be put to it clearly and a personal acceptance of baptism included in the acceptance of confirmation. The catechesis will also need to make it clear how the Eucharist completes initiation and will prepare the one being confirmed to enter fully into the mystery of the Eucharist. However, account has to be taken of the fact that in the common practice of the Latin Church the first catechesis of those baptized in infancy will not be preparing them for confirmation but for their first eucharistic communion. Theology is bound to point out the anomalies of this practice. It cannot but encourage pastoral choices to change it, by having children confirmed before their First Communion. Where the common practice is maintained, theology will at least urge that the catechesis for First Communion includes a retrospective catechesis of baptism and inculcates a sense of and desire for confirmation.

At whatever age people are initiated they require a continuous retrospective catechesis of the sacraments of initiation. The framework for it is provided in the liturgical year, which offers a catechumenate experience for the whole Church during Lent and a baptismal reenactment during the Easter Vigil; it further recalls confirmation by prolonging the Easter giving of the Spirit into the celebration of Pentecost. The time after Easter provides a setting for a retrospective, mystagogical catechesis of initiation. Because it is the heart and center of the liturgical year, the Easter Eucharist, with its dramatic elaboration on Holy Thursday and Good Friday, invites a catechesis of how the Eucharist completes baptism and confirmation and becomes the constantly repeated sacramental core of Christian life. Perhaps the most important skill that a theologian, concerned to affirm the unity of Christian initiation, would want a catechist to have is this ability to make the Eucharist the center of all sacramental catechesis. The Eucharist, indeed, needs to be understood in the light of baptism and confirmation. But that understanding will be communicated effectively if everything that is taught about baptism and confirmation reaches forward to the Eucharist. The life experiences and situations on which the catechesis of these sacraments draws must be of the sort that are open to the gift of eternal life that the Eucharist sacramentalizes.

## FROM LIFE TO FULLNESS OF LIFE

Christian initiation is a movement from life toward the fullness of life. The movement continues throughout the life of a Christian and is always being influenced by the sacraments of initiation. These sacraments can never be far from the mind of pastoral ministers. In their catechesis and preaching there will always be something of a "mystagogical" attention to the way the life situations of the people they minister to are touched by their having been baptized, confirmed, and given eucharistic communion. The ministers will be helping Christians to let these sacraments progressively penetrate and transform their life experiences. The life experiences that are open to the mystery of eternal life and to the passages that need to be negotiated in order to gain it and grow in it are the serious, not the trivial ones. Trivial life experiences have been offered earlier in this book as providing superficial analogies that might help the theological understanding of one or other of the sacraments. But one must not expect such superficial experiences to let people feel how the sacraments bring their human life to the fullness of life. The kind of experiences that are capable of doing that are deep moments, such as when human limitations and the passage of time are felt to be overcome, moments of self-transcendence and of unqualified happiness. They may be moments of discovery in the intimacy of love, moments of vision in the search for truth, moments of delight in the perception of beauty, moments of success in some treasured project, moments of power being exercised decisively for the well-being of some group. But they also may be moments of emptiness and defeat, of social helplessness and the failure of dreams, in which self-transcendence is experienced in yielding oneself in trust to another. Such moments can offer precious human ways of letting the divine gift of eternal life that is given in Christian initiation take deep hold of a human life and bring it toward fulfillment in God.

The specifically religious experience of people will need to be carefully handled in the catechesis and pastoral care that prepares for and follows initiation. It will need to be gathered, sometimes painfully, into the great vision of the Trinitarian God that is given in initiation. The movement from life to the fullness of life that has to be presented in the catechesis of initiation is a movement toward God, who is the goal as well as the giver of eternal life. People can have widely differing experiences of God, not all of them life-giving. One cannot assume that people who come out of an explicitly religious culture, even a Christian one, understand the word God in a way that corresponds to the reality of the one who is revealed and named Father by Jesus. Nor can one be always sure that the personal experience of every candidate will be making the name Father evoke someone who is loving and life-giving. And one may, perhaps, have to wrestle theologically with the feelings of those who want God to be also experienced as and named Mother. The Trinitarian theology that for so long has accompanied the rites of initiation is not always ready-made for catechesis. And this can be true, too, of the theology of grace. Catechesis may have to face the possibility that a candidate for initiation might be so bereft of life-giving personal relationships that the whole idea of receiving life from another, be it a divine or a human person, or one who is both divine and human, has to be put very carefully to them. When people are locked into self-centeredness—whether from fear or selfishness—their relationships with others are fraught with myth and fantasy. There is in everyone something of this tendency to see others, not as they really are, but as they might fulfill one's own felt needs. Catechesis has the task of helping people to break out of self-centeredness and to accept the mysterious other, the God of our Lord Jesus Christ, who gives life in the Christian sacraments. To present Christian initiation merely as human self-fulfillment carries the risk of reducing the Trinitarian theology, that alone can account for the mystery that is in the rites, to what is at best a healing, satisfying myth and at worst an escapist fantasy.

Everything that happens in Christian initiation is believed to happen in and through Christ. The theological word about sacraments is also a Christological word. The catechist realizes that what a candidate for initiation thinks about Christ is affected by what he or she thinks about what it is to be divine and what it is to be human; and then, by how they conceive someone being both divine and human. People can be brought to a sense of the divine in Christ in a way that leaves them with problems about his being human. It takes some intellectual daring and tenacity to affirm full humanness in one who is fully divine. It takes great pedagogical skill to communicate this truth, not just as an intellectual judgment but as a fact of life, on which those who are being initiated are staking their future. How that humanness is appreciated must be related to how the candidate perceives what it is to be human; for if Jesus is not thought to be human in the same sense that the candidate experiences what it is to be human, he cannot be really accepted as Savior. And yet he has to be presented as perfect in his humanness, with a perfection befitting one who is Son of God. It seems easier to attribute perfect goodness and saving power to Jesus in his divinity than to make the laborious and risky effort to understand how he was perfectly good and grace-filled in his humanity, with the same kind of holiness by which other humans are made holy; and that he is active as our Savior in the sacraments of initiation truly as a good man. Even when Jesus is recognized as perfectly human, and as uniquely perfect in his way of being human, there is still the pedagogical problem of dealing with the different images people have of "the perfect man." These may be derived from stories about Jesus himself heard in childhood, or from the way he is presented in Christian art. They may be derived from ancient myths about heroes or modern myths about superstars. Or they may be derived from scientific anthropologies that give their own profile of human perfection. Catechists will have to use the images that speak to a candidate for initiation in order to convey the humanness and human saving power of Jesus. But they will always measure the images they use against the theological teaching of Christian faith. Otherwise, the call to life that is contained in the sacraments of initiation may not be heard as a call to the fullness of life that is in Christ, but to some scaled-down version of it.

Initiation into eternal life in Christ is initiation into the Church that is his Body gathered together and animated by his Spirit. As Body of Christ, gifted by the Spirit and structured in a variety of ministries, the Church is a sociological as well as a theological reality. It shares the fortunes of human society and becomes part of its history. At the same time it is the temple of the Spirit, and as such, an eschatological and missionary reality in the last times of the world. This mystery of the Church has to be presented to those being initiated as it is realized in a particular local community. It is in such a local community that they are being given access to the universal Church. To be initiated into the Church is also a sociological experience and requires sociological options. They cannot be neglected by catechesis on the pretext that initiation is entry into the mystery of Christ and his Spirit. The mystery is certainly more than a sociological reality, but it is realized in sociological and historical choices, as it was in Christ's own life. The theology of Christian initiation deals in general terms with the worldly implications of the gift of eternal life. Catechesis has to help candidates to discover what those implications are in their own particular situation. It has to take account of how they experience the reality of the society to which they belong: how they are living its successes and failures, its tensions and divisions; how they relate to the poor and what responsibility they are prepared to take for social structures. In particular it will help candidates to discover the social significance that the Church they are entering has in their own local world. They will have to identify with the role that the local church has and take some responsibility for it. They will have to be given confidence in the prophetic and priestly gifts that initiation brings them, and some assurance that these gifts will strengthen and when necessary change the role of the local church in the world it touches. On the basis of that assurance they can have the confidence to take on the mission that members of the Church have for the salvation of the world.

It is on the issue of giftedness that the catechesis of initiation will take the understanding of initiation beyond the sociological into the distinctive realm of the Spirit. The tradition of faith suggests that it is in the experience of being gifted, and in the interiority that necessarily accompanies it, that the Holy Spirit is recognized and accepted by believers. To explain convincingly to people that the Holy Spirit is given to them in Christian initiation one needs to be able to call on some real demonstration that the Church they are entering encourages the spiritual gifts of its members and builds itself up from their complementarity. The task of the catechist is made difficult when the local church to which people are being initiated does not reflect these great truths about the manifold gifts of the Holy Spirit and the way their interaction builds up the Church as the Body of Christ. At the same time the experience of giftedness that is used to communicate a sense of what the Holy Spirit means in initiations is of the sort that is in keeping with the gospel of Christ and with the faith of the apostles. It is of the sort that respects the ministerial structures of the Church and obeys those in authority. Life experiences of the Spirit that are divisive and insensitive to the bonds of communion within the Church are not good material for a catechesis of initiation.

A catechesis of initiation has to help candidates for initiation to make the signs and symbolic actions used in the sacraments, and explained in sacramental theology, become real signs of life. The symbolism is not always immediately evident. Some storytelling has to be done to let it come through. Other uses of the same symbol, or analogous symbols, can be appealed to. One can do a certain amount of this in general theology but a catechist will be able to do it on the basis of the known life experiences of those being initiated. The theologian will want to warn against letting this use of analogy turn into a hankering after imitation. To reduce any part of the rite of Christian initiation to an imitation of the rites of human growth and human fellowship would be to compromise its sacramentality. A rite in which the God of salvation is acting through Christ in the Church can have real similarities with rites that evolve in human culture. One can be invited to live it with the same imagination that one puts into the familiar rites of one's spontaneous culture. But the sacramental rite has imperatives that arise from the mystery it holds within it. It is not merely a creation and projection of human life; it is also a projection and an offer of the divine life that fills it. If a true sense of God and of eternal life is being communicated in the catechesis, if the mystery of Christ and the gift of his Spirit in the Church is being recognized, the demands that sacramentality makes in the rites of initiation will be more readily appreciated.

## Life Choices

It is in helping candidates to discover the personal decision that the grace of the sacraments of initiation calls forth that pastoral ministers enter most deeply into their life situations. Moral choices have to be made within and about real-life situations if the grace of the sacrament is to be life-giving. The kinds of choice that are presented to candidates for initiation must be of sufficiently profound and even dramatic seriousness to match the mystery of life and death that is being played out in the sacramental rites. Baptism is the giving of new life through dying to an old life. It calls for a life-and-death decision. What have to be presented in a catechesis of the sacrament are situations that candidates would experience as matters of life and death. Nothing else will convince them about the seriousness of baptism and stir them to the kind of moral decision it requires. Confirmation sacramentalizes the eschatological gift of the Spirit and the effect that it has on human relations with God and on human responsibility for the salvation of the world. Candidates for initiation will have experiences of taking responsibility for their own lives, of doing so under hostile pressure from others, of having to take responsibility for others. They will have some special experiences of being "the last resort," of situations in which they have a feeling that "the end of the world has come"; they will know what it is to "stand up and be counted" in such situations, because of confidence in their own inner resources. The theology of confirmation suggests that it is out of reflection on such situations that the moral challenge of the sacrament will be given realism and continuity with real life. The Eucharist calls people to choose solidarity with and in the Body of Christ in the belief that this is what gives eternal life now and forever. The choices in favor of human solidarity that can be used in a catechesis of the Eucharist must be those that are life-giving, that are reconciling, that want to be a force for unity within the whole human family rather than a sectarian going apart from others, that commit one to work and suffer and sacrifice for the sake of joy, that can live with the disappointment of not having everything all at once and be prepared to wait in hope. Anything less will not serve to convey the mystery that is being entered into in the decision to accept eucharistic fellowship.

The catechetical process of presenting the grace of the sacraments of initiation in continuity with the choices of real life makes it possible for that grace really to transform the life of those who are initiated, and to build up the Church as a community that can transform the real world. The grace of initiation will be ready to be prolonged in the other four sacraments that mark the critical moments of human life in the Church and the world. It will affect decisions that the initiated make singly and together about the whole range of human concerns. It will touch the secular with the sacred, but with a sacredness that is not an escape from the secular, because it is embodied in the secular. It will be an incarnational grace. As the incarnation filled the human reality of Jesus with the life of God, the sacraments will take the reality of human lives and fill them with the life of God, making them in the process not less but more fully human.

## TELLING THE STORY OF SALVATION

The concerns outlined in this Epilogue about the theological quality of the catechesis of initiation are drawn from dogmatic, moral, and sacramental teaching. Careful doctrine about faith and morals is indispensable for the life of God's People, and the creed is at the heart of every catechesis. It must, however, be recognized that it is not doctrinal formulations that ultimately make people live. As was suggested in the Introduction to this book, peoples and communities live by stories, and it is their stories that they act out in their rites. No one knows this better than a good catechist. A catechist will share the theologian's concern about the true meaning of eternal life, of the word "God," of the incarnation, of the Trinitarian mystery of Father, Son, and Spirit, of the Church . . . . But he or she will find these great truths as they emerge and are remembered in the story of God's People: as they are written in its scriptures and woven into life in its traditions about saints and sinners, in its pilgrimages to holy places, in the monuments left behind by the growth and decline of local churches, in the tragic residue of doctrinal disputes and heresies, in the firm judgments of councils, in the variety of liturgical families and schools of spirituality. These stories—but especially those of the origins that are written in scripture—are what a catechist will tell and retell in a way that makes them stories for today. Theological sensitivity will ensure that they are told in depth, with accuracy and consistency; good pedagogy will help candidates to identify with the stories and make them their own; a feeling for ritual will communicate a sense of how the rites of initiation can make the story of salvation life-giving for people of today.

## THE LAST WORD

If the tone of this Epilogue is becoming somewhat oratorical it is perhaps a hint that the last word about the sacraments of initiation might belong, not to the theologian nor to the catechist, but to the preacher. The theologian does the thinking and the catechist the teaching, but it is the preacher who does the talking at an actual celebration of the sacraments. His is the prophetic word that points to the Lord's anointed summoned to the sacramental celebration and says to him or to her "you are the one." The story of salvation is coming true here and now for an individual person in the sacramental rite. The story of the newly initiated is, from now on, being written into the story of salvation, and its unfolding in their lives will be celebrated in every Eucharist that they join. The preacher needs to know both the story of salvation and the story of the people who are being initiated and celebrating, if he is to tell how the two stories are being brought together in the sacramental rite. He needs to be a theologian and he needs to have some of the skills of the catechist and of the liturgist. But his own gift is different from theirs, and he does best when he builds on their gifts and does not duplicate them. He tells what is happening here and now, and why it is happening, and what is needed to make it happen to the full.

The time comes, however, for the preacher, too, to be silent. The final word is not about the sacrament or about the story of salvation: it is the sacramental word itself. It is said by the minister(s), who perform the priestly task of making the rite. It is the climax of all the words that surround and build up the sacrament and points it toward the participant. It is the personal word of Christ in which his present intentions toward this person are revealed. It is received in faith by the whole Church as embodying the presence and the power of Christ. It is the word that finally demands belief, and the here and now consequences of belief, from those who are taking part in the sacrament. It is the word spoken within the rite that finally gives life.

# Appendix
## Further Reading

### INTRODUCTION

**General Introductions to Christian Liturgy**

Martimort, A. G. and others, *The Church at Prayer*. Trans. from French; revised edition, 4 vols. Collegeville, MN: The Liturgical Press and London: Chapman, 1986–1988.

Fink, P. E., SJ, ed., *The New Dictionary of Sacramental Worship*. Collegeville, MN: The Liturgical Press, 1990.

Jones, C., Wainwright, G., Yarnold, E., SJ, and Bradshaw, P., eds., *The Study of Liturgy*, London: SPCK, Oxford: Oxford University Press, Revised edition 1992.

Chupungco, Ansgar, OSB, ed., *Handbook for Liturgical Studies. Introduction to the Liturgy*. Vols. I–V. A Pueblo Book. Collegeville, MN: The Liturgical Press, 1997.

Jones, C., Wainwright G., Yarnold, E., SJ, and Bradshaw, P., eds., *The Study of Liturgy*. London: SPCK and Oxford: Oxford University Press, revised edition, 1992, Part One: "A Theology of Worship" by J. D. Crichton, "The Word of God in Worship" by C. M. Norén, "Ritual" by M. Searle.

**Rites and Their Place in Human Life**

van Gennep, A., *The Rites of Passage*. Chicago: University of Chicago Press, 1960 (originally written 1908).

van der Leeuw, G., *Religion in Essence and Manifestation*. London, 1938.

Dillistone, F. W., *Christianity and Symbolism*. London: Collins, 1955.

Zaehner, R. C., *At Sundry Times*. London: Faber and Faber, 1958.

Eliade, M., *Patterns in Comparative Religion*. London: Sheed & Ward, 1958.

Eliade, M., *The Sacred and the Profane*. New York: Harcourt, Brace and Company, 1959.

Bouyer, L., *Rite and Man*. Trans. from French, Notre Dame: Notre Dame Press, 1963.

Turner, V. W., *The Ritual Process*. New York: Cornell University Press, 1969.

Bocock, R., *Ritual in Industrial Society*. London: Allen & Unwin, 1974.

Fourez, F., sj, *Sacraments and Passages*. Notre Dame, Indiana: Ave Maria Press, 1983.

Valenziano, C., "Liturgy and Anthropology: The Meaning of the Question and the Method for Answering It," in Chupungco, A., osb, ed. *Handbook for Liturgical Studies. Introduction to the Liturgy.* Vols. I–V. Collegeville, MN: The Liturgical Press, 1997, vol. II, 11, pp.189–225.

Bell, C., *Ritual. Perspectives and Dimensions*. Oxford/London: Oxford University Press, 1997.

**Word and Rite:**

Bouyer, L., *Rite and Man*. Trans. from French. Notre Dame: Notre Dame Press, 1963.

Rahner, K., "The Word and the Eucharist" in *Theological Investigations* 4. London, 1966, pp. 253–286.

Shea, J., *Stories of Faith*. Chicago: Thomas More Press, 1980.

Shea, J., *Stories of God: An Unauthorized Biography*. Chicago: Thomas More Press, 1978.

Navone, J., sj, *Seeking God in Story*. Collegeville, MN: The Liturgical Press, 1990.

Tracy, D., *The Analogical Imagination*. New York: Crossroads, 1998 (especially in his treatment of "manifestation" and "proclamation").

# CHAPTER 2. RITES CALLED SACRAMENTS

References to specialized studies on *musterion* and *sacramentum* in individual Fathers can be found in dictionaries and manuals of Patrology.

## Patristic and Magisterial texts on "Sacrament":

Palmer, P., sj, *Sacraments and Worship. Liturgy and Doctrinal Development of Baptism, Confirmation, and the Eucharist.* London: Longmans, Green and Co., 1957.

## *Musterion/Sacramentum* in the First Three Centuries (Clement, Origen, Tertullian):

Neunheuser, B., osb, *Baptism and Confirmation.* Trans. from German. New York: Herder and Herder, 1964, Chapters 1–4.

## The Mystery Religions:

Rahner, H., sj, *Greek Myth and Christian Mystery.* Trans. from German. London: Burns & Oates, 1963.

## The Mystagogical Catecheses:

Yarnold, E., sj, *The Awe-Inspiring Rites of Initiation. The Origins of the R.C.I.A.* 2nd edition. Collegeville, MN: The Liturgical Press, 1994.

## The Sense of Sacramentality in Patristic Exegesis:

Danielou, J., sj, *The Bible and the Liturgy.* Trans. from the French. Notre Dame: University of Notre Dame Press, 1965; paperback edition. *Bible and Liturgy.* University of Notre Dame Press, 2002.

## "Sacrament" in Saint Augustine:

Neunheuser, B., osb, *Baptism and Confirmation.* Trans. from German. New York: Herder and Herder, 1964, Chapter 5.

## Historical Material with Distinctive Theological Interpretation:

Casel, O., osb, *The Mystery of Christian Worship.* Trans. from German of 1932 and incorporating subsequent editions, London: Darton, Longman & Todd, 1962; paperback edition. New York: Crossroads Publishing Company, 1999.

## Critique of Casel's Position on "Mystery":

Bouyer, L., *Liturgical Piety.* Notre Dame: Notre Dame Press, 1956; published also as *Life and Liturgy.* London: Sheed & Ward, 1956, Chapter 7.

Dalmais, I., OP, "Principles of the Liturgy" in Martimort, A. G. and others, *The Church at Prayer.* Trans. from French; revised edition, 4 vols. Collegeville, MN: The Liturgical Press and London: Chapman, 1986–1988, vol. I, pp. 266–271.

## Sacraments in Orthodoxy:

Ware, T., *The Orthodox Church.* New edition. London: Penguin Books, 1997, Chs. 13, 14, 15.

Schmemann, A., *Sacraments and Orthodoxy.* New York: Herder & Herder, 1965.

## The Middle Ages and Saint Thomas:

Marsh, T., "The Sacramental Character" in *Sacraments,* ed. D. O'Callaghan. Dublin: Gill & Son, 1964.

Gallagher, J., *Significando Causant. A Study of Sacramental Causality.* Fribourg: Editions Universitaires, 1965.

Walsh, L. G., OP, "Sacraments" in *The Theology of Thomas Aquinas.* Edited by R. van Nieuwenhove and J. Wawrykow. Notre Dame: University of Notre Dame Press, 2005, pp. 326–364.

## Sacramental Theory and Practice in the Later Middle Ages:

Jungmann, J. A., SJ, *The Mass of the Roman Rite: its origins and development (Missarum Sollemnia).* New rev. and abridged edition of *Missarum Sollemnia,* 2 vols., (1949), New York: Benziger Brothers, 1959.

Vogel, Cyrille, *Medieval Liturgy. An Introduction to the Sources.* Revised and translated from French (1981) by W. G. Storey and N. K. Rasmussen, OP, Washington, DC: The Pastoral Press, 1986.

## The Reformers' Understanding of "Sacrament" with Reference to the Eucharist:

Brilioth, Y., *Eucharistic Faith and Practice, Evangelical and Catholic*. Trans. from Swedish. London: SPCK, 1930, 1956.

Thompson, B., *Liturgies of the Western Church*. Cleveland/New York, 1962; Philadelphia: Fortress Press, 1980.

## The Decrees of the Council of Trent on Sacraments:

Duval, A., OP, *De Sacraments au Concile de Trente*. Paris: Edition du Cerf, 1985.

Tanner, N. P., SJ, ed., *Decrees of the Ecumenical Councils*. Vols. I and II. London and Washington: Sheed & Ward and Georgetown University Press, 1990, pp. 684–713.

Neuner, J., SJ, and Dupuis, J., SJ, eds., *The Christian Faith: In the Doctrinal Documents of the Catholic Church*. 7th Revised Edition, Staten Island, NY: Alba House, 2001.

## The Decrees of Trent on Sacraments, and Protestant Positions and Post-Tridentine Developments in Catholic Theology:

Leeming, B., SJ, *Principles of Sacramental Theology*. London: Longmans, 1956.

Power, D. N., OMI, *The Sacrifice We Offer. The Tridentine Dogma and Its Reinterpretation*. Edinburgh: T. & T. Clark, 1987.

## Catholic Liturgy from Trent to Vatican II:

Bouyer, L., *Liturgical Piety*. Notre Dame: University of Notre Dame Press, 1956; published also as *Life and Liturgy*. London: Sheed & Ward, 1956, Chapters 4–5.

Pecklers, K. F., SJ, "History of the Roman Liturgy from the Sixteenth until the Twentieth Centuries," in vol. I, 10, pp. 153–178 of Chupungco, A., OSB, ed. *Handbook for Liturgical Studies. Introduction to the Liturgy*. Vols. I–V. A Pueblo Book, Collegeville, MN: The Liturgical Press, 1997.

## Ecumenical Sacramental Theology:

Van Beck, F. J., sj, *Grounded in Love: Sacramental Theology in an Ecumenical Perspective*. Washington, DC: University Press of America, 1981.

Fahey, M. A., ed., *Catholic Perspectives on Baptism, Eucharist and Ministry*. A discussion of the ecumenical "Lima Document," Baptism, Eucharist and Ministry (1982: Faith and Order Paper #111). Lanham, MD: Catholic University Press of America, 1986.

Thurian, M., ed., *Churches Respond to BEM: Official Responses to the "Baptism, Eucharist and Ministry" Text*. Vols. I–VI, Faith and Order Papers 129, 132, 135, 137, 143, 144. Geneva: WCC, 1986–1988.

*Baptism, Eucharist and Ministry 1982–1990. Report on the Process and Responses*. Faith and Order Paper No. 149. Geneva: WCC, 1990.

## Post-modern Theology of Sacraments:

Segundo, J. L., sj, *The Sacraments Today*. New York: Orbis Books, 1973.

Chauvet, L.-M., *Symbol and Sacrament: A Sacramental Re-reading of Christian Existence*. Trans. from French. Collegeville, MN: The Liturgical Press, 1995.

Osborne, K. B., ofm, *Christian Sacraments in a Postmodern World: A Theology for the Third Millennium*. Mahwah, NJ: Paulist Press, 1999.

Power, D. N., *Sacrament: The Language of God's Giving*. New York: The Crossroad Publishing Company, 1999.

John Paul II, Encyclical Letter *Fides et Ratio: On the Relationship between Faith and Reason*, Staten Island, NY: Pauline Books and Media, 1998, n. 91.

Rosemann, P. W., "Postmodern Philosophy and J.-L. Marion's Eucharistic Realism," in *The Mystery of Faith. Reflections on the Encyclical Ecclesia de Eucharistia*. J. McEvoy and M. Hogan, eds. Dublin: Columba Press, 2005, pp. 224–244.

# CHAPTER 3. A THEOLOGY OF SACRAMENT

Roguet, A. M., op, *Christ Acts Through the Sacraments*. Trans. from French. Collegeville, MN: The Liturgical Press, 1954.

Leeming, B., sj, *Principles of Sacramental Theology*. London: Longmans, 1956.

Bouyer, L., *Liturgical Piety*. Notre Dame: University of Notre Dame Press, 1956; published also as *Life and Liturgy*. London: Sheed & Ward, 1956.

Vagaggini, C., osb, *Theological Dimensions of the Liturgy*. Trans. from Italian. Collegeville, MN: The Liturgical Press, 1959.

Rahner, K., sj, *The Church and the Sacraments*. Trans. from German. Freiburg/New York/London: Herder and Herder, 1963.

Schillebeeckx, E., op, *Christ, the Sacrament of Encounter with God*. London/New York: Sheed & Ward, 1963.

O'Neill, C. E., op, *Meeting Christ in the Sacraments*. New York: Alba House, 2007.

O'Neill, C. E., op, *Sacramental Realism. A General Theory of the Sacraments*. Wilmington, DE: Glazier, 1983.

Martos, J., *Doors to the Sacred: A Historical Introduction to Sacraments in the Catholic Church*. Revised, Updated Edition. Tarrytown, NY: Triumph Books, 2001.

Vorgrimler, H., *Sacramental Theology*. Trans. from German by L. M. Moloney. Collegeville, MN: The Liturgical Press, 1992.

McPartlan, P., *Sacrament of Salvation*. Edinburgh: T&T Clark, 1995.

Drumm, M., *Passage to Pasch*. Dublin: Columbia Press, 1998.

Cook, B., *Sacraments and Sacramentality*. Mystic, CT: Twenty-Third Publications, 2002.

McCabe, Herbert, *The New Creation*, new edition, New York and London: Continuum, 2010.

# Chapter 4. Baptism: The Rite

## The Rite of Baptism:

*Ordo baptismi parvulorum*, promulgated 15 May 1969. Published in ICEL English translation as *Rite of Baptism for Children*, 2nd edition, 1973.

*Ordo initiationis christianae adultorum*, promulgated 6 January 1972; emended second printing containing *Praenotanda de initiatione christiana*, 1974. Published in ICEL English translation as *Rite of Christian Initiation of Adults* (interim version, 1974; definitive edition, 1985). Both available in official editions, but also in *The Rites of the Catholic Church as Revised by the Second Vatican Council*. New York:

Pueblo, 1976; new translation of the introductions in *Documents on the Liturgy 1969–1979*. Collegeville, MN: The Liturgical Press, 1982.

## Presentation of the Rite:

Crichton, J. D., *Christian Celebration: Understanding the Sacraments*. 3rd edition. London: Chapman, 1992.

Kavanagh, A., *The Shape of Baptism: The Rite of Christian Initiation*. New York: Pueblo, 1978.

## On Jewish antecedents:

Delorme, J., "The Practice of Baptism in Judaism at the Beginning of the Christian Era" in George, A., and others, *Baptism in the New Testament. A Symposium*. Trans. from French (1956). London: Chapman, 1964.

de Vaux, R., OP, *Ancient Israel. Its Life and Institutions*. Trans. from French, London: Darton, Longman & Todd, 1961. Vol. 2, *Ancient Israel. Religious Institutions*, in McGraw-Hill Paperback Edition, 1965.

Beckwith, R. T., "The Jewish Background to Christian Worship" in C. Jones, G. Wainwright, E. Yarnold, SJ, and P. Bradshaw, eds. *The Study of Liturgy*. London: SPCK and Oxford: Oxford University Press, revised edition, 1992.

## History of the Rite of Baptism:

Whitaker, E. C., *Documents of the Baptismal Liturgy*. 2nd edition. London: SPCK, 1970; Revised Expanded Edition, E. C. Whitaker and Maxwell Johnson, Collegeville, MN: The Liturgical Press, 2003.

Cabié, R., "Christian Initiation" Vol. III, Chapter 1 of Martimort, A. G. and others, *The Church at Prayer*. Trans. from French; revised edition., 4 vols. Collegeville, MN: The Liturgical Press and London: Chapman, 1986–1988.

Nocent, A., OSB, "Christian Initiation during the First Four Centuries" in Chupungco, A., OSB, ed. *Handbook for Liturgical Studies. Introduction to the Liturgy*. Vols. I–V. Collegeville, MN: The Liturgical Press, 1997–2000, vol. IV, pp. 5–28.

Nocent, A., OSB, "Christian Initiation in the Roman Church From the Fifth Century Until Vatican II," in Chupungco, A., OSB, ed.

*Handbook for Liturgical Studies. Introduction to the Liturgy.* Vols. I–V. Collegeville, MN: The Liturgical Press, 1997–2000, vol. IV, pp. 49–90.

Studer, B., osb, "Liturgical Documents of the First Four Centuries," in Chupungco, A., osb, ed. *Handbook for Liturgical Studies. Introduction to the Liturgy.* Vols. I–V. Collegeville, MN: The Liturgical Press, 1997–2000, Vol. I. 12, pp. 199–224.

Johnson, M. E., *The Rites of Christian Initiation. Their Evolution and Interpretation.* Collegeville, MN: The Liturgical Press, 1999.

### The General Anthropology of Rites of Initiation:

Fourez, F., sj, *Sacraments and Passages.* Notre Dame, Indiana: Ave Maria Press, 1983.

Van Gennep, A., *The Rites of Passage.* Original French edition, 1908. Republished Chicago: University of Chicago Press, 1960.

Eliade, M., *Rites and Symbols of Initiation* (first published as *Birth and Rebirth*). New York/London: Harper and Row, 1958.

# Chapter 5. Baptism: The Word

### Scriptural Teaching on Baptism in Biblical Dictionaries:

Articles on "Baptism" in Biblical Dictionaries

Cullmann, O., *Baptism in the New Testament.* Trans. from German. London: SCM Press, 1950 and 1973.

George, A., and others, *Baptism in the New Testament. A Symposium.* Trans. from French (1956). London: Chapman, 1964.

Beasley-Murray, G. R., *Baptism in the New Testament.* Grand Rapids: Eerdemans, 1984.

Schnackenburg, R., *Baptism in the Thought of St Paul.* New York, 1964.

Dunn, J. D. G., *Baptism in the Holy Spirit.* London: SCM Press Ltd., 1970.

### History of Doctrine about Baptism:

Neunheuser, B., osb, *Baptism and Confirmation.* Trans. from German. New York: Herder and Herder, 1964.

## Patristic Texts on Baptism:

Palmer, P., SJ, *Sacraments and Worship: Liturgy and Doctrinal Development of Baptism, Confirmation, and the Eucharist*. London: Longmans, Green and Co., 1957.

Yarnold, E., SJ, *The Awe-Inspiring Rites of Initiation: The Origins of the R.C.I.A.* 2nd edition, Collegeville, MN: The Liturgical Press, 1994.

## On Saint Thomas:

Cunningham, J. J., OP, *Baptism and Confirmation*. Vol. 57 of Thomas Aquinas, *Summa Theologiae* (IIIa, qq. 66–72) London and New York: Blackfriars in conjunction with Eyre & Spotiswoode and McGraw-Hill, 1975.

## On the Issue of Faith and Baptism, Reflecting a Reformation Debate:

Barth, K., *The Teaching of the Church Regarding Baptism*. Trans. from German of 1943. London: SCM Press, 1948.

Cullmann, O., *Baptism in the New Testament*. Trans. from German. London: SCM Press, 1950 and 1973.

J. Duplacy, J., "Salvation by Faith and Baptism in the New Testament" in A. George and others, *Baptism in the New Testament: A Symposium*, trans. from French (1956). London: Geoffrey Chapman, 1964.

## On Ecumenical Developments:

Fahey, M., ed., *Catholic Perspectives on Baptism, Eucharist and Ministry: A Study Commissioned by the Catholic Theological Society of America*. Lanham, MD, 1986.

Root, M. and Saarinen, R., eds., *Baptism and the Unity of the Church*. Geneva: WCC Publications, 1998.

Best, T. F. and Heller, D., *Becoming a Christian. The Ecumenical Implications of Our Common Baptism*. Faith and Order Paper No. 184. Geneva: WCC Publications, 1999.

## General Theology of Baptism:

Wainwright, G., *Christian Initiation*. Richmond, VA: John Knox Press, 1969.

Marsh, T. A., *Gift of Community. Baptism and Confirmation*. Wilmington, DE: Glazier, 1984.

Osborne, K. B., ofm, *The Christian Sacraments of Initiation. Baptism, Confirmation, Eucharist*. New York: Paulist Press, 1987.

## On Baptizing Children:

Jeremias, J., *Infant Baptism in the First Four Centuries*, Trans. from German. London: SCM Press, 1960; Philadelphia: Westminster Press, 1962.

Jeremias, J., *The Origins of Infant Baptism*. Trans. from German. Naperville, IL: A.R. Allenson, 1963.

## On Infants Who Die without Baptism:

The International Theological Commission, *The Hope of Salvation for Infants who Die without Being Baptized*. Vatican, 2007. Text in *Origins*: CNS Documentary Service, vol. 36, no. 45.

# CHAPTER 6. CONFIRMATION: THE RITE

## The Rite of Confirmation: Liturgical Books:

*Ordo confirmationis* promulgated 22 August 1971 (includes the Apostolic Constitution *Divinae consortium naturae* of Pope Paul VI, promulgated 15 August 1971). Published in ICEL English translation as *Rite of Confirmation* (1975).

*Ordo initiationis christianae adultorum*, promulgated 6 January 1972; emended second printing containing *Praenotanda de initiatione christiana*, 1974. Published in ICEL English translation as *Rite of Christian Initiation of Adults* (interim version, 1974; definitive edition, 1985). Both available in official editions, but also in *The Rites of the Catholic Church*. New York: Pueblo, 1976; new translation of the introductions in *Documents on the Liturgy 1963–1979*. Collegeville, MN: The Liturgical Press, 1982.

## History and the Significance of the Rite:

Neunheuser, B., osb, *Baptism and Confirmation.* Trans. from German, New York: Herder and Herder, 1964.

Milner, A., op, *The Theology of Confirmation.* Cork, Ireland: Mercier, 1971.

Fisher, J. D. C., *Confirmation Then and Now.* Chicago, Mundelein, IL: Hillenbrand Books, 2005.

Fisher, J. D. C., *Christian Initiation in the Mediaeval West.* Chicago, Mundelein, IL: Hillenbrand Books, 2004.

Fisher, J. D. C., *Christian Initiation, the Reformation Period.* Chicago, Mundelein, IL: Hillenbrand Books, 2006.

Austin, G., *Anointing with the Spirit. The Rite of Confirmation: The Use of Oil and Chrism.* Collegeville, MN: The Liturgical Press / A Pueblo Book, 1985.

Kavanagh, A., *Confirmation: Origin and Reform.* New York: Pueblo, 1988.

Turner, P., *Confirmation: The Baby in Solomon's Court.* Chicago, Mundelein, IL: Hillenbrand Books, 2005.

Turner, P., *Sources of Confirmation. From the Fathers Through the Reformers.* Collegeville, MN: The Liturgical Press, 1993.

# Chapter 7. Confirmation: The Word

## Biblical Material on the Holy Spirit and Confirmation:

"Holy Spirit" in Dictionaries of the Bible.

Schweizer, E. and others, "Pneuma" in G. Friedrich, ed. *Theological Dictionary of the New Testament.* VI, Grand Rapids: Wm B. Eerdmans, 1964, pp. 332–452.

Lampe, G. M. H., *The Seal of the Spirit.* 2nd edition, London: Longmans, 1967.

Congar, Y. M.-J., op, *I Believe in the Holy Spirit.* Trans. from French; 3 vols. London: Chapman, New York: Seabury, 1983.

Congar, Y. M.-J., op, *Un peuple messianique.* Paris: Editions du Cerf, 1975.

## Patristic Texts on the Holy Spirit:

Patout Burns, SJ, and G. M. Fagin, SJ, eds., *The Holy Spirit.* Message of the Fathers of the Church. Wilmington, DE: Glazier, 1984.

## Doctrinal Tradition and Systematic Study:

Thornton, L. S., *Confirmation, Its Place in the Baptismal Mystery.* Westminster, London: Dacre Press, 1954.

Bohen, M., *The Mystery of Confirmation.* New York: Herder and Herder, 1963.

Cunningham, J. J., OP, *Baptism and Confirmation.* Vol. 57 of Thomas Aquinas, *Summa Theologiac* (IIIa, qq. 66–72). London and New York: Blackfriars in conjunction with Eyre & Spotiswoode and McGraw-Hill, 1975.

Marsh, T. A., *Gift of Community. Baptism and Confirmation.* Wilmington, DE: Glazier, 1984.

## Ecumenical Questions:

Argenti, C., "Chrismation" in *Ecumenical Perspectives on Baptism, Eucharist and Ministry.* Geneva: WCC, 1983, pp. 46–67.

## A Suitable Age for Confirmation:

Congar, Y. M.-J., OP, *I Believe in the Holy Spirit.* Trans. from French; 3 vols., London: Chapman, New York: Seabury, 1983, vol. III, pp. 217–227.

Wilde, J. A., ed., *When Should We Confirm? The Order of Initiation.* Chicago: Liturgy Training Programs (Archdiocese of Chicago), 1989.

# CHAPTER 8. EUCHARIST: THE RITE

## The Rite of Mass

### *The Missal of Paul VI*

The rite as given in the Missal of Paul VI is presented in general works on liturgy dating from after 1970. In reading works that predate 2002 account has to be taken of the fact that a revised edition of the Missal, with a revised edition of the General Instruction, was published that year in Latin. To general works on the liturgy can be added:

Crichton, J. D., *Christian Celebration: The Mass*. London: Chapman, 1971; republished 1981.

Emminghaus, J., *The Eucharist: Essence, Form, Celebration*. Trans. from German, Collegeville, MN: The Liturgical Press, 1978.

## Biblical Origins (Covenant Assemblies, Passover, Blessing Prayers, Table Liturgies):

Bouyer, L., *Liturgical Piety*. Notre Dame, IN: University of Notre Dame Press, 1956; published also as *Life and Liturgy*. London: Sheed & Ward, 1956.

Bouyer, L., *Eucharist: Theology and Spirituality of the Eucharistic Prayer*. Trans. from French. Notre Dame, IN: University of Notre Dame Press, 1968.

Audet, J. P., "Esquisse historique du genre litteraire de la 'bénédiction' juive et de l' Eucharistie chrétienne," *Revue Biblique* 65 (1958), 370–399; trans. as "Literary Form and Contents of a Normal *Eucharistia* in the First Century" in *The Gospels Reconsidered*. Oxford, 1960.

Jeremias, J., *The Eucharistic Words of Jesus*. Trans. from 3rd German edition. London: SCM Press, 1966.

Leon-Dufour, X., *Sharing the Eucharistic Bread: The Witness of the New Testament*. Trans. from French. New York: Paulist Press, 1987.

Jaubert, A., *The Date of the Last Supper*. Trans. from French, New York: Alba House, 1965.

## Sources of the Roman as Well as of Other Rites:

Palmer, P., sj, *Sacraments and Worship. Liturgy and Doctrinal Development of Baptism, Confirmation, and the Eucharist*. London: Longmans, Green and Co, 1957.

Deiss, J., *Early Sources of the Liturgy*. New York, 1967. Published as *Springtime of the Liturgy*. Collegeville, MN: The Liturgical Press, 1979.

Jaspers, R. C. D. and Cuming, G. J., *Prayers of the Eucharist: Early and Reformed*. 3rd edition. New York: Pueblo Publishing Company, 1987.

Massa, E., *Celebration of the Eucharist: The Origin of the Rite and the Development of its Interpretation*. Collegeville, MN: The Liturgical Press, 1999.

### The General History of the Roman Mass:

Dix, G., *The Shape of the Liturgy*. London, 1945; published by Continuum, 2005.

Jungmann, J.A., SJ, *The Mass of the Roman Rite: its origins and development (Missarum Sollemnia)*. New rev. and abridged edition of *Missarum Sollemnia*, 2 vols., (1949). New York: Benziger Bros., 1959.

Cabié, R., *The Eucharist*. Vol. 2 of *The Church at Prayer*, ed. A. G. Martimort, trans. by M. J. O'Connell. Collegeville, MN: The Liturgical Press, 1986.

### The Eucharistic Prayer, with particular reference to the Roman Canon:

Vagaggini, G., OSB, *The Canon of the Mass and Liturgical Reform*. Trans. from Italian, New York: Alba House, 1967.

Bouyer, L., *Eucharist: Theology and Spirituality of the Eucharistic Prayer*. Trans. from French, Notre Dame, IN: University of Notre Dame Press, 1968.

Massa, E., *The Eucharistic Prayer of the Roman Rite*. Trans. from Italian. New York: Pueblo Publishing Company, 1986.

### The Rites Developed by the Reformers:

Thompson, B., *Liturgies of the Western Church*. Cleveland/New York, 1962; Philadelphia: Fortress Press, 1980.

### The "Rite Zairois":

Egbulem, C., OP, "An African Interpretation of Liturgical Inculturation: The 'Rite Zairois'" in Downey, M. and Fragomeni, R., eds., *A Promise of Presence. Studies in Honor of David Power*. Washington, DC: The Pastoral Press, 1992, pp. 227–250.

## On Ritual Meals:

Van der Leeuw, *Religion in Essence and Manifestation*. Trans. from German. London: Allen and Unwin, 1938; with additions from 2nd German edition, Gloucester: Peter Smith, 1967.

Guzie, T., *Jesus and the Eucharist*. New York: Paulist Press, 1974.

Hellwig, M., *The Eucharist and the Hunger of the World*. New York: Paulist Press, 1976.

Fitzpatrick, P. J., *In Breaking of Bread. The Eucharist and Ritual*. Cambridge: Cambridge University Press, 1993.

Smith, D. E., *From Symposium to Eucharist: The Banquet in the Early Christian World*. Minneapolis: Fortress Press, 2003.

# CHAPTER 9. EUCHARIST: THE WORD FROM THE NEW TESTAMENT TO AQUINAS

## New Testament

See articles on "Breaking of bread," "Lord's Supper," "Eucharist" in biblical dictionaries, and from commentaries on eucharistic passages in the Synoptics, Paul, and John; also:

Thurian, M., *The Eucharistic Memorial* I: *The Old Testament*, II: *The New Testament*. Trans. from French, London: Lutterworth Press, 1961.

Delorme, J., and others, *The Eucharist in the New Testament*. Baltimore/Dublin: Helicon Press, 1964.

Jeremias, J., *The Eucharistic Words of Jesus*. Trans. from 3rd German edition, London: SCM Press, 1966.

Barrett, C. K., *A Commentary on the First Epistle to the Corinthians*. New York: Harper & Row, 1968.

Leon-Dufour, X., *Sharing the Eucharistic Bread: The Witness of the New Testament*. Trans. from French. New York: Paulist Press, 1987.

## Patristic texts on the Eucharist in:

Palmer, P., SJ, *Sacraments and Worship. Liturgy and Doctrinal Development of Baptism, Confirmation, and the Eucharist*. London: Longmans, Green and Co, 1957.

Sheerin, J., ed., *The Eucharist*. Message of the Fathers of the Church 7. Wilmington, DE: Glazier, 1986.

## On the Eucharistic theology of the Fathers:

Van der Meer, F., *Augustine the Bishop*. Trans. from Dutch, London, New York: Sheed & Ward, 1961.

Kilmartin, E. J., sj, *The Eucharist in the Primitive Church*. Englewood Cliffs, NJ: Prentice-Hall, 1965.

Rordorf, W. and others, *The Eucharist of the Early Christians*. Trans. from French. New York: Pueblo Publishing Company, 1978.

Halliburton, R. J., "The Patristic Theology of the Eucharist" in *The Study of Liturgy*. ed. C. Jones, G. Wainwright and E. Yarnold, London: SPCK and Oxford: Oxford University Press, revised edition, 1992.

## Orthodox Theology of Eucharist:

Schmemann, A., *The Eucharist: Sacrament of the Kingdom*. New York: St. Vladimir's Seminary Press, 1988.

## On Medieval Theology of the Eucharist:

Aquinas, Thomas, *Summa Theologiae*, Pars IIIa, qq. 73–83; ed. and English trans. W. Barden, op, vol. 58 (qq. 73–78), Blackfriars edition. London/New York: Eyre and Spottiswoode, 1965; vol. 59 (qq. 79–83) ed. and English trans. T. Gilby, op, 1975.

de Lubac, H., sj, *Corpus Mysticum: The Eucharist and the Church in the Middle Ages*. Trans. from French, 2nd edition. 1949. Notre Dame: Notre Dame University Press, 2007.

McCue, J. F., "The Doctrine of Transubstantiation from Berengar through the Council of Trent" in *Lutherans and Catholics in Dialogue, The Eucharist*. Washington/New York, 1967.

Schillebeeckx, E., op, *The Eucharist*. New York: Sheed & Ward, 1968.

Pelikan, J., *The Growth of Medieval Theology* (600–1300), vol. III of *The Christian Tradition*. Chicago: University of Chicago Press, 1978.

Macy, G., *The Theologies of the Eucharist in the Early Scholastic Period. A Study of the Salvific Function of the Sacrament according to the Theologians c. 1080–1220*. Oxford: Clarendon Press, 1984.

Power, D. N., *The Eucharistic Mystery. Revitalizing the Tradition*. New York: Crossroad, 1992.

Kilmartin, E. J., SJ, *The Eucharist in the West. History and Theology.* Ed. R. J. Daly, SJ, Collegeville, MN: The Liturgical Press, 1998.

## Chapter 10. Eucharist: The Word from the Reformers of Trent to Vatican II and Beyond and Chapter 11. Systematic Theology of the Eucharist

### On late medieval theology and the teaching of the Reformers:

Clark, F., SJ, *Eucharistic Sacrifice and the Reformation.* 2nd edition. Chulmleigh, Devon: Augustine Publishing Co., 1980.

Brilioth, Y., *Eucharistic Faith and Practice, Evangelical and Catholic.* Trans. from Swedish. London: SPCK, 1930; new impression, 1965.

Dix, G., *The Shape of the Liturgy.* London, 1945; new edition, London/New York: Continuum, 2000.

Thompson, B., *Liturgies of the Western Church.* Cleveland/New York/Philadelphia: Fortress Press, 1980.

### On the teaching of the Council of Trent:

Rahner, K., SJ, "The Presence of Christ in the Sacrament of the Lord's Supper" in *Theological Investigations* 4. London: Darton, Longman & Todd, 1966, pp. 287–311.

Schillebeeckx, E., OP, *The Eucharist.* New York: Sheed & Ward, 1968.

Power, D.N., OMI, *The Sacrifice We Offer. The Tridentine Dogma and its Reinterpretation.* Edinburgh: T. & T. Clark, 1987.

### Modern works on the Eucharist are mentioned in the text. On theories of transignification/transfinalization:

Powers, J. M., SJ, *Eucharistic Theology.* New York: Herder & Herder, 1967.

O'Neill, C., OP, *New Approaches to the Eucharist.* Dublin: Gill & Son, 1967.

## Eucharistic theology inspired by Vatican II in:

McGoldrick, P., ed., *Understanding the Eucharist*. Dublin, 1969.

Lash, N., *His Presence in the World. A Study of Eucharistic Worship and Theology*. London, 1968.

## Postmodern Eucharistic Theology:

Power, D. N., *The Eucharistic Mystery. Revitalizing the Tradition*. New York: The Crossroad Publishing Company, 1992.

## For Contemporary Ecumenical Discussion:

McAdoo, H. R., ed., *Modern Eucharistic Agreements*. London: SPCK, 1973.

Thurian, M., *The Mystery of the Eucharist—An Ecumenical Approach*. London/Oxford: Mowbray, 1981.

Thurian, M., "The Eucharistic Memorial, Sacrifice of Praise and Supplication" in *Ecumenical Pespectives on Baptism, Eucharist and Ministry*. Geneva: WCC, 1983, pp. 90–103.

Tillard, J.-M.R., OP, "The Eucharist, Gift of God," in *Ecumenical Perspectives on Baptism, Eucharist and Ministry*. Geneva: WCC, 1983, pp. 104–118.

Kilmartin, E. J., SJ, "The Lima Text on Eucharist" in *Catholic Perspectives* on *Baptism, Eucharist and Ministry: A Study Commissioned by the Catholic Theological Society of America*, ed. M. Fahey. Lanham, MD/New York/London, 1986, pp. 135–160.

Reumann, J., *The Supper of the Lord: The New Testament, Ecumenical Dialogues, and Faith and Order on Eucharist*. Philadelphia: Fortress Press, 1985.

Power, D. N., OMI, *The Sacrifice We Offer. The Tridentine Dogma and Its Reinterpretation*. Edinburgh: T. & T. Clark, 1987.

Gros, J., Elder, E. R., and Wondra, E. K., eds., *Common Witness to the Gospel. Documents on Anglican-Roman Catholic Relation 1983–1995*. Washington, DC: United States Catholic Conference, 1997.

Walsh, L.G., OP, "An ecumenical reading of Aquinas on the Eucharist" in M. Klöeckener and A. Join-Lambert, eds., *Liturgia et Unitas*. Fribourg: Universitäetsverlag Freiburg Schweiz, 2001.

# Bibliography

The scriptures are quoted from the Revised Standard Version of the Bible: Old Testament, copyright 1952; New Testament, 1st edition copyright 1946; 2nd edition copyright 1971; the Apocrypha, copyright 1957; Third and Fourth Book of Maccabees and Psalm 151, copyright 1977. All above copyrights held by the Division of Christian Education of the National Council of the Churches of Christ in the United States of America.

The rites of the sacraments are referred to in the ICEL English translation, available in official editions, but also in *The Rites of the Catholic Church*. New York: Pueblo, 1976; new translation of the introductions in *Documents on the Liturgy 1963–1979*. Collegeville, MN: The Liturgical Press, 1982.

The Fathers are quoted in translations, which are acknowledged in the text by the name of the translator and described in detail in this Bibliography.

References to the *Summa* of Saint Thomas Aquinas are to: *Summa Theologiae*. 60 vols. London and New York: Blackfriars in conjunction with Eyre & Spotiswoode and McGraw-Hill, 1963–1975.

Texts from the *magisterium* are quoted in the translation of J. Neuner, SJ, and J. Dupuis, SJ, apart from those of Vatican II which are from the edition of A. Flannery, OP; reference is also made to the translation of N. P. Tanner (full references below).

The following works are referred to in the text:

Anglican-Roman Catholic International Commission (ARCIC), "Eucharistic Doctrine" in *The Final Report*. Windsor, 1971: also in *Modern Eucharistic Agreements*. London: S.P.C.K. and in *Growth in Agreement*. Eds. H. Meyer and L. Vischer, New York: Paulist Press and Geneva: WCC, 1984.

Aquinas, Thomas, *see* Barden; Bourke; Cunningham; Gilby.

Argenti, C., "Chrismation" in *Ecumenical Perspectives on Baptism, Eucharist and Ministry*. Geneva: WCC, 1983, pp. 46–67.

Audet, J. P., "Esquisse historique du genre litteraire de la 'benediction' juive et de l' 'Eucharistie' chrétienne," *Revue Biblique* 65 (1958), 370–399; trans. as "Literary Form and Contents of a Normal *Eucharistia* in the First Century" in *The Gospels Reconsidered*. Oxford: Blackwell, 1960.

Austin, G., OP, *Anointing with the Spirit. The Rite of Confirmation. The Use of Oil and Chrism*. New York: Pueblo Publishing Co., 1985.

Barden, W., OP, *The Eucharistic Presence*. Vol. 58 of Thomas Aquinas, *Summa Theologiae* (IIIa, qq. 73–78). London and New York: Blackfriars in conjunction with Eyre & Spotiswoode and McGraw-Hill, 1965.

Barrett, C. K., *A Commentary on the First Epistle to the Corinthians*. London: Hendrickson 1993.

Barth, K., *The Teaching of the Church Regarding Baptism*. Trans. from German of 1943. London: SCM Press, 1948.

Beasley-Murray, G. R., *Baptism in the New Testament*. London: Macmillan & Co, 1962; Grand Rapids: Eerdemans, 1984.

Beekenkamp, W. H., ed. *Berengarius of Tours, De sacra coena adversus Lanfrancum*. The Hague, 1941.

Bell, C., *Ritual, Perspectives and Dimensions*. Oxford/London: Oxford University Press, 1997.

Benoit, P., OP, *see* Delorme and others.

Berengarius, *see* Beekenkamp.

Best, T. F. and Heller, D., *Becoming a Christian. The Ecumenical Implications of Our Common Baptism*. Faith and Order Paper No. 184. Geneva: WCC Publications, 1999.

Bocock, R., *Ritual in Industrial Society*. London: Allen and Unwin, 1974.

Bohen, M., *The Mystery of Confirmation*. New York: Herder and Herder, 1963.

Boismard, M. E., OP, *see* George and others; Delorme and others.

Bourke, D., *The Sacraments*. Vol. 56 of Thomas Aquinas, *Summa Theologiac* (IIIa, qq. 60-65). London and New York: Blackfriars in conjunction with Eyre & Spotiswoode and McGraw-Hill, 1975.

Bouyer, L., *Eucharist: Theology and Spirituality of the Eucharistic Prayer*. Trans. from French, Notre Dame: Notre Dame University Press, 1968.

Bouyer, L., *Liturgical Piety*. Notre Dame: Notre Dame Press, 1956; published also as *Life and Liturgy*. London: Sheed & Ward, 1956.

Bouyer, L., *Rite and Man*. Trans. from French, Notre Dame: Notre Dame Press, 1963.

Brilioth, Y., *Eucharistic Faith and Practice, Evangelical and Catholic*. Trans. from Swedish, London: SPCK, 1930; new impression, 1965.

Brown, R. E., ss, *The Gospel According to John*. Anchor Bible 29, 29a; 2 vols. Garden City, NY: Doubleday, London: Chapman, 1966, 1971.

Brown, R. E., ss, *An Introduction to the Gospel of John*. Ed. F. J. Moloney. New York: Doubleday, 2003.

Brown, R. E., ss, *The Community of the Beloved Disciple*. New York: Paulist Press, 1979.

Browne, C. G., and Swallow, J. E., editors and translators. *Select Orations of Saint Gregory Nazianzen*. LNPF ser. 2, vol. 7. Buffalo and New York, 1900. Reprinted Grand Rapids, 1952.

Cabié, R. and others, *The Eucharist*. Vol. II of *The Church at Prayer*, ed. A. G. Martimort. Trans. from French. Collegeville, MN: The Liturgical Press, 1986.

Cabié, R. and others, *The Sacraments*. Vol. III, of *The Church at Prayer*, ed. A.G. Martimort. Trans. from French. Collegeville, MN: The Liturgical Press, 1988.

Calvin, J., *A Short Treatise on the Lord's Supper*. Trans. from French by J. K. S. Reid. Library of Christian Classics XXII, Philadelphia, 1954.

Casel, O., OSB, *The Mystery of Christian Worship*. Trans. from German of 1932 and incorporating subsequent editions. London, 1962; paperback edition, New York: Crossroads Publishing Company, 1999.

Castelot, J. J. and Cody, A., osb, "Religious Institutions of Israel" in R. E. Brown, ss, J. A. Fitzmyer, R. E. Murphy, o.carm., eds. *The New Jerome Biblical Commentary*. London: Geofrey Chapman, 1989.

Chauvet, L.-M., *Symbol and Sacrament. A Sacramental Re-reading of Christian Existence*. Trans. from French. Collegeville, MN: The Liturgical Press, 1995.

Chupungco, A., osb, ed. *Handbook for Liturgical Studies. Introduction to the Liturgy*. Vols. I–V. A Pueblo Book. Collegeville, MN: The Liturgical Press, 1997.

Clark, F., sj, *Eucharistic Sacrifice and the Reformation*. 2nd edition. Chulmleigh, Devon: Augustine Publishing Co., 1980.

Congar, Y. M.-J., op, *The Mystery of the Church*. 2nd edition. Baltimore: Helicon Press, 1965.

Congar, Y. M.-J., op, *I Believe in the Holy Spirit*. Trans. from French; 3 vols. London: Chapman, New York: Seabury, 1983.

Congar, Y. M.-J., op, *Un peuple messianique*. Paris: Edition du Cerf, 1975.

Cook, B., *Sacraments and Sacramentality*. Mystic, CT: Twenty-Third Publications, 2002.

Crichton, J. D., *Christian Celebration: the Mass*. London: Chapman, 1971; republished 1981.

Crichton, J. D., *Christian Celebration: Understanding the Sacraments*. 3rd edition. London: Chapman, 1992.

Cullmann, O., "The Meaning of the Lord's Supper in Primitive Christianity" in *Essays on the Lord's Supper*. Richmond: John Knox Press, 1958.

Cullmann, O., *Baptism in the New Testament*. Trans. from German. London: SCM Press, 1950 and 1973.

Cullmann, O., *Le foi et le culte dans l'église primitive*. Neuchâtel, 1963; pub. in part in *Early Christian Worship*. London: SCM Press, 1953.

Cunningham, J. J., op, *Baptism and Confirmation*. Vol. 57 of Thomas Aquinas, *Surma Theologiae* (IIIa, qq. 66–72). London and New York: Blackfriars in conjunction with Eyre & Spotiswoode and McGraw-Hill, 1975.

Cyprian, St., *see* Donna, Deferrari.

Dalmais, I., op, "Principles of the Liturgy" in Martimort, A. G. and others, *The Church at Prayer*. Trans. from French; revised edition, 4 vols. Collegeville, MN: The Liturgical Press and London: Chapman, 1986–1988.

Danielou, J., sj, *The Bible and the Liturgy*. Trans. from French. Notre Dame: University of Notre Dame Press, 1965; paperback edition. *Bible and Liturgy*. University of Notre Dame Press, 2002.

Deferrari, R. J., editor and translator. *St. Cyprian, Treatises*. The Fathers of the Church. A New Translation, vol. 36. Washington, DC: The Catholic University of America Press, 1958.

de Ghellinck, J., *Pour l'histoire du mot 'Sacramentum.'* Louvain, 1924.

de la Taille, M., sj, *Esquisse du Mystère de la foi*. Paris, 1925.

de la Taille, M., sj, *Mysterium Fidei*. Paris, 1921.

de Lubac, H., sj, *Corpus Mysticum: The Eucharist and the Church in the Middle Ages*. Trans. from French, 2nd edition. 1949. Notre Dame: Notre Dame University Press, 2007.

de Vaux, R., OP, *Ancient Israel. Its Life and Institutions*. Trans. from French. London: Darton, Longman & Todd, 1961. Vol. 2, *Ancient Israel. Religious Institutions*, in McGraw-Hill Paperback Edition, 1965.

Deiss, J., *Early Sources of the Liturgy*. New York: Alba House, 1967. Published as *Springtime of the Liturgy*. Collegeville, MN: The Liturgical Press, 1979.

Delorme, J. and others, *The Eucharist in the New Testament*. Trans. from French. Baltimore/Dublin: Helicon Press, 1964.

Delorme, J., *see* George and others.

*Didaché*, *see* Kleist.

Dillistone, F. W., *Christianity and Symbolism*. London: Collins, 1955.

Dix, G., *The Apostolic Tradition of St. Hippolytus of Rome*. 2nd edition, intro. H. Chadwick. London, 1968.

Dix, G., *The Shape of the Liturgy*. London: Dacre Press, 1945; published by Continuum, 2005.

Donna, R. B., CSJ, *St. Cyprian, Letters (1–81)*. The Fathers of the Church. A New Translation, vol. 51. Washington, DC: The Catholic University of America Press, 1964.

Drumm, M., *Passage to Pasch*. Dublin: Columba Press, 1998.

Dunn, J. D. G., *Baptism in the Holy Spirit*. London: SCM Press Ltd, 1970.

Duplacy, J., *see* George and others.

Dupont, J., OSB, *see* Delorme and others.

Durrwell, F. X., CSSR, *Holy Spirit of God*. Trans. from French. London: Geoffrey Chapman, 1986, Cincinnati: Servant Books, 2006.

Egbulem, C., OP, "An African Interpretation of Liturgical Inculturation: The 'Rite Zairois'" in Downey, M. and Fragomeni, R. eds., *A Promise of Presence. Studies in Honor of David Power*. Washington, DC: The Pastoral Press, 1992, pp. 227–250.

Eliade, M., *Rites and Symbols of Initiation* (first published as *Birth and Rebirth*). New York/London: Harper and Row, 1958.

Eliade, M., *Patterns in Comparative Religion*. London: Sheed & Ward, 1958.

Eliade, M., *The Sacred and the Profane*. New York: Harcourt, Brace and Company, 1959.

Emminghaus, J., *The Eucharist: Essence, Form, Celebration*. Trans. from German. Collegeville, MN: The Liturgical Press, 1978.

Fahey, M., ed., *Catholic Perspectives on Baptism, Eucharist and Ministry: A Study Commissioned by the Catholic Theological Society of America*. Lanham, MD, 1986.

Filthaut, T., *La théologie des mystères. Exposé de la controverse*. Paris and Tournai: Desclée, 1954.

Fink, P. E., SJ, ed., *The New Dictionary of Sacramental Worship*. Collegeville, MN: The Liturgical Press, 1990.

Fisher, J. D. C., *Christian Initiation in the Mediaeval West*. Chicago/Mundelein: Hillenbrand Books, 2004.

Fisher, J. D. C., *Christian Initiation, the Reformation Period*. Chicago/Mundelein: Hillenbrand Books, 2006.

Fisher, J. D. C., *Confirmation Then and Now*. Chicago/Mundelein: Hillenbrand Books, 2005.

Fitzpatrick, P. J., *In Breaking of Bread. The Eucharist and Ritual.* Cambridge: Cambridge University Press, 1993.

Flannery, A., OP, ed., *Vatican Council II. The Conciliar and Post-Conciliar Documents.* Revised edition. Dublin: Dominican Publications and Northport, NY: Costello Publishing Company, 1996.

Fourez, F., SJ, *Sacraments and Passages.* Notre Dame, Indiana: Ave Maria Press, 1983.

Gallagher, J., *Significando Causant. A Study of Sacramental Causality.* Fribourg: Editions Universitaires, 1965.

Galot, J., SJ, *La nature du caractère sacramentel.* 2ème ed., Paris-Louvain: Desclée de Brouwer, 1958.

George, A., SM, and others, *Baptism in the New Testament. A Symposium.* Trans. from French (1956). London: Chapman, 1964.

Giblet, J., *see* George and others.

Gietl, J., ed., *Roland Bandinelli, 'Sententiae.'* Fribourg: Editions Universitaires, 1891.

Gilby, T., OP, *Holy Communion*, vol. 59 of Thomas Aquinas, *Summa Theologiae* (IIIa, qq. 79–83). London and New York: Blackfriars in conjunction with Eyre & Spotiswoode and McGraw-Hill, 1975.

Gore, C., *The Body of Christ.* London: J. Murray, 1901.

Gregory of Nazianzus, *see* Browne and Swallow.

Gros, J., Elder, E. R. and Wondra, E. K., eds., *Common Witness to the Gospel. Documents on Anglican-Roman Catholic Relation 1983–1995.* Washington, DC: United States Catholic Conference, 1997.

Guillet, J., SJ, *see* George and others.

Guzie, T., *Jesus and the Eucharist.* New York: Paulist Press, 1974.

Halliburton, R. J., "The Patristic Theology of the Eucharist" in C. Jones and others, eds, *The Study of Liturgy.* London: SPCK and Oxford: Oxford University Press, revised edition, 1992, pp. 245–251.

Heine, R. E., trans., *Origen. Commentary on the Gospel according to John, Book 1–10.* The Fathers of the Church, A New Translation, vol. 80. Washington, DC: The Catholic University of America Press, 1989.

Hellwig, M., *The Eucharist and the Hunger of the World.* New York: Paulist Press, 1976.

Hill, C. and Yarnold, E., SJ, eds., *Anglicans and Roman Catholics: The Search for Unity.* London: SPCK/CTS, 1994.

Hippolytus, St., *see* Dix.

Holeton, D. R., "Confirmation in the 1980s" in *Ecumenical Perspectives on Baptism, Eucharist and Ministry.* Geneva: WCC, 1983, pp. 68–89.

Irenaeus, St., *see* Keble.

The International Theological Commission, *The Hope of Salvation for Infants who Die without Being Baptized.* Vatican, 2007. Text in *Origins*: CNS Documentary Service, vol. 36, no. 45.

James, E. O., *Sacrifice and Sacrament.* London: Thames & Hudson, 1962.

Jaspers, R. C. D. and Cuming, G. J., *Prayers of the Eucharist: Early and Reformed.* 3rd edition. New York: Pueblo Publishing Company, 1987.

Jaubert, A., *The Date of the Last Supper.* Trans. from French, New York: Alba House, 1965.

Jeffrey, S. M., "Christian Initiation: A Pastoral Perspective on Restored Order" in *Antiphon* 9 (2005), 245–252.

Jeremias, J., *Infant Baptism in the First Four Centuries.* Trans. from German. London: SCM Press, 1960; Philadelphia: Westminster Press, 1962.

Jeremias, J., *The Eucharistic Words of Jesus.* Trans. from 3rd German edition. London: SCM Press, 1966.

Jeremias, J., *The Origins of Infant Baptism.* Trans. from German. Naperville, IL: A. R. Allenson, 1963.

John Paul II, *Encyclical Letter Fides et Ratio: On the Relationship between Faith and Reason*, Vatican, 1998.

Johnson, M. E., *The Rites of Christian Initiation. Their Evolution and Interpretation.* Collegeville, MN: The Liturgical Press, 1999.

Jones, C., Wainwright G., Yarnold, E., sj, and Bradshaw, P., eds., *The Study of Liturgy.* London: SPCK and Oxford: Oxford University Press, revised edition, 1992.

Jungmann, J. A., sj, *The Mass of the Roman Rite: Its origins and development (Missarum Sollemnia).* New rev. and abridged edition of *Missarum Sollemnia*, 2 vols., 1949. New York: Benziger Bros., 1959.

Kavanagh, A., osb, *The Shape of Baptism: The Rite or Christian Initiation.* New York: Pueblo Publishing Company, 1978.

Keble, J., trans. *Five Books of St Ireneus, Bishop of Lyons, Against Heresies.* Library of Fathers of the Holy Catholic Church 42, Oxford, 1872.

Kelly, J.N.D., *Early Christian Doctrines.* 4th edition. London: Adam & Charles Black, 1968.

Kilmartin, E. J., sj, "The Lima Text on Eucharist" in Fahey M., ed., *Catholic Perspectives on Baptism, Eucharist and Ministry: A Study Commissioned by the Catholic Theological Society of America.* Lanham, MD, 1986.

Kilmartin, E. J., sj, *The Eucharist in the Primitive Church.* Englewood Cliffs, NJ: Prentice-Hall, 1965.

Kilmartin, E. J., sj, *The Eucharist in the West. History and Theology.* Ed. R. J. Daly, sj, Collegeville, MN: The Liturgical Press, 1998.

Kittel, see Schweizer.

Kleist, J. A., sj, trans. *The Didaché, The Epistle of Barnabas, The Epistles and the Martyrdom of St. Polycarp, The Fragment of Papias, The Epistle to Diognetus.* Ancient Christian Writers 6. Westminster, MD: The Newman Press, London: Longmans, Green and Company, 1948.

Kleist, J. A., sj, trans. *The Epistles of St. Clement of Rome and St. Ignatius of Antioch.* Ancient Christian Writers 1. Westminster, MD: The Newman Press, London: Longmans, Green and Company, 1961.

Lampe, G.M.H., *The Seal of the Spirit.* 2nd edition. London: Longmans, 1967.

Lang, H., *Aurelia Augustini. Textus eucharistici selecti.* Florilegium Patristicum fasc. 35, Bonn, 1933.

Leeming, B., sj, *Principles of Sacramental Theology.* London: Longmans, 1956.

Leenhardt F. J., "This Is My Body" in *Essays on the Lord's Supper.* Trans. from *Cahiers Theologiques* 37. Neuchâtel/Paris, 1955. London, 1958.

Leon-Dufour, X., *Sharing the Eucharistic Bread: The Witness of the New Testament.* Trans. from French. New York: Paulist Press, 1987.

Lepin, M., *L'Idée du Sacrifice de la Messe d'après les théologiens depuis l'origine jusqu'à nos jours.* Paris: Beauchesne, 1957.

Ligier, L., "From the Last Supper to the Eucharist" in L. Sheppard (ed.), *The New Liturgy.* London: Chapman, 1970, pp. 113–150.

Ligier, L., "The Origins of the Eucharistic Prayer. From the Last Supper to the Eucharist." *Studia Liturgica* 9 (1973), 161–185.

Luther, Martin, *The Pagan Servitude of the Church.* Trans. and ed. B. L. Woolf in *The Reformation Writings of Martin Luther.* Vol. I. London, 1953; repr. in J. Dillenberger, *Martin Luther, selections from his writings.* New York: Doubleday, 1961.

Macy, G., *The Theologies of the Eucharist in the Early Scholastic Period. A Study of the Salvific Function of the Sacrament According to the Theologians c. 1080–1220.* Oxford: Clarendon Press, 1984.

Marsh, T. A., "The sacramental Character" in D. O'Callaghan, ed. *Sacraments.* Dublin: Gill, 1964.

Marsh, T. A., *Gift of Community. Baptism and Confirmation.* Wilmington, DE: Glazier, 1984.

Martimort, A. G. and others, *The Church at Prayer.* Trans. from French; revised edition, 4 vols. Collegeville, MN: The Liturgical Press and London: Chapman, 1986–1988.

Martos, J., *Doors to the Sacred. A Historical Introduction to Sacraments in the Christian Church.* London: Chapman, 1981; Revised edition, Tarrytown, NJ: Triumph Books, 2001.

Mascall, E. L., *Corpus Christi.* London: Longmans, 1953.

Massa, E., *The Eucharistic Prayer of the Roman Rite.* Trans. from Italian, New York: Pueblo Publishing Company, 1986.

Massa, E., *Celebration of the Eucharist: The Origin of the Rite and the Development of its Interpretation.* Collegeville, MN: The Liturgical Press, 1999.

Masure, E., *The Christian Sacrifice.* Trans. from French. London: Burns, Oates & Washbourne, 1944.

Masure, E., *The Sacrifice of the Mystical Body.* Trans. from French. London: Burns & Oates, 1954.

McAdoo, H. R., *Modern Eucharistic Agreement.* London: SPCK, 1973.

McCabe, Herbert, *The New Creation*, new edition, New York and London: Continuum, 2010.

McCue, J. F., "The Doctrine of Transubstantiation from Berengar through the Council of Trent" in *Lutherans and Catholics in Dialogue. The Eucharist.* Washington/New York, 1967; also in *The Harvard Theological Review* 61 (1968), 385–430.

McGoldrick, P., ed. *Understanding the Eucharist.* Dublin: Gill, 1969.

McPartlan, P., *Sacrament of Salvation.* Edinburgh: T&T Clark, 1995.

Meyer H. and Vischer L., eds. *Growth in Agreement. Reports and Agreed Statements of Ecumenical Conversations on a World Level.* New York: Paulist and Geneva: WCC, 1984.

Milner, A., OP, *The Theology of Confirmation.* Cork: Mercier Press, 1971.

*Modern Eucharistic Agreement.* Foreword by Bishop Alan C. Clark, Introduction by Bishop H. R. McAdoo, London: SPCK, 1973.

Mollat, C., SJ, *see* Delorme and others; *see* George and others.

Moloney, R., SJ, *Our Eucharistic Prayers.* Wilmington, DE: Glazier, 1986.

Navickas, J. C., *The Doctrine of St. Cyprian on the Sacraments.* Würzburg, 1924.

Navone, J., SJ, *Gospel Love. A Narrative Theology.* Wilmington, DE: Glazier, 1985.

Navone, J., SJ, *Seeking God in Story.* Collegeville, MN: The Liturgical Press, 1990.

Neuner, J., SJ, and Dupuis, J., SJ, eds. *The Christian Faith in the Doctrinal Documents of the Catholic Church.* Fifth revised and enlarged edition. London: HarperCollins Religious, 1992; New York: Alba House, 1996.

Neunheuser, B., OSB, *Baptism and Confirmation.* Trans. from German. New York: Herder and Herder, 1964.

Nielen, J. M., *The Earliest Christian Liturgy.* Trans. from German. St. Louis/London, 1941.

Nocent, A., OSB, "Christian Initiation during the First Four Centuries" in vol. IV (2000), pp. 5–28 of Chupungco, A., OSB, ed. *Handbook for Liturgical Studies. Introduction to the Liturgy.* Vols. I–V. A Pueblo Book. Collegeville, MN: The Liturgical Press, 1997.

Nocent, A., OSB, "Christian Initiation in the Roman Church From the Fifth Century Until Vatican II" in vol. IV (2000), pp. 49–90; Chupungco, A., OSB, ed. *Handbook for Liturgical Studies. Introduction to the Liturgy.* Vols. I–V. A Pueblo Book. Collegeville, MN: The Liturgical Press, 1997.

O'Callaghan, D., ed. *Sacraments.* Dublin: Gill, 1964.

O'Neill, C. E., OP, *Meeting Christ in the Sacraments.* New York: Alba House, 2007.

O'Neill, C. E., OP, *New Approaches to the Eucharist.* Dublin: Gill & Son, 1967.

O'Neill, C. E., OP, *Sacramental Realism. A General Theory of the Sacraments.* Wilmington, DE: Glazier, 1983.

Origen, *see* Heine.

Osborne K. B., OFM, *Christian Sacraments in a Postmodern World. A Theology for the Third Millennium.* New York: Paulist Press, 1999.

Osborne, K. B., OFM, *The Christian Sacraments of Initiation. Baptism, Confirmation, Eucharist.* New York: Paulist Press, 1987.

Palmer, P., SJ, *Sacraments and Worship: Liturgy and Doctrinal Development of Baptism, Confirmation, and the Eucharist.* London: Longmans, Green and Co., 1957.

Patout Burns, SJ, and G. M. Fagin, SJ, eds. *The Holy Spirit.* Message of the Fathers of the Church 3. Wilmington, DE: Glazier, 1984.

Pecklers, K. F., SJ, "History of the Roman Liturgy from the Sixteenth until the Twentieth Centuries," in vol. I, 10, pp. 153–178 of Chupungco, A., OSB, ed. *Handbook for Liturgical Studies. Introduction to the Liturgy.* Vols. I-V. A Pueblo Book. Collegeville, MN: The Liturgical Press, 1997.

Pelikan, J., *The Growth of Mediaeval Theology (600–1300)*. Vol. III of *The Christian Tradition*. Chicago: University of Chicago Press, 1978.

Power, D. N., omi, *Sacrament. The Language of God's Giving*. New York: The Crossroad Publishing Company, 1999.

Power, D. N., omi, *The Eucharistic Mystery. Revitalizing the Tradition*. New York: The Crossroad Publishing Company, 1992.

Power, D. N., omi, *The Sacrifice We Offer. The Tridentine Dogma and Its Reinterpretation*. Edinburgh: T. & T. Clark, 1987.

Powers, J. M., sj, *Eucharistic Theology*. New York: Herder & Herder, 1967.

Quasten, J., *Patrology*. 3 vols., Westminster, MD: Spectrum Publishers, 1950, 1953, 1960; vol. IV, ed. A. Di Bernardino. Westminster, MD: Christian Classics Inc., 1991.

Rahner, H., sj, *Greek Myth and Christian Mystery*. Trans. from German. London: Burns & Oates, 1963.

Rahner, K., sj, "Introductory Observations on Thomas Aquinas' Theology of the Sacraments in General" in *Theological Investigations* 14. Baltimore/London, 1980, pp. 149–160.

Rahner, K., sj, "The Presence of Christ in the Sacrament of the Lord's Supper, in *Theological Investigations* 4. London: Darton, Longman & Todd, 1966, pp. 287–311.

Rahner, K., sj, "The Word and the Eucharist" in *Theological Investigations* 4. London: Darton, Longman & Todd, 1966, pp. 253–286.

Rahner, K., sj, *The Church and the Sacraments*. Trans. from German. Freiburg/New York/London: Herder and Herder, 1963.

Reumann, J., *The Supper of the Lord: The New Testament, Ecumenical Dialogues, and Faith and Order on Eucharist*. Philadelphia: Fortress Press, 1985.

Roguet, A. M., op, *Christ Acts Through the Sacraments*. Trans. from French. Collegeville, MN: The Liturgical Press, 1954.

Rordorf, W. and others. *The Eucharist of the Early Christians*. Trans. from French. New York: Pueblo Publishing Company, 1978.

Root, M. and Saarinen, R. eds. *Baptism and the Unity of the Church*. Geneva: WCC Publications, 1998.

Rosemann, P. W., "Postmodern Philosophy and L.-L. Marion's Eucharistic Realism" in *The Mystery of Faith. Reflections on the Encyclical Ecclesia de Eucharistia*. Eds. J. McEvoy and M. Hogan. Dublin: The Columba Press, 2005, pp. 224–244.

Ryan, J. B., *The Eucharistic Prayer*. New York: Paulist Press, 1974.

Schillebeeckx, E., op, *Christ the Sacrament of Encounter with God*. Trans. from Dutch. London and New York: Sheed & Ward, 1963.

Schillebeeckx E., op, *The Eucharist*. London and New York: Sheed & Ward, 1968.

Schmaus, M., *Dogma 5: The Church as Sacrament*. Trans. from German. London: Sheed & Ward, 1975.

Schmemann, A., *Sacraments and Orthodoxy*. New York: Herder & Herder, 1965.

Schmemann, A., *The Eucharist: Sacrament of the Kingdom*. New York: St. Vladimir's Seminary Press, 1988.

Schnackenburg, R., *Baptism in the Thought of St. Paul*. Trans. from German. London: Basil Blackwell, New York: Herder and Herder Oxford, 1964.

Schweizer, E. and others, "Pneuma" in Kittel, G. Friedrich, ed. *Theological Dictionary of the New Testament*. Vol. VI. Grand Rapids: Wm B. Eerdmans, 1964, pp. 332–452.

Segundo, J. L., sj, *The Sacraments Today*. Trans. from Spanish. New York: Orbis Books, 1973.

Shea, J., *Stories of Faith*. Chicago: Thomas More Press, 1980.

Shea, J., *Stories of God: An Unauthorized Biography*. Chicago: Thomas More Press, 1978.

Sheerin, J., ed. *The Eucharist*. Message of the Fathers of the Church 7. Wilmington, DE: Glazier, 1986.

Souter, A., trans. *Tertullian's Treatises Concerning Prayer, Concerning Baptism*. London: SPCK, 1919.

Studer, B., osb, "Liturgical Documents of the First Four Centuries" in Chupungco, A., osb, ed. *Handbook for Liturgical Studies. Introduction to the Liturgy*. Vols. I–V. Collegeville, MN: The Liturgical Press, 1997–2000, vol. I, 12, pp.199–224.

Talley, T., "The Eucharistic Prayer of the Ancient Church according to Recent Research: Results and Reflections." *Studia Liturgica* 11 (1976), 138–158.

Tanner, N. P., sj, ed. *Decrees of the Ecumenical Councils*. Vols. I and II. London and Washington: Sheed & Ward and Georgetown University Press, 1990.

Tertullian, *see* Souter.

Thompson, B., *Liturgies of the Western Church*. Cleveland: Collins, New York: World Publishing Co., 1958; Philadelphia: Fortress Press, 1980.

Thornton, L. S., *Confirmation, Its Place in the Baptismal Mystery*. Westminster, London: Dacre Press, 1954.

Thurian, M., "The Eucharistic Memorial, Sacrifice of Praise and Supplication" in *Ecumenical Perspectives on Baptism, Eucharist and Ministry*. Geneva: WCC, 1983, pp. 90–103.

Thurian, M., ed., *Churches Respond to bem: Official Responses to the "Baptism, Eucharist and Ministry" Text*. Vols. I–VI, Faith and Order Papers 129, 132, 135, 137, 143, 144. Geneva: WCC, 1986–1988.

Thurian, M., "The Eucharistic Memorial, Sacrifice of Praise and Supplication" in *Ecumenical Perspectives on Baptism, Eucharist and Ministry*. Geneva: WCC, 1983, pp. 90–103.

Thurian, M., *The Eucharistic Memorial* I: *The Old Testament*, II: *The New Testament*. Trans. from French. London: Lutterworth Press, 1961.

Thurian, M., *The Mystery of the Eucharist—an Ecumenical Approach*. Trans. from French (1981). London & Oxford: Mowbray, 1983; Grand Rapids, MI: W. B. Eerdmans Pub. Co., 1984.

Tillard, J.M.R., op, *The Eucharist: Pasch of God's People*. Trans. from French. New York: Alba House, 1976.

Tracy, D., *The Analogical Imagination*. New York: Crossroad, 1981.

Tremel, B., op, see George and others.

Turner, P., *Confirmation: The Baby in Solomon's Court*. New York: Paulist Press, 1993.

Turner, P., *Sources of Confirmation. From the Fathers Through the Reformers.* Collegeville, MN: The Liturgical Press, 1993.

Turner, V. W., *The Ritual Process.* New York: Cornell University Press, 1969.

Vagaggini, C., OSB, *Theological Dimensions of the Liturgy.* Trans. from Italian. Collegeville, MN: The Liturgical Press, 1959.

Vagaggini, G., OSB, *The Canon of the Mass and Liturgical Reform.* Trans. from Italian. New York: Alba House, 1967.

Van Beck, F. J., SJ, *Grounded in Love: Sacramental Theology in an Ecumenical Perspective.* Washington, DC: University Press of America, 1981.

Van Buchem, L. A., *L'Homélie Pseudo-Eusébienne de Pentecôte.* Nijmegen, 1967.

Van der Leeuw, *Religion in Essence and Manifestation.* Trans. from German, London: Allen and Unwin, 1938; with additions from 2nd German edition, Gloucester: Peter Smith, 1967.

Van der Meer, F., *Augustine the Bishop.* Trans. from Dutch. London, New York: Sheed & Ward, 1961.

Van Gennep, A., *The Rites of Passage.* Original French edition. 1908; republished Chicago: University of Chicago Press, 1960.

Vogel, C., *Medieval Liturgy. An Introduction to the Sources.* Revised and translated from French (1981) by W. G. Storey and N. K. Rasmussen, OP, Washington, DC: The Pastoral Press, 1986.

Vonier, A., OSB, *A Key to the Doctrine of the Eucharist.* Original edition 1925; revised edition in *The Collected Works of Abbot Vonier.* Vol. II. London: Burns, Oates, 1952; Westminster, MD: Newman Press, 1958.

Vorgrimler, H., *Sacramental Theology.* Trans. from German. Collegeville, MN: The Liturgical Press, 1992.

Wainwright, G., *Christian Initiation.* Richmond, VA: John Knox Press, 1969.

Wainwright, G., *see* Jones and others.

Walsh, L.G., OP, "An ecumenical reading of Aquinas on the Eucharist" in *Liturgia et Unitas.* Eds. M. Klöckener and A. Join-Lambert. Fribourg: Universitäetsverlag, 2001.

Walsh, L.G., OP, "Sacraments" in *The Theology of Thomas Aquinas.* Edited by R. van Nieuwenhove and J. Wawrykow. Notre Dame: University of Notre Dame Press, 2005, pp. 326–364.

Walsh, L.G., OP, "The Presence of the Mystery of Christ in the Broken Bread" in J. McEvoy and M. Hogan, SSC, eds. *The Mystery of Faith. Reflections on the Encyclical Ecclesia de Eucharistia.* Dublin: Columba Press, 2005, 140–160.

Ware, T., *The Orthodox Church.* New edition. London: Penguin Books, 1997.

WCC, *Baptism, Eucharist and Ministry.* Faith and Order Paper No. 111. Geneva: WCC, 1982.

WCC, *Baptism, Eucharist and Ministry 1982–1990. Report on the Process and Responses.* Faith and Order Paper No. 149. Geneva: WCC, 1990.

Whitaker, E. C., and Johnson, M. E., *Documents of the Baptismal Liturgy.* Revised and expanded edition. The Liturgical Press: Collegeville, MN: The Liturgical Press, 2003.

Wilde, J. A., ed. *When Should We Confirm? The Order of Initiation*. Chicago: Liturgy Training Publications (Archdiocese of Chicago), 1989.

Wilkin, V., SJ, *From Limbo to Heaven. An Essay on the Economy of Redemption*. London: Sheed & Ward, 1961.

Yarnold, E., SJ, *see* Jones and others.

Yarnold, E., SJ, *The Awe-Inspiring Rites of Initiation. The Origins of the R.C.I.A*. 2nd edition. Collegeville, MN; The Liturgical Press, 1994.

Zaehner, R. C., SJ, *At Sundry Times*. London: Faber and Faber, 1958.

# INDEX

*Msgr. Reynold Hillenbrand*
*1904–1979*

Monsignor Reynold Hillenbrand, ordained a priest by Cardinal George Mundelein in 1929, was Rector of St. Mary of the Lake Seminary from 1936 to 1944.

He was a leading figure in the liturgical and social action movement in the United States during the 1930s and worked to promote active, intelligent, and informed participation in the Church's liturgy.

He believed that a reconstruction of society would occur as a result of the renewal of the Christian spirit, whose source and center is the liturgy.

Hillenbrand taught that, since the ultimate purpose of Catholic action is to Christianize society, the renewal of the liturgy must undoubtedly play the key role in achieving this goal.

**Hillenbrand Books** strives to reflect the spirit of Monsignor Reynold Hillenbrand's pioneering work by making available innovative and scholarly resources that advance the liturgical and sacramental life of the Church.

# About the Liturgical Institute

The Liturgical Institute, founded in 2000 by His Eminence Francis Cardinal George of Chicago, offers a variety of options for education in liturgical studies. A unified, rites-based core curriculum constitutes the foundation of the program, providing integrated and balanced studies toward the advancement of the renewal promoted by the Second Vatican Council. The musical, artistic, and architectural dimensions of worship are given particular emphasis in the curriculum. Institute students are encouraged to participate in its "liturgical heart" of daily Mass and Morning and Evening Prayer. The academic program of the Institute serves a diverse, international student population—laity, religious, and clergy—who are preparing for service in parishes, dioceses, and religious communities. Personalized mentoring is provided in view of each student's ministerial and professional goals. The Institute is housed on the campus of the University of St. Mary of the Lake/Mundelein Seminary, which offers the largest priestly formation program in the United States and is the center of the permanent diaconate and lay ministry training programs of the Archdiocese of Chicago. In addition, the University has the distinction of being the first chartered institution of higher learning in Chicago (1844), and one of only seven pontifical faculties in North America.

For more information about the Liturgical Institute and its programs, contact: usml.edu/liturgicalinstitute. Phone: 847-837-4542. E-mail: litinst@usml.edu.